PROTEST POLITICS IN GERMANY

PROTEST POLITICS IN GERMANY

MOVEMENTS ON THE LEFT AND RIGHT SINCE THE 1960s

ROGER KARAPIN

THE PENNSYLVANIA STATE UNIVERSITY PRESS
UNIVERSITY PARK, PENNSYLVANIA

LIBRARY OF CONGRESS CATALOGING-IN-PUBLICATION DATA

Karapin, Roger.
　Protest politics in Germany : movements on the Left and Right since the 1960s / Roger Karapin.
　　p.　cm.
　Includes bibliographical references and index.
　ISBN 978-0-271-02986-3 (pbk : alk.paper)
　1. Protest movements—Germany—Case studies.
　2. Political participation—Germany–Case studies.
　3. Social movements—Political aspects—Germany.
　4. Right and left (Political science).
　I. Title.

HN445.5.K37　2007
322.40943—dc22
　　　　　　2007008467

Copyright © 2007 The Pennsylvania State University
All rights reserved
Printed in the United States of America
Published by The Pennsylvania State University Press,
University Park, PA 16802-1003

The Pennsylvania State University Press is a member of the Association of American University Presses.

It is the policy of The Pennsylvania State University Press to use acid-free paper. This book is printed on Natures Natural, containing 50% post-consumer waste, and meets the minimum requirements of American National Standard for Information Sciences—Permanence of Paper for Printed Library Material, ANSI Z39.48–1992.

TO
Silke, Anna, and Lukas

CONTENTS

List of Tables and Figures		ix
Preface and Acknowledgments		xi
	Introduction: Explaining Protest Politics in Germany	1
1	Political Interactions and German Protest Movements Since the 1960s	17
2	Urban Renewal Conflicts in Hanover and West Berlin	61
3	Nuclear Energy Conflicts at Wyhl and Brokdorf	117
4	Immigration Conflicts in Munich and Rendsburg County	161
5	Immigration Conflicts in Hoyerswerda, Rostock, and Riesa	191
6	Conclusions	219
	Notes	259
	References	279
	Index	303

TABLES AND FIGURES

TABLES

1	Main Features of the Cases	5
2	The Interactive Political Process Theory: Variables and Their Effects on the Size and Type of Protest	40–41
3	Explaining the Size and Duration of Protests in Ten Cases	221–222
4	Explaining the Types of Participation in Nine Cases	228–229

FIGURES

1	The Making Opportunities Argument	38
2	Political Interactions Affecting Three Types of Participation	48

PREFACE AND ACKNOWLEDGMENTS

This book takes an interactive political process approach to studying protest movements in contemporary Germany.[a] I argue that interactions between protesters, political elites, and authorities can explain why large, influential protests occur and why protest activity takes conventional, nonviolently disruptive, or militant forms. This claim applies very generally in Germany—to left-wing and right-wing movements and to protest in the western and eastern parts of the country—and I expect it is valid in other industrialized democracies, too. This book is also an attempt to rebut certain structural theories of protest, those that focus on social structures, socioeconomic change, and political institutions. To provide broad support for my arguments, I have studied nine cases of conflict between protesters and authorities, arranged mostly in contrasting pairs within three policy areas. The cases include leftist protests about urban renewal and nuclear energy, and rightist protests about immigration. Hence, this book is unusual in several ways: it compares left-wing and right-wing movements; it uses contrasting cases; and it assesses the relative utility of political process and structural theories for explaining this wide range of empirical materials. By undertaking different kinds of comparison within one country, I also aim to reveal something of the texture of its politics.

I initially tried to see how the strategic choices of protest groups affected outcomes. But I became interested in a more powerful force: mutually reinforcing actions by protest groups, their elite allies, and their adversaries in the state. Daring protest actions, alliances between protest groups, support for protests from elite allies, the nature and timing of reforms, and specific police practices together have major effects on the course of protest movements.

    a. In this book, "Germany" refers to the Federal Republic of Germany, i.e., West Germany before October 1990 and unified Germany thereafter.

As I grappled with the case materials of this book and the interpretative possibilities laid out by the available theories, I was drawn consistently into a debate with structural explanations, which I found in theories of new politics, new social movements, political opportunity structures (the static variant), and ethnic competition. These seemed to argue that protesters and their opponents do what immovable external conditions require. Most prominent among those structural conditions were social structures, large socioeconomic trends, and political institutions. I found it important to test the limits of those explanations while I developed political process accounts of protest.

The approach I have taken is not the only kind of political process theory that can be usefully applied to this subject. Others have successfully used theories of protest cycles or waves,[1] syntheses of political institutions and processes,[2] and a contextualized, contingent political process theory[3] to explain mobilization, protest strategies, and policy outcomes. Political process theories often do not distinguish between causes of protest that are structural and those controlled by actors.[4] However, my interest in the relative contributions of structures and agency led me to focus on the ways that political interactions produce large protests of different types and to contrast my interactive approach with more structurally oriented theories of political opportunities.

Of course, I do not mean that political interactions are wholly independent of social and political structures, or that political actors are free to create, shape, steer, or prevent protests as they wish. Rather, my claim is that the interactions identified here are significantly independent of structures. There is much scope for human agency, in the form of decisions and actions by protesters, public officials, and other political leaders. The reader can experience the exact contours of this claim in the chapters that follow, in which I also try to improve our understanding of the conditions under which actors can make a difference.

This book would not have been possible without the help of countless people during the project's many phases. From the start of my fieldwork, researchers in Germany pointed me toward sources of all kinds and provided me with a sounding board for my emerging findings. Thanks especially to Dieter Rucht, Roland Roth, Margit Mayer, Klaus Selle, Hubert Heinelt, Werner Bergmann, Rainer Erb, and Ruud Koopmans. Approximately one hundred members of protest groups, nonprofit organizations, political parties, and administrative bodies gave me their time, recollections, and insights in interviews. Only a fraction of them are cited in the notes, but they all contributed to my understanding of protest politics in Germany. I would also like to thank those who opened archives and libraries to me in Berlin, Hanover, Kiel, Stuttgart, Munich, Hoyerswerda, Rostock, and Dresden.

As much as I learned from fieldwork, my interpretations of the case materials depended on the work of many theorists of protest and politics. Bill Gamson, Dieter Rucht, Sidney Tarrow, and Charles Tilly provided inspiration through their incisive writing and gave me invaluable encouragement and guidance through their generous responses to my written work. In addition, many others read chapters in draft form and gave me helpful comments. The theoretical framework of the book and an earlier version of Chapter 5 were discussed at the Workshop on Contentious Politics, Columbia University. I would like to thank the following for their comments in that forum, and others who commented on later versions of the theory chapter: Talya Blokland, Gerard Braunthal, Brian Burgoon, Alice Holmes Cooper, John Glenn, Carol Hager, Jack Hammond, Michael Hanagan, Herbert Kitschelt, Hanspeter Kriesi, John Krinsky, Marc Lerner, Tony Levitas, Roy Licklider, Howard Lune, Andy Markovits, David Meyer, Ann Mische, Kelly Moore, Tibor Papp, Dieter Rucht, Salvador Sandoval, Damir Skenderovic, Narendra Subramanian, Sidney Tarrow, Wayne te Brake, and Charles Tilly.

My thanks go also to those who commented on early versions of the empirical chapters: Suzanne Berger, Josh Cohen, Bill Gamson, Ellen Immergut, Andy Markovits, Charles Sabel, Caren Addis, Antonio Bothelho, Brian Burgoon, Carol Conaway, Richard Deeg, Eric Fernald, Dan Grossman, Wade Jacoby, Jennie Purnell, James Rosberg, Narendra Subramanian, Werner Bergmann, Jack Hammond, Michael Hanagan, Jeffrey Herf, Christopher Husbands, John Krinsky, Roy Licklider, David Meyer, Francesca Polletta, Dieter Rucht, Damir Skenderovic, John Skrentny, Charles Tilly, and Helmut Willems. Earlier versions of Chapters 4 and 5 were published previously in *German Politics and Society* and *Comparative Politics*, respectively.[5] I would like to thank those journals' anonymous reviewers for their comments, and their editors for permission to use material from those articles. More recent incarnations of the manuscript benefited from careful reading by Eva Bellin, Joe Foudy, Jack Hammond, and Damir Skenderovic. Belinda Davis, Herbert Kitschelt, and David Meyer provided detailed comments that helped me sort the wheat from the chaff. Andrew Lewis improved the book in countless small ways through his copyediting suggestions. With so much highly skilled help, how could I go wrong? But I probably did, at least some of the time. When you find one of the book's remaining flaws, you will know it is my responsibility.

I found that writing this book required emotional as well as intellectual resources. I will never forget the friends who have listened to me talk about my work and have helped me see what is valuable and what is less so. I especially want to thank Brian Burgoon, Francoise Carre, Janice Goldman, Emine Kiray, Tony Levitas, Ariel Lublin, Sharon Moran, Lee Perlman, Damir Skenderovic, Silke Springorum, and Narendra Subramanian. I also want to thank my mother, Gisela Franken Karapin, whose stories inspired my interest in German politics, and my late father, Peter Paul Karapin, who showed me the value of learning.

In this era, sustained intellectual work depends on institutional support. My heartfelt thanks to those who personally took an interest in my work, provided moral support, and at the right moments helped mobilize essential institutional resources on my behalf. Suzanne Berger, Josh Cohen, and Andy Markovits did so at M.I.T. and Harvard, as did Ken Sherrill and Andy Polsky at Hunter College. Sandy Thatcher was a steady beacon guiding me through the entire publication process.

Money does not make the world go round, but it sure helps pay the bills associated with research. The Fulbright Commission, Social Science Research Council, and the Research Foundation of CUNY funded my field work, the latter through PSC-CUNY Awards 665523, 668538, and 62670-0031. At Hunter College, I especially want to thank President Jennifer Raab and Dean Judith Friedlander, who provided crucial last-minute support that made it possible for me to finish the book and see it published in a timely manner. Hunter College also provided assistance through Eugene Lang and Ruth G. Weintraub Faculty Development Awards and a Presidential Incentive Grant.

I dedicate this book to my wife Silke Springorum and to our children, Anna and Lukas. Thank you for bearing with me as this project took longer than any of us imagined, and for your delightful companionship—an everyday reminder of life outside and beyond this book.

INTRODUCTION:
EXPLAINING PROTEST POLITICS IN GERMANY

My research for this book began with urban renewal politics in the Kreuzberg borough of Berlin, which I see as a microcosm of leftist[a] protest politics in the Federal Republic of Germany before and after unification. In the early 1970s, officials in West Berlin, Hanover, and many other West German cities planned urban renewal projects that would demolish thousands of apartments and displace tens of thousands of people from residential neighborhoods ("clear-cut renewal").[b] Public housing corporations and private developers, who stood to benefit from state construction subsidies, supported the plans, and leaders in the main political parties gave their tacit consent. Small groups of long-time residents and leftist university students formed citizen initiatives[c] to oppose clear-cut renewal. Activists met with residents to formulate demands for a halt to demolition and for more citizen participation. But officials ignored the protesters or shunted them into unproductive meetings to discuss plans that would not be altered. The protesters lacked access to top decision makers, had no organized constituency, and had little support from political parties.

Yet the small protest groups in West Berlin built a large, intense movement that successfully opposed demolition and displacement. I later found that a similar process had occurred in the Linden section of Hanover, though the protests there were smaller and tamer. In both cases, small

   a. Below and in Chapter 1, I define "left" and "right" in terms of the ideologies of committed activists and the political parties with which protesters tended to form alliances.
   b. *Kahlschlagsanierung.*
   c. *Bürgerinitiativen.*

groups mobilized thousands of people to sign petitions, illegally occupy vacant apartments, or attend demonstrations. They gained publicity, negotiated with officials, won concessions, initiated a debate about the ends and means of urban renewal policy, and provoked splits within and between the political parties in parliament. In West Berlin, urban renewal protests helped drive the Social Democrats out of government in 1981, while in Hanover, urban renewal and other protest groups helped the city's Green Party end the Social Democrats' majority control of government that same year. Urban renewal protesters also won major policy reforms. They blocked the old policies of demolition and displacement and gained new policies of renovating apartments for existing residents. After the reforms, protest participation continued at high levels in the two cities. Thousands of residents attended tenant assemblies and neighborhood commission meetings, and nonviolently disruptive protests also continued.

Despite their similarities, these two urban renewal conflicts differed greatly in the forms of participation used by protesters. In Hanover-Linden, protesters used mainly conventional methods, such as meetings and a petition, supplemented by a small number of sporadic housing squats and other nonviolently disruptive actions by leftists and other young protesters. Militant actions, such as attacks on police or property or displays of force at demonstrations, were almost completely absent.

The Kreuzberg conflict was much more intense, as thousands of protesters engaged in illegal activity, both nonviolent and violent, and the height of conflict lasted for five years (1977–82), compared with about one year (1973) in Linden. Although citizen initiatives in Kreuzberg met and negotiated with officials, they also sparked a massive squatter movement, which involved over 160 apartment buildings and thousands of participants. Centered in Kreuzberg, the squatter movement spread to other West Berlin neighborhoods and helped generate the autonomist movement. Autonomists fundamentally opposed the West German political and economic systems and used militant methods, such as battling with police at demonstrations and violently defending squatters against eviction. Militant protests resurged in the late 1980s; through the mid-1990s, on every May Day, Kreuzberg continued to be a site for shows of force and battles between several hundred autonomists and large contingents of riot police.[d] At the same time, nonviolent protests continued on many issues, such as the occupation of a bridge to protest road expansion a few years after the fall of the Berlin Wall.

d. *Bereitschaftspolizei.*

The Berlin-Kreuzberg conflict, it seemed to me, contradicted central claims made by theories of new politics and new social movements. Many observers saw this conflict as a major example of new social movements in West Germany. But the context was a working-class neighborhood rather than a more postmaterialist setting, the issues were largely material (low-rent housing and physical planning),[e] and nonviolent protests were intermingled with threats and violence by protesters as well as police. Furthermore, protesters were not simply radically opposed to established parties and institutions, but rather were interdependent with them. They gained crucial support from some Social Democrats and other political elites, and they participated heavily in tenant advising and neighborhood commissions—new local institutions that protesters themselves had demanded.

These features pointed me toward political rather than socioeconomic causes of the protest. But what could explain the mix of conventional, disruptive, and militant protests? Political institutional theories offered one set of answers, but I did not find a structural explanation convincing for a movement whose protest forms changed so often and so dramatically. Hence, I developed a political process explanation of the Kreuzberg conflict. I then embarked on comparing Kreuzberg to other urban renewal conflicts, and to other policy areas, and found that those comparisons supported the process theories more than the structural theories. In the early 1990s, as I finished a comparative study of leftist movements,[1] right-wing protest against immigration surged in newly unified Germany. The anti-immigration movement presented a completely different set of actors in a new policy area and a novel political context, including postcommunist conditions in the eastern part of the country. Nonetheless, I found that the dynamics of this movement displayed remarkable similarities to the leftist cases.

Questions and Cases

As shown by the Kreuzberg and Linden examples, protest groups[f] in Germany sometimes have attracted large numbers of participants to their

---

e. However, issues of countercultural identity and autonomy were also important for alternative and autonomist groups, who were major actors within this conflict.

f. "Protest groups" and "protesters" refer to groups that mobilize to influence policy or public opinion but lack routine access to state resources and decision-making. This concept is similar to that of a challenging group (Tilly 1978, 52; Gamson 1990, 14–18) or a social movement organization (Zald and Ash 1966).

movements,[g] have mobilized over long periods, and have influenced government policy. These examples also show that how protesters participated in politics differed across localities and regions even within the same policy area. Some conflicts were marked mainly by conventional methods, while in others, disruptive yet nonviolent methods became important. Still other conflicts were dominated by protesters' militant threats and violence against property or people, which often intermingled with police violence against protesters.

The core questions of this book concern the size of protest movements and the diverse forms that protests take. Why did protest groups mobilize large numbers of people to oppose government policies, sometimes over periods of many years? Why did protesters in different conflicts use such different methods? To address these questions, I examine nine cases of protests in three different policy areas, with contrasting cases within each area (see Table 1). Besides the local urban renewal movements in Hanover and West Berlin, these include sustained regional movements against nuclear energy at Wyhl and Brokdorf, and brief local protest campaigns against immigration by asylum seekers in two western German localities (Munich-Südpark and Kronshagen) and three eastern German localities (Hoyerswerda, Rostock, and Riesa). I chose cases with a strong local or *Land*-level[h] focus because the great majority of protests in Germany have targeted those levels of government,[2] and because this allowed me to select comparable, largely independent cases while holding constant the many factors associated with each policy area. The cases include left-leaning movements, in urban renewal and nuclear energy, and campaigns that were part of the right-leaning movement against immigration by asylum seekers.

Protest Movements in Germany Since the 1960s

The manifold political changes in Linden and Kreuzberg illustrate many of the ways protest movements have helped shape democratic politics in

---

g. By a "movement," I mean one or more protest groups that engage in sustained collective action against some common opponents and with some common goals. The protest groups in a movement may often act independently of one another and may mobilize different or overlapping constituencies (cf. Tilly 1984b, 304, and Tarrow 1994, 3–4).

h. A *Land* is one of Germany's sixteen federal states; before unification, West Germany contained eleven *Länder*, including West Berlin, which was still overseen by the Western Allied powers.

Table 1. Main Features of the Cases

Case	Policy area	Levels of government (governing party)	Size of protests	Duration of main protests	Types of participation
		Western Germany			
Hanover-Linden	Urban renewal	City (SPD) Borough (SPD)	Large	1972–92	Conventional and disruptive
Berlin-Kreuzberg	Urban renewal	Land (SPD until 1981, then CDU) Borough (SPD)	Very large	1969–96	Conventional, disruptive, and militant
Wyhl	Nuclear energy	Land (CDU) National (SPD; CDU from 1982)	Very large	1974–83	Conventional and disruptive
Brokdorf	Nuclear energy	Land (CDU) National (SPD; CDU from 1982)	Very large	1974–86	Conventional, militant, some disruptive
Munich-Südpark	Immigration	City (SPD) Borough (SPD) Land (CSU)	Medium	1992–94	Conventional, some disruptive, some militant
Kronshagen	Immigration	Town (CDU) Land (SPD)	Small	1992–94	Conventional
		Eastern Germany			
Hoyerswerda	Immigration	County (CDU-SPD) Land (CDU)	Very large	1990–91	Militant, some conventional
Rostock	Immigration	City (SPD-CDU) Land (CDU)	Very large	1991–92	Militant, some conventional
Riesa	Immigration	County (CDU-SPD) Land (CDU)	Small	1991–94	Conventional and militant (both minor)

Germany and other advanced industrial democracies from the 1960s to the present. In this period, movements have mobilized on a wide range of issues, beginning with the student movements that rippled through many Western countries in the 1960s. The movements' concerns have been diverse, including war, university policies, housing, women's rights, civil liberties, the natural environment, nuclear energy, nuclear weapons, gay rights, ethnic minority rights, international economic policies, abortion rights, and immigration.[3i] The nature of the protests and their outcomes were varied and complex. Protest groups introduced new forms of political participation, raised new issues, enlivened public debates, and influenced policy reforms. Protesters also used violence, made antisystem demands, and provoked authorities to escalate their repressive responses.

Germany is an especially interesting country in which to study contemporary protest politics. Compared with other advanced industrial democracies, both leftist and rightist movements have been strong in Germany since the 1960s. Movements in Germany have also been very diverse in their goals, their methods, and the outcomes of their campaigns, representing the wide range that is found in Western democracies as a whole.[4] Leftist movements, such as the antinuclear movement, peace movement, women's movement, and local urban renewal movements, grew in West Germany in the 1970s and 1980s, and they remained active in the 1990s.[5] I call them leftist or left-leaning because they drew on socialist and communist[j] activists and tended to be allied with the center-left Social Democratic Party (SPD) and with interest groups associated with that party, such as the Protestant churches and labor unions. Later, during and after the rapid, unexpected unification of West and East Germany in 1989–90, a strong national anti-immigration movement grew, including anti-foreigner[k] violence and citizen initiatives

    i. Aside from anti-immigration and anti-abortion movements, the largest movements have been left-leaning.

    j. The latter were organized in small sectarian groups known in Germany as *K-Gruppen* ("C-groups").

    k. I use "foreigner" (*Ausländer*) to refer to members of non-German ethnic groups, who usually are not German citizens; this follows the common usage in German politics and in scholarly work. Foreigners include "guest workers," asylum seekers, short-term contract workers (in former East Germany), and refugees, but not ethnic German "resettlers" from historically German parts of eastern Europe, who have automatic rights to German citizenship. Foreigners can often remain in Germany for many years or indefinitely and hence can be considered immigrants. However, the use of the term "foreigner" is probably more accurate because it reflects the difficulty that non-

opposed to immigration.[1] This movement[m] was especially strong in the eastern part of the country, a postcommunist setting where democratic institutions were new and democratic experience lacking in the early 1990s. The anti-immigration movement was a right-wing movement, since it included neo-Nazi activists and skinheads using Nazi symbols and it was supported by the nationalist wing of the center-right Christian Democratic Union (CDU) and Christian Social Union (CSU) more than by the other parliamentary parties.

Finally, protest movements in postwar Germany developed in a political system that initially lagged behind many other Western democracies. In the 1950s and 1960s, most West German citizens were relatively passive, political elites (party and interest group leaders) tended to pursue consensus, and relations between the two were marked by authority, obedience, and distance. Yet these problems were greatly ameliorated between the late 1960s and the late 1980s, as citizens became more active and politicians more responsive. Examining protest politics since the 1960s can help us understand the processes by which democracy was strengthened in West Germany, as well as the extent to which Germany's democratic deficits have continued.

The Main Arguments of the Book

The overarching claim of this book is that protest movements are shaped more by political interactions than by social structures, socioeconomic change, or political institutions. In brief, interactions among protest groups, political elites,[n] and public officials explain why large, successful protests develop and why protesters use different types of participation. I identify the following general mechanisms:[6] the formation of alliances

---

Germans have in gaining citizenship and becoming integrated into German society and politics.

  l. Since most foreigners were long-term residents of Germany, and hence de facto immigrants, I will refer to conflicts over their arrival or presence as conflicts over immigration.

  m. I consider this a movement in the sense that protest groups on the right engaged in sustained challenges against some common opponents and with some common goals. This broad concept of "movement" contrasts with that used by some German authors, who have applied narrower criteria, including durability and cohesiveness (Hellman 1996; Koopmans and Rucht 1996; Hellman and Koopmans 1998).

  n. By political elites, I mean non-state actors who have routine access to state resources and decision-making, such as party and interest group leaders.

between protest groups, the protesters' innovation of tactics, the formation of alliances between protesters and elites, reforms made by state actors in response to protests, and police responses to protest. If appropriate interactions occur and reinforce each other, then small protests grow into large, influential movements. Interactions involving alliances, reforms, and policing also explain why conventional, nonviolently disruptive, or militant kinds of participation become important in a given conflict. More specifically, I make four arguments.

THE LIMITS OF SOCIOECONOMIC AND INSTITUTIONAL THEORIES

The first argument is that neither socioeconomic factors nor political institutions adequately explain the size or type of protest when one leaves the aggregate, national[o] level and examines local and regional variations. Scholars have explained the rise of left-wing movements in terms of a shift toward postindustrial society and postmaterialist values. But large, long-lived protest movements against clear-cut renewal occurred in places where young, affluent, educated groups were either normally represented or underrepresented (Chapter 2). For their part, scholars studying anti-immigration protests, especially violent ones, have usually explained them as the result of immigration, unemployment, and socioeconomic marginalization, which lead to material competition between different ethnic groups. But the large, violent anti-immigration protests in Hoyerswerda and Rostock did not occur in the most economically distressed parts of eastern Germany, or derive from social structures where unemployment or immigration posed unusually large threats of ethnic competition. Indeed, large protests occurred in a great variety of social and political settings, in rural *Länder*[p] governed by the Christian Democrats, large cities ruled by Social Democrats, and medium-sized eastern industrial areas with Grand Coalition (CDU-SPD) governments. Furthermore, pairs of cases in all three policy areas were marked by similar social structures yet very different types of protest.

Other authors have argued that political institutions are responsible for differences in movement strategies. For Germany, the argument is that policymaking institutions make political elites unresponsive to protesters, which leads protesters to adopt confrontational and violent meth-

---

[o]. I use "national" to refer to the country as a whole, and "federal" to refer to institutions at the federal level.

[p]. Plural of *Land*.

ods, while the institutions of policy implementation are weak, leading protesters to use conventional actions. However, the paired comparisons of nuclear energy and immigration conflicts in Chapters 3 and 5 show that conflicts with very similar sets of political institutions nonetheless gave rise to movements with very different strategies—conventional or nonviolently disruptive or militant. Furthermore, the right to participate in public hearings or commissions was not a stable feature of the polity that merely conditioned movements, but rather, the pressure of protests often led authorities to expand institutional access, especially in urban renewal (Chapter 2).

It is not that socioeconomic and institutional factors are irrelevant. Social structures can help explain who took part in various kinds of protests and what interests were at stake, while political institutions provide necessary, permissive conditions for the development of movements. But in the nine cases studied here, these factors cannot explain why large protests occurred when and where they did, or why protesters in particular conflicts adopted the methods that they did. To explain these, it is necessary to turn to political interactions.

MAKING OPPORTUNITIES

My second argument is that protest groups in Germany were able to mobilize strongly in many cases because protesters, allies, and opponents acted in mutually reinforcing ways. Protest depends on opportunities provided by institutions and powerful actors, but if institutions are sufficiently open and potential elite allies are available, then protest groups can help expand the political opportunity structure. This, in turn, makes continued and intensified protest mobilization possible. However, protesters can initiate the process of opportunity expansion only if they use bold, surprising tactics and form alliances with other protesters who use complementary strategies. When they do these things, protesters can have two kinds of opportunity-expanding effects. They can win support from party leaders or other political elites, and they can trigger mistakes by public officials in the timing of reforms and use of police.

Daring actions can attract media attention, which helps win the support of elite allies and may give protesters control of key resources, both of which increase their chances of success. Examples include housing squats in West Berlin and Hanover and the attempts to occupy construction sites in the nuclear energy conflicts at Wyhl and Brokdorf. Alliances between protest groups with different, complementary strategies allow a movement to combine the respectability of moderate groups with the risk-taking of radical groups. This makes it easier to recruit elite allies and negotiate with authorities, and it helps protect protests from state repression.

When political elites give support to protest groups, they increase the chance that the protesters will attain their goals, while also reducing the risk of repression. This promotes protests because people are more likely to join movement activities if chances for success are high and the costs and risks of participation are low. In Germany, protesters in left-leaning movements, such as in urban renewal and nuclear energy, found elite allies mainly in the SPD and Protestant churches, and later in the Green parties. Anti-immigration groups benefited from allies mainly in the CDU and CSU, and secondarily in the SPD. Furthermore, protesters gained support from a wide range of parties and officials at the lowest levels of government (village, neighborhood, town, or borough).

Protesters benefit not only from supporters, but also from their opponents' mistakes. Although public officials prefer to avoid opposition to their policies, protests sometimes catch them off guard, surprising them with the intensity or breadth of discontent, or by specific protest methods that give protesters control of important assets, such as the nuclear plant site at Wyhl or apartment buildings in West Berlin. In such circumstances, officials sometimes respond in ways that inadvertently provoke or facilitate protests. Officials can make four kinds of mistakes: (1) maintaining or increasing threats to residents in the face of protests; (2) overreacting to protests through overly harsh or undifferentiated repression by police and other officials; (3) creating or expanding public participation measures while refusing to make substantive policy reforms; and (4) tolerating illegal protests.

Public officials may provoke further protests if they respond by ignoring protests, trying to show unshakable resolve, or even accelerating the policies that are under attack. Local residents sometimes feel threatened or outraged by this kind of official response and increase their support for nearby protest actions. A different kind of provocation occurs when authorities meet protesters with a strong police force, arrests, and prosecution. The first attempts at repression may be overbearing and counterproductive, if police fail to differentiate between violent and nonviolent protesters or crack down in unusually harsh ways. Overreactions may increase solidarity among different protest groups and prompt elites to support the protesters, complicating later attempts at repressing militant actions.

However, officials can also facilitate protests, when they create or expand citizen participation measures while remaining intransigent on the substance of policy. Protesters may respond by using the new institutional access to organize residents, publicize their grievances, gain some encouraging concessions, and drive a wedge between elites. Finally, when protest groups use new kinds of illegal tactics, either nonviolent or violent, authorities sometimes respond passively, which serves as an open invitation for those groups and others to accelerate the illegal activity.

When protests win elite allies and trigger authorities' mistakes, as they did in most of the cases in this book, protest actions, elite divisions, and authorities' mistakes may become mutually reinforcing. During the rising phase of a protest movement, these interactions may simultaneously expand the threats that protesters face, the opportunities that they perceive, and the level of protest participation that they achieve. However, this process is far from inevitable. Although protesters can help make their own opportunities in some circumstances, in others, the potential elite allies are lacking, or protest groups fail to come up with innovative tactics or to form alliances with other protesters pursuing complementary strategies. In such cases, protests remain small, brief, or both.

INTERACTIONS AND THE TYPES OF PROTEST

The book's third argument is that the types of participation used by protesters also depend on how protest groups, public officials, and political elites interact. Conventional participation, nonviolently disruptive protests, and militant actions[q] are the results of choices that people make about which strategy to adopt, whether or not to publicly support a protest group using a given strategy, and whether or not to participate in particular actions. However, the leaders of protest groups and the participants in them do not choose autonomously. They respond to the opportunities and constraints presented by public officials, other protest groups, and elite allies. Therefore, political interactions strongly influ-

---

q. My aim is to explain significant militant actions, rather than violence as such. As I define it in Chapter 1, militancy includes threatening as well as violent behavior. Militancy usually leads to violence, but whether it does and the scale of the violence depend partly on situational factors such as tactical decisions by police, protesters, and bystanders and the centralization or dispersal of the targets of violence (see Chapter 6).

ence whether conventional participation, nonviolent protests, or militant actions are used by significant numbers of people over the course of conflicts, some of which may last many years. Six kinds of political interactions, relating to alliance patterns, reforms, and policing, are important here: (1) protest groups making alliances with other protest groups pursuing complementary strategies; (2) political elites supporting or discouraging specific kinds of actions; (3) authorities making procedural reforms that open routine access to officials; (4) government officials failing to adopt major substantive policy reforms that reduce the level of threat to residents; (5) authorities making policy concessions, apparently in response to particular protests; and (6) police overreacting or underreacting to unconventional protests.

A protest group's allies can encourage or discourage it from using particular methods. Where disruptive or militant protesters get support from a protest group with more moderate positions and milder methods, the latter lends its respectability to the riskier activities, reducing the risk of state repression. For their part, elite allies can restrain or encourage protest groups that are on the verge of shifting toward disruptive or militant activity. Elite support or opposition to particular actions affects the likelihood of repression and hence indirectly affects the kinds of actions that protesters will attempt and sustain.

In addition, the timing of policy reforms affects the kinds of actions that protesters will see as most effective for reaching their goals. When authorities refuse to adopt major policy reforms in response to initial protests, protesters often shift toward nonviolent disruption or militancy and violence. A different effect concerns the timing of reforms. When authorities make concessions in response to protests, they inadvertently encourage protesters to use the same type of protest again. In addition, authorities promote conventional protests, by directly lowering the costs of such actions, when they provide routine access to official decision makers.

Finally, authorities affect the nature of a conflict through the ways they use police to repress certain forms of political activity, since this directly affects the costs and risks of participation. Consistent, proportionate repression that distinguishes between different kinds of protest activity tends to be effective at reducing protests. When police and the public officials commanding them are passive, protesters can use the apparent weakness in state authority to pursue either disruptive or militant protests. However, overreactions by police can also indirectly promote militancy, by increasing support that protesters receive from other protest groups and elite allies.

EXPLAINING LEFT AND RIGHT, EAST AND WEST

My fourth argument is that the interactive processes I have described had surprisingly similar effects on the activity levels and strategies of protest groups on the left and the right, and on protesters in the western and eastern *Länder*. Admittedly, leftist and rightist protesters differed in their social backgrounds, ideological origins, forms of organization, participatory repertoires, and the nature of violence they threatened and engaged in. Leftists attacked mainly property and police officers who defended it, while rightist violence was mostly against relatively powerless people, especially foreigners, but also homeless people and leftists.[7] By comparing leftist and rightist protests, and using "militant" to describe the strategies of both leftist groups (communists and autonomists) and rightist groups (neo-Nazis and skinheads), I do not mean they are similar in these or other important ways.[r] Indeed, I will focus on explaining two major differences between leftists and rightists in Germany: rightists have been much more likely to use threats and violence, and much less likely to use nonviolently disruptive methods, than leftists have. In addition, I will explain why right-wing violence has occurred disproportionately in the East compared with the West.

Although protest politics on the left and right, and in the East and West, are usually analyzed separately,[8] I argue that they have important commonalities in their causal dynamics. Similar cycles of opportunity expansion led to large, influential protests in both leftist and rightist conflicts, and in western and eastern cases. Where conventional, disruptive, or militant participation occurred, it was produced by similar patterns of

---

r. My use of the term "militant" for both leftists and rightists may remind some readers of contemporary political uses of the "extremist" label in Germany. Some social scientists argue that using this overarching concept for left-wing and right-wing actors obscures important differences between left-wing and right-wing "extremists." See, for example, Kopke and Rensmann 2000; Butterwegge 1996, 64–78; Jaschke 1994; and Stöss 1991. For opposing views, see Backes and Jesse 1996 and Pfahl-Traughber 1992. Although I analyze left-wing and right-wing movements in similar terms, concerning protest levels and broadly defined participation types, I do not mean to imply that left-wing and right-wing militants engage in a similar quality and quantity of violence, or are likely to cooperate because of common interests or ideological elements. Nor do I mean that all their effects are similar, or that they pose similar or equivalent risks to the stability of democratic institutions and civil liberties in contemporary Germany.

strategic interaction, regardless of the protesters' ideological orientation or regional location. Where right-wing skinheads and neo-Nazis undertook massive riots against foreigners in the East, the causes were similar to those that produced militant protests by leftists in the West: a combination of provocative actions by authorities, inadequate routine access to officials, support for the militants by conventional or disruptive protesters, and police passivity. As in the leftist cases, anti-immigration protests remained conventional where officials granted routine access and moderate protesters did not form alliances with disruptive or militant groups.

Moreover, the differences in the types of protest used by leftists and rightists across Germany were mainly due to differences in how protesters, authorities, and potential allies interacted, as I argue in Chapters 1 and 6. For example, there was more nonviolent disruption on the left than on the right partly because leftist activists innovated disruptive methods and rightist activists did not. In addition, the Social Democrats were more supportive of disruptive protests than Christian Democrats were. There was more violence on the right than on the left partly because authorities were more tolerant of right-wing violence than left-wing violence. Anti-foreigner violence rates were higher in the East than in the West partly because the collapse of the communist system in 1989 and 1990 created several years of chaos in administration and policing. This made it more likely that local officials would house foreigners in persistently provocative ways and less likely that they would protect foreigners from attack. However, even in the East, public officials in some locations avoided provocative housing policies and used police and citizen participation effectively enough to prevent major violence against asylum seekers.

The Plan of the Book

Chapter 1 grounds this study's questions in the democratic politics of Germany, examines the limits of socioeconomic and institutional theories of German movements, and details the interactive political process approach used here. It also discusses the reasons for choosing the policy areas and the local and *Land*-level cases that are included.

Comparative case studies occupy the next four chapters. Chapter 2 analyzes large, ultimately successful protest movements against government plans to demolish housing and displace residents in Hanover-

Linden and Berlin-Kreuzberg from the late 1960s to the early 1990s. This chapter also compares the divergent paths taken by protests in the two cities. In Linden, authorities incorporated citizen initiatives into official decision-making, disruptive protests were limited, and militant threats or violence were absent. In Kreuzberg, although residents were also included on official bodies, the conflict was more intense, including a massive squatter movement with nonviolently disruptive and militant wings.

Chapter 3 turns to regional nuclear energy conflicts. It analyzes the development of long-lived, large-scale movements against planned nuclear power plants at Wyhl and Brokdorf from the early 1970s to the mid-1980s, protests that led to the cancellation of the Wyhl plant and a national stalemate on nuclear energy policy. This chapter also contrasts the nonviolent site occupation and the negotiations between protest groups and the *Land* government at Wyhl with the repeated militant actions, clashes between protesters and police, and lack of effective dialogue at Brokdorf.

The next two chapters concern different aspects of the anti-immigration movement. They analyze protests by resident groups, skinheads, and neo-Nazis against foreigners in Munich neighborhoods, small towns in Schleswig-Holstein, and three localities in eastern Germany in the early 1990s. Chapter 4 concerns conflicts in Munich and Schleswig-Holstein, where resident initiatives used mostly conventional methods to protest the siting of shelters for asylum seekers. Chapter 5 explains the large anti-foreigner riots in two eastern German localities, Hoyerswerda and Rostock, through a comparison to Riesa, which had relatively little violence.

Finally, Chapter 6 examines how well the cases support the interactive political process theory. It also explains differences between the action repertoires of left-wing and right-wing movements in Germany and assesses the relative contributions of the interactive theory, structural theories, and theories of protest cycles.

1 POLITICAL INTERACTIONS AND GERMAN PROTEST MOVEMENTS SINCE THE 1960S

Movements and Democracy in the Postwar Period

WEAKNESSES AND STRENGTHS IN GERMAN DEMOCRACY

While the questions of this study are motivated by general issues that protest movements raise for democracy in Western countries, the questions are particularly relevant for Germany. Although West German institutions met the formal requirements of representative democracy after the creation of the Federal Republic in 1949, most political scientists agree that West German democracy had important deficits for at least its first two decades. In the first place, political participation was limited and a participatory culture was lacking among elites and citizens. The leaders of the main political parties feared disorder and distrusted citizen participation, concerns which were institutionalized in the Basic Law (the constitution) in 1949.[1] The Basic Law limited the power of the Bundestag in favor of the government, did not permit referenda on federal legislation, and allowed state actors to ban anticonstitutional political parties and other organizations. Although the Social Democrats in opposition and the labor unions supported protests against rearmament, NATO membership, and nuclear weapons in the 1950s, those movements collapsed when party and union leaders withdrew their support in order to return to purely institutional forms of participation.[2] While voter turnout was high, citizens' participatory repertoire was mostly limited to voting and passive membership in interest groups.[3] West Germans had few positive feelings about their political institutions, and most believed they could not do anything "to change an unjust or unfair law" at the federal level.[4] West German citizens tended to be passive, obedient, and dutiful, largely lacking the civic culture found in the United States and Britain. Unconventional forms of participation such as marches, boycotts, and unauthorized strikes were less common in the 1950s than they have been from the late 1960s onward.[5]

Party competition was another area of weakness for democracy in this period. Political parties are a crucial focus for elite competition in Germany, since the parties enjoy official status, according to the Basic Law and the 1967 Law on Political Parties. But by the 1960s, West Germany's parties cooperated and sought consensus more than they competed against each other for public support.[a] Within the framework of the modified proportional representation system, the federal parliamentary parties were reduced to only three by the 1960s: the CDU-CSU,[b] the SPD, and the Liberal Party.[c] Changes in the composition of the federal government occurred at long intervals and, until 1998, only as a result of party leaders' decisions rather than election outcomes. By the 1960s, the parliamentary parties had converged on accepting the social market economy and integration into the European Community and NATO.[6] De facto convergence between the Social Democrats and Christian Democrats led to formal cooperation in Grand Coalition governments, which ruled at the federal level from 1966 to 1969.

Finally, politicians and public officials in West Germany were highly unresponsive to protests in the 1950s and 1960s. The movements against rearmament and nuclear weapons in the 1950s, which included demonstrations involving over 300,000 people in 1958, collapsed after the Federal Constitutional Court banned the movement's use of unofficial referenda and the Social Democratic and union leadership withdrew their support.[7] Authorities met leftist protesters with repression and attempts to discredit them by associating them with communism, rather than by making concessions or including them in debate.[8]

At the same time, West Germany's democratic institutions have had some important strengths, which since the 1960s have provided a con-

---

a. In addition, consensual relations among elites have been supported by a moderately strong pattern of neocorporatist relations between the state and the major interest groups (Katzenstein 1987, 42; Schmitter 1981, 294; Helm 1993, 18, 21–22).

b. A long-term coalition at the federal level between the Christian Democratic Union and its Bavarian affiliate, the Christian Social Union.

c. The Freie Demokratische Partei (Free Democratic Party).

text in which protest groups could gain elite allies, be partly sheltered from state repression, and expand their mobilization. That is, political institutions have provided permissive conditions for the development of large protest movements. First and foremost, parliamentary government, the rule of law, and civil liberties became well established in the first decades of the Federal Republic, providing the basis for elite competition and political participation. Second, the electoral law creates the potential for more party competition than actually existed in the 1960s. The proportional representation system for parliamentary elections at all levels of government makes a multiparty system likely, even though there are restrictions on the smallest parties, which must gain five percent of the vote or relative majorities in three electoral districts in order to qualify for any seats. The five-percent hurdle proved surmountable by the Greens in the early 1980s, and may even have benefited that party by providing incentives for its diverse factions to join forces and remain unified.[9]

Third, the decentralized federal system, a product of early German political history and the Allied occupation, creates many chances for meaningful participation in subnational politics. Subnational political systems included eleven *Länder* (sixteen after unification) and approximately sixteen thousand municipal and county governments, each with its own administration, in the 1970s. Much policymaking is controlled or strongly influenced by subnational officials. *Land* and local administrative agencies employ about 88 percent of all civil servants and control about 45 percent of all tax revenue, and, until a 2006 reform, about 60 percent of all federal legislation was subject to an absolute veto power by representatives of the *Länder* in the upper house, the Bundesrat.[10] Therefore, the subnational levels of government provided important opportunities for new issues, participants, and party competition in the 1960s. Decentralized federalism created opportunities for competition among politicians and public officials at different levels of government, even in policy areas where federal institutions had a large role.[11] Issues could percolate from lower to higher levels, leading to increases in party competition in the political system as a whole, especially after local politics became more politicized along party lines beginning in the 1960s.[12]

Fourth, the political parties have been potentially important sites for democratic politics and the transmission of demands from below. The parties have large memberships, and party organizations extend down to the local level. The Basic Law and subsequent legislation require parties to maintain a degree of internal democracy, and this provides a basis for factional conflict within the parties.[13] In 1968, the SPD and the Liberal Party, the parties most important for left-wing protesters in the 1970s, claimed 730,000 and 57,000 members, respectively. By 1983, the Christian Democratic parties had grown to 920,000 members, which offered potential access to the party system to right-wing protesters.[14] Even in the 1950s and 1960s, local party organizations and affiliated bodies such as youth organizations possessed much autonomy from federal and *Land* party leaders.

Indeed, factions have been well established in the largest parties. The Social Democrats in the 1970s and 1980s contained a left wing that was opposed to capitalism and favored increased citizen participation and environmental protection, as well as a right wing that was close to the trade unions and supported the status quo on those issues. In the 1980s and 1990s, the Christian Democratic parties included a right wing that had nationalist leanings and was opposed to immigration, a moderate conservative wing, and a leftist grouping that supported workers' rights.[15] Partly as a result, debates within the parties sometimes have been vigorous on particular issues, even though party leaders have largely dominated decision-making processes.[16]

Finally, the court system is independent of the other branches of government and well articulated down to district levels. This creates the potential for outside groups to challenge government actions in the courts and for judges to side with them against the government, although the opponents of movements have also used the courts to block proactive policy reforms such as abortion liberalization.[17]

LEFTIST MOVEMENTS AND DEMOCRACY SINCE THE 1960S

In light of the democratic defects of the 1950s, the changes in West German politics from the late 1960s to the late 1980s were momentous. During those twenty years, two intertwined developments occurred: left-leaning protest movements grew, and Germany's democracy became invigorated and hence more similar to other advanced industrial democracies. After the student movement and Extra-Parliamentary Opposition rose and declined in the late 1960s, many students and recent graduates helped organize local residents on environmental, urban, women's, and social problems. Together with mainly middle-class adults, they helped set into motion what contemporaries called a "citizen initiative movement" beginning in the early 1970s. Over the next two decades, strong movements developed, with goals, allies, and activists that placed them mainly on the left. At the same time, by pursuing noneconomic issues, using unconventional methods, and relying on informal organization, the new movements differed from the traditional left, as represented by the Social Democrats and labor unions.[d]

In this period, left-leaning protest groups worked against nuclear power plants, for renewable energy, against slum clearance, for neighborhood preservation, against highway construction, and for inexpensive housing and mass transit. They mobilized against new industrial facilities and pollution, for women's equality and autonomy, against nuclear missiles, for self-managed economic units, for increased citizen participation, and for the interests of the unemployed, the mentally ill, the homeless, foreigners, and residents of Third World countries. These movements mobilized a massive amount of political participation. During one peak period, from 1981 to 1983, an estimated three to four million people participated in protests annually. By 1989, 12 percent of West Germans said they had participated in a citizen initiative, up from 5 percent in 1980, and this figure rose to 16 percent in unified Germany in 1992. Leftist protests continued at high levels after unification, with an estimated five million protest participants in 1992, and the total number of protests in the 1990s was similar to the 1980s. During those two decades, protests occurred about three times more often than they had in the 1950s.[18]

Although many of these activists eschewed identification with political parties and with traditional left-right politics, it is appropriate to consider these protest movements as leftist or left-leaning on the whole.[e] Their

---

d. The newness of these movements was overstated by much of the literature on new social movements. The left-wing protesters' supposedly new features can be found in the early phases of many movements, and the new movements had features that overlapped with those of "old politics," such as a degree of formal organization, use of conventional participation, and alliances with elites (D'Anieri, Ernst, and Kier 1990; Klandermans 1990; Kriesi 1993; Tarrow 1989b, 61–68; 1994, 147–48). Even in Germany, where the claims to newness are perhaps most credible, some important protest groups (e.g., communist and autonomist groups) made significant use of old-left ideas (Marxism, revolutionary socialism, and anticapitalism), organizational practices (cadre groups and infiltration of other organizations), and methods (provocative street violence). The inexactness of the term "new social movement" has become even more apparent with the appearance, in the 1980s and 1990s, of right-wing movements that have some "new" features (cf. Kriesi 1995, 11 and note 2).

e. While this is not a perfect term, the alternatives are more problematic. "New social movements" exaggerates the newness and separateness of these groups and the differences between leftist and rightist protest. "Left-libertarian" fails to capture the

goals placed them on the left in that they opposed concentrated political authority and supported equality in various spheres, such as the relations between citizens and the state, nature and humanity, residents and business enterprises, tenants and landlords, females and males, and poor states and rich states.[f] These movements included many activists who were inspired by Marxist socialism and were organized in communist, "undogmatic left," and autonomist groups, the last beginning in the early 1980s. Moreover, these protest groups found allies mainly in leftist or center-left political parties and in interest groups linked to those parties: the left wings of the SPD and the Liberal Party, the Protestant churches, some labor unions, and later the Greens.[19] The supporters of these protest groups overlapped strongly with the supporters of left-wing parties, and most saw themselves as leftists.[20]

While these movements grew and became institutionalized in many ways by the 1980s,[g] Germany's democratic deficits shrank. Citizens became more active and less deferential, politicians and officials sometimes openly made concessions to protest groups, and the political culture shifted away from a subject culture toward a civic culture.[21] Academic observers saw many causes for this strengthening of democracy. Some held that democratic institutions helped socialize younger Germans into democratic values while older, more authoritarian cohorts died off.[22] Others argued that socioeconomic developments such as peacetime prosperity and mass education and communication promoted a shift toward citizen participation and other postmaterialist values.[23] Changes in the party system were arguably both causes and effects of the transforma-

---

important illiberal elements on the left (communists, autonomists, and militant strategies), while "left-ecological" seems to exclude groups interested in housing policy, nuclear disarmament, or women's rights. Although some participants in these movements were clearly right-wing, especially some leaders in the environmental movement and the early Green parties, they made up a small minority and did not prevail within the Green parties or among voters when leftists and rightists came into conflict in the Greens around 1980 (Biehl and Staudenmeier 1995, chap. 2; Markovits and Gorski 1993, 193–96).

f. Despite much criticism of the left-right distinction, and its changing meanings in the Western countries over the last two hundred years, it remains useful (Ignazi 2003, chap. 1). For a similar conceptualization of the left and right based on social equality and freedom, in opposition to inequality and authoritarianism, see Bobbio 1996, chaps. 6–7.

g. These include the formation of the Green parties, the acceptance of public subsidies by alternative and women's groups, and the growth of environmental organizations (Kitschelt 1989; Dalton 1994; Cooper 2004, 214–16).

tion. The party system became more competitive after the Social Democrats shifted to the political center with their 1959 Bad Godesberg program and the Liberals shifted toward coalition with the Social Democrats in the late 1960s. This made alternation between the two main parties of government possible, a development reinforced by the founding of the Green parties and their consistent winning of parliamentary seats beginning in the early 1980s. Social Democrats and Greens began forming coalition governments at *Land* and local levels, as they ultimately did at the federal level in 1998, presenting a clear alternative to the bloc of Christian Democratic and Liberal parties.[24]

But the changes in German democracy cannot be adequately explained by reference to elite and institutional politics, socioeconomic developments, and political culture. Those explanations leave out the contributions made by political actors. Citizen initiatives and other protest groups of the 1960s, 1970s, and 1980s, together with their allies among political elites, created a vibrant and democratic kind of protest politics. They broadened the participatory repertoire, increased party competition, and made officials more responsive. Protest groups contributed to these changes by working within the SPD and by pressuring it from outside. Their efforts led the party to move, unevenly and slowly, toward movement positions on citizen participation, the environment, and many other issues beginning in the early 1970s. Through mostly nonviolent conflicts with authorities, they helped socialize West Germans, especially the younger generations, into a more activist kind of citizenship. They also publicized the key issues later used by the Green parties, helped found those upstart parties, and supported their early campaigns.[h]

The other problem with the socioeconomic approach to the left-leaning movements is its inattention to militancy, violence, and extremism. Many studies that link political participation at the national or aggregate level to postmaterialist values focus almost exclusively on nonviolent participation.[25] They see the leftist movements as part of a more democratic, more participatory "new politics." Similarly, authors in the new social movement perspective have seen them as the carriers and embodiment of a new, more democratic political paradigm with the potential to de-

---

h. Voters and activists were attracted to the Greens largely because they adhered to the demands of the left-leaning protest groups, especially regarding nuclear energy, environmental protection, nuclear disarmament, and increased democratic rights (Frankland and Schoonmaker 1992, 92; Pappi 1991, 462–65; FGW 1987, 39).

mocratize civil society and politics.²⁶ⁱ Indeed, there is much research to support this view. These groups did contribute to increased participation and a broader repertoire of nonviolent participatory methods, and the vast majority of participants in these movements were nonviolent.ʲ

However, this perspective fails to account for the growth of antisystem groups, militancy, and violence within left-wing movements. Nor does this work examine the relation of militant actions, including violence, to other forms of political participation. Yet beginning in the late 1960s, left-wing antisystem groups formed, gained adherents, and committed acts of political violence. These groups included communists and autonomists, as well as underground terrorist organizations engaged in armed struggle against the state, such as the Red Army Faction, the June 2nd Movement, and the Revolutionary Cells. The number of activists that the government classified as anarchists and "social revolutionaries," who were mostly autonomists, rose from 2,000 in 1982 to about 5,400 in 2003.²⁷

Largely because of the activity of these groups, left-wing political violence grew greatly from the 1950s to the 1980s in West Germany, as it did in some other Western countries such as the Netherlands and Italy.²⁸ Even though the vast majority of participants in left-leaning protests were nonviolent, the annual rate of leftist violence in West Germany approximately doubled from 1965–79 to 1980–89.ᵏ Federal authorities reported about eight hundred acts of left-wing violence per year in the 1990s, 80 to 90 percent of them by autonomists, including about sixty-five arson attacks and one hundred injuries annually.²⁹ Rising violence by protesters went hand in hand with the growing use of state repression against leftist protesters, including regulations barring suspected radicals from state employment (the 1972 Radicals Decree), massive use of police to intimidate or even trap protesters, the criminalization of demonstrators in the 1980s, increasing armament of police forces, and prosecutions for

---

i. A polar opposite view is that the leftist movements undermined or threatened representative democracy (Crozier, Huntington, and Watanuki 1975; Kaase 1982, 187; Kaltefleiter and Pfalzgraff 1985; cf. also Klages 1981).

j. For example, Rucht found that only 0.2 percent of protesters and 8.4 percent of protests were violent in 1950–93 (Rucht 1999, 357–58; cf. also Koopmans 1992, 17; Barnes et al. 1979, 545, 549; Dalton 1996, 76).

k. Neidhardt and Rucht 1999, 151–52; Koopmans 1993, 643; 1992, 264; author's calculations. Rucht analyzes protests by all kinds of groups, which were largely left-wing groups in this period; he also finds that violent protests tripled from the 1950–64 period to the 1965–79 period.

the broadly defined crime of supporting a terrorist association (Paragraph 129a of the criminal code).[30]

UNIFICATION AND THE ANTI-IMMIGRATION MOVEMENT IN THE EARLY 1990s

After 1989, democracy in the Federal Republic changed again, in wholly unexpected ways, with the sudden democratization of East Germany and its rapid unification with West Germany. Small ecology, peace, and human rights groups in East Germany, which organized under the protection of the Protestant Church in the 1980s, grew into a prodemocracy movement that helped bring down the Honecker regime. Although the transition to representative democracy and unification became possible only because of the decay and collapse of communist regimes in Eastern Europe and the Soviet Union, the prodemocracy movement also played a key role. In 1988 it began nonviolent public protests, which culminated in mass demonstrations of up to 500,000 people in Leipzig and other cities in the fall of 1989. The demonstrations led to roundtable negotiations with the communist government beginning in December 1989 and to free multiparty elections in March 1990.[31]

The unification of West and East Germany in October 1990 meant the extension of West German political institutions to the former East Germany, but there were many unforeseen consequences. While the official unemployment rate remained over 15 percent in the eastern *Länder* during the 1990s, an East-West cleavage became established in national politics. The former East German Communist Party,[l] renamed the Party of Democratic Socialism, gained representation in the parliaments of the eastern *Länder* and in the Bundestag in the 1990s.[32] The East German prodemocracy movement temporarily enjoyed a major role in national politics but the movement and the eastern Green parties that it spawned quickly faded to the margins of politics in the new eastern *Länder*.[33]

Furthermore, the first few years after unification coincided with the most important right-wing protest movement in postwar German history, a nationwide movement against immigration that peaked in the early 1990s.[m] Citizen initiatives, neo-Nazis, and skinheads mobilized in

l. Sozialistische Einheitspartei Deutschlands.
m. After the brief rise and decline of the National Democratic Party in the late 1960s, broad-based right-wing movements were absent in the 1970s and 1980s. However, neo-Nazi groups were significant, according to authorities, who counted between

efforts to drive out asylum seekers and other foreigners and to bring about more restrictive policies on immigration and foreigner rights. Skinheads endorsed vague versions of neo-Nazi goals, focused on radical opposition to foreigners ("Foreigners out!"), and often used threats and violence. The anti-immigration movement was right-wing in that it promoted social and political inequality (Germans over members of other ethnic groups), recruited many activists from neo-Nazi groups, and found its allies on the right. The Christian Democratic parties, the right wing of the SPD, and new far-right parties (the Republicans and the German People's Union),ⁿ supported the anti-immigration movement, though they usually did not openly support the militant groups.[34] From 1991 to 1993, skinheads, other right-wing youths, and neo-Nazis carried out about 6,300 violent crimes, including about 1,300 arson attacks, mostly against foreigners' housing, and they injured about 2,100 people.[35] This was a massive increase compared with the 1980s. Anti-foreigner violence occurred disproportionately in eastern Germany, where 31 percent of all right-wing arson attacks occurred, although it has only 20 percent of the population.[36] Protests against immigration declined sharply after the Bundestag and Bundesrat voted in May 1993 to restrict asylum rights by amending Article 16 of the Basic Law.

Most analyses of the anti-immigration movement in Germany have exaggerated its differences from the leftist movements.ᵒ Aside from analyses of far-right parties, almost all work on anti-immigration protest focuses on neo-Nazis and skinheads, and hence on extremist ideology and violence.[37] Although some studies have related right-wing mobilization to the politics of immigration,[38] even this literature has mostly ignored nonviolent protests and the activities of citizen initiatives that were opposed to immigration and used conventional or disruptive methods.[39] In part this is because right-wing protesters as a whole have been focused more on threats and violence and less on nonviolently disruptive methods than leftist groups.[40] However, at least in the western *Länder,* citizen

---

one thousand and two thousand neo-Nazis and an average of eighty violent actions and over thirty injuries by right-wing extremists annually in the 1980s (BV 1980, 18, 21–40; 1989, 109; 1990, 88; data on actions from BV 1980–89, author's calculations; Assheuer and Sarkowicz 1992, 22–25; Stöss 1991, 167).

n. The Republikaner and the Deutsche Volksunion.

o. As with the left-wing movements, the explanations offered for the right-wing protests have focused on socioeconomic factors—unemployment, modernization losers, and immigration—as well as neo-Nazi ideology and the loss of identity (e.g., Heitmeyer 1992; Tuttle 1994; Merkl 1993).

initiatives, led by middle-class adults, often mobilized nonviolently against immigration by asylum seekers. They mainly used conventional methods, sometimes resorted to nonviolent disruption, and pursued reformist goals. In short, movements on the left and right all have contained a range of strategies, demands, and social constituents. In this respect, they are more similar than they are often portrayed to be.

The Limits of Socioeconomic and Institutional Theories

SOCIOECONOMIC EXPLANATIONS OF "NEW SOCIAL MOVEMENTS" AND ANTI-FOREIGNER VIOLENCE

A variety of socioeconomic theories have been used to explain the development of protest movements. Although these theories help explain who participates in protest actions, they have difficulty explaining why large protests and long-lived movements occur at some times and in some places and not others, and why protests take conventional, disruptive, or militant forms. While social structural change may create the potential for protests, political factors are required to convert that potential into action.[41]

Theories of postmaterialism, new social movements, and new politics explain the rise of protest in industrialized democracies as the result of social changes associated with the rise of postindustrial society.[42] These changes include increased affluence and almost uninterrupted economic growth, the expansion of service occupations, mass communications, and higher education, and the security provided by the long period of international peace in the Western countries after 1945. As a result of these changes, many citizens have acquired greater political skills and have shifted from materialist values, such as economic growth, toward postmaterialist values, such as environmental protection and citizen participation. Hence, according to the theory, younger, educated, middle-class people have increasingly engaged in elite-challenging political behavior, including unconventional protests.

These socioeconomic changes can help explain why young people with high levels of education participated disproportionately in left-leaning citizen initiatives and other protest groups in Germany and in other Western countries.[43] Changes related to postindustrialization seem to be necessary conditions for the success of left-libertarian, ecological parties,[44] and they may be necessary for the development of movements related to those parties, such as the environmental, women's, and peace movements. However, postindustrial social structures are not sufficient to produce large increases in protest. Protests and political participation increased markedly in Germany from the 1960s to the 1980s, a period when indicators of postindustrialization also advanced. However, this pattern did not hold in all countries undergoing postindustrial changes, such as France and the United States, which did not have large, long-term increases in protests or unconventional participation during the 1970s and 1980s.[45] In addition, as I argue in Chapter 2, strong leftist protests in West Germany did not require highly postindustrial social structures.

Socioeconomic changes[p] have also been used to explain protests, and especially violence, against foreigners or ethnic minorities. In contrast to theories of leftist movements, the relevant theories refer to the materialist dimension of postwar economies and to problems in their recent economic development. According to the theory of ethnic competition, economic restructuring, the bifurcation of labor markets, and high unemployment in many West European countries since the 1970s have increased the ranks of modernization losers. Prominent in this group are young males with few job skills and poor employment prospects. In this view, surges in immigration or unemployment, or local concentrations of those phenomena, lead to interethnic competition for jobs, housing, and other material resources. The working-class groups who are most threatened by foreigners blame them for their problems, and hence carry out violence against them.[46] Indeed, these factors can help explain why perpetrators of anti-foreigner violence have been overwhelmingly young, male, and working class.

Moreover, at first glance, these socioeconomic factors seem to explain the surge in right-wing protests against foreigners in the early 1990s, a period when immigration to Germany and unemployment in eastern Germany increased rapidly. The foreign population of Germany rose by 2.6 million people between 1987 and 1993, largely because of immigra-

p. I focus here on objective conditions rather than subjective perceptions of competition between Germans and foreigners, because comparative subnational data on subjective grievances are not available. Moreover, if subjective grievances are not caused by objective conditions, then such grievances may well be products of mobilization processes rather than causes of them.

tion by refugees and asylum seekers from Eastern Europe, Asia, and Africa; in addition, over 1 million ethnic German "resettlers" arrived from historically German parts of Eastern Europe in this period.[47] Meanwhile, the collapse of the former East Germany's state-run economy led to massive unemployment there beginning in 1991.[q]

However, immigration and unemployment were correlated with anti-foreigner violence only at the most aggregate levels. Closer examination of the evidence shows that in Germany in the early 1990s, there was little if any relationship between unemployment and immigration, on the one hand, and the timing or location of violence against foreigners on the other. Krueger and Pischke's cross-sectional study, which included all 543 counties and separate analyses of eastern and western Germany from 1991 to 1993, found that the sites of anti-foreigner violence did not correlate with unemployment rates or other measures of economic distress.[48] Although unemployment and anti-foreigner violence both were higher in eastern Germany than in western Germany in the early 1990s, there is no relationship between unemployment and anti-foreigner violence in different areas within western Germany, and unemployment was actually negatively related to violence within eastern Germany. My analysis of fifty-four localities within the *Land* of Saxony also found that violence was greatest in areas with unemployment lower than the *Land* average.[r] In addition Krueger and Pischke found that there was no significant relationship between violence and either manufacturing wage levels or workforce skill levels in western Germany.[49]

Nor can increases in unemployment rates explain the rapid increase in anti-foreigner violence in the western *Länder* in the early 1990s. In western Germany rightists committed over 1400 attacks against persons and caused over 660 injuries in 1991–92, with about 85 percent of their

q. Industrial production collapsed in 1990 and had fallen 70 percent by the beginning of 1991, and the real rate of unemployment reached about 40 percent by mid-1991. Although only 12 percent of the workforce were officially unemployed in July 1991, an additional 17 percent were on "short-time" (often "zero-hours short-time"), and others were in retraining or public works programs (Collier 1993, 96; Baylis 1993, 85).

r. This analysis included major attacks on immigrant worker housing and asylum shelters in the counties and cities of Saxony during the peak violence periods of 1991 and 1992. Fifty percent of localities with relatively low unemployment had major shelter attacks, while only 22 percent of places with relatively high unemployment had such attacks.

victims being foreigners.⁵⁰ˢ This rate of violence was about eight times higher than the average rate from 1978 to 1990.ᵗ But overall unemployment and youth unemployment rates in the western *Länder* were actually declining while violence was increasing. Unemployment rates reached a low point in 1991, much lower than their peak in the mid-1980s. While the economy of eastern Germany collapsed during 1991, the economy in the western part of the country continued to expand, and unemployment there fell from 7.9 percent in 1989 to 6.3 percent in 1991.ᵘ

In addition, there is little or no relationship between anti-foreigner violence and the location of foreigners. Only 1.2 percent of the eastern German population were foreigners at the end of 1992, compared with 9.7 percent in the western part of the country.⁵¹ Yet eastern Germany had a disproportionately high share of the anti-foreigner violence. Moreover, violence and other crimes by right-wing extremists show little if any relationship to the foreign share of the population within the western *Länder* or within the eastern *Länder*.⁵²

The strongest evidence for the socioeconomic theory is the connection between the rising numbers of asylum seekers and the rising violence against them in the early 1990s. Asylum seekers were the main targets of the violence, including some of the most dramatic attacks by skinheads in this period. New applications for asylum reached 100,000 annually in 1988 and peaked at an average of over 330,000 per year from 1991 to 1993, the period when anti-foreigner violence also peaked.⁵³ But this correlation permits different interpretations. One is that asylum seekers presented competitive threats to many Germans and that interethnic competition became violent. However, there is little evidence of competition for scarce material resources, since asylum seekers were usually barred from employ-

---

s. In "attacks against persons," I include official counts of bombings, arson attacks (*Brandanschläge*), bodily injuries, and deaths, while excluding counts of property damage. The attacks in eastern and western Germany continued at about the same annual rates in 1993, although official data no longer distinguished between the two parts of the country.

t. In that period, about 45 attacks and 35 injuries were recorded per year in western Germany (data from BV 1978–90, author's calculations). In nominal terms, the increase in attacks was about sixteen-fold. But about half of this increase was due to a loosening of the criteria for classifying attacks as "right-extremist-motivated" (BV 1991, 76, 125–26 n. 9; 1990, 124). Although police data are far from perfect, they are the most comprehensive available, and they are largely corroborated by newspaper accounts (see the graphs in Koopmans 1996b, 205, and 1997, 160).

u. It rose, but only slightly, to 6.6 percent in 1992 (BFA 1993, 42–43, 81; *die tageszeitung* [*taz*], 7 August 1997).

ment and were forced to live in low-standard housing in which Germans would not want to live. In addition, if ethnic competition were occurring, then anti-foreigner attitudes would be linked to increases in violence in Germany. But the proportion of the population holding the most negative attitudes toward asylum seekers actually declined from 1990 to 1992 and was lower in the eastern than in the western *Länder*.[54]

In Chapter 5, I present an alternative explanation of how immigration by asylum seekers helped trigger protests, including anti-foreigner violence, in Germany. In the first place, I argue that immigration caused cultural conflicts rather than material conflicts. Residents' complaints about asylum seekers concerned issues that were seen very differently by people from different cultures, such as noise, hygiene, or public deportment, rather than competition over jobs, apartments, or other material goods.[55] Furthermore, the local importance of these cultural conflicts depended on political interactions. Cultural conflicts were aggravated or reduced by government policies on the distribution, housing, and management of asylum seekers, and the size of protests was affected by the availability of local allies for anti-immigration protesters. Similarly, whether conflicts became violent or remained nonviolent depended on political processes, not the numbers of asylum seekers.

SOCIAL STRUCTURES AND TYPES OF PROTEST

According to social structural theories, how individuals participate depends on their socialization and access to political resources. Those writing about right-wing protesters argue that violence is most likely to come from youths, males, and working-class participants because of their authoritarian socialization, economic deprivation, and insecurity.[56] By contrast, those focusing on leftist protests have emphasized that nonviolently disruptive protests can be expected from young members of the new middle classes because of their high levels of education and experience of affluence.[57]

Studies of who participates in protest movements in Germany often bear out these expectations. Right-wing skinheads, left-wing autonomists, and members of communist groups, all of whom often engage in violence, consist almost entirely of male youths and young adult men. By contrast, small property owners and citizen initiatives dominated by them often have preferred conventional kinds of participation, reflecting their stake in the status quo, communication skills, and easier access to elites. Those engaged in nonviolently disruptive protests tend to have intermediate social positions, as university students or recent graduates.[58]

However, the social structural theory leaves much unexplained even at the individual level. Social position influences but does not determine how people participate. Young, highly educated participants in the leftist protest groups used the full range of protest methods. Autonomists and members of other militant left-wing groups were drawn from university students and recent graduates and not mainly from manual workers.[59] Workers in Germany often carry out nonviolently disruptive actions, such as strikes and demonstrations.[60] Older middle-class residents sometimes moved from conventional to disruptive protest methods, or at least openly supported the latter.[61] The perpetrators of anti-foreigner violence were not usually unemployed, and were much more likely to be skilled than unskilled workers.[62]

Moreover, explaining what kinds of individuals participate does not help much in explaining why conflicts become conventional, disruptive, or militant. Social structures can explain little here because movements often draw on socially diverse constituencies and protesters try to use multiple forms of participation.[63] In addition, protest groups and movements are often factionalized on the question of how to participate. In all the major conflicts I studied in Germany, a wide range of social groups (youths and adults, working class and middle class) were available and at least somewhat mobilized. But the strategies and tactics that dominated the conflicts nonetheless varied greatly from place to place. In Germany, it was easy to find quite different protest strategies used in areas with similar social structures, such as in predominantly working-class neighborhoods in large western German cities undergoing urban renewal (see Chapter 2), rural agricultural areas with proposed nuclear facilities in western Germany (Chapter 3), and declining industrial counties in eastern Germany with small influxes of asylum seekers (Chapter 5). The interactive political process approach can help account for these differences in protest types across conflicts.

POLITICAL INSTITUTIONAL THEORIES OF PROTEST TYPES

A second major approach focuses on political institutions, viewed as stable features of political opportunity structures.[64,v] According to the institu-

---

v. Although authors using this approach differ somewhat in the institutions and mechanisms that they propose, there is consensus on certain theoretical claims, which I will state as they apply to Germany.

tional theory, if a political system's policymaking structures are open, then protest groups will use assimilative, conventional strategies rather than confrontational ones, and they can attain procedural reforms. However, proponents of this theory argue that in Germany the policymaking structures are institutionally closed compared with other countries. The party system is small, the five percent clause inhibits new party formation, a referendum process is usually not available, political parties are strongly organized, and relations between interest groups and the state are moderately corporatist. In addition, German elites have a stable, prevailing strategy for dealing with protesters, which involves excluding and repressing them.[65] Since they face closed policymaking structures, movements in Germany use disruptive or militant protests, and are unlikely to gain procedural reforms. On the other hand, the strength or weakness of policy implementation structures also affects movements, and in Germany, this points in a different direction. Germany has weak implementation structures, because of decentralized federalism, an independent judiciary, and little state control over the private sector. These weaknesses lead protest groups to undertake conventional actions, such as litigation.

Institutional aspects of political opportunity structures can help explain some general differences in protests across countries, such as the greater use of confrontational strategies in France, the reliance on direct democracy methods in Switzerland, and the focus of most protesters on the local and *Land* levels in Germany.[66] But the institutional approach also has several major limitations. First, a national, aggregate level of analysis is of little help in explaining differences between movements or between *Länder* or localities in Germany's system of decentralized federalism. As I show in the case chapters, political environments for protest groups in Germany are more productively defined in terms of specific political jurisdictions and policy sectors, which for many policy areas means defining them at local or *Land* levels.[67]

Second, political institutions, understood in such general terms, cannot explain many observed differences in protest group strategies within Germany, even within political contexts defined subnationally in terms of particular policy areas. All the cases in this book unfolded in political contexts with relatively closed policymaking structures and weak implementation structures, yet few of them exhibited the mix of strategies that the institutional theory predicts. Indeed, in the pairs of urban renewal and nuclear energy conflicts analyzed in Chapters 2 and 3, protest groups in similar political institutional settings adopted strategies ranging from conventional to disruptive to militant.

Finally, this kind of institutional theory focuses on fixed features of institutions and charts their effects on political contention. Hence, it neglects possible reciprocal causation, in contrast to neo-institutionalist theory.[68] But not all institutions that influence the size and type of protest are fixed. Sometimes authorities respond to protests by creating or reshaping institutions, as when courts expand the right to demonstrate.[69] In the cases studied in this book, protest groups often expanded procedural rights that aided routine political participation. Urban renewal protests led to the establishment of neighborhood committees in West Berlin and Hanover (Chapter 2), and the antinuclear protesters at Wyhl gained a series of formal negotiations and an agreement regulating their participation with *Land* authorities (Chapter 3).

An Interactive Political Process Approach

In the following, I lay out an interactive political process theory designed to explain why large and sometimes long-lived protests develop and why protesters use conventional, disruptive, or militant methods. This theory builds on political process theories, but with a greater emphasis on agency than is common in such theorizing. Political process theorists hold that political opportunity structures affect movements, and they also argue that movements can influence opportunity structures.[70] However, as McAdam notes, theorizing about the latter is much less developed than work on the former.[71] While recognizing that movements depend on a degree of institutional openness as a permissive condition,[72] the approach I take here focuses on the changeable or volatile aspects of the political environment.[73] By focusing on mutually reinforcing actions by protest groups, elite allies, and public officials, I try to identify how protesters sometimes help make their own opportunities.

More specifically, I argue that the size and type of protests are affected by three kinds of interrelated processes that themselves can be influenced by protesters' actions: alliance formation, reforms by public officials, and the policing of protest. Although for the sake of clarity I separate the arguments about protest size and protest type here, there is necessarily some overlap between them when it comes to explaining why large disruptive or militant protests develop.

This theory rests on the assumption that actors pursue power and policy goals to a large extent as though they were making rational calculations. In industrialized democracies such as Germany, public officials and political elites have policy, electoral, and public order goals. Officials prefer to maintain order and pursue their original policies without yielding power to protest groups, yet they will give ground on policy and even on participation rights if necessary to avoid uncontrollable disorder or electoral failures. Some opposition politicians will be more responsive to protest than authorities, because they are more sensitive to electoral threats and incentives and to pressure from party members, and are less concerned about public order, than are authorities. The same holds for interest group leaders with regard to pressure from members of their own organizations. For their part, protesters have policy and participation goals, but prefer to avoid unnecessary risks or costs of participating. Hence, they tend to adopt methods that seem effective, and they do not waste much energy on lost causes.

However, this is a contingent analysis, which recognizes that there will always be a residue of unexplained action. Although actors usually pursue their goals rationally, the theory yields indeterminate results because actors have potentially conflicting goals and their choices depend on actions by others, which may be changing rapidly or otherwise unpredictable. In addition, the theory does not assume anything close to perfect rationality. Hence, it does not explain why authorities sometimes misjudge their opponents, why protesters do or do not try innovative, risky types of actions, why elite allies come forward or fail to do so, or why authorities sometimes make colossal, unforced errors in policing. Still, structural theories do not provide convincing explanations of these features either. Although one cannot always predict when and how actors will act in these ways, the interactive political process theory argues that they can do so, and that their actions are significantly independent of structural constraints.

My theory complements the theory of protest cycles or waves advanced by Tarrow, Koopmans, and others,[74] which focuses on how interactions among actors produce shifts in protest strategies. While the theory of protest cycles helps explain the development of a large set of interrelated movements at the national level, the interactive political process theory is better suited for explaining how protest develops in particular conflicts (see Chapter 6). In addition, my theory further articulates some of the mechanisms proposed by McAdam, Tarrow, and Tilly in their theory of contentious mobilization.⁷⁵ In explaining why protests become large, I agree with those authors on the importance of innovative collective actions and opportunity spirals, in which protesters, political elites, and authorities interact in ways that reinforce each other.⁷⁶ʷ

HOW PROTESTERS MAKE OPPORTUNITIES

Protest groups can make opportunities for themselves by influencing the political environments that constrain them. According to political process theories, each protest group operates in a political environment created by formal political institutions and elite alignments. This political environment affects protests by providing threats, success chances, facilitation, or repression. Public officials make threats when they openly intend to harm the interests of a group or begin to do so.ˣ To say that the chances of success are high means that protests are likely to produce gains for the group's interests, including the blocking of threats by state actors. Authorities facilitate protest when they lower the costs and risks of taking collective action, or keep them low. Repression refers to high or increasing costs or risks, which can also undermine the organizational capacity for further protests. Other things being equal, protest groups are most likely to mobilize if threats, success chances, and facilitation are high, and repression is low.⁷⁷ Institutional openness, elite divisions, support from elite allies, and low levels of state repression tend to promote mobilization by increasing the chances of success and reducing the costs and risks of protesting.⁷⁸ In addition, the types of participation used by protesters are affected by the specific pattern of facilitation and repression, as described below.

---

w. However, my theory is more modest in what it attempts to explain and in its scope. Unlike Tilly, Tarrow, and McAdam, I do not aim to explain collective-identity formation or protest outcomes, and the scope of my theory is limited to protest movements in industrialized democracies.

x. This concept of threats by state actors is a subset of the concept of suddenly increased grievances (Walsh and Warland 1983). Sudden grievances are important in many different theories of movements, including theories of collective behavior (Smelser 1962), political process (Tilly 1978, 133–35; Tarrow 1989a, 38–51, 337; Meyer 1993, 54), new social movements (Habermas 1975, 1981, 1984; Klandermans and Tarrow 1988, 8; Brand 1982, 63ff.), and ethnic competition (Olzak 1992). In my political process approach, I include grievances that are increased by state actions because they are part of the interactions between authorities and protest groups. I exclude grievances that increase due to socioeconomic changes such as unemployment or immigration.

Bold Protests and Alliances Between Protest Groups

Although the political environment affects protest movements, movements also affect the political environment. Through interactions with public officials and elite allies, protesters can help make opportunities for themselves, which aids their further mobilization.[79]

But how do protesters do this? Not all protests lead to expanded opportunities and rising mobilization. Indeed, most protests remain brief and insignificant, failing to attract much attention from news media, opponents, bystanders, or researchers. Protest groups make opportunities only when they form alliances with protesters using complementary strategies and undertake bold, surprising actions—and thereby win elite support or trigger mistakes by authorities. In other words, large protests occur because protesters, reformist elites, and overconfident officials expand opportunities together, often unintentionally, through mutually reinforcing actions.[y] A cycle occurs, in which protest groups act boldly and form alliances with each other, elite allies express support, and authorities make mistakes. Those responses increase the protest group's opportunities or the threats it faces, and thus lead to continued, intensified, or larger protests (see Figure 1). The cycle of opportunity expansion may then begin again, this time at a higher level of protest and with a greater degree of elite support. This process unfolded in the rising phases of the urban renewal and nuclear energy conflicts, and in the Hoyerswerda and Rostock immigration conflicts. In the leftist movements, durable changes in opportunity structures sometimes led to long-term increases in protests, which lasted more than a decade after major reforms were adopted. By contrast, where a cycle of opportunity expansion does not occur, protests remain weak and conflicts small, as in the Kronshagen and Riesa conflicts over asylum seekers and the early phase of the Kreuzberg conflict over urban renewal.

y. Many theorists study how mutually reinforcing actions, triggered in part by protesters, contribute to the development of large movements. McAdam, Tarrow, and Tilly (2001, 243) examine "opportunity spirals," while Joppke (1990; 1993, 13, 222 n. 25), drawing on Blumer (1978), studies "circular interaction" and "feedback," and Willems (1997, 476–78) analyzes "self-reinforcing processes." Sharp (1973, chap. 12) has analyzed "political jiu-jitsu," and Smithey and Kurtz (1999) the "paradox of repression." For the concept of "positive feedback" in systems approaches to political science, see Jervis 1997. Positive feedback between labor movements and elites or authorities has also been identified as an important element in welfare-state development (Castles 1978; Esping-Andersen 1985, 37–38; Rothstein 1990; Skocpol 1988; Pierson 1994).

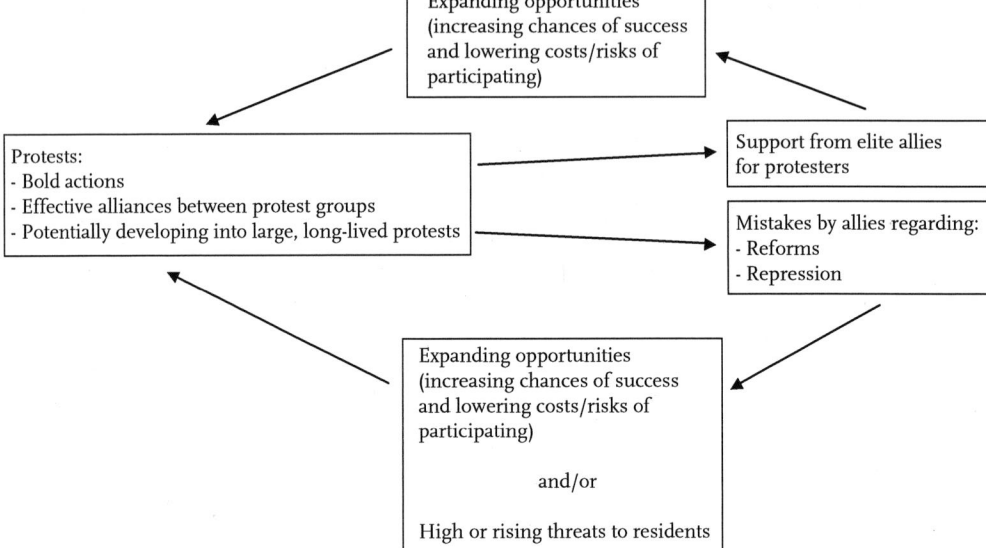

Figure 1. The Making Opportunities Argument

Opportunity expansion depends on bold, risky actions and alliances between protesters with complementary strategies (see Table 2). Actions that are risky or costly to protesters can be effective at expanding opportunities because such actions may gain media and public attention, demonstrate a high degree of protester commitment, and give protesters control over crucial resources, such as buildings or construction sites.[80] Publicity may affect public opinion, thus giving party leaders electoral incentives to support protesters. Innovative tactics can be especially effective in getting attention and throwing authorities off balance, making rapid, effective repression less likely even if the actions are illegal.[81] Alliances between different kinds of protest groups make it possible for protesters to undertake riskier actions, since groups using conventional methods can lend respectability or resources to groups willing to try illegal actions, and also can serve as spokespersons or negotiators after disruptive actions are taken.[82] Moreover, such alliances present an unpredictable new force that may shake up existing alignments among elites.

Gaining Elite Allies

Although protest groups can help make their own opportunities, they are able to do so only when they receive crucial assistance from political elites, especially leaders in political parties and interest groups.[83] Protesters' allies are often weak insiders, who are somewhat marginalized from the most powerful elites and therefore are potentially interested in gaining power through an alliance with a protest group.[84] In Germany, elite allies for protesters have come mainly from the local and *Land* levels, and more often from opposition parties than from parties in government. However, protesters' allies have sometimes been politicians, and even public officials, at higher levels of government than those targeted by the protesters. Elite allies can promote protests in many ways. By publicly advocating similar positions, elites raise protesters' chances of success. By pressing for the adoption of procedural reforms, they lower the costs of participation for protest groups. By publicly accepting a protest group as a legitimate actor or defending the right to protest, they can hinder repression by authorities.[85]

Interactions between the student movement and the center-left parties in the late 1960s show how early protests can win elite allies and thus expand opportunities for later protests. In response to dramatic protests and anti-authoritarian demands by the student movement in the late 1960s, reformist Social Democrats and Liberals led by Federal Chancellor[z] Willy Brandt (SPD) opened their parties, and especially their youth wings, to young leftists. Over 200,000 people joined the Social Democratic Party between 1968 and 1972, most of them under thirty-five years old, and the party's youth organization, the Young Socialists, grew to 350,000 members in 1975.[86] With the influx of new activists, the parties suddenly contained reformist elements that could publicly support and even help organize protest groups. Indeed, in 1971, the Young Socialists declared a "double strategy," which meant working for change within institutions while protesting outside them.[87] Some Young Socialists worked their way up the SPD hierarchy over the next two decades, becoming increasingly capable of supporting reformist positions. Hence they raised the chances of success for protest groups, although their positions also became much more moderate as their careers advanced.[aa] Hence, the early interactions between the student movement, the SPD, and the Liberals set the stage for the opportunity-expanding alliances between left-leaning protesters, Social Democratic leaders, and other

z. The *Bundeskanzler* is the head of government.
aa. For example, Walter Momper became West Berlin's mayor from 1989 to 1990, and Gerhard Schröder was premier of Lower Saxony from 1990 to 1998 and federal chancellor from 1998 to 2005.

Table 2. The Interactive Political Process Theory: Variables and Their Effects on the Size and Type of Protest

Kind of action or interaction	Effects on the size of protests	Effects on the type of protest
Bold actions by protesters	May gain attention, win elite allies, trigger authorities' mistakes, hence promote large protests	Introduce disruptive or militant protests to a conflict
Alliances between conventional and disruptive groups	Enable riskier actions that win allies or trigger official mistakes, hence expand opportunities and promote large protests	Promote disruptive actions
Alliances between either conventional or disruptive groups and militant groups	Enable riskier actions that win allies or trigger official mistakes, hence expand opportunities and promote large protests	Promote militant actions
Political elites' support for protesters	Increases chances of success, reduces repression risks, hence promotes large protests	Steers protesters toward or away from particular kinds of protest
Procedural reforms by authorities	Lower costs of organizing, may increase chances of success, hence promote larger protests	Lower costs of conventional protests, hence promote them
Authorities' failure to adopt major reforms; continued or accelerated threats	Maintains a high level of threat, hence promotes large protests	Makes previous protests seem ineffective, hence promotes a shift to riskier (i.e., disruptive or militant) actions.

Table 2. (Continued)

Kind of action or interaction	Effects on the size of protests	Effects on the type of protest
Authorities' concessions in response to protests	May indicate rising chances of success or declining threats; indeterminate effects	Make protests seem effective, hence promote the type of protest that triggered the concessions
Police or other authorities' use of harsh or undifferentiated repression	May promote alliances between protesters and elite support for them, hence may promote large protests	By promoting alliances between conventional and disruptive groups, promotes disruptive actions By promoting alliances of conventional or disruptive groups with militant groups, promotes militant protests
Police passivity in the face of illegal protests	Lowers the costs and risks of protests, hence promotes large protests	Lowers the costs and risks of disruptive or militant actions, hence promotes these kinds of actions
Police or other authorities' use of proportionate, differentiated, flexible repression	Raises the costs and risks of some protests, hence hinders large disruptive or militant actions	Raises the costs and risks of disruptive or militant actions, hence reduces the use of those kinds of actions

elites in the urban renewal and nuclear energy cases analyzed in Chapters 2 and 3.

The rise of the Green parties to parliamentary representation in the early 1980s is another important example of protest movements increasing the availability of elite allies and hence expanding opportunities for later protests. Between 1977 and 1980, communist activists, other leftists, and members of citizen initiatives founded Green and alternative parties.[88] These parties affiliated to become the Greens, which contested elections at local, *Land,* and federal levels, and won 5.6 percent of the national vote in 1983. The Green parties soon became left-ecological parties advocating policies taken largely from the demands of the locally oriented citizen initiatives, the peace movement, the women's movement, and human rights groups. In the 1980s, their federal program emphasized ecology, grassroots democracy, feminism, and nonviolence.[89] By pressuring the Social Democrats to adopt more reformist positions on issues such as nuclear energy and environmental protection in the 1980s, the Greens raised the chances of success for protest groups mobilizing on those issues.[90] Green party organizations and parliamentary groups also supported protest groups by organizing demonstrations, criticizing police actions, and pressing for parliamentary inquiries, which reduced protesters' costs of action and risks of state repression. While Social Democratic leaders were usually careful to endorse only legal protests, Green politicians often supported and participated in illegal nonviolent actions, and they sometimes offered implicit approval of militant violence.[91]

Similarly, interactions between protest groups and political elites in the 1980s helped make elite allies available for the anti-immigration protesters of the early 1990s. Protests by local groups against shelters for asylum seekers, which began in 1978 in southern West Germany and were often encouraged by local officials,[92] helped motivate and publicly justify anti-immigration campaigns by Christian Democratic politicians. These legislative campaigns occurred in 1980, 1982, 1985–86, and 1991–93 at the *Land* and federal levels, with the main targets shifting from "guest workers" to asylum seekers.[93] Under pressure from citizen initiatives opposed to asylum seekers and growing electoral competition by far-right parties, many Christian Democrats and some Social Democrats joined the anti-asylum campaigns in the early 1990s, when the issue dominated the national political agenda for several years.[94] These campaigns weakened the taboo on publicly expressing anti-immigration views in Germany, which has existed because such views are associated with racism, the Third Reich, and the Holocaust.[95] Besides making opposition to immigration more respectable, the campaigns politicized immigration issues and created opportunities to influence federal policy. Hence, in the 1990s the debate over asylum rights encouraged protests by a variety of groups opposed to immigration, who used nonviolent as well as violent tactics.[96] By the early 1990s, large elite divisions on the asylum issue also made local elite allies available to groups opposing asylum shelters, which influenced the development of local protests (see Chapter 4).

Triggering and Benefiting from Authorities' Mistakes

Protest groups can also trigger mistakes by authorities regarding the timing of reforms and the use of police. By a "mistake," I mean official actions that expand opportunities or threats and hence make further or accelerated protests more likely, presumably inadvertently.[97] I assume that authorities prefer to avoid strong opposition to their policies, especially in the form of disruptive or militant protests. When protests emerge, authorities are often able to reduce opposition through a combination of consultation, concessions, and the proportionate, differentiated, and flexible use of police against unconventional protests.[98] However, protests may catch authorities off guard if they involve new policy areas, new localities, new tactics, new alliances between protest groups, or rapidly growing support from dissenting elites. Hence, especially in the initial phases of a movement, authorities may make mistakes in their efforts to reduce protests.[99]

Authorities can make mistakes that either provoke or facilitate protests. One kind of provocative mistake occurs when government officials ignore protests that have popular or elite support and when they continue or even accelerate the implementation of unpopular policies in the face of opposition. In addition, police may repress protests with unusually harsh methods or without differentiating between violent and nonviolent protesters. This can increase elite allies' support for protesters, as well as the solidarity among different protest groups.[100]

Leftist protests in Germany were strongly spurred by authorities' provocative mistakes, although officials' threats by themselves cannot explain large protests.[bb] Beginning in the late 1960s and continuing into the 1990s, public officials in West Germany greatly increased their activity in localities, especially through the planning of highways, airports, nuclear energy facilities, other industrial facilities, and the reconstruction of urban neighborhoods. These activities threatened many West Germans with increased pollution, the risk of nuclear accidents, and higher rents, and hence provoked the formation of citizen initiatives and the initiation of protest campaigns.[101] In addition, the decision to station medium-range nuclear missiles in West Germany in the 1980s provided a major spur to the peace movement, as did the German government's support for the United States in the 1991 Gulf War.[102] Furthermore, even where state actions provoked nonviolent protests that gained significant public and elite support, officials often adhered rigidly to their original plans or reacted harshly to the protests. Such responses could reinforce public and elite support for the protest groups' claims, and thus helped expand political opportunities, as they did in urban renewal and nuclear energy (see Chapters 2 and 3).

Similarly, officials adopted a variety of policies toward asylum seekers that made them more threatening to German residents and hence triggered intense protests against the newcomers. The distribution of asylum seekers to small towns and rural areas that had little experience with foreigners increased the chance for cultural conflicts, while bans on employment made it more likely that some asylum seekers would engage in petty crime or other disturbing behaviors. Moreover, the construction of large group shelters for asylum seekers, even in the face of protests, concentrated the conflicts in certain neighborhoods (see Chapters 4 and 5).

Public officials can also make mistakes that facilitate protests. One such mistake occurs when they grant routine participatory rights to protest groups while remaining intransigent on the substance of policy. In Germany, protests in many policy areas were facilitated by participation rights that were adopted in response to the student movement and citizen initiatives of the 1960s. Brandt and others in the first SPD-Liberal

---

bb. Mobilization was weak or nonexistent in many cases where threats increased (Kitschelt 1980; Rucht 1984; Kriesi et al. 1995, 148–61), including Kronshagen, Riesa, and the early phase of the Kreuzberg conflict in this book. A threat or grievance explanation also cannot explain why participation sometimes remains at high levels even after threats have been greatly reduced, as in the urban renewal conflicts. Nonetheless, a threshold level of threat seems necessary to explain large protests (see Chapter 6).

government (1969–72) acted to promote increased participation under the slogan "dare more democracy."[103] The right to demonstrate was expanded, and the voting age was lowered from twenty-one to eighteen. Moreover, residents gained new or expanded participation rights regarding state activity on transportation, urban renewal, energy facilities, and air pollution.[104] New legal requirements gave them the right to attend hearings or enter formal objections to government plans. This offered citizen initiatives some chances for success, at least in terms of delaying unwanted projects. It also lowered their costs of organizing residents and publicizing their grievances, gave them an obvious strategic focus, and provided forums where they could gain some encouraging concessions and drive a wedge between elites.[105]

Facilitating mistakes also occur when police tolerate illegal protests, or when authorities make concessions to such actions. These mistakes lead to larger protests and to increases in the particular kind of protest that is tolerated or rewarded. The case chapters show that officials' toleration of illegal and even violent protests was important in many conflicts in Germany. Authorities tolerated housing squats in Hanover, a huge squatter movement and occasionally rioting in West Berlin, and the occupation of the nuclear construction site at Wyhl. Official toleration and passivity were even more important for right-wing actions against foreigners. The surge of anti-foreigner violence in the late 1980s and early 1990s was facilitated by the passivity of many police, prosecutors, judges, and local and *Land* officials, who tended to see neo-Nazi and skinhead actions as apolitical and did not adequately protect the foreigners (see Chapters 5 and 6).[106]

STRATEGIC INTERACTION AND THE TYPE OF PROTEST

Protest Strategies and Strategic Shifts

This study identifies protests as either conventional, nonviolently disruptive, or militant. This classification captures two distinctions important in the protest politics of Germany and many other industrialized democracies, as well as in much of the literature on protest movements: between conventional and unconventional participation, and between nonviolent and violent methods.[cc] Although these somewhat crude dis-

---

cc. For the sake of simplicity, my classification departs somewhat from those used in work with protest event data, which distinguish among conventional, demonstrative, and confrontational types of nonviolent protests (Koopmans 1992, 264; Neidhardt and Rucht 1999, 151).

tinctions ignore the great variety of protest methods and subcategories of methods,[107] they are nonetheless important for protesters, elites, authorities, news media, and the public. While conventional forms of participation involve only procedures that are specified and understood in advance, unconventional protests are open-ended in terms of how the action will develop.[108] Because they are unpredictable, unconventional actions can upset political routines. In protest politics, the break from conventional to unconventional activity is widely noticed and often very salient, though exactly where the divide occurs depends on the observer and on many contextual features. In addition, many unconventional actions become more predictable as they are used repeatedly and authorities adjust to them.[109] A second major dividing line, that between nonviolent disruption and militancy, is crossed when protesters physically harm persons or property, or threaten to do so. In Germany, this line is very important to most participants, targets, and bystanders, who tend to assume or fear that all kinds of violence are related and that those threatening violence will sometimes use it. Because these two distinctions are so salient, they strongly affect strategic decisions by protesters, their potential supporters, and authorities.

These types of participation correspond to three basic strategies used by protest groups, although a particular group or movement may use more than one strategy.[dd] The conventional strategy is to use or promote routine forms of participation, such as voting, petitions, and hearings, with a willingness to bargain and compromise with opponents. In Germany, groups using a conventional strategy usually have reformist goals, seeking relatively small changes in particular policies.[ee] The disruptive strategy entails the disruption of political or economic routines in nonviolent ways in order to get public attention, gain public support, influence elites, seize control of important resources, spur broad policy debates, and gain policy reforms. Disruptive activity may be relatively mild, involving demonstrative action forms such as rallies, demonstrations, or symbolic actions. Or it may be severe, involving noncooperation or nonviolent interventions, such as boycotts, site occupations, squatting, and blockades.[110] Disruptive actions are often illegal and are intended to

---

dd. Internally factionalized groups and movements that consist of multiple protest groups, such as those studied in this book, are likely to pursue more than one of the strategies.

ee. Groups' goals and strategies tend to correlate because they are both influenced by ideologies and because other actors expect them to correlate.

strengthen protesters' bargaining positions. Disruptive groups in Germany tend to have radical goals, seeking far-reaching, fundamental changes in policy, but within the general confines of the present political and economic system.

Finally, the militant strategy is to try to intimidate and coerce opponents by threatening or engaging in violence. Militant methods include the communication of threats, hostile confrontations with police or other groups, sabotage, arson attacks, beatings, and killings. Militant groups in Germany have almost always had antisystem goals, fundamentally opposed to the political, economic, or social system. The militant strategy will not always involve much violence, since violence also depends on tactical decisions by protesters, their adversaries, and bystanders (see Chapter 6). However, other things being equal, if militant actions increase, so will protester violence. However, sometimes the main form of militant activity that is observed is an act of violence, especially in the immigration conflicts analyzed in Chapters 4 and 5, and much systematic data concerns violence. I distinguish between militancy and violence where militant threats were important but resulted in little violence.

Why were some conflicts in Germany dominated by conventional actions, others by nonviolently disruptive protests, and still others by militant threats and violence? In a trivial sense, the forms of participation used in a conflict depend on the strategies used by protesters. But protesters involved in a conflict often pursue multiple strategies, and their predominant methods may change over time. An existing protest group may shift its strategy or shift its attention to a new issue, a new group may form with a new strategy, a different group of activists may join in protests or an existing group may demobilize, and people who are not core activists in any group may shift their participation from one group to another. Hence, the types of protest used in a conflict cannot be traced to fixed strategies of the protest groups available in a given location.

Political Interactions and Protest Types

To explain which types of protest become most important in a given conflict, it is necessary to examine interactions among protest groups, their allies, and their opponents. As in explaining large protests, the key variables center on alliance formation, reforms, and police practices (see Table 2 and Figure 2). These factors affect protesters' expectations about the likely effectiveness of different kinds of actions, the direct costs and

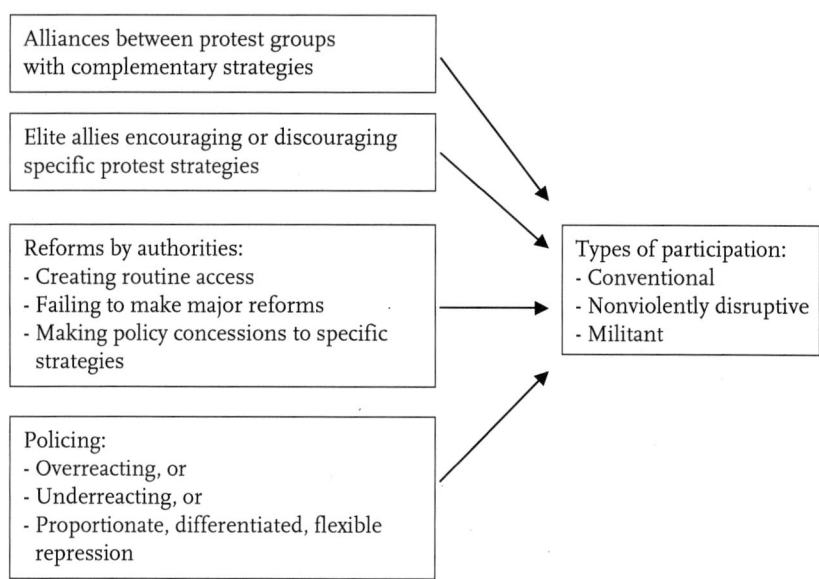

Figure 2. Political Interactions Affecting Three Types of Participation

risks of taking action, and protesters' capacities for undertaking costly actions. The factors listed in Table 2 may also reinforce each other in various ways.

First, alliances between protest groups, or between them and elites, strongly affect the predominant type of participation. Protest types vary according to the costs and risks associated with them. Under most circumstances, conventional methods involve the lowest costs and risks, militant actions involve the highest, and disruptive methods fall in between. Protest groups differ in their tolerance for risky or costly forms of protest, but alliances between groups can overcome the limitations of any one group. Disruptive or militant actions are more likely to become significant if a disruptive or militant group gains support from a group with a conventional strategy, since such groups possess respectability and access to elites, which reduces the likelihood of state repression.[111] Thus, groups using conventional methods may promote nonviolent protests by disruptive groups, as they did in Linden and Kreuzberg, and at Wyhl.

Similarly, conventional or disruptive groups may support militant groups, which can make it more difficult for authorities to repress the militants. Militants may try to use nonviolent protesters' tacit support by trying to mix with the latter at public events, thus inhibiting the police or provoking police to attack in ways that spur further protests. Nonviolent protesters may also make repression of militants more difficult in other ways. They may make it politically difficult to ban demonstrations, they can distract police, and they often attract news media, whose presence may deter police from using hard tactics against militants. Crowds of nonviolent protesters complicated police efforts against militants in Kreuzberg, Brokdorf, Hoyerswerda, and Rostock.

Elite allies can also influence the type of protest, by responding favorably or unfavorably to the pursuit of certain strategies.[112] An elite response to a particular kind of protest sends a message to protesters that elite support and hence the chances of success may depend on the strategy pursued. It also may convey to authorities that elites will or will not object to the state's repression of certain forms of protest. For example, when elites expressed their support for housing squats as a means of influencing urban renewal policy in West Berlin in the early 1980s, this made evictions less likely. Some elites also encouraged squats in Linden, rioting in Kreuzberg, the nonviolent site occupation at Wyhl, purely nonviolent demonstrations away from the construction site at Brokdorf, and conventional actions in most of the cases in this book. Conversely, if an elite ally expresses reservations about supporting a group should it shift toward disruptive or militant actions, the chances of state repression will rise, and the group may be deterred. When Social Democratic and Protestant Church leaders warned that demonstrations at the Brokdorf nuclear construction site would become violent, many nonviolent protesters stayed away from those actions. Elites also discouraged squats in Linden in the late 1970s and 1980s and in Kreuzberg in the late 1980s.

Second, reforms also affect strategies in several ways. Most obviously, if authorities make procedural reforms that increase low-cost access to public officials, such as through public hearings, formal consultation of protest groups, or litigation, they will promote conventional participation.[113] Low-cost access to officials became available to some extent in all the cases in this book, especially in the urban renewal cases after the peak of protest, and this access strongly promoted conventional participation.

Furthermore, the timing of substantive policy reforms has two different kinds of effects on participation, both of which involve protest groups learning about the effectiveness or ineffectiveness of particular methods. The first effect explains why disruptive or militant protests become important. This effect occurs when officials refuse to make major policy reforms in response to growing protests, even though they may make minor concessions. Facing official intransigence, protesters will tend to shift toward an approach that is more risky and costly but might gain them public attention, allies, or the control of important new resources.[114] That is, they shift from conventional to disruptive or militant strategies, or from a disruptive to a militant approach. For example, after citizen initiatives using litigation and other conventional methods found they were having no effect on official plans to site nuclear plants at Wyhl and Brokdorf, they turned toward the disruptive strategy of occupying construction sites or began to support other protest groups who were willing to do so. For similar reasons, conventional protesters shifted toward housing squats in Hanover and West Berlin, toward small disruptive and militant actions in Munich, and toward supporting riot violence in Rostock.

The second effect of policy reforms can explain why either conventional, disruptive, or militant actions get reinforced. Much research on protesters' action repertoires shows that repertoires change incrementally as actors experiment around the edges of their customary practices and tend to adopt the kinds of actions seen to be effective in meeting their goals.[115ff]

If authorities adopt reforms in response to actions by protest groups, this reinforces the kinds of actions that the authorities appeared to reward, whether those actions were conventional, nonviolently disruptive, or militant.[116] Protesters notice what seems to work and tend to repeat it, whether the reforms are minor concessions or major policy changes. For example, when squats led authorities to give apartments to low-income tenants in Hanover and West Berlin, this encouraged further squats. Favorable responses by officials or politicians also reinforced rioting in West Berlin, a nonviolent site occupation at Wyhl, militant demonstrations at Brokdorf, anti-foreigner violence in Hoyerswerda and across Germany, and conventional participation in Munich, Kronshagen, and many other cases.

Finally, authorities, especially the police, may make mistakes by either

---

ff. Moreover, over the last two centuries in the Western countries, the rise of national states and capitalist industrial economies has made repertoires "modular," that is, easily diffusible from one actor or context to another (Tarrow 1993; 1994, 35–45; Tilly 1986, 1995a; Rucht 1990b, 160–61). Hence, the main constraints on the strategies that protesters use are those given by their allies and opponents in a given conflict.

overreacting or underreacting to disruptive or militant protests. Especially in the early stages of a conflict, police may use harsh, undifferentiated repression of all protesters, or they may appear to tolerate illegal protests.[117] Either response is likely to inadvertently promote further protests. Police repression that is considered overly harsh or disproportionate in light of customary standards will increase the support that the targeted group receives from its constituents and allies, especially if specific events such as the killing of protesters create martyrs for protesters.[118] Similarly, if police repress both disruptive and militant protesters in an undifferentiated way, this may increase cooperation among different kinds of protest groups and may provoke elite support for both kinds of protesters.[119] Although repression raises the costs of protesting, police overreactions may indirectly increase opportunities so much that the net effect of the repression is to promote protests. Harsh repression is much more likely to backfire if other factors from the interactive theory are already present, especially alliances between protest groups, elite support for protesters, and unpopular government policies.[gg] The squatter movement in Kreuzberg and the nuclear conflicts at Wyhl and Brokdorf are good examples of police overreactions that were counterproductive.

A different kind of mistake regarding repression occurs when police are passive in the face of illegal actions, whether the actions are nonviolent or violent. Police passivity in that context signals greatly reduced risks and thus strongly encourages those kinds of actions. Police passivity was an important factor in Hoyerswerda and Rostock, as well as in Kreuzberg and at Wyhl and Brokdorf.

By contrast, where police use proportionate, differentiated, flexible repression, they reduce disruptive or militant protests. Differentiated actions are useful for dividing protesters, while proportionate actions are necessary to avoid triggering increased support for unconventional protests from elite allies, moderate protesters, and the public. Flexibility is needed to keep police responses proportionate when protests vary in intensity. This kind of repression is especially effective where the illegal protesters lack prior support from more moderate protest groups or elite allies. It helped limit squats in the North Linden section of Hanover, reduce violence at Kreuzberg demonstrations in the 1990s, and prevent attacks on foreigners in Riesa.

gg. Much literature on the variable effects of police repression focuses on contextual variables; see Schock 2005, 42–44, for a review.

Explaining Left-Right and East-West Similarities and Differences

As I have described, analyses of leftist and rightist protesters in Germany have usually exaggerated the differences in their forms of activity, and have also seen their mobilization as caused by quite different socioeconomic factors. Leftist groups are seen as largely nonviolent and driven by affluent, postindustrial society. Rightist groups are seen as violent and driven by socioeconomic marginalization and immigration pressures. However, as I show in the case studies, the places where leftist groups protested most strongly were not characterized by unusually postindustrial conditions, and the largest right-wing protests were not in locations with unusually high unemployment or immigration rates. More generally, I argue that leftist and rightist movements were not primarily driven by divergent socioeconomic trends, but rather were caused and shaped by similar political processes.

Major protests occurred on the left and right because a certain pattern of political interaction unfolded on both sides of the political spectrum. Public officials imposed threats, protest groups formed alliances and launched daring protests, officials remained intransigent, and some elites offered support. The protest groups responded with larger or intensified actions, and this gained them additional elite support and triggered mistakes by authorities, leading to more solidarity among protest groups and additional elite support, and hence to further mobilization. This pattern was strikingly similar for protest groups on the left and the right, and in the eastern and western *Länder*.[hh]

The protest methods used by leftists and rightists, and by western and eastern protesters, also depended on the same kinds of strategic interaction. Immigration conflicts were largely conventional and nonviolent in the eastern case of Riesa and the western cases of Munich-Südpark and Kronshagen because of common interactive processes in these three cases: officials gave access to protesters; they made concessions to conventional protests; and moderate protesters did not form alliances with militants. Where right-wing skinheads and neo-Nazis undertook massive militant protests, including days of rioting, in the eastern cities of Hoyerswerda and Rostock, the causes were similar to those shaping the militant protests by West German leftists more than a decade earlier in West

---

hh. Similarly, Koopmans has showed that right-wing mobilization responded to the same kinds of changes in political opportunities as left-wing protests did (Koopmans 1995, 1996d, 1996b).

Berlin and Brokdorf. In all these cases, militant protests resulted from a combination of provocative actions by authorities, inadequate routine access to officials, support for the militants by conventional or disruptive protesters, and police passivity.

Leftist and rightist movements, in both the western and eastern *Länder*, used many of the same strategies.[ii] Nonetheless, right-wing protesters were much more likely to use militant and violent methods, especially against persons (such as beatings and arson attacks on occupied housing), and much less likely to use methods of nonviolent disruption, than were leftists. According to Koopmans's analyses of events reported in national newspapers in 1990–94, only 18 percent of right-wing actions were conventional, only 15 percent were nonviolently disruptive, and fully 67 percent were violent. By comparison, 26 percent of protests by left-wing movements from 1975 to 1989 were conventional, the bulk (62 percent) were nonviolently disruptive, and only 12 percent were violent.[120][jj]

As I argue in Chapter 6, these left-right differences in the types of protest were due to many interactive factors. The Social Democrats supported disruptive protests more than did the Christian Democrats, and authorities repressed right-wing militancy much less consistently than left-wing militancy. Furthermore, there were important differences in strategic innovation by leftist activists in the 1960s and 1970s and by rightist activists in the 1990s, and important differences in leftist and rightist activists' attitudes toward democracy.

Why was there a higher rate of anti-foreigner violence in the eastern *Länder* than in the western *Länder*? In addition to the economic crisis explanation, addressed earlier in this chapter, two main explanations have been offered: eastern German political culture and political processes related to unification.

Some have argued that the higher rate of violence is due to a political culture in eastern Germany that is more authoritarian, more xenophobic

---

ii. During the 1990–97 period, about 70 percent of all nationally reported protests in the eastern *Länder* were nonviolent, compared with about 85 percent of protests in the western *Länder*; these figures include protests against immigration (Rucht 2003, 163).

jj. In these figures, threatening actions without overt violence are included with other nonviolently disruptive actions, which overstates the percentage of nonviolently disruptive actions and understates the proportion of militant or violent actions, especially for the right. The action repertoire of the leftist movements did not change much in the 1990s compared with the 1980s (Rucht 2002).

or racist, and more supportive of violence.[121] In this view, the experience of forty years of communist dictatorship, following the twelve years of the Third Reich, left eastern Germans with a highly authoritarian political culture on the eve of unification. Moreover, the East German government did not allow discussion of the Third Reich or a process of strong national identity formation, so, it is argued, eastern Germans are more susceptible to extreme nationalistic claims and anti-foreigner ideas than westerners.[122] Therefore, unification involved a loss of identity and status, and many easterners responded with extreme nationalism, resentment, and violence against foreigners.

However, opinion research does not provide clear support for the political culture explanation. The evidence on authoritarianism is mixed, with some studies finding adults but not youths more authoritarian in eastern than in western Germany.[123] While there is evidence that youths in the eastern *Länder* were more xenophobic than their western counterparts,[124] this is not true for residents of the eastern *Länder* as a whole. In fact, easterners were slightly less opposed to asylum seekers (the main group under physical attack), much less concerned with asylum seekers as a political issue, and more concerned about right-wing extremism than westerners.[125] In response to an open-ended question, only 8 percent of easterners named the asylum issue as an important problem in September 1991, rising to only 21 percent in October, compared with 45 and 73 percent of westerners, respectively.[kk] Moreover, whatever role eastern Germany's political culture may have played, it has been rather stable and hence cannot fully account for violence that came in a large wave and then declined rapidly after 1993. In addition, the preponderance of violence was not a general feature of eastern movements in the 1990s, but mainly limited to the anti-immigration movement. Leftist movements used mainly nonviolent methods in the East, as they did in the West.[126]

By contrast, others argue that the political processes of unification led to a collapse in state and societal authorities, which allowed violence by right-wing youths to increase. With the collapse of the state-run economy and political order, social control by parents, teachers, youth organization leaders, youth clubs, and local politicians declined sharply.[127] Law en-

---

kk. In September, seven problems were named more often by easterners (unemployment, economic development, unification, pensions, wages, rents, and peace; FGW data, in Wochenschau 1991, 212). Economic issues remained the most important ones for easterners throughout the early 1990s surge in anti-foreigner violence.

forcement agencies were confused, disorganized, and undergoing restructuring, and the police and courts responded weakly when violence began.[128] Foreigners became targets because local neo-Nazi activists, strongly influenced by neo-Nazis from western *Länder*, encouraged eastern skinheads to adopt a right-wing stance and to mobilize against foreigners.[129]

The evidence in Chapter 5 supports and elaborates on the political unification explanation. Failures in local government policy, leading to sharp cultural conflicts and extremely weak policing, were important causes of the riots in Hoyerswerda and Rostock. Moreover, weaknesses in public administration and in the mainstream political parties can also help explain why conventional participation against immigration was more limited in the East than in the West. Public officials and politicians in the East often did not provide openings for residents to participate in routine ways. At the same time, the Riesa case shows that anti-immigration protests did not necessarily lead to significant militant protests or violence against foreigners in the eastern *Länder*. Riesa shows that officials could proactively incorporate citizens in discussions, site asylum shelters carefully, and use police to prevent anti-foreigner violence.

Research Design and Methods

Protest movements varied greatly from place to place in contemporary Germany. In order to capture and explain this diversity, I compare cases of large protests which had contrasting kinds of participation (see Table 1). Of course, the comparative case study approach meant that I needed to focus on a small number of conflicts out of hundreds of possible cases.

Yet at the same time, I wanted this study to reach general conclusions about German protest politics in the period from 1969 to 1995.[11] To make my findings more generalizable, I selected cases in three different policy areas and followed many of the cases over long periods of time. This gave

---

11. The scope of this study is limited to instrumental, policy-oriented protest groups, i.e., those that have tried to influence what government and other state actors do (cf. Kriesi et al. 1995, chap. 4). Although anti-immigration groups often mobilized directly against foreign residents, their actions were targeted, or were seen to be targeting, the authorities who control the making and implementation of immigration policy. I have excluded groups that tried to change opinions, consciousness, or societal practices but not state actions, such as most of the alternative movement and important aspects of the women's movement (Brand, Büsser, and Rucht 1986).

me a rather broad coverage of German movements,^mm while also setting up two kinds of comparisons that helped me identify the causes of large protests and of different types of protest.

First, comparisons of contrasting cases within a given policy area (a most-similar-systems approach) gave me important differences to explain, and at the same time allowed me to control for many structural conditions that were similar within each policy area.[130] Those structural conditions included the levels of government involved in the conflict, urban versus rural location, the partisan control of government at the outset of the conflict, and the location of the conflict within national cycles of protest in Germany. By making comparisons within the western *Länder* (Chapters 2–4) and within the new eastern *Länder* (Chapter 5), I also controlled for the myriad differences between the western and eastern parts of the country.

The second kind of comparison is of similar protests in different policy areas (a most-different-systems approach).[131] Some sets of cases were similar in the size and duration of protests, while others were similar in the types of protest. Comparing cases with these similarities allowed me to search for common causal dynamics that were present despite the different structural contexts associated with the different policy areas.^nn The causes I identified are the processes of strategic interaction between protest groups, authorities, and elites already described.

To investigate the cases, I gathered information from interviews, local and national newspapers, government documents, reports by protest groups, and other documents. These sources revealed many small, undramatic actions that, taken together, were important to the development of the movements. Since they usually were not reported in national newspapers, they are not included in event data projects that are based on

---

mm. However, I did not include leftist protests in eastern Germany (cf. Rucht, Blattert, and Rink 1997 and Rink 2000), or cases of small-scale right-wing violence against foreigners (cf. Willems et al. 1993).

nn. For example, nuclear energy and urban renewal conflicts had structural features that were very different from each other. Nuclear energy plants were planned in rural areas, in *Länder* with conservative-led governments, and were subject mainly to *Land*-level policies. They also involved highly technical issues on which authorities presumed citizens to be incompetent, and involved large, indivisible investments, making the stakes of each local conflict high. By contrast, urban renewal plans were made for densely populated urban areas, mostly in cities where governments were traditionally led by the SPD, and were subject to municipal-level policies. Residents could be expected to understand many of the issues, and the programs involved investments that could be steered in a fine-grained way, facilitating compromises.

national news sources.⁰⁰ I relied heavily on interviews and documents for the urban renewal cases, while an extensive secondary literature was available for the nuclear energy cases, which I supplemented with local newspapers. For the immigration cases, since I found the right-wing protest groups much less accessible than those on the left, I relied heavily on local newspapers, supplemented with expert and elite interviews. I assembled the materials into case chronologies to trace common and divergent processes.[132] Although the study's multiple questions meant that my focus in each case study was rather broad, I limited my attention to the main issues and actors in each conflict.ᵖᵖ

Why did I choose conflicts over urban renewal, nuclear energy, and immigration? These three policy areas had characteristics that helped me answer my questions about protest politics in Germany as a whole, though of course the picture I draw here is necessarily far from complete. First, the conflicts in each of these areas were important in the context of German politics. These three policy areas involved large amounts of state activity, major protests, and significant changes in policy when compared with other contemporary German movements. They include two of the most important left-wing movements and the only major right-wing movement since the 1960s. Second, they involved locally based protests directed at a variety of levels of government: local for urban renewal; *Land* and federal for nuclear energy; and local, *Land*, and federal for immigration. In this regard, the cases chosen are roughly representative of protest politics in Germany.[133]

Finally, each of these three policy areas included multiple, local or *Land*-based conflicts that were largely independent of each other, which

---

oo. Local newspapers, for example, include many more local or regional protest events than do national newspapers (Hocke 1999, 150).

pp. Each case included state actions in a given policy area and geographic location (*Land*, municipality, or neighborhood), campaigns by a variety of protest groups directed at blocking or influencing state actions, and the policy and procedural responses by officials, party leaders, and other elites. To make the case studies manageable, I included only protest activity relevant to the main policy issues. I left out aspects such as protest groups' attempts to influence secondary policies, for example, groups trying to improve social services in urban renewal areas, to promote renewable energy or conservation as an alternative to nuclear energy, or to gain control of bars and youth centers in areas with anti-immigration mobilization. I also left out attempts to effect cultural change and efforts to build organizations, networks, and communities largely apart from the mainstream German society, though cultural change and organizational networks were potentially important sources of the movements' resiliency and policy influence.

aided the comparative analysis.[qq] These three policy areas also include conflicts that varied greatly in the type of protest. In urban renewal, some conflicts remained largely conventional (such as Darmstadt, Hanover-Linden, and Wiesbaden), while squatters became important in other cities (Frankfurt, Cologne, West Berlin, and Freiburg). In a few places, repeated, violent confrontations between autonomists and authorities developed (Berlin-Kreuzberg, Hamburg-Hafenstrasse, and Hanover-Nordstadt).[134] Antinuclear conflicts ranged from mostly nonviolent, disruptive, and long-lived (Wyhl and Gorleben), to short and militant (Kalkar and Grohnde), to long and militant (Brokdorf), to strongly mixed (Wackersdorf).[135] Immigration conflicts also varied greatly across *Länder* and localities, with nonviolent participation in many locations throughout Germany, especially western Germany, and large-scale riots in a few places in the new eastern *Länder*. Even in the East, there was much variation, since significant violence occurred in less than half of the communities that received asylum seekers in the early 1990s.[136]

To choose the contrasting cases within each policy area, I mainly looked for cases of large conflicts[rr] that varied greatly in the kind of protest at the peak of conflict, that is, when authorities took decisive action that led to a decline in unconventional protests. This gave me a large amount of variance to explain. But I also wanted to avoid a potential problem. Work on protest cycles cautioned me that earlier, high-profile conflicts might greatly influence later conflicts. To the extent that cases proved to be interdependent, I wanted to choose cases that tended to influence other cases more than they were influenced by the others. Therefore, I chose cases that occurred fairly early in the national cycle of left-wing protest (which began in the 1960s) and in the right-wing protest cycle (which began around 1989), and that were among the most important conflicts in terms of state activity, mobilization, and publicity.

Therefore, after studying Berlin-Kreuzberg with its repeated battles between leftists and police, I chose to examine Hanover-Linden, which had milder protests. Kreuzberg became a high-publicity case, exemplary for radical and antisystem protesters, while Linden was a model for those seeking to resolve urban renewal conflicts through expanded conventional participation, and both conflicts were under way in the early 1970s.

qq. Although national and international contexts, as well as external movements, affected the conflicts, the effects of those factors were limited and strongly mediated by local or *Land* conditions.
rr. Hence, cases with small or moderate amounts of protest are underrepresented.

I chose Wyhl, since it is an exemplary case of nonviolently disruptive protest, and then Brokdorf as the ideal contrast, given the role of high-publicity violence by protesters and police in that conflict. With these two cases, I include the earliest significant conflicts over nuclear energy, as well as two of the largest and most influential ones. Finally, I turned to immigration conflicts. I first studied the anti-foreigner riots in Hoyerswerda, which occurred near the start of the early 1990s wave of right-wing protests, and then investigated why Riesa, another case in the eastern German *Land* of Saxony, had little anti-foreigner violence though it had a large and active skinhead group. Later I sought cases of predominantly nonviolent anti-immigration protests in the early 1990s, which led me to Munich neighborhoods and the small town of Kronshagen in Schleswig-Holstein, places chosen because their structural conditions were very different from each other, although initially I knew little about the types of protests to be found there.

2 URBAN RENEWAL CONFLICTS IN HANOVER AND WEST BERLIN

In the 1970s and 1980s the Linden section of Hanover and the Kreuzberg borough of West Berlin became the sites of major conflicts over the goals and means of urban renewal policy. In several ways, these two conflicts exemplify the importance of political interactions. In both Linden and Kreuzberg, large, sustained, and ultimately successful movements against municipal policies of demolition and displacement developed because protest groups repeatedly expanded political opportunities by winning allies and triggering officials' mistakes. In both cases, too, political participation increased in the long term because earlier protests made the political environment more favorable for later protesters. Although both conflicts were large and sustained, more people participated in protests in Kreuzberg than in Linden, and the peak phase of protests in Kreuzberg lasted five years, from 1977 to 1982, compared with only fourteen months (1972–73) in Linden.

Linden and Kreuzberg also are examples of quite different types of protest. In Linden, protesters used mainly conventional methods (meetings, assemblies, and petitions), supplemented to a significant degree by nonviolently disruptive methods (housing squats). By contrast, protesters in Kreuzberg frequently used nonviolent disruption and militancy, including a massive squatting campaign, repeated confrontations with police, and rioting, as well as conventional activities, such as tenant advising. These differences in types of protest were due to differences in alliances between protest groups, the timing of reforms, and police practices.

In the following sections, I sketch the basic chronologies of the conflicts and then examine the limitations of socioeconomic and institutional theories in explaining these cases. In the bulk of the chapter, I present an interactive political process explanation of the protests, divided into two phases. In the rising phases of the movements, I focus on how protest and opportunities for protest expanded together, more so in Kreuzberg than in Linden, and on why the types of protest diverged in the two conflicts. Next, I explain why protest participation in both cases increased in the long term, after major reforms were adopted, and also explain the strategies used after the peaks of these conflicts. The conclusions compare the two cases, summarizing the causes of the large, long-lived protests and the differences in protest types. There I also address a possible structural explanation of the differences between the cases.

A Chronology of the Hanover-Linden Conflict

Beginning in 1970, the Hanover city administration began to implement plans to demolish almost 30 percent of the existing, low-rent housing in South Linden, a working-class neighborhood of twelve thousand residents. The city's goals included building new housing and a major highway link, reducing the population by displacing many existing residents, and attracting higher-income residents. When the plans became public in June 1972, middle-class residents formed the Independent Citizen Initiative,[a] and leftist students formed a group called Housing Emergency Action[b] to oppose the city's clear-cut renewal plans. They demanded housing renovation for existing residents and resident participation in urban renewal decisions, a program I call "neighborhood renewal." The citizen initiative collected over 2,300 signatures on a petition and began to meet with representatives of the City Planning Office,[c] while Housing Emergency Action carried out a series of housing squats and other illegal protests.

When the two groups joined forces to occupy a building on Kaplan Strasse in July 1973, they quickly achieved major reforms. Two days after the squat, the city council gave the Independent Citizen Initiative a veto power over housing evictions and demolitions in South Linden, and the next month, the Planning Office halted the formulation of block plans

a. Unabhängige Bürgerinitiative.
b. Aktion Wohnungsnot.
c. Stadtplanungsamt.

and finally produced plans for new construction in the neighborhood. At the same time, a major split developed within the Hanover Social Democrats, and within months, the city council and administration adopted a major shift in policy under pressure from the left wing of the SPD.[1] Citizen initiatives gained seats on newly created, neighborhood-level renewal commissions,[d] where they had a veto power over eviction and demolition decisions. The protesters also gained access to a planning advisor[e] who helped them produce expert plans to counter those produced by the city. The city itself also employed community workers[f] to help low-income residents participate. Through a detailed, city-financed counterplanning process held from 1973 to 1976, the Independent Citizen Initiative and its political allies achieved much of the neighborhood renewal program.[2] The result for both South and North Linden was a drastic reduction in the scale of demolition and a halt to involuntary displacement. The highway construction was abandoned, much of the housing was renovated, and the neighborhoods remained largely working class (about 52 percent manual workers), with a stable mixture of Germans and foreigners (about 25 percent foreigners).[3]

After the most important reforms were adopted, conventional and disruptive participation continued in South Linden, and protests began in North Linden, which city administrators defined as an official urban renewal area in 1976. They began to implement plans to demolish rear buildings (those in the interiors of residential blocks) in order to increase the value of the front-building apartments (those facing the street). Those plans were opposed by several newly formed protest groups: the North Linden Citizen Initiative,[g] the North Linden Tenant Group,[h] and several groups of young squatters. Conventional participation was high in the renewal commissions in both Linden neighborhoods, but disruptive protests against demolitions also continued from 1977 to 1981, especially surrounding three large housing squats and a rent strike in North Linden.[i] Some of these were spurred by an influx of protesters inspired

---

d. A *Sanierungskommission* in South Linden and one in North Linden.
e. *Anwaltsplaner.*
f. *Gemeinwesenarbeiter.*
g. Bürgerinitiative Linden-Nord.
h. Mietergruppe Linden-Nord.
i. These were the Benno Strasse rent strike, the Viktoria Strasse squats and protests, the Stärke-Koch Strasse squat, and the Velvet Strasse squat (*Stadtpost*, June–November 1979, May–July 1980, September–October 1980, May 1981; *taz*, 11 June 1981; *Neue Presse*, 23 March, 6 April 1981; *Lindenblatt*, November 1979; Warnken, Burucker, Krüger, Peter, Ützmann, first E. Barkhoff, and second Becker interviews).

by the late 1970s youth protests and squatter movements in Zurich, West Berlin, and other cities, as well as the movement against nuclear energy.[4]

But militant actions were rare in Linden. In contrast to the role played by eastern Kreuzberg within West Berlin, Linden did not attract the most militant groups in Hanover. Even though many autonomists lived in North Linden, in the late 1980s and 1990s they commuted to protest actions in the Nordstadt neighborhood, two kilometers distant, and undertook very few actions in Linden.[j] When punks and autonomists held highly publicized Chaos Days in Hanover each August in 1994, 1995, and 1996, participants from many German cities converged on Hanover-Nordstadt, but they did not mount actions in Linden.[k]

A Chronology of the Berlin-Kreuzberg Conflict

In the Kottbusser Tor neighborhood of Kreuzberg, initially home to 33,000 people, official plans in the late 1960s foresaw the demolition of 84 percent of the housing. In 1966, the West Berlin Construction and Housing Ministry[l] began allowing urban renewal corporations to evict tenants and demolish buildings, which prompted leftist students to form several groups to mobilize residents in opposition. Yet protests remained small and official responses were very limited from 1968 to 1976. In 1975, a new construction minister invited public participation in urban renewal decisions in the adjoining Kreuzberg neighborhood, an area with 41,000 residents called "SO36."[m] In response, new groups formed and mounted effective opposition to official plans. They demanded urban renewal for the sake of existing residents and with resident participation. The SO36 Citizen Initiative[n] publicized these demands and began to

---

j. Autonomists vandalized bank offices in North Linden in 1986, and a hundred young leftists rioted there in 1992 (*Hannoversche Allgemeine Zeitung* [*HAZ*], 29 October 1986, 24 August 1992). These actions were isolated and had little if any connection to urban renewal issues.

k. These involved major militant actions. About two hundred demonstrators and two hundred police were injured in the 1995 riots (*taz*, 8 August 1994, 7 August 1995, 12 June, 19 August 1996; Geiling 1996, 251).

l. Senat für Bau- und Wohnungswesen.

m. Named for the postal district Südost 36, or "Southeast 36."

n. Bürgerinitiative SO36.

squat buildings threatened with demolition, while the SO36 Association⁰ negotiated with officials.

As policy became stalemated, a squatter movement spread through Kreuzberg and several other West Berlin boroughs in 1979–82, and the police and the courts largely tolerated it. An estimated three to five thousand participants took control of about 165 buildings, most of them in Kreuzberg, making the West Berlin squatter movement by far the largest in West Germany from the 1960s to the 1980s.[5] National news coverage made Kreuzberg synonymous with the leading edge of left-alternative protest.[6] The West Berlin squatter movement was centered in Kreuzberg and the adjoining borough of Schöneberg, and included housing activists and participants in the alternative movement.

Squatters used nonviolently disruptive methods and also engaged in militant confrontations with police at demonstrations and during evictions. Their actions grew dramatically during the last months of Mayor Dietrich Stobbe's (SPD) government and contributed to its resignation in January 1981. Squats continued to spread during the brief successor government led by Hans-Jochen Vogel (SPD), and protests by the squatter movement continued under the new government formed by Richard von Weizsäcker (CDU) in June 1981. Between December 1980 and September 1981, squatters and their supporters took part in at least fifty-three marches, blockades, or riots, fifteen of them drawing a thousand or more participants. The demonstrations were mostly peaceful, especially the larger ones. But at least thirty-four of these actions involved some violence, including four days of rioting in December 1980 and the repeated large-scale destruction of shop windows on the city's luxury shopping street, the Kurfürstendamm.[7] Small-scale, less public attacks on property also rose, apparently linked to the squatter movement, such as gluing shut the entrance doors to banks or firebomb attacks against the police and SPD offices.[8]

The squatter movement and a general crisis in urban renewal policy helped force the Social Democrats out of the West Berlin government in 1981, ushering in eight years of CDU-led government, first under Weizsäcker and then, beginning in 1984, under Eberhard Diepgen.ᵖ Initially, policy stalemate and a large squatter movement continued under the

o. Verein SO36.
p. At first, Weizsäcker's government was tolerated by Liberal deputies, before a formal CDU-Liberal coalition was created in 1983.

Christian Democrats, who were internally divided.[q] Leading Christian Democratic officials took a hard-line stance against the protesters, especially the squatters. But the protesters received various kinds of support from Christian Democratic reformers, Social Democratic politicians, leaders of the Alternative List (AL),[r] and many other elites who became "godparents" for squatted buildings.

Ultimately, the stalemate was broken by the new Kreuzberg borough government, which was controlled by the SPD and AL after 1981, and the Urban Renewal Division of the International Building Exposition,[s] which was created in the late 1970s with weak planning authority in Kreuzberg. In 1983, the West Berlin parliament adopted twelve principles of "Careful Urban Renewal," which officially implemented the protesters' main neighborhood renewal goals.[9] Demolitions and other major decisions became subject to veto by tenants, who were aided by city-funded tenant advisors and by resident representatives on the neighborhood committees in SO36 and in Kottbusser Tor.[t] About half of the West Berlin squats were legalized, and squatters gained access to public funds for building repairs, while many other squatters were evicted, with tense confrontations and sometimes violence between them and police.[10] As a result, very little housing was demolished in Kreuzberg after 1980, and although 20 percent of eastern Kreuzberg's housing was publicly renovated between 1979 and 1988, there was very little displacement of residents out of the neighborhood. These neighborhoods remained largely working class (about 54 percent manual workers), with a foreign population share that rose and stabilized at around 40 percent in the late 1980s.[11,u]

As in Linden, the reforms were followed by further protests. Thou-

---

q. Within the new *Land* government, reformers such as Construction Minister Rastemborski and Social Minister Fink saw important overlaps between the demands of the alternative movement and a neoconservative approach to social problems involving more self-help and less state finance. But hard-liners, led by Interior Minister Heinrich Lummer, emphasized internal security and favored demolition and displacement as a means to reduce the base enjoyed by protest groups in Kreuzberg and Schöneberg (Bodenschatz 1987, 205).

r. The Alternative Liste für Democracy and Environmental Protection.

s. The Bereich Stadterneuerung of the Internationale Bauausstellung, also known as IBA-Altbau.

t. The Stadtteilausschuss SO36 and the Erneuerungskommission Kottbusser Tor.

u. These demographic patterns continued even after the unification of Berlin suddenly put eastern Kreuzberg near the new center of the city and led to rising rents (*taz*, 31 August 1995, 18 August 1997).

sands of residents participated in building assemblies organized by the new tenant advisors, and weekly meetings of the neighborhood committees attracted large turnouts when decisions were controversial. Disruptive, nonviolent protests also remained important. Housing activists and autonomists carried out six squatting actions against homelessness and housing vacancy under the CDU-Liberal *Land* government in 1987–89.[12] After the opening of the Berlin Wall in November 1989 and the democratic election of a reformist East Berlin government in May 1990, officials planned to widen a bridge linking Kreuzberg with the East Berlin borough of Friedrichshain and to open it to car traffic. Their plans sparked an illegal traffic blockade in May 1992, which was part of a large action to block traffic on the inner ring of highways in Berlin, and a nonviolent occupation of the bridge in July.

Militant activity also resurged in Kreuzberg, with a series of threatening demonstrations, riots against property, and battles with police on every May Day from 1987 to 1997. Estimates of the hard core of autonomists at Kreuzberg demonstrations ranged up to one thousand people, who could mobilize up to ten thousand supporters for demonstrations.[13] In some years, such as 1987 and 1989, injuries numbered in the hundreds, and property damage exceeded one million deutschmarks.[14] Although the autonomists proclaimed revolution as their goal, the May Day events remained tied to urban renewal politics in terms of the autonomists' goals and allies.[v]

The Limits of Socioeconomic and Institutional Explanations

The social structures of Linden and Kreuzberg cannot explain why major conflicts between protesters and authorities occurred, why protests were larger in Kreuzberg than in Linden, or why protesters participated in different ways in the two cases. When protests began, Linden and Kreuzberg were rather similar working-class neighborhoods and were much less affluent and postindustrial than most locations in West Germany. The neighborhoods did not have unusually large concentrations of young, middle-class people with postsecondary educations, the social group most likely to participate in left-leaning protest movements.

---

v. Autonomists sought to prevent an upscaling of Kreuzberg and to gain additional space by occupying buildings.

Linden is a section of Hanover, a city of about a half million residents that is the political capital of the *Land* of Lower Saxony in western Germany. Linden is cut off from the more prosperous parts of Hanover by the Leine River. In the 1970s, South Linden and North Linden had a higher proportion of residents with working-class occupations and a lower concentration of residents with postsecondary degrees than did Hanover as a whole and than did West Germany.[w] In addition, when protests began, the Linden neighborhoods probably did not have unusually large numbers of young Germans.[x]

Social conditions were not highly postindustrial in the Kreuzberg section of West Berlin (population 2.1 million), either. Before the unification of Germany and of Berlin in 1990, Kreuzberg was one of West Berlin's twelve political boroughs. The Cold War had partitioned the city and left West Berlin physically and economically isolated from the rest of West Germany. The city was dependent on subsidies from the federal government in Bonn, which rose to about 8 billion deutschmarks in 1986. Kreuzberg is a working-class borough with about 160,000 residents, and in the late 1960s, its two eastern neighborhoods (known as Kottbusser Tor and SO36) contained a compactly built mixture of apartment buildings and industrial workshops dating mostly from the late nineteenth century. Housing was at a low standard, often with toilets in stairwells or courtyards, and the eastern neighborhoods, surrounded by the Berlin Wall on three sides, were isolated from the more prosperous parts of West Berlin. Eastern Kreuzberg was the poorest area in West Berlin, with much smaller proportions of white-collar workers, civil servants, and graduates of postsecondary institutions than the average for West Berlin or West Germany.[y] Similarly, the borough's share of juveniles and young

---

w. Manual workers were 53 percent of Linden residents who were employed, compared with 39 percent in Hanover and 45 percent in West Germany in the 1970s. Only 8 percent of the neighborhood population in 1970 had degrees from *Hochschulen* and *Fachhochschulen*, versus 14 percent in Hanover (*Statistischer Vierteljahresbericht Hannover* 1971, I:38, IV:85, author's calculations; FGW 1976, 11).

x. At the start of urban renewal, 21 percent of the population in the Linden urban renewal areas consisted of Germans eighteen to thirty-five years old, which is probably not much, if at all, higher than the average for Hanover or West Germany, although comparable data are not available (Karapin 1993, 521).

y. The average income there was 27 percent lower than in the city as a whole in 1979 (Bezirksamt Kreuzberg 1987, Appendix 6, 1). Only 29 percent of neighborhood residents were white-collar workers or civil servants, compared with 46 percent for West Berlin and 41 percent for West Germany in the 1970s (*Berliner Statistik, Sonderheft* 230 [December 1974], 174–85; author's calculations; FGW 1976, 11). Only 9 percent

adults at the start of urban renewal was only slightly above average for West Berlin.[z] Indeed, Kreuzberg's social structure remained mostly working class from the early 1970s to the early 1990s, a period during which political participation linked to left-wing protesters grew enormously.[aa]

After major reforms were initiated, large numbers of young, politically active Germans were attracted to both Linden and Kreuzberg, where they created dense organizational networks and contributed to high levels of protest in later years.[bb] These changes were the results of the earlier protests in these neighborhoods. The widely publicized conflicts of the 1970s gave Linden and Kreuzberg reputations as politically active areas, and the neighborhood renewal reforms ensured low-cost housing. Rather than postindustrial social structures causing these conflicts, the social structures were themselves altered by the initial periods of protest and the ensuing urban renewal reforms.

Finally, there is little evidence to support the claim that the Kreuzberg protests were especially militant because they attracted many working-class participants. Working-class youths were present in about equal proportions in Linden and Kreuzberg, while the degree of militant activity varied greatly between the two cases. Moreover, the social backgrounds of the militant and disruptive protesters in Kreuzberg were not very distinct. According to police sources, the militant squatters and later the autonomists were mixed in terms of age and occupational background, including large proportions of pupils, postsecondary students, working-

---

had postsecondary degrees in 1970, in contrast to 16 percent in West Berlin (*Berliner Statistik, Sonderheft* 239 [July 1975], 26–29; *Sonderheft* 229 [December 1974], 126–27).

z. In the Kreuzberg borough, 4.7 percent of the residents were between fifteen and twenty years old and 30.0 percent were between twenty and forty years old in 1970, compared with 4.2 and 27.8 percent for West Berlin, respectively (*Berliner Statistik, Sonderheft* 239 [July 1975], 26–29; *Sonderheft* 227 [September 1974], 122–23; *Sonderheft* 229 [December 1974], 122–23).

aa. Even in the late 1980s, its shares of residents with postsecondary degrees, white-collar workers, and civil servants were still far below the averages for West Berlin (*Berliner Statistik, Sonderheft* 403 [April 1989], 29, 41).

bb. Young adult Germans (aged eighteen to thirty-five years) increased their share of the population in Linden to 33 percent in 1987, compared with only 27 percent in Hanover as a whole (*Statistischer Vierteljahresbericht Hannover*, Sonderband 1989, 12–13). In eastern Kreuzberg, this age group rose from 27 percent of the population in 1973 to 35 percent in 1981 and 44 percent in 1986. This compares with an increase of only three percentage points in West Berlin as a whole (data from Statistisches Landesamt Berlin; *Berliner Statistik, Sonderheft* 227 [September 1974], 122–25; *Sonderheft* 403 [April 1989], 14–15, 18).

class apprentices, and unemployed youths.¹⁵ Other sources state that both the militant groups (who were strongest in Kottbusser Tor) and the radical-disruptive protesters (strongest in SO36) consisted largely of middle-class young males and were led by current or former university students.¹⁶ The latter included activists from undogmatic left student groups, who influenced the autonomists' political goal of confronting the state.¹⁷

The political institutional settings of Linden and Kreuzberg were also similar in most ways,^cc and thus cannot explain the differences in the amount or kinds of protest in the two cases. In Hanover and West Berlin, and in unified Berlin after 1990, the executive is chosen by and responsible to a regularly elected parliament,^dd which consists of party groups. The main lines of policy are set by the executive and the parliament, and party leaders head the administrative departments that implement policy. The Hanover City Planning Office and the West Berlin Construction and Housing Ministry had a significant degree of autonomy in the drawing up of urban renewal plans, purchase of property, and designation of renewal agents; however, the heads of these administrative agencies were ultimately responsible to the mayor and the partisan majority of parliament. The urban renewal plans in both cities operated under the loose constraints of federal regulation under the 1971 Urban Renewal Law, which also provided important subsidies to municipalities.¹⁸^ee The law required participation by the affected residents, but was so vague on this score that meaningful participation depended on local governments choosing to elaborate participation rights that went well beyond the federal law.^ff

The party systems were also very similar in the two cities. In the early

cc. One major difference, in the relations between housing corporations and public administration, is treated in the conclusions to this chapter.

dd. The House of Deputies (Abgeordnetenhaus) in West Berlin, with about 140 members in the 1970s and 1980s, elected the mayor (*regierender Bürgermeister*) and ministers (*Senatoren,* collectively the *Senat*). The city council in Hanover, with 65 members, elected the mayor and executive committee (*Verwaltungsausschuss*) in the 1970s and 1980s (Gunlicks 1986, 80–81); in 1996, the Hanover mayor became directly elected.

ee. Federal subsidies exceeded 200 million deutschmarks each year beginning in 1973, and rose to an average of over 600 million deutschmarks annually in 1986–90 (BRBS 1988, 10).

ff. The law required the "discussion" of the overall plans with affected residents, which could be fulfilled by merely holding informational meetings (Heise 1981, 151–52 and notes 91 and 103; Selle 1986, 106; Karapin 1993, 134–38).

1970s, the parliamentary parties were the SPD, CDU, and Liberal Party. The Social Democrats formed the dominant party, governing alone in Hanover from the 1960s until 1981 and leading the government in West Berlin from 1954 to 1981. In each city, a party related to leftist and ecological movements (the Alternative List in West Berlin and the Green-Alternative Citizen List in Hanover) gained parliamentary seats beginning around 1980. However, an important difference in the political contexts is the degree of electoral stability. Until 1981, the SPD achieved stable electoral results in Hanover, with an absolute majority from 1956 through the 1976 elections, although the party lost eight percentage points in 1981, when the Greens began to contest council seats.[19] By contrast, the SPD's vote share in West Berlin declined sharply and nearly continuously, from 62 percent in 1963 to 38 percent in 1981.[20] But, ironically, despite the greater importance of electoral competition in West Berlin in the 1970s, the Social Democrats there were less responsive to protest than they were in Hanover.

Differences in the scale of local political institutions might help explain why disruptive and militant actions became more important in Kreuzberg than in Linden, but these differences are smaller than they initially appear. West Berlin had four times the population of Hanover, and enjoyed the status of a *Land,* with legislative authority comparable to the other ten *Länder* in West Germany before unification.[gg] Hence West Berlin's government was more remote from most residents and perhaps for that reason less responsive to protests.

However, these formal differences in size and authority were tempered by a degree of political decentralization within West Berlin compared with relative centralization in Hanover. In West Berlin, borough councils were directly elected, and the boroughs had large, comprehensive administrations.[21] The borough of Kreuzberg had only 160,000 residents in 1970. The West Berlin Construction Ministry and the construction departments of the borough governments shared authority over the urban renewal program in West Berlin, and each could veto planning decisions. By contrast, in Hanover, legislative and government institutions were limited to the citywide level until borough councils were created in 1981, and there was no borough-level administration even after that date, although the Hanover political parties were organized at the neighborhood level.[22]

gg. Hanover was under the jurisdiction of the *Land* of Lower Saxony.

The Rise of Major Protest Movements and the Divergence of Strategies

THE THREAT POSED BY CLEAR-CUT RENEWAL POLICIES

One reason that large, sustained protest movements developed in Kreuzberg and Linden is that official urban renewal plans in both cities posed major threats to neighborhood residents. In South Linden, a neighborhood with about twelve thousand residents, the Hanover City Planning Office and its agent, a city-owned housing corporation,[hh] intended to use federal urban renewal subsidies to demolish almost 30 percent of the existing, low-rent housing. Public officials planned to remove lower-income groups, build new high-rise housing for higher-income white-collar employees working in the Hanover city center, and divide South Linden by a six-lane highway link.[23] Much of the existing population was to be displaced to other neighborhoods. By the middle of 1973, about 120 apartments had been destroyed and many others purchased by the city and allowed to deteriorate, but the promised new construction was not forthcoming.[24] In 1976, the city began implementing similar, though more modest, plans in North Linden, a neighborhood of 21,000 residents about one kilometer distant.[25]

Similarly, in West Berlin, officials sought to "improve the socioeconomic structure" of urban neighborhoods by replacing poor people, old people, and guest workers with middle-income German families.[26] Inspired by urban renewal programs in the United States, they sought to reduce density, remove conflicts between industrial and residential uses, demolish old, run-down buildings, and build new higher-standard housing. The West Berlin plans called for urban renewal agents to buy buildings that contained fifty-five thousand apartments, remove the tenants, destroy the apartments, and build twenty-seven thousand new apartments in several densely populated inner boroughs of the city. These agents were mostly city-owned or private housing corporations officially recognized by the *Land*, and they operated with heavy public subsidies. The Kottbusser Tor urban renewal area in Kreuzberg, initially with thirty-three thousand residents, was one of the largest in the country.[27] When the *Land* government's renewal plans came to include the nearby SO36

---

hh. The Gemeinnützige Baugesellschaft Hannover.

neighborhood in 1976, a large proportion of its approximately forty-one thousand residents were also threatened with displacement.²⁸

Besides displacing residents from their neighborhoods, the construction of new housing in the 1970s meant higher rents. Most of the housing to be constructed was publicly subsidized "social housing,"^ii where rents were regulated according to the terms of the federal subsidy programs. However, rents in social housing built in this period were much higher than rents in old apartment buildings, because of high interest rates and construction costs.^jj

The clear-cut renewal plans were unpopular with most residents. In an official survey of 5,500 households in 1976, 95 percent of North Linden residents said they preferred to continue living in their neighborhood. Moreover, 82 percent said they wanted to live in an old building, which would minimize rent increases, compared to only 13 percent who preferred to live in a new structure. In fact, 45 percent preferred their present apartment in its present condition, compared with 33 percent who wanted a renovated or new apartment.²⁹ Similarly, in Kreuzberg, half the residents surveyed in 1975 said they wanted to live in renovated prewar apartments within the borough.³⁰ Because of these housing preferences, citizen initiatives opposed to clear-cut renewal were popular. According to a 1975 survey, three-fourths of Kreuzberg residents thought that citizen initiatives were needed to advance residents' interests, and residents evaluated protests positively by a three to one margin.³¹

The threats of demolition and displacement triggered protests. When the City of Hanover made public its urban renewal plans in June 1972, the local SPD organization called for a neighborhood assembly, at which the administration presented its plans. Five hundred people attended, with the crowd spilling out of the meeting hall. A majority of those present supported urban renewal but wanted it done "carefully." Two weeks later, at another public meeting, a group from the SPD organization in Linden^kk helped form the Independent Citizen Initiative. This protest group was dominated by long-time, middle-class Linden residents, including small landlords and shopkeepers, others interested in improving the neighborhood's image, and some tenants.³² While the majority of

ii. *Sozialwohnungen.*

jj. Rising rent subsidies paid to tenants (*Wohngeld*) made up little of the difference (Neef 1981, 335; Statistisches Bundesamt 1987, 127–28; Ulbrich 1988, 86).

kk. This was the Linden-Limmer section of the party, which I simply call the Linden SPD organization.

the group's members favored conventional methods of protest, it also contained a significant minority that favored disruptive methods.[ll]

In Kreuzberg, too, protests were triggered by a combination of visible threats from state activities and the efforts of activists, in this case from the student movement in the late 1960s. The first construction became visible in Kottbusser Tor in the summer of 1968, when a row of sixteen-story high-rises was begun. Immediately, architecture students, other leftist students, and assistant professors began organizing residents against demolition and displacement and in favor of rent controls and tenant rights.[33]

However, threats by officials, even combined with the efforts of activists, were not sufficient to produce a large movement. Although threats of state action quickly sparked protests in Kreuzberg, a large movement against clear-cut renewal did not emerge there between 1968 and 1976. Indeed, the threats in Kreuzberg were much larger than those in South Linden in the early 1970s, but protests were larger in South Linden. The failure of the early protest groups in Kreuzberg was not due to the lack of imaginative, disruptive tactics, the co-optation of leaders into public participation forums, or the absence of an adequate population of young Germans.[mm] Rather, they failed because the protesters were not able to win elite allies. In Linden, protesters gained local Social Democratic support within one year, and their movement grew rapidly. But in Kreuzberg, elite allies were unavailable, and protests remained small for the first eight years of the conflict. For similar reasons, clear-cut renewal met with few protests and was carried out successfully during the 1960s and 1970s in other West Berlin boroughs, such as Wedding.

---

ll. This faction consisted of alternative planners and architecture students, left-wing Social Democratic activists, and Housing Emergency Action members who attended the Independent Citizen Initiative's meetings (Gerlach and Holland 1976, 267 n. 10).

mm. Three groups of leftist students, assistant professors, and Young Socialists attempted a variety of disruptive approaches from 1968 onward, similar to Housing Emergency Action's activities in Linden. For example, leftist activists held demonstrations in June 1968 and May 1969, met real estate speculators at the airport and gave them informal tours of the neighborhood, and drove Kreuzberg residents to massive suburban housing projects in order to shock them with the sight of the new high-rise dwellings. Youths also occupied part of a disused hospital in May 1971 and gained a legalized youth center there. In addition, resident representatives used official forums to resist demolition (Heise 1981; Pirker et al. 1975, 59–62). The young German population share in Kreuzberg was slightly above average for West Berlin (*Berliner Statistik, Sonderheft* 227 [September 1975], 122–23).

PROCEDURAL REFORMS COMBINED WITH POLICY INTRANSIGENCE

In the long run, another interactive process also promoted large protest movements in Linden and Kreuzberg: initial protest actions triggered mistakes by public officials, who granted protesters procedural reforms while continuing to pursue unpopular urban renewal policies. As protesters gained some access to officials, it became easier to organize opposition, while protesters saw continued protests as necessary in order to gain influence. The combination of procedural reforms and policy intransigence also affected the type of protest. It directly encouraged routine participation, but also led some protesters to shift toward more disruptive methods because they came to see conventional protests as ineffective.

Soon after it formed in June 1972, the Independent Citizen Initiative demanded that government ensure affordable rents and move the proposed highway link underground, and the group began conventional protests. It held meetings, and in September, it presented municipal officials with a petition containing 2,368 signatures, collected during a three-month period from among the 12,000 residents of South Linden.[34] The petition demanded "humane" dwellings for all residents and no increase in traffic on the street slated for expansion. In later statements during this period, the citizen initiative made demands that included additional elements of its emerging position in favor of neighborhood renewal: less demolition, less displacement of residents, and more say for the group in the city's decision-making.[35]

These early protests led Hanover officials to grant procedural concessions, but without budging from their policy of demolition and displacement. The Hanover City Planning Office agreed to meet regularly with the Independent Citizen Initiative, beginning in late 1972. In December, the Planning Office also agreed to the citizen group's demand for a city-financed, independent advisor to help the group articulate its interests. The Planning Office approved a three-year contract for a planning advisor to help the citizen initiative develop a counterplan, which city officials promised only to consider.[36] But city administrators still withheld information about their plans and carried out what the protesters saw as a policy of neglecting and demolishing buildings.[37]

The combination of procedural reforms and intransigence on the substance of policy encouraged further protests and a shift toward more disruptive methods, especially housing squats. Disruptive protests were undertaken first by a new group, Housing Emergency Action, and then by the Independent Citizen Initiative. Housing Emergency Action formed in late 1972 as a new-left neighborhood group[nn] of current and former students, with between ten and twenty-five active members and the ability to mobilize up to one hundred leftists from around Hanover.[38] The group aimed to politicize urban renewal issues in order to build general opposition to West Germany's capitalist system. It included a small communist faction that refused dialogue with state actors in principle and opposed the Independent Citizen Initiative as a tool of the city administration. But most members of Housing Emergency Action saw a need for a local group to negotiate with the city, and hence wanted to work with the citizen initiative while undertaking disruptive, popular protests in order to strengthen the latter's negotiating position.[39] Housing Emergency Action's most important activities in South Linden were housing squats. Between January and July 1973, this group occupied five vacant city-owned buildings on behalf of poor families while also distributing leaflets, a newsletter, and posters informing residents of the threats posed by demolition and displacement.

At this time, during the first half of 1973, the lack of reform in renewal policy led to frustration and a strategic shift by the Independent Citizen Initiative. The group failed to gain influence on a Catholic convent's plans for a nursing home, and the city continued demolitions without producing block-by-block construction plans for comment by the citizen initiative.[40] Finally, after an especially unproductive meeting with city administrators, the citizen initiative held a meeting that no city representative attended, which was an unusual circumstance. At that meeting, a majority of the citizen group decided to join with Housing Emergency Action in squatting a building on Kaplan Strasse that was slated for demolition to make way for an underground parking garage.[41] However, the extent and duration of the citizen initiative's strategic shift was limited by the responses of Hanover authorities to the Kaplan Strasse squat. Because officials rapidly adopted major policy reforms, they undermined support for disruptive tactics and helped prevent the growth of a squatter movement in Linden.

In Kreuzberg, too, early protests helped lead to procedural reforms that made it easier for protesters to organize opposition to clear-cut renewal. The procedural reforms were adopted by Harry Ristock, a leftist Social Democratic leader in West Berlin, who was appointed construction

nn. *Stadtteilgruppe.*

minister in 1975. Ristock's appointment and his reformist approach resulted partly from construction scandals, which had showed that setting policy mainly to benefit construction companies and housing corporations could discredit the SPD. However, earlier protests in West Berlin were also important in spurring Ristock's reform efforts. Residents' opposition to demolition in the Charlottenburg borough led, in 1974-75, to an experiment in renovation on behalf of existing residents, which achieved political popularity while aiming at a thirty-percent cost savings compared with clear-cut renewal.[42] Meanwhile, in the Kottbusser Tor area, residents' opposition to clear-cut renewal had led to a gradual expansion of participation rights from 1970 to 1975, and the continued resistance of the residents' representatives on various official committees showed the difficulty of getting residents to accept demolition and displacement policies.[43]

Therefore, Ristock began seeking allies among representatives of local groups and other elites in Kreuzberg in his efforts to reorient urban renewal policy away from demolition and toward a program of "Urban Repair." When a citizen participation experiment was proposed by a Protestant pastor[oo] in Kreuzberg and was supported by the national-level German Protestant Church Convention,[pp] Ristock instituted their proposal: a "Strategies for Kreuzberg" competition. This competition solicited proposals to improve conditions for residents in eastern Kreuzberg and provided state funding for the winners.[44]

The Strategies for Kreuzberg competition aided the protesters in many ways. It gave opponents of clear-cut renewal access to 250,000 deutschmarks in prize money, provided by the *Land*. Among the groups ultimately funded in 1978 was the SO36 Association, which took a leading role in organizing opposition to urban renewal policy. Moreover, since the competition led to the distribution of four thousand copies of a publicity brochure and to a series of public meetings critical of clear-cut renewal in the spring of 1977, it raised residents' awareness of urban renewal issues in SO36 just before the *Land* began major activities in that neighborhood. By soliciting residents' suggestions about how to revitalize SO36, it encouraged them to think about the neighborhood's prob-

---

oo. Klaus Duntze, who had been an advocate of intact inner-city neighborhoods since 1972 (cf. Duntze 1972).

pp. The Evangelische Kirchentag is a nationwide, week-long meeting of members of the Protestant Church, which, during the 1970s and 1980s, discussed a range of controversial social and political topics. In 1977, it took place in West Berlin.

lems and about solutions that government policy could promote. Within two months, 129 applications had been submitted. Finally, to judge the applications, authorities created a forum, the Project Commission, which consisted of twelve officials and twenty-two citizen members, who were representatives of residents and neighborhood groups chosen by the *Land* and borough governments. The Project Commission unexpectedly became a target for protest and a means for disruptive protesters to gain access to negotiations.[45]

At the same time that they lowered the costs of mobilizing protests, the officials in the Construction Ministry and the Kreuzberg Construction Department[qq] accelerated the threats of demolition and displacement. First, officials had an abandoned firehouse in eastern Kreuzberg demolished in May and June 1977, despite opposition by a local group, which illegally occupied the building, and by most of the citizen representatives on the Project Commission.[46] The second, more far-reaching mistake was introducing a new housing renovation program that threatened to displace residents throughout the SO36 neighborhood. In June 1977, Ristock announced that 70 million deutschmarks in federal subsidies[rr] would be channeled into extensive renovation rather than demolition in this neighborhood. He presented the program as part of a "Turnaround in Urban Renewal." However, this program would have displaced residents out of the neighborhood through the loss of housing units and higher rents, since it required the demolition of all rear and side buildings and a high standard of renovation for the remaining apartments.

The threat to low-cost housing was sharpened by mistakes in the renovation program's implementation. Kreuzberg borough council members revealed that a list of buildings to be renovated already existed and that the program would have nothing to do with the Strategies competition.[47] These plans encouraged real estate speculators, especially firms set up to provide tax shelters, to buy buildings and leave them vacant in 1978–80. Since they could combine subsidies from the new renovation program with those provided through the Berlin Subsidy Law and social housing laws, speculators had strong financial incentives to leave buildings vacant or force tenants out, and then to either demolish the buildings or allow

qq. Kreuzberg Bauressort.
rr. From the Zukunftsinvestionsprogramm, which was intended to provide a total of 20 billion deutschmarks in macroeconomic stimulus (*taz*, 3 December 1987; Dittrich and Habeny 1980, 10–11; Schreiber 1982, 50; Verein 1989b, 25).

them to decay.⁴⁸ According to a public admission by Ristock, there were ten thousand empty apartments in West Berlin at the end of 1980; unofficial estimates ranged up to forty thousand.⁴⁹

Under pressure from the citizen members of the Project Commission, the Construction Ministry made a major procedural concession concerning the renovation program, but this only fueled protests because the substantive reforms were too minor to mollify the local activists. In January 1978, the ministry created a Renovation Funding Committee,⁵⁵ with five representatives from the residents, two from the ministry, and three from the borough administration. This committee gained power to decide whether buildings should be demolished, renovated, or left alone.ᵗᵗ But since it operated by consensus, the committee was unable to influence a significant reform away from demolition and displacement, and given its narrow scope, it could do little about the rapidly growing problem of speculative vacancy in SO36.⁵⁰

This combination of facilitated participation and rising threats of displacement also encouraged protesters to shift toward increasingly disruptive methods, and thus to initiate the squatter movement. In response to being circumvented by the authorities in the firehouse conflict, ten of the citizen members of the Project Commission formed the Stammtisch group,ᵘᵘ which met weekly in a local bar and was open to all residents but not to administration officials. Some members of the Stammtisch later formed a new group, the SO36 Citizen Initiative, in October 1977. By the end of 1979, this loosely organized citizen initiative grew to include many participants in the alternative movement. The SO36 Citizen Initiative had thirty to forty active members and fifty to one hundred members at its quarterly meetings, before it contracted to a small core of housing policy activists in the early 1980s. Its active participants included many university students, as well as shopkeepers, young architects, and other professionals.⁵¹

Although the group's members had diverse conceptions about how demolition could be stopped and what broader political changes that would require, it consistently supported neighborhood renewal goals. These included providing residents a voice through tenant advising and

---

ss. This was the "ZIP Committee," named after the renovation program, the Zukunftsinvestionsprogramm.

tt. However, administrators bound themselves to its decisions only informally.

uu. Named after the colloquial term for a table at a bar that is regularly occupied by the same people.

public demonstrations, protecting residents against demolition and displacement, and reforming traditional urban renewal policy.[52] Frustrated with the failures of the Renovation Funding Committee, the SO36 Citizen Initiative in February 1979 turned to squatting actions aimed at the property owners with the largest numbers of vacant apartments in the neighborhood.[vv] As major reforms in urban renewal failed to materialize, squats spread to other parts of Kreuzberg and to other boroughs in West Berlin, reaching a peak of 165 apartment buildings in May 1981. When even large-scale squatting actions failed to produce major reforms, many protesters shifted to militant actions such as violent demonstrations and the militant defense of squats threatened by evictions from 1980 to 1982, or supported those who did.

MAKING ALLIANCES BETWEEN PROTEST GROUPS

Cooperation between protest groups using complementary strategies was crucial in helping urban renewal protesters launch disruptive or militant actions that expanded the opportunities for further protests. Disruptive and militant groups were willing to risk arrest, prosecution, or police violence, while citizen and tenant initiatives that preferred conventional protests were better placed to develop alternative policy proposals and negotiate with authorities. Potential elite allies were more willing to endorse illegal actions such as squats, and thus to help shield them from repression, if comparatively respectable citizen initiatives were participating in the squats or publicly supporting them. In turn, disruptive or militant actions, especially housing squats, expanded political opportunities by gaining publicity, attracting the attention of reformist elites, and sometimes provoking mistakes in policing. I describe how these protests won the support of elite allies in the next section. Here I focus on the cooperation among diverse protest groups in producing housing squats and other dramatic actions. This cooperation was longer and more continuous in Kreuzberg than in Linden.

In South Linden, despite their sharply contrasting approaches and tensions, Housing Emergency Action and the Independent Citizen Initiative generally cooperated and had an effective division of labor. At a meeting of the citizen initiative in January 1973, Housing Emergency

---

vv. These were a *Land*-owned housing corporation, the Berliner Wohn- und Geschäftshaus, which had about three hundred empty apartments, and private tax shelter firms, which owned 19 percent of the neighborhood's housing in 1980 (Gude 1988).

Action defined itself as not working with the city administration. Whereas the citizen initiative met quietly with members of the City Planning Office, Housing Emergency Action sought to generate publicity and communicate with Linden residents through dramatic public actions and its widely read newsletter.[53] When Housing Emergency Action carried out a series of illegal housing squats, mostly on behalf of poor families, the citizen initiative then negotiated with the city to legalize the squats, usually with success.[ww] Although at first the citizen initiative studiously avoided endorsing or participating in these actions, it also implied that it might change its policy if the city remained too unresponsive.[54] Ultimately, when the two protest groups together occupied the Kaplan Strasse building in July 1973, they symbolically demonstrated their solidarity against the city administration. Their joint action suddenly gave the local movement against clear-cut renewal significant power, because it created great uncertainty about the extent to which moderate groups like the Independent Citizen Initiative would resort to disruptive methods. Therefore, the squat drove a wedge between reformers and conservatives in the Hanover government and city council.

In West Berlin, cooperation among protest groups was much more complex and longer-lived than in Hanover, making it possible for the West Berlin squatter movement to undertake massive illegal actions while gaining elite support. The Urban Renewal Division of the International Building Exposition, borough-level party organizations, prominent intellectuals, and other elites came to support the squatter movement even though it included a militant wing. This was possible because the housing policy groups, which used a conventional strategy, helped give the squatter movement respectability and a capacity to criticize clear-cut renewal and offer detailed reform proposals.

The SO36 Citizen Initiative worked in an explicit division of labor with the SO36 Association, which was set up in June 1978 as a result of a winning entry in the Strategies for Kreuzberg competition. The SO36 Association was funded by the *Land* to advise tenants and landlords on apartment renovation, and it sought acceptance by officials as a negotiating partner. By contrast, the SO36 Citizen Initiative aimed to keep more distance from the state, in order to more effectively organize protest actions and publicize opposition to the ministry's plans. However, the

---

ww. At times, Housing Emergency Action also negotiated with the city, despite its slogans to the contrary (Buchholz 1973, 43–44).

memberships of the SO36 Citizen Initiative and the SO36 Association overlapped considerably, and citizen initiative members usually controlled the Association's three-member board from 1978 until 1984, when the citizen initiative ceased activities.[xx]

The cooperative actions of these two groups sparked the West Berlin squatter movement, which began in eastern Kreuzberg in 1979. The SO36 Citizen Initiative first tried conventional, legal means. It petitioned a housing corporation, which was a major property owner in SO36, to maintain and rent its apartments, and appealed to *Land* authorities to enforce the law on the "deliberate removal of housing units" from the housing market. After these lawful efforts failed, members of the citizen initiative illegally occupied two of the housing corporation's apartments and began repairing and renovating them, with the support of the SO36 Association, in February 1979.[55] Thus, "rehab-squatting"[yy] became a crucial tactic in a nonviolently disruptive approach to reforming urban renewal policies. The image of the rehab-squatter, displayed prominently in the SO36 Citizen Initiative's posters that advertised its squats, was a cheerful young man carrying tools, ready to invest his labor in order to take control of speculators' buildings and reverse the physical destruction of the neighborhood.[56]

West Berlin experienced an extraordinarily large squatter movement in part because the alliance of protest groups supporting the rehab-squatting approach soon became much broader. During 1979 and 1980, a loose alliance formed between housing policy activists in the SO36 Citizen Initiative, the SO36 Association, and the Dresdener Strasse Tenant Initiative[zz] on the one hand, and activists in two externally inspired movements, the alternative and autonomist movements, on the other. The alternative movement in West Germany grew in response to the failures of militant protests at Brokdorf (see Chapter 3) and the failures of the Red Army Faction, a left-wing terrorist group, in the face of rising state repression in 1976–77.[aaa] Participants in the movement, known as "alter-

---

xx. There was a break in cooperation between November 1980 and June 1981, after which the citizen initiative reasserted control over the Association's board (Verein 1989b, 49; Laurisch 1981, 100; Thörnig interview; *Der Tagesspiegel* [*Tsp*], 3 April 1979; Sonnewald and Raabe-Zimmermann 1983, 52).

yy. *Instandbesetzung*, a neologism combining *Instandsetzung* (building repair) and *Besetzung* (occupation).

zz. Mieterinitiative Dresdener Strasse.

aaa. The alternative movement also had roots in the countercultural practices of the 1960s student movement, including small residential communes.

nativers," were fundamentally opposed to what they saw as the hierarchical and bureaucratic economic and political system of West Germany. They created "alternative projects," which were self-managed experiments in living and working.[57] West Berlin was especially attractive for alternativers from West Germany for several reasons. The city's economic and political isolation from the rest of West Germany before 1989 offered a greater degree of cultural autonomy, military conscription was not enforced, and the urban renewal areas, with their low rents and lively protest politics, were especially large.[58]

The first squats in SO36 attracted members of the alternative movement, who quickly predominated in the squatter movement. The alternativers generally supported neighborhood renewal goals while seeking to control buildings that would house their alternative projects. They were ambivalent regarding protest strategies. Some allied with the housing policy activists and tried to organize local residents against displacement, using conventional and disruptive methods. Others aligned with the remnants of communist groups to form the core of a militant opposition that rejected the West German political and economic system and sought confrontations with the state.[59]

The alliance between the housing policy activists and alternativers involved a division of labor that was effective in gaining elite allies and pressuring authorities. The alternativers contributed by occupying an increasing number of buildings in 1980–81, bold actions that attracted much media and elite attention. The citizen and tenant initiatives contributed information about the specifics of urban renewal policy and reform demands, which they publicized in neighborhood festivals, banners hung from squatted buildings, and information published by the *Südost Express*. The latter was a neighborhood newspaper, which published information about vacant buildings and notorious speculators in order to direct squatters toward appropriate targets. The publicity work linked the squatter movement to demands for the reform of urban renewal policy, and hence made it possible for elites to support the squatters as a justifiable and perhaps necessary response to the failures of government policy.[60]

As the squatter movement grew, the actions of its militant faction often overshadowed those of other protesters in news coverage and authorities' perceptions. Beginning in 1980, squats in Kreuzberg attracted substantial numbers of militant protesters, some of whom soon began calling themselves "autonomists," an identity inspired in part by a militant movement among Italian students and workers in the late 1970s.[61] The autonomists' leaflets and periodicals declared their complete rejection of the West German political system and their eagerness to engage in potentially violent confrontations with the state.[62] For example, a leaflet that announced the "Tuwat[bbb] Spectacle," a nationwide gathering and demonstration in West Berlin planned by Kreuzberg squatters in August 1981, explained that "the West Berlin government has declared war on us . . . wants to annihilate our living space and our personal connections . . . we will carry out demonstrations that will teach them naked dread."[63] In January 1981, squatter councils in Kreuzberg and Neukölln called for the creation of an autonomous republic, and also explained the autonomists' strategic use of violence: "Our hostages are their panes of glass, their [police] vans, their property. Make it expensive for them!!! All they can understand is money!"[64]

The squatter movement grew from December 1980 to September 1981 on the basis of a strong alliance between conventional protesters and disruptive and militant squatters. Protesters were unified behind a common set of demands in opposition to clear-cut renewal and housing speculation, and in defense of the squatter movement. Soon after the December 1980 riots, the citywide "Squatter Council,"[ccc] a loosely structured weekly forum with representatives from most squatted buildings, demanded an amnesty and the release of all arrested demonstrators as a precondition for any negotiations concerning housing squats. It maintained this position until January 1982, when it allowed squatters of individual buildings to negotiate to legalize their squats.[65] The amnesty demand was strongly supported by an influential group of nonviolently disruptive, reformist squatters in eastern Kreuzberg, who were about to sign a purchase agreement for a large complex of buildings,[ddd] but broke off negotiations in solidarity with the rest of the squatter movement. The SO36 Citizen Initiative also circulated an appeal to a broad range of groups asking them to support the amnesty demand, reminding them that the squatter movement was a response to the ineffectiveness of tenants' less dramatic urban renewal protests.[66] Other, relatively respectable actors such as the SO36 Association and employees of the Urban Renewal Division also supported particular squats and opposed evictions.[67]

    bbb. Slang meaning "do something," an ironic reference to the *Tunix* ("do nothing") festival held by alternativers in 1978.
    ccc. Besetzerrat.
    ddd. Known as the Kerngehäuse, on Cuvry Strasse.

Solidarity among the squatters remained largely intact for over a year, with only a few groups of squatters reaching agreements on their buildings before 1982.[68] During this period, the broad alliance of protesters helped protect militants from police repression at demonstrations and prevent their eviction from squatted buildings.

GAINING ELITE ALLIES

As a result of their first actions and the attendant publicity, the protest groups in Linden and Kreuzberg gained support from Social Democratic politicians and other elites. Elite support increased the chances that protests would be successful, made repression less likely, and thus encouraged further mobilization. Support from elites was broader and more continuous in Kreuzberg than in Linden, making longer and more massive protests possible in the former. Elite allies also shaped the nature of participation, by steering protesters away from disruptive actions in Linden and by endorsing disruptive and sometimes militant protests in Kreuzberg.

In Hanover, the Independent Citizen Initiative's initial protests won it support from Social Democratic politicians and from a planning advisor hired by the City Planning Office. The Hanover Social Democrats responded to the citizen initiative's petition in the summer of 1972 by endorsing the group's demands in general terms. In the campaign for the October 1972 city council elections, the SPD even called for "careful urban renewal for all neighborhoods,"[69] though this slogan had no effect on city policy.

Moreover, the planning advisor, hired by the city in response to the Independent Citizen Initiative's first actions, served as an important ally for that group. The advisor, Klaus-Jürgen Holland, provided information and technical expertise useful for criticizing and countering the City Planning Office's plans. Moreover, although Planning Office officials had intended that the planning advisor would mediate between them and the Independent Citizen Initiative, Holland defined his role as purely an advisor to the latter, and helped to shore up its independence from the administration.[eee] Holland gave the citizen initiative a veto right over his appointment and soon stopped informing the Planning Office of the

---

eee. For example, Holland insisted that the citizen group control its own agenda, which he encouraged in part by not attending all of its meetings.

group's plans, while continuing to funnel information about the city's plans to the citizen initiative.[70]

When protesters carried out disruptive actions, they gained further allies. Housing Emergency Action's squats and other protests gained support from the neighborhood newspaper *Lindenblatt* and from the Linden SPD. Furthermore, when the Independent Citizen Initiative and Housing Emergency Action illegally occupied a building on Kaplan Strasse on 30 July 1973, they gained much elite attention and triggered a major split within the Hanover Social Democrats. The day after the squat, city councillors spoke at a rally outside the squatted building, where Social Democratic and Liberal leaders expressed sympathy with the protesters.[71] By contrast, Christian Democratic leaders soon called for repressive measures, such as cutting off funds for the planning advisor and turning over the Independent Citizen Initiative's membership list to the administration.[72]

Furthermore, many within the Hanover SPD endorsed the squats and called for major reforms away from clear-cut renewal. In late August, the delegate assembly of the Linden SPD organization, in a unanimous vote, denounced the Planning Office's renewal policy and threatened to carry out additional squats if other means of influence did not become available. A major split within the Hanover party followed when the mayor, Herbert Schmalstieg (SPD), came out strongly against squats, stressing their illegality.[73] In response, the head of the city council's construction committee, Klaus-Peter Beck (SPD), expressed solidarity with the Kaplan Strasse squat at a special meeting of the Independent Citizen Initiative. Beck said it was unthinkable to demolish the building.[74] A few days later, the conflict escalated when a Young Socialist group illegally occupied a building in the outlying neighborhood of Buchholz and held a meeting there.[75]

In West Berlin, politicians were much slower to respond to protests. Before 1977, public officials and housing corporation managers formed a consensus on the clear-cut renewal program, and most party politicians ignored the neighborhood-level issues it raised. However, potential elite allies finally became sufficiently available in the mid-1970s, which made it possible for protesters to win their support and thus expand opportunities further. Potential allies became available for three reasons: clear-cut renewal produced obvious problems; protests in the Kottbusser Tor area and other parts of West Berlin showed the continued unpopularity of the policy; and the 1975 elections placed sympathetic elites in positions to assist the movement.

By the mid-1970s, the problems with clear-cut renewal in West Berlin had become glaring. Existing apartment buildings were deteriorating, the construction of most new housing was delayed, and what construction had been completed was costly and unpopular. Land speculators, in collusion with Construction Ministry officials, held buildings vacant until they could obtain higher prices, which delayed the urban renewal program and created a growing and highly visible problem of vacant, deteriorating apartment buildings at a time when affordable housing was scarce.[76] Although Kreuzberg's urban renewal activities had begun in 1965, eight years later only 20 percent of the new apartments originally planned had been built, and many were in unpopular high-rise housing projects. The New Kreuzberg Center, a massive complex in the heart of Kottbusser Tor that was finished in 1974 and went bankrupt in 1978, symbolized the problems of clear-cut renewal. Its massive commercial space was too expensive to be rented, and it blocked access to the side streets, ruining business for the small shops there. The complex's roofs offered a view of barbed wire instead of the promised roof gardens, leading tenants to nickname their home the "New KZ." This was a play on words involving the complex's official abbreviation NKZ (for Neues Kreuzberger Zentrum) and the colloquial German abbreviation for concentration camp (KZ, for *Konzentrationslager*).

Furthermore, from the 1971 to the 1975 West Berlin elections, the Social Democrats lost eight percentage points and fell to 43 percent of the vote. They failed to gain an absolute majority of parliamentary seats and were forced to form a coalition government with the Liberals. As part of the change in government, the leftist Harry Ristock (SPD) replaced the conservative Klaus Riebschläger (SPD) as construction minister. In part, Ristock's appointment resulted from construction scandals in the early 1970s, which increased the power of leftists, including some Kreuzberg Social Democratic leaders, within the West Berlin party and led to Ristock's appointment as an attempt to improve the SPD's image in construction policy.[fff]

Ristock became a crucial ally for urban renewal protesters in Kreuz-

---

fff. Riebschläger was later forced out of the cabinet in a construction scandal (Rädler interview; Ulsen and Claassen 1982, 140–43; *Der Spiegel* 29 [17 February 1975], 58–60).

berg, and he undertook a series of policy initiatives that increased opportunities and resources for protesters. In May 1976, he announced an emphasis on "Urban Repair" rather than wholesale demolition, but ran into opposition from the housing corporations and the middle-level civil servants allied with them in the Construction Ministry.[77] Ristock then tried to undermine the clear-cut renewal bloc in three ways. I have already described two of them: the Strategies for Kreuzberg experiment in citizen participation, developed with leaders in the Protestant Church, and the use of new federal subsidies for housing renovation rather than demolition.

In addition, Ristock created a new planning apparatus in Kreuzberg, which immediately became poised to serve as an ally for local protesters. In June 1978, the West Berlin parliament approved the creation of the International Building Exposition in order to stage an extensive architectural exhibition in West Berlin. It included an Urban Renewal Division, which was given the task of renewing Kottbusser Tor with the participation of the existing population.[78] The Urban Renewal Division employed about eighty planners, architects, and social scientists who worked in parallel with the Construction Ministry.

The Urban Renewal Division was inclined to form alliances with protesters for several reasons. Although it was a potential rival to Ristock's own administration, it was initially in a weak position, with little funding, an uncertain jurisdiction, and no clear authority to steer the three large, unwilling housing corporations that owned much of the housing in Kottbusser Tor.[79] Moreover, its top personnel had previous positive experiences with protest groups. The director, Hardt-Waltherr Hämer, had worked with a tenant initiative in Berlin-Charlottenburg to implement experimental renovation plans. Hämer chose four assistants who had backgrounds in progressive urban planning and architecture and who had been influenced by the 1960s student movement.[80]

Hence, in 1979, Hämer and his assistants supported the Dresdener Strasse Tenant Initiative, which was the officially recognized representative of residents in Kottbusser Tor, as well as squatters in that neighborhood. The Urban Renewal Division publicly backed the tenant initiative's demands and elaborated and publicized them as twelve principles of "careful urban renewal."[81] The main elements of this neighborhood renewal program were renewal for the needs of existing residents and businesses, the preservation and improvement of the existing building stock, and the integration of residents and shopkeepers into the planning process through local decision-making bodies. The Urban Renewal Division critiqued official plans and developed alternatives, drawing on its professional expertise and reputation, which gave it access to major media and attracted support from international experts in architecture and urban renewal.

Elite support for protesters became more extensive when the squatter movement began. This helped reduce the chance of evictions or other state repression, and hence allowed both the movement against clear-cut renewal to grow and the specific tactic of housing squats to spread. The Urban Renewal Division and the Kreuzberg section of the Alternative List party gave early support to the squatter movement.[82] The Cultural Political Society of Bonn[ggg] awarded the SO36 Association and the SO36 Citizen Initiative a prize for their "exemplary neighborhood work" in November 1979, and the citizen initiative used the press attention at the award ceremony to announce additional squats.[83] Moreover, as the government's crisis in urban renewal policy grew during 1980, politicians from the governing parties, including the West Berlin parliamentary deputy Walter Momper (SPD) and the Liberal Party organization in Berlin-Tiergarten, openly supported the building occupations.[84] In October, the director of the Urban Renewal Division wrote to Mayor Dietrich Stobbe (SPD), asking for no police evictions of squats.[85] The Urban Renewal Division also aided squatters in a variety of ways, by calling for the police to release those arrested at pro-squatting demonstrations, by making technical arguments and creating plans for preserving squatted buildings that were slated for demolition, and by developing models for self-help renovation by squatters.[86,hhh]

Even when a large militant faction became important in the squatter movement, the movement as a whole received much elite support. In part this was because a crackdown by the political prosecutor's office in 1981–82 drove together a broad coalition against the *Land* government. Furthermore, when the Christian Democrats took over the West Berlin government in June 1981, the threat of squat evictions increased, and elites responded with a "godparentship movement," in which respectable organizations and prominent individuals expressed their long-term support for illegal squatting actions in particular buildings. A Protestant

---

ggg. Kulturpolitische Gesellschaft, Bonn.

hhh. Squatters and the Urban Renewal Division also came into conflict concerning details, and in some cases, entire buildings (Laurisch 1981, 99–100, 197).

church and a neighborhood center, which had been created by the 1977 Strategies competition, announced the first godparentships in June 1981. The godparents came to include well-known writers (such as Günter Grass), labor unions, youth groups of political parties, the Berlin Tenant Association,[iii] the West Berlin Liberal Party's executive board, officials in the Kreuzberg borough administration, unions within the West Berlin branch of the German Labor Federation,[jjj] and even a solitary police officer, who was immediately suspended from duty.[87] The godparents organized local support and created favorable publicity for squatters, by participating in sleep-ins, holding university lectures in squatted buildings, and publishing their sometimes euphoric impressions of the squatters' experiments with collective living and working.[88] Their support hindered evictions, prolonged the high-mobilization period of the West Berlin squatter movement, and ultimately encouraged a policy shift toward neighborhood renewal.

THE TIMING OF CONCESSIONS TO PROTESTS

One reason the Kreuzberg protests were much more militant than those in Linden is the timing of concessions to protests. In Linden and Kreuzberg, authorities made concessions to disruptive protests after refusing to adopt reforms when protesters used conventional methods, and thus encouraged the repeated use of disruptive protests in both cases. However, in Kreuzberg, militant protests seemed even more effective at producing concessions than nonviolent disruption. This made it more likely that some protesters would try militant actions in later years and that other protesters and some elites would support them.

In Linden, when Housing Emergency Action began a series of nonviolent, disruptive, and often illegal protests in January 1973, they usually gained concessions from authorities. Since disruptive actions seemed to be working, the group continued to carry them out, and it gained increasing support from local residents, as well as from some Social Democratic leaders. For example, after a five-year-old girl was hit by a car at a dangerous intersection, Housing Emergency Action members blocked the road, painted a pedestrian crossing on it, and continued blocking traffic until the paint dried. When police arrived on foot, according to Housing Emer-

---

iii. Berliner Mieterverein.
jjj. Deutscher Gewerkschaftsbund.

gency Action members, the audacity of the action and the favorable reactions of bystanders, who helped block traffic, surprised the police and deterred them from arresting anyone.[89] City authorities repeatedly had paint removed from this location, but ultimately a Social Democratic councillor endorsed an official pedestrian crossing, and the city installed one.[90]

Housing Emergency Action's squats also gained the group local support and some visible results from the city administration. Local residents donated furniture ("Not just junk, either," according to one participant), and the city allowed poor families to live in the buildings legally.[91] Housing Emergency Action's successes with disruptive actions, compared with the Independent Citizen Initiative's lack of progress through conventional methods, encouraged the latter group to make a temporary but decisive shift toward a disruptive strategy in the crucial Kaplan Strasse squat.

In Kreuzberg, too, concessions to nonviolently disruptive actions encouraged protest groups to use disruptive methods later. After the firehouse was occupied and demolished, the Stammtisch group threatened to boycott the Project Commission, which immediately produced concessions from borough officials on the Commission. As the group demanded, legal charges were dropped against the firehouse squatters, and the head of the Kreuzberg Construction Department (Wolfgang Kliem, CDU) was barred from the Project Commission because of his role in the firehouse demolition. The officials also agreed in principle that the Project Commission would be able to participate in the funding decisions for the new renovation program.[92] After disruptive methods—the occupation of the firehouse and a threatened boycott—had produced these results, some Stammtisch members formed the SO36 Citizen Initiative, a group interested in further disruptive actions, in October 1977.

Moreover, that citizen initiative's squatting actions in eastern Kreuzberg quickly gained concessions and hence encouraged other squats by making it seem likely that they too would be effective. The February 1979 squats were staged just weeks before *Land*-wide parliamentary elections in West Berlin. Presumably because the ruling Social Democrats wanted to avoid negative publicity, the *Land*-owned housing corporation that owned the apartments immediately negotiated leases with the squatters and agreed to rent forty other empty apartments.[93] Squats also seemed to produce some results in overall urban renewal policy where none had been forthcoming earlier. In August 1979, the SO36 Association and the

Urban Renewal Division, with support from Kreuzberg SPD leaders, had key demands met by Construction Ministry and borough officials: the institution of independent tenant advising and extension of the Urban Renewal Division's jurisdiction.[94] After early squats had gained these concessions, squats spread to twenty-four buildings in eastern Kreuzberg by November 1980.

Authorities also made concessions to militant protests, which created what some called "the myth of the stone"[kkk] and thereby encouraged further militant actions. In May 1980, mild protests by residents against the construction of a high wall in a park in Kottbusser Tor—an especially provocative action given the park's proximity to the Berlin Wall—were largely ineffective, even though a thousand residents signed a petition. But a violent protest seemed to be more effective. In May, a large group of protesters engaged in a tense confrontation with police, in which an officer fired his revolver and the crowd demolished the wall. In response, the borough government called a citizen assembly and officially complied with the residents' demand that the wall not be built.[95]

This dynamic was repeated on a larger scale in December 1980. Clashes between police and squatters, who built barricades to protect squatted buildings, led to four days of highly publicized riots. The rioting moved from Kottbusser Tor to the Kurfürstendamm, about five kilometers to the west, and resulted in sixty-six arrests.[96] The *Land* government responded to the riots by announcing that it was negotiating with squatters and would offer leases and some funds for renovation.[97] These concessions were more public than any the government had made during the previous year and a half of nonviolent squats. They foreshadowed the major concessions that the *Land* government would make to the disruptiveness and militancy of the squatter movement in 1981 and 1982, when the government shifted toward a policy of Careful Urban Renewal, legalized about half of the squatted buildings, and gave squatters access to public subsidies. Because of their successes at the peak of conflict, many militant squatters gained an exaggerated impression of their own strength and felt that a "Free Republic of Kreuzberg" was an attainable goal.[98] Official concessions to militant actions encouraged militant protesters to continue confrontations with police at squatted buildings and demonstrations in 1981–83 and long afterward, and they also encouraged other protesters and elite allies to support the militants.[99]

kkk. That is, the impression that violence was effective, which was sometimes but not always an accurate impression.

PASSIVITY AND OVERREACTION BY POLICE AND OTHER PUBLIC OFFICIALS

Police practices affected both the size and type of protests in Hanover and West Berlin. Decisive, consistent policing limited the scale of protests, especially illegal actions, in Linden. Authorities responded to squats decisively, either with rapid legalizations, as in South Linden in the early 1970s, or with prompt evictions combined with offers of substitute housing, as in the Velvet Strasse squats in North Linden in the 1980s. By contrast, in Kreuzberg, police vacillated between passivity and undifferentiated repression in the early 1980s. These responses allowed illegal protests to expand, increased solidarity among protesters and their elite allies, and thereby helped make the Kreuzberg conflict massively disruptive and militant. Police acted as they did in Kreuzberg partly because of constraints posed by inadequate urban renewal reforms and broad alliances among a variety of protesters and their elite supporters.

In the first place, official passivity in response to squats in West Berlin helped create a very large protest movement against demolition and displacement. Passivity also encouraged that movement to shift toward squats and the defense of squats, which occurred in both nonviolently disruptive and militantly violent ways. The first rehab-squats gained good publicity as a commonsense solution to the vacancy problem and revealed that authorities had no effective means of countering such actions. Government officials tolerated squats because they saw no other immediate solution to the problems of housing vacancies and a shortage of low-cost apartments. Urban renewal policy remained stalemated after the inconclusive results of the March 1979 *Land* elections, as the housing corporations, speculative landlords, and their allies in the Construction Ministry resisted reforms.[100] When officials failed to evict the squats, this gave protesters a green light to occupy more buildings. Indeed, until May 1981, police leaders and administrative court judges generally tolerated housing squats and implicitly supported reformist housing policy goals, thus operating partly as allies for the squatter movement. The police chief, Klaus Hübner (SPD), announced in October 1980 that squatting could be addressed only through housing policy, not police measures. Hence, the police generally minimized their interventions and reacted flexibly in order to preserve room for political negotiation. Police evicted squats from only 8 buildings before May 1981, while tolerating the illegal occupation of over 160 apartment buildings.[101]

In his inaugural address in February 1981, Mayor Vogel (SPD) formalized this rather tolerant strategy, calling it the "Berlin Line of Reason."[lll] According to the Berlin Line, police were to hinder new squats if at all possible, but existing squats were to be evicted only when certain, rather stringent conditions were fulfilled, including that the owner sought an eviction and had a credible intention to begin renovation or demolition work immediately.[102] An upper administrative court decision in April 1981 supported the Berlin Line by confirming that property owners did not have a general claim on the *Land* to evict squatters if an eviction might lead to severe riots.[103] Somewhat ironically, the Berlin Line promoted an alliance between squatters and housing policy activists, by encouraging squatters to target landlords who had created speculative vacancy rather than landlords involved in orderly urban renewal activities.

Furthermore, a government crisis developed in the winter of 1980–81, when four days of rioting by squatters and a construction scandal paralyzed the West Berlin government. The squatter movement might have been much smaller had it not coincided with this crisis. The scandal was the "Garski affair," which involved 120 million deutschmarks in improper state subsidies to a private contractor. Revelation of the affair forced the economics and finance ministers to resign in January 1981, and Stobbe's entire government followed suit later that month.[104] After a new SPD-Liberal government led by Vogel took over, the CDU and Alternative List conducted a highly popular petition drive to force new elections.[105] Vogel's government called new elections for May and, in the interim, took a timidly reformist approach, trying only limited urban renewal reforms. As the crisis in urban renewal continued between December 1980 and May 1981, the squatter movement experienced about four-fifths of its growth.

At the same time, some public officials also used harsh, undifferentiated repression, which was largely counterproductive because it increased the solidarity among different segments of the squatter movement and created some elite support for the squatters. While most authorities met the squats passively until September 1981, prosecutors and some judges pursued a crackdown by ordering police raids on squatted buildings and conducting harsh criminal proceedings. The crackdown was led by the *Land* political prosecutor's office,[mmm] which

---

lll. "Berliner Linie der Vernunft."
mmm. The politische Staatsanwaltschaft.

possessed much independence from elected officials, controlled the criminal cases being brought against demonstrators, and gained support from some judges.[nnn] The political prosecutor blocked the efforts of other judges to grant bail to those arrested at the December riots and sought long sentences for them.[106] Trials were held in high-security courtrooms normally reserved for left-wing terrorists. Some trial judges passed down unusually severe sentences (twelve to thirty months imprisonment, some without parole) for those arrested in the December riots.[107] This attempt at deterring sympathizers backfired, as the harsh measures led many supporters to see the defendants as victims of a police state.[108] The long prison terms also provoked demonstrations with violence during the first part of 1981. Harsh measures continued under Weizsäcker's government, when large-scale evictions of squats began, leading to the accidental death of a demonstrator in September 1981, which created a martyr for the squatter movement.

The political prosecutor also ordered police to search squatted buildings, which often led to harsh or undifferentiated repression. Police officers were supposed to follow overarching principles of the Berlin Line, such as reacting proportionately to squatters' actions and differentiating between violent and nonviolent protesters. But police commanders were often unable to control their officers, who allowed themselves to be provoked and reacted opportunistically.[109] While searching squatted buildings, police often damaged personal belongings or destroyed renovation work. Raids and arrests also did not differentiate between disruptive and militant squatters. Between December 1980 and October 1982, police made 1,400 arrests and initiated 7,800 criminal investigations of 3,800 different people, but achieved only 186 convictions, suggesting that most of those arrested did not belong to the hard core of the militant squatters.[110]

The squatters were resilient in the face of this repression, partly because it was not very thoroughgoing; the police did not evict squats and could not even prevent new ones in this period. Moreover, undifferentiated and harsh repression inadvertently led other protesters, and even some elites, to increase their support for the squatter movement as a whole, including the militants. A few days after the December 1980 bat-

---

nnn. The political prosecutor's office was under the justice minister, while the police were under the interior minister. The police had the task of carrying out searches for the *Land* prosecutor, as well as their own searches.

tles between police and demonstrators, the superintendent of the Protestant Church in Kreuzberg, Gustl Roth, announced that support among the Kreuzberg population for the squatters was "complete."[111] The Urban Renewal Division, the SO36 Citizen Initiative, and the Alternative List also supported releasing demonstrators arrested in December 1980, which lent support to the Squatter Council's demand for an amnesty.[112] Many left-wing organizations and individuals also expressed solidarity with all squatters against the state by endorsing the amnesty demand. In addition, the godparentship movement responded to the crackdown and the threat of evictions under the new Christian Democratic government by mobilizing a wide range of elite support for housing squats beginning in June 1981.

After the Peak of Protest: Expanded Opportunities, New Threats, and Resurgent Protests

At their peaks, the protests in the Linden and Kreuzberg conflicts not only changed urban renewal policy, but also expanded the opportunities for protests in the long term. As a result, protest levels many years after the adoption of major reforms remained much higher than at the start of the conflicts in the early 1970s. Protests continued at high levels partly because new neighborhood-level institutions were created, making participation easier, and because elite allies became more available for protesters, making it more likely that participation would be successful. Moreover, state actions continued to threaten residents' interests, and this also spurred protests. In addition, the success of neighborhood renewal attracted concentrations of young, educated Germans interested in protest movements.

As during the rising phase of the conflicts, the types of protest after the peak depended on interactions between protesters, elite allies, and police. Procedural reforms and the rise of new low-level elite allies led to a great increase in conventional participation in Linden and Kreuzberg. At the same time, the support of local elite allies and the police responses to protests led to sporadic disruptive actions in Linden, and to a major resurgence of disruptive and militant activity in Kreuzberg.

CONVENTIONAL PARTICIPATION: NEW INSTITUTIONAL ACCESS AND ELITE ALLIES

Rather than facing fixed institutions, the protesters in Linden and Kreuzberg helped change local institutions in ways that expanded opportunities for participation in the post-peak period. The main procedural reforms in urban renewal policymaking closely reflected the demands made by protesters.

In Linden, public officials implemented renewal commissions and hired planning advisors and community workers. These procedural reforms aided routine participation by reducing the costs of taking action and by making elite allies available for protesters. At the end of 1973, a renewal commission was created in South Linden, with six residents and six party politicians. The commission decentralized major planning decisions normally made by the city council, giving them to a regular forum that met weekly in the neighborhood. A similar commission was created in North Linden a few years later. Residents gained the right to speak on all agenda items, and resident groups such as the Independent Citizen Initiative gained voting rights and hence strong influence on the decisions that were made in those bodies and formally confirmed by the city council.[113] Social Democratic councillors and the representatives of local citizen initiatives formed a working majority on each renewal commission.[ooo]

In addition, the city expanded funds for planning advisors, who eased participation by resident groups and served as low-level elite allies for them. Both preexisting and new resident groups gained a right to assistance from planning advisors, who helped them articulate their interests in meetings with the City Planning Office. The planning advisors provided protest groups with technical resources that made it much easier for them to participate in the formulation and implementation of local policies, including the city administration's urban renewal plans and its distribution of publicly subsidized apartments. Finally, the city also hired additional community workers, who were social workers employed to organize and assist groups in low-income urban neighborhoods. Within limits, the community workers supported political participation by local residents.[114]

In Kreuzberg, the procedural reforms were slightly different, reflecting protesters' demands there, but they had similar effects in facilitating routine participation through the mid-1990s.[115] Tenant advisors, rather than planning advisors, became available as low-level elite allies for po-

---

ooo. Representation for the Independent Citizen Initiative and later resident groups depended on the support of elite allies in the SPD, the Liberal Party, and, after 1981, the Greens. The party representatives had the right to appoint most of the resident representatives, but they customarily reserved those seats for the local citizen initiatives (*HAZ*, 2 October, 2 November 1973; second E. Barkhoff interview).

tential protesters. Soon after taking office in 1981, under the pressure of the squatter movement, Construction Minister Ulrich Rastemborski (CDU) instituted city-funded, "landlord-independent" tenant advising. The *Land* paid for tenant advising for all tenants who were affected by proposed demolition, renovation, or new construction in West Berlin's urban renewal areas, and also in areas where urban renewal was being considered, such as SO36.[ppp] In the mid- and late 1980s, the West Berlin *Land* paid for about twenty-five independent tenant advisors in eastern Kreuzberg, who were mostly former protesters organized in alternative projects and directly employed by the SO36 Association and the Dresdener Strasse Tenant Initiative. Since proposals affecting a building now required a consensus of all tenants, the tenant advisors gained the power to limit renovation or demolition work to the amount that the poorest tenants in the building assemblies said they could afford.[116]

Activists in Kreuzberg also gained *Land*-created neighborhood committees in SO36 in 1980 and in Kottbusser Tor in 1982. As in Linden, the neighborhood committees were attractive sites for participation because their composition and customary rules gave residents and their representatives the ability to influence authoritative decisions. The neighborhood committees met weekly or biweekly in storefront offices or community centers, and anyone could attend and speak. The SO36 Neighborhood Committee included five resident representatives[qqq] (one of whom chaired the meetings) and three representatives apiece from the Construction Ministry, the borough council, and the Urban Renewal Division. The Neighborhood Committee sought to reach decisions by consensus, and both the Construction Ministry and the Kreuzberg borough council's urban planning committee bound themselves, in an oral agreement, to implement the committee's decisions.[117]

The new institutions in Linden and Kreuzberg ushered in a large volume of routine participation by resident representatives, other residents, tenant advisors, community workers, and local politicians in the period after the adoption of major reforms. The planning-advising process involved resident groups in years of detailed planning in Linden, while the independent tenant advising in SO36 involved 4,500 tenants between

---

ppp. The West Berlin regulations concerning tenant advising were elaborations of the social planning provisions of the federal Urban Renewal Law (Herberg-Reidenbach 1989; Karaciyan interview).

qqq. Chosen by the SO36 Association, which had a stable, mainly middle-class German membership of about four hundred people through the 1980s, including fifty active members in 1989 (Senat von Berlin 1983, 7; Sauter interview).

1980 and 1988 alone.[118] Renewal commissions continued to meet weekly in South Linden through 1988 and through the early 1990s in North Linden. In Kreuzberg, too, the neighborhood committees met until the mid-1990s, as long as large-scale public investment for urban renewal in eastern Kreuzberg continued, though the flow of money and hence the volume of planning decisions dropped greatly after 1989.[rrr] The renewal commissions and neighborhood committees became dominated by politicians, resident representatives, tenant advisors, and civil servants. Yet a wide variety of actors routinely used these bodies to debate issues publicly, form alliances, and make compromises with each other that created the substance of careful urban renewal.

Moreover, conflicts continued in many cases, and they usually led to surges in participation in these bodies by residents, as low-level elites mobilized them or supported their demands. In North Linden, block assemblies held for residents affected by the city administration's plans typically attracted thirty to fifty residents each. In cases of controversy, as many as a hundred people sometimes attended block assemblies and then took their demands to renewal commission meetings, triggering public debates and sometimes official concessions about rear-building demolitions and other issues.[119] Similarly, in Kreuzberg, tenants' preferences and landlords' plans still conflicted in some instances. When this occurred, many tenants appeared at the neighborhood committee meetings, and their contributions sometimes served as a check on the agreements reached by the committees.[120] In Kottbusser Tor, where former squatters often remained at loggerheads with their opponents, residents used the neighborhood committee to oppose landlords, the Construction Ministry, and the Urban Renewal Division, and consensus between residents and officials remained distant.[121] Finally, when disruptive protests occurred in Linden and Kreuzberg, the protesters often went to the renewal commissions and neighborhood committees to make their demands, seek allies, and negotiate with landlords and officials.

ELITE ALLIES FOR DISRUPTIVE AND MILITANT PROTESTERS

As in the period of rising protests, elite allies encouraged or discouraged certain protest strategies in the post-peak period. Local politicians on the

---

rrr. After the unification of Berlin, the *Land* shifted its urban renewal funds to badly decayed neighborhoods in the former East Berlin. Kreuzberg's subsidies were slated to be cut from 81 million deutschmarks in 1990 to half that amount in 1993 (*taz*, 1 February, 20 July, 1 November 1990; Verein 1992).

renewal commissions and neighborhood committees encouraged conventional protests, by frequently supporting protesters who brought their demands to public meetings. Elite allies also encouraged disruptive actions in both cases, and militant actions in Kreuzberg.

In Linden, support from Social Democratic politicians and community workers was important in encouraging disruptive actions. There was more elite support and more disruptive protest in North Linden than in South Linden.[sss] In North Linden, the two neighborhood-based groups that carried out most of the disruptive protests,[ttt] the North Linden Citizen Initiative and the North Linden Tenant Group, were initially organized by activists from the Linden SPD, though the groups quickly became largely independent of the Social Democrats. Both groups became active around 1978, when urban renewal activity increased in North Linden. They used formal participatory rights to support a mildly disruptive strategy, received support from the Social Democrats on the renewal commission, and hence were able to achieve partial successes.[122] Community workers and planning advisors employed by the city also aided some disruptive protesters, directly or indirectly.[uuu]

In Kreuzberg, a wider range of allies became available to potentially support disruptive actions. The 1981 elections brought the Alternative List into power in alliance with the Social Democrats in the Kreuzberg borough government, an arrangement that later helped inspire an SPD-AL coalition in the West Berlin government from 1989 to 1991. The Alternative List was a leftist party aligned with Green parties elsewhere in West Germany. It advocated social movements and demanded radical democracy in many areas of politics and society, such as civil liberties, women's issues, social policy, and schools.[123] Having gained 16 percent of the vote for the Kreuzberg borough council, its strongest showing in the city, the Alternative List was able to appoint the director[vvv] of the Kreuzberg Construction Department in 1981. It chose Werner Orlowsky, a former activist from the Dresdener Strasse Tenant Initiative, a shop-

---

sss. Henning, A. Barkhoff, and Burucker interviews. In addition, the protest groups in North Linden were more open to new participants than the Independent Citizen Initiative was in South Linden (Henning, A. Barkhoff, Burucker, Sancho-Rico, Deiters, Grube, Grubert, and E. Barkhoff interviews).

ttt. Described in note i.

uuu. Burucker, E. Barkhoff, Ützmann, and Ronge interviews. However, there were also clear limits to the facilitation of protest by local state actors. The city barred community workers from doing publicity work or making political demands themselves.

vvv. *Baustadtrat.*

keeper who was a strong advocate of neighborhood renewal. Moreover, from 1981 on, reformist factions in the Kreuzberg SPD and Alternative List formed a working alliance on urban renewal issues in the Kreuzberg borough council. Orlowsky and these borough councillors made use of important institutional resources for influencing the new urban renewal policy, including their power to develop and approve all block-level construction plans in Kreuzberg, subject to approval by the Construction Ministry.[124]

Three elite allies were most important for protesters in eastern Kreuzberg. Orlowsky, who directed the Construction Department from 1981 until 1989,[www] was exceptionally open to talking and strategizing with protesters ranging from reformists to autonomists. The Kreuzberg Alternative List, whose deputies made up 26 percent of the Kreuzberg borough council from 1985 to 1989, was strongly committed to supporting left-wing movements in a wide variety of areas, including urban renewal and housing.[125] Finally, the SO36 Association's tenant advisors and community workers were leading actors in the local neighborhood committee and block assemblies, and hence were easily accessible to all residents.

These elite actors encouraged disruptive actions in many ways. They conditionally supported and sometimes instigated protests. They also helped protesters link their demands, which often were very particular at the outset, to broader issues on the neighborhood renewal agenda. "Neighborhood Palavers"[xxx] served as important meeting grounds between protesters and their allies. The palavers were irregular public discussions, attracting between two and four hundred people, which were called by the SO36 Association or the neighborhood committees in connection with major events such as the autonomist-led riots in 1987–89.[126] Moreover, from 1989 to 1991, the SPD and Alternative List formed a new *Land* government, led by Mayor Walter Momper (SPD), who had been a Young Socialist tenant organizer in 1970 and had supported a Kreuzberg squat in 1980. The formation of a left-leaning SPD-AL government created the perception that disruptive protests for more affordable housing might be met with concessions, and this led to a small wave of squats in eastern Kreuzberg. However, the new government ordered the eviction of seven squatted buildings in March 1989.[127]

www. His successor, Franziska Eichstädt, was likewise appointed by the Alternative List and initially was expected to continue Orlowsky's favorable orientation toward protesters.

xxx. *Kiezpalaver.*

Elite allies also spurred protests against homelessness in the late 1980s. Tenant advisors and a community worker at the SO36 Association began publicizing this issue early in 1988. After it was revealed in November that twenty-five homeless people had gradually squatted a vacant apartment building, Orlowsky and the SO36 Association helped find them temporary housing.[128] In addition, when squatters protested against vacancy in the late 1980s, they often acted with the support or encouragement of the SO36 Association and some local politicians. Although autonomists were sometimes involved, these actions remained nonviolent and oriented toward negotiations.[129]

Similarly, after unification, a large conflict over the expansion of traffic on a bridge involved broad alliances between protesters and elites, which undergirded a series of long, disruptive protests. After Berliners breached and largely destroyed the Berlin Wall in November 1989, only a canal separated eastern Kreuzberg from the neighboring borough of Friedrichshain in what was formerly East Berlin. The *Land* government planned to widen a disused bridge[yyy] linking the two boroughs and to open it to car traffic, as part of larger highway expansion plans in unified Berlin. Resident representatives in Kreuzberg's neighborhood committees initiated opposition to the bridge expansion in August 1991, and residents living near the bridge sued the *Land* in administrative court in an effort to block construction. The Alternative List and at times the West Berlin SPD encouraged and supported them. In July 1992, between fifty and one hundred autonomists began to occupy the bridge, setting up tents, huts, and construction wagons. The mayor of the Friedrichshain borough, Helios Mendiburu (SPD), supported the occupation, praising it for providing "political pressure." The occupation remained nonviolent even though the autonomists were evicted four days later. The conventional protesters and their elite allies had influenced the autonomists to stick to a nonviolently disruptive strategy.[130]

It may be surprising that some elites in Kreuzberg also, albeit rather indirectly, supported militant actions by autonomists, especially in the late 1980s. After the May Day riots in 1987 and 1988, Orlowsky, the SO36 Association, the borough government, the local Protestant church, and the Kreuzberg organizations of the Alternative List and the SPD implicitly supported the rioters. These local elites used the sudden media attention on the neighborhood to provide facts about poverty in eastern

---

yyy. The Oberbaumbrücke.

Kreuzberg and to criticize the *Land* government's attempts to undermine neighborhood renewal, its weak response to youth unemployment, and its police tactics. They strongly implied that government policies caused the riots and that there were common interests between local residents and the autonomists.[131] The autonomists' most consistent supporter was a major faction of the *Land*-level Alternative List, especially the party's Kreuzberg organization. Members of this faction accepted violence as a means of opposing the state, and they gave the autonomists strong support, including attendance at May Day demonstrations.[zzz] Reformist protesters also provided support for the autonomists from 1987 to 1989. The clashes between autonomists and police often began at large public street festivals held by reformist groups on the Lausitzerplatz, a square in eastern Kreuzberg. Moreover, while autonomists battled with police, other demonstrators hindered police maneuvers or destroyed property themselves.[132]

Elite support for the autonomists can be explained in terms of the previous conflict history. At the peak of conflict in the early 1980s, these low-level elite actors, as well as reformist protesters, had come to see militancy as important for enhancing their own negotiating positions with landlords and the *Land* government. Therefore, linking the threat of riots to demands for concessions, or to demands for preserving the post-1982 status quo in neighborhood renewal policy, became part of the normal political discourse in the 1980s in eastern Kreuzberg. For example, in 1985, protesters held these signs outside an SPD meeting as they demonstrated in favor of Orlowsky's reappointment as director of the Kreuzberg Construction Department:

> 1981—Riots—Orlowsky becomes director. 1985—No more trouble—Orlowsky is supposed to go

and

> Without Orlowsky as the Construction Department director, Kreuzberg will be turned upside down.[133]

---

zzz. The Alternative List had been deeply divided about political violence since its inception. For example, in 1981, half of the party's electorate approved of the use of violence by squatters (FGW 1981, 25). The party's overall position was a stalemate in which party leaders neither openly supported violence by protesters nor denounced it. When pressed on the issue, they drew attention to police violence (see Bühnemann,

NEW THREATS TO RESIDENTS

In both cities, the period of major conflict and reforms was followed, about five years later, by authorities' attempts to undermine neighborhood renewal reforms and return to demolition practices. This created new threats for residents and spurred new disruptive or militant protests. In North Linden, the key issue was the demolition of rear buildings, which the city administration began in the late 1970s. Demolition plans and activities triggered a series of squatting conflicts and a rent strike, mostly in North Linden, from 1977 to 1981. After the Linden Social Democrats resolved in 1981 to oppose such demolitions because of an acute housing shortage,[134] demolition attempts and disruptive protests became less frequent.[aaaa]

In West Berlin, Weizsäcker's CDU-led *Land* government, which was elected in May 1981, created new threats that were much larger than those in Linden, and these provoked large protests. This government was deeply divided between reformists and hard-liners. During the 1981 election campaign, the Christian Democrats attacked the Social Democrats for permitting the squatter movement to develop, sharply criticized the Berlin Line as too lenient, called for a crackdown on rioters and squatters, and promised a return to law and order if elected.[135] However, the party's reformers were more in tune with most voters, who saw affordable housing as the most important issue and favored a compromise between the squatters and the government.[136] A large majority (63 percent) approved of nonviolent rehab-squats, and only 19 percent thought it important to prevent squats.[137]

Thus, the CDU-led governments of the 1981–89 period were ambivalent about urban renewal policy. Although they ultimately initiated neighborhood renewal reforms in 1982–83, they also made a series of new threats to the neighborhood renewal groups. Soon after taking office, Weizsäcker's government threatened to evict squats, which sparked the mobilization of elites as godparents in support of the squatters. After the adoption of Careful Urban Renewal policies, several years of relative calm followed, which were broken when hard-liners in the *Land* govern-

---

Wendt, and Wituschek 1984, 162–83; author's observation of Alternative List board meeting, 19 August 1987; and *taz*, 1 October 1987, 20 February 1988, 31 January, 16 November 1990).

aaaa. However, later protests included two squatting actions in 1989 (Burucker and Ützmann interviews).

ment undertook several new policies that threatened groups in Kreuzberg. These new threats led to an upsurge of protests, especially the riots and squats of the late 1980s.

Between 1987 and 1989, the *Land* government worked to end general rent controls in West Berlin and threatened to return to demolition and displacement policies. The government also undertook symbolically important actions against eastern Kreuzberg, including a police blockade of the Kreuzberg borough during a visit to West Berlin by U.S. President Ronald Reagan in 1987. After Rastemborski resigned as construction minister in 1983 and the hard-liner Klaus Franke (CDU) replaced him, the tone of *Land* government policy toward Kreuzberg was set increasingly by the hard-line interior minister Heinrich Lummer and his successor Wilhelm Kewenig (both CDU). In addition, the unexpected unification of Berlin also led to new threats to residents of eastern Kreuzberg. Not only were the *Land* government's transportation policies suddenly up for grabs, but also, since eastern Kreuzberg lay just a few kilometers south of the future center of unified Berlin, it was seen as a potentially valuable piece of real estate, which could attract private investment that would drive out low-income residents.[138]

THE EFFECTIVE AND INEFFECTIVE USE OF POLICE

In Linden, the ways that authorities used police in response to protests de-escalated conflicts and made large militant protests unlikely. Authorities responded to squats in ways that split militants, and sometimes disruptive protesters, from conventional protesters and potential elite allies. Public officials were quick to give in to the component of squatters' demands that dealt with housing policy. They usually offered squatters substitute housing if they left voluntarily, and squats during an acute housing shortage in 1980–81 led the city administration to make vacant housing available to others seeking apartments.[139] The apparent generosity of this practice gave the city government public support and neutralized potential opposition from resident groups.

These concessions left the government rather free to use police to force out squatters in North Linden, especially since they lacked cooperative relationships with the Linden SPD and with resident groups in the neighborhood. A crucial conflict occurred on the Velvet Strasse in 1981. Squatters there refused substitute housing and insisted on staying in their squatted buildings, because they wanted to build a political group in North Linden. They were evicted by about two hundred police, who carried them from the rooftops and later presented them with a bill for 100,000 deutschmarks to cover the costs of the eviction.[140] The authorities' strategy was effective in preventing alternativers and autonomists from creating any large center in North Linden, such as the squatted chocolate factory in the nearby neighborhood of Nordstadt, which became a major site for autonomist activity.

By contrast, police practices in Kreuzberg increased solidarity between militants, reformist protesters, and their elite allies, thus enhancing the potential for militant actions. Police and other authorities vacillated between passivity and undifferentiated repression in the late 1980s, a period when the *Land*'s policies also seemed very insensitive to low-income tenants. Police actions helped provoke May Day riots through unexpectedly aggressive actions, undifferentiated attacks on autonomists and bystanders, and sudden retreats from the field of battle. For example, on 1 May 1987, after protesters overturned a police van near a large street festival in SO36, riot police responded by using tear gas and clubs to chase away all festival participants, including the nonviolent members of neighborhood groups along with the autonomists. Rioting and widespread looting ensued, in which many residents participated. Later, police and firefighters withdrew completely for much of the night, allowing rioting to continue. Over one hundred people were injured and forty-seven were arrested.[141] These kinds of police responses aided militant protests because they increased solidarity within the autonomist groups and strengthened the more aggressive factions within them. They also made reformist elites and other residents more willing to support militants; in the late 1980s, local elites responded to May Day riots by expressing sympathy with the rioters rather than denouncing them.[142]

In addition, local elite support for the autonomists grew after provocative actions by authorities in June 1987, during a visit to West Berlin by President Reagan. In the wake of the May Day riots the previous month, the SO36 Association and local churches organized a boycott of the *Land* government's gala celebration of Berlin's 750th anniversary. Mayor Eberhard Diepgen denounced his opponents in Kreuzberg as "anti-Berliners," and the government increased the police forces for Kreuzberg while creating a unit of specially trained riot police.[143] Moreover, on the day of Reagan's speech at the Brandenburg Gate, *Land* authorities physically blockaded the Kreuzberg borough, cutting it off from the rest of West Berlin by street or subway. Police conducted searches and identity checks on the streets leading out of the eastern part of the borough. Ironically, while Reagan called on Soviet leader Gorbachev to "open this gate! ... tear down this wall!" his hosts were taking extraordinary measures to abridge freedom of movement a few kilometers away in West Berlin. The Kreuzberg borough government responded to the blockade by refusing to hold local celebrations of the city's 750th anniversary.[144]

But after an SPD-AL government took office in West Berlin in March 1989, two changes occurred that gradually reduced the autonomists' ability to mount large militant actions in Kreuzberg. First, low-level elites and reformist protest groups withdrew their support for autonomists, because of a conflict over housing squats that were directed against the new *Land* government. Autonomists occupied seven buildings in March, six of them in Kreuzberg, but the SO36 Association and its tenant advisors opposed the squats. They argued that the buildings were slated for renovation and return to tenants under the provisions of the Careful Urban Renewal program. These local housing experts saw the autonomists as unfairly trying to take apartments that would go to tenants or to alternative or autonomist projects that were on the borough's waiting list for apartments.[145] Since the squatters were politically isolated, the new *Land* government quickly evicted them, and even all the Alternative List's ministers supported the evictions.[146]

The evictions led to an open break between the autonomists and many of their former allies in Kreuzberg. Autonomists destroyed the plate glass windows of the SO36 Association's main office and shouted down representatives of the Kreuzberg Alternative List at a large assembly in western Kreuzberg.[147] Eventually, that party's organization split openly on the issue of whether autonomists were suitable allies in housing policy. The SO36 Association announced it would not participate in future May Day festivals, in order to avoid creating a "mass that can be maneuvered for senseless actions."[148] However, after 1989, the citywide and Kreuzberg Greens/Alternative List[bbbb] continued to implicitly endorse violence at some of the annual May Day confrontations, by issuing statements justifying particular riots as understandable consequences of social and political problems.[149]

The second change concerned the use of police. The new interior min-

---

bbbb. After unification, the West Berlin Alternative List became part of the *Land*-level Green party (Bündnis 90/Grüne), while its Kreuzberg organization changed its name to the Grüne/Alternative Liste.

ister, Erich Pätzold (SPD), tried to introduce a policing strategy aimed at de-escalating conflicts by avoiding overreactions to militant actions at the 1989 May Day events in Kreuzberg. But police leaders in the field apparently instructed the police to remain very passive; consequently, de-escalation efforts that year were ineffective.[150] For hours, autonomists went on the offensive against police and local property in the name of opposing the SPD-AL *Land* government, while the police gave them free rein, producing spectacular television images of police crouching under hails of stones rather than retreating or attacking. Then, the police struck back indiscriminately.[151]

However, in ensuing years, the police generally used the new de-escalation strategy, even under CDU-SPD governments beginning in 1991. When confronting autonomists at May Day demonstrations, police increasingly avoided overreacting to the autonomists while being more active in protecting property in the neighborhood.[cccc] The new police strategy was popular with local residents, many of whom now saw the autonomists as a threat and wanted the police to defend against them. This was a complete reversal of residents' perceptions in the late 1980s, when police had engaged in unprovoked attacks on all kinds of protesters and had hunted small groups of bystanders and militants through the streets at night. In response to the de-escalation strategy, local elites and resident groups further reduced their support for the autonomists.

This new constellation led to lower levels of violence, and within a few years it also helped reduce the level of militant activity in Kreuzberg, which shifted to eastern Berlin. Each May, about a thousand autonomists held "Revolutionary May Day" demonstrations at which they threatened violence, and five to ten thousand people joined them in protest marches. But with little support from allies and little chance of benefiting from police overreactions, the autonomists shifted their activity away from violence and toward shows of force and ritualistic expressions of fundamental opposition. This reduced the scale of property damage and injuries at Kreuzberg May Day events in the years after 1991. Typically, German autonomists and Turkish youths destroyed some property and got into small battles with police, and police used force and made several hundred arrests.[152] Partly because they lacked much support in Kreuzberg, militants began to shift their demonstrations and rioting to the Friedrich-

---

cccc. Police used undifferentiated actions in 1993, but this was exceptional.

shain, Prenzlauer Berg, and Mitte boroughs in eastern Berlin beginning in 1993.[dddd]

Summary and Conclusions

MAKING OPPORTUNITIES

Large, influential protests against clear-cut renewal unfolded in Linden and Kreuzberg for similar reasons (see Table 3 on page 222). In response to the large threats posed by demolition and displacement policies, protesters undertook bold actions, especially housing squats, and formed effective alliances with other protest groups pursuing complementary strategies. Their innovative tactics and unexpected alliances gained them popular support and won support from some elites. The Kaplan Strasse squat turned a large part of the Hanover SPD, and especially its youth wing, into allies for the Independent Citizen Initiative. The West Berlin squatter movement gained the support of a wide range of elites, including Social Democrats, Protestant Church leaders, the Urban Renewal Division of the International Building Exposition, some union organizations, and well-known intellectuals.

Initial protests triggered important mistakes by authorities. Public officials in both cities extended participatory rights without making real changes in demolition and displacement policies. While Hanover officials used police flexibly and in a differentiated way, West Berlin authorities responded with a combination of passivity and overreaction that was almost optimal for promoting a large squatter movement. Authorities there tolerated squats, but police also raided squats and repressed protesters in harsh and undifferentiated ways in the early and late 1980s.

In Kreuzberg, the authorities' intransigent pursuit of demolition policies and the alliances between protest groups were longer-lived than in Linden, the support from elites more extensive, and police mistakes much more egregious, and hence the protests were also larger and more widespread than in Linden. But in both cases, early protests expanded opportunities for protests in the long term, as protesters gained new neighborhood-level institutions and elite allies in the SPD or in new left-

---

dddd. Another reason for this shift may be the split that developed between traditional autonomists and a new Stalinist organization, the Revolutionary International Movement, which appealed to younger leftists.

ecological parties. Therefore, in Linden as in Kreuzberg, major protests continued for over a decade after major policy reforms were adopted.

POLITICAL INTERACTIONS AND TYPES OF PROTEST

Why were disruptive and militant protests much more significant in Kreuzberg than in Linden? The strategic choices made by protest groups and those they mobilized in Linden and Kreuzberg depended on alliance patterns, the timing of reforms, and the use of police (see Table 4 on page 228).

First, alliances between different protest groups, or the absence of alliances, strongly affected the kinds of participation in the Linden and Kreuzberg conflicts. In both cases, conventional and disruptive groups cooperated in a division of labor, which allowed them to undertake a broader range of actions. However, in South Linden, the alliance between conventional and disruptive protesters was weaker and shorter-lived than in Kreuzberg, and thus it did not support the launching of large-scale or long-term disruptive actions. In addition, the main conflict in Linden was settled about five years before the West German alternative movement emerged, so the alternativers and other radicals who came to Linden in the late 1970s found it difficult to locate vacant buildings and gain allies among conventional protesters and local elites. Hence, the alternativers in Linden mounted few disruptive actions, and most of them gave up in North Linden after the Velvet Strasse eviction in 1981.

By contrast, in Kreuzberg, alliances among protest groups were broad and long-lived, and this created major opportunities for both disruptive and militant protesters. The alliance between the disruptive protesters in the SO36 Citizen Initiative and the conventional protesters in the SO36 Association burgeoned to include a wide range of groups during the squatter movement. Furthermore, in Kreuzberg, the alternative movement of the late 1970s coincided with an increase in speculative vacancy and the rise of political opportunities. As a result, alternativers were available as allies for the housing policy activists in the Kreuzberg squatter movement. Militants enjoyed support from a wide range of protest groups, in both the early 1980s and the late 1980s.

The squatter movement in West Berlin might have remained a largely disruptive movement with support from conventional protest groups and elites. However, alliances among protest groups extended to include militants, who were willing to defend squatted buildings violently and to clash with police at demonstrations. Under the pressure of a crackdown by the political prosecutor and some judges during the crucial 1980–82 period, most squatters and housing activists closed ranks behind the militants' demands for the legalization of all squats and an amnesty for those arrested.

Second, the support of elite allies also shaped the nature of participation by protest groups in these two conflicts. In Linden, allies from the SPD strongly supported the conventional actions of the Independent Citizen Initiative. Social Democratic leaders only reluctantly endorsed protests by the Housing Emergency Action group, and they gave significant support to a squatting action only when the Independent Citizen Initiative participated in one. In Kreuzberg, elites gave much more support for illegal protests. Leaders in the SPD (especially Ristock), the Protestant Church, the Urban Renewal Division, and the Alternative List supported groups using conventional methods (the SO36 Association) and disruptive strategies (the SO36 Citizen Initiative). In addition, as conflicts mounted between the squatters and authorities, a variety of elites, including the godparents and a church official, lent support to the entire squatter movement, including its militant wing. The support of some elites for militants revived again in the late 1980s, when autonomists rioted against a *Land* government seen as hostile to Kreuzberg and to neighborhood renewal policies.

Third, the nature and timing of reforms also strongly affected the strategies protesters used, partly by encouraging alliances between some protesters and elites. Procedural reforms that granted routine access to public officials led to much conventional participation in both cases. In South Linden, administrators' provision of a planning advisor and the erection of renewal commissions led protest groups to focus on making detailed arguments about official plans in routine forums. In Kreuzberg, the representation of local groups on the Project Commission and the Renovation Funding Committee, the funding of the SO36 Association and other groups through the Strategies for Kreuzberg competition in 1978, and the initiation of *Land*-funded tenant advising in 1980 led to much conventional participation by opponents of demolition and displacement.

Delays in substantive urban renewal reforms help explain why protesters' methods shifted away from a purely conventional strategy in both cases, and why they shifted much more in Kreuzberg than in Linden. In Linden, authorities' intransigence on clear-cut renewal policies led to a shift toward squats by Housing Emergency Action and ultimately also by the Independent Citizen Initiative. But compared with Kreuzberg, substantive reforms occurred quickly in Linden, within a year instead of a decade, before disruptive protests had become widespread and before militant actions had been attempted.

Participation in Kreuzberg could have more closely resembled that in Linden, if officials had adopted reforms much sooner. However, disruptive protests led authorities in the Kreuzberg case to make only minor reforms, and they continued policies that promoted speculative vacancy and demolition. Their ineffective policy response encouraged elite divisions, alliances between protest groups, and the growth of a large squatter movement using disruptive and militant actions. Similarly, if officials had not reimposed threats to Kreuzberg residents after 1986, the rioting and other militant protests of the late 1980s and 1990s would have been much smaller or altogether absent.

The timing of reforms also encouraged the long-term use of disruptive methods in Linden and a mix of disruption and militancy in Kreuzberg. In both cases, conventional actions, when undertaken alone, met only with procedural reforms, not with changes in the substance of urban renewal policy. By contrast, authorities made concessions in response to squats and other disruptive protests (in Linden), and in response to both nonviolent rehab squats and militant actions by parts of the squatter movement (in Kreuzberg). Since those kinds of actions seemed effective, protesters were encouraged to use them later, even many years after the peak of protest, and conventional protest groups became inclined to support protesters who used the riskier, more effective methods.

Finally, police strategies and tactics contributed greatly to the disruptive and militant protests in Kreuzberg, and to the absence of militancy in Linden. In Kreuzberg, the responses of police and other authorities were nearly optimal for promoting disruptive and militant protests. On the whole, authorities vacillated between passivity and overreaction. Police usually tolerated squats, but no authorities legalized them, thus creating a large gray area of illegal but officially accepted activity. At the same time, the political prosecutor, police, and some judges repressed squatters in ways that did not differentiate between violent and nonviolent protesters or that were seen as overly harsh. Police overreactions occurred in a setting where the movement against clear-cut renewal already had substantial support from residents, protest groups, and some elites, and hence the policing mistakes strengthened alliances among those actors.

By contrast, Hanover authorities used an effective mix of concessions and the consistent, proportionate repression of illegal protests. They used police cautiously when confronted with disruptive protests in the early 1970s, when such protests had broad local support. But in the late 1970s and early 1980s, they repressed most squatters, after first using procedural and policy reforms to isolate illegal protesters from potential supporters. Harsher responses by authorities in the early 1970s might have led the Independent Citizen Initiative, or its allies in the SPD, to give Housing Emergency Action stronger and more public support than they did. That could have produced a larger squatter movement and perhaps led to the use of militant tactics in South Linden.

STRUCTURAL EXPLANATIONS AND THE SQUATTER MOVEMENT

Is there a structural explanation for the differences in political interactions in Kreuzberg and Linden? The prime candidate is a feature of the political institutional setting identified by Harald Bodenschatz and his colleagues: the unusually close links between interest groups and the administration in West Berlin, combined with the federal subsidies that were uniquely available to the city in the 1970s and 1980s because of its location in the middle of East German territory.[153] Bodenschatz argues that these factors caused the Social Democratic governments in West Berlin to be unusually intransigent in the face of protests against demolition and displacement policies, implying that this is what caused the protests there to be large, disruptive, and militant.

Certainly this is an important difference in the political contexts of the two conflicts. In both Hanover and West Berlin, housing corporations played a major role in implementing housing and urban renewal policy. After the destruction caused by World War II, they helped to build and manage about half of the publicly subsidized housing stock in large West German cities.[154] These corporations, which included state-owned and private entities with public utility[eeee] status, benefited from a system of state subsidies for construction coupled with limits on rents and profits.[155] Moreover, the role of housing corporations and other interest groups in urban renewal differed across the two cities. In Hanover, the

eeee. *gemeinnützig.*

one city-owned housing corporation that was to carry out the clear-cut renewal program had no special influence on the city's Planning Office, which supervised urban renewal. But in West Berlin, the housing corporations, tax shelter firms, and public Housing Credit Bank[ffff] had much influence on, and sometimes corrupt relationships with, the upper and middle ranks of the massive West Berlin Construction Ministry, which had three thousand employees in the 1970s. These interest groups formed a powerful bloc in favor of clear-cut renewal, while federal aid created a subsidy culture among Construction Ministry officials and private actors in the city. The role of ministry officials in giving out subsidies led to construction-related scandals beginning in the 1970s.[156]

In Bodenschatz's view, these economic factors determined urban renewal politics in West Berlin.[157] Economic factors ensured that the government would pursue clear-cut renewal policies even while construction costs and local protests rose sharply during the late 1970s. Only because the economic costs of property acquisition and new construction rose too high and reductions in federal subsidies loomed, making clear-cut renewal economically infeasible, did government shift to neighborhood renewal policies in order to cut costs.

Although the subsidy culture and the clear-cut renewal bloc had important effects on urban renewal politics in West Berlin, by themselves they cannot explain why reforms were delayed so long, or why they occurred when they did. In the first place, financial considerations did not dictate the nature of urban renewal policies or the timing of reforms. Neighborhood renewal was often as expensive as new construction, and the shift to neighborhood renewal in 1982 was accompanied by continued high levels of public spending on urban renewal and large federal subsidies to West Berlin, including housing subsidies.[158][gggg]

Furthermore, the role of the clear-cut renewal bloc was a changeable, not permanent, feature of West Berlin politics. After the Christian Democrats took over the West Berlin government in 1981, the bloc rapidly lost influence, and *Land* and borough officials overturned the clear-cut renewal policy. This could have occurred in the late 1970s, given appropriate political leadership within the Social Democrats, who controlled the West Berlin government, the construction minister's office, and the

ffff. Wohnungsbaukreditanstalt.
gggg. The federal share of West Berlin's revenue was basically stable during the 1980s, making up 52.4 percent in 1980 and 50.6 percent in 1990 (Strom 2001, 80–81).

Kreuzberg borough government. By 1979, the size and intensity of opposition to clear-cut renewal, as well as the policy's internal problems and the SPD's electoral decline, indicated a need for a major shift in policy. But the leaders of the West Berlin SPD were slow to respond. Why did they fail to make the shift to neighborhood renewal, at the latest after rehab-squatting began in 1979?

The failure of SPD leadership was due to contingent political reasons, none of which was an inevitable outgrowth of the state, party, or interest group system in West Berlin at this time. In particular, the government crisis in December 1980 and January 1981 provided great opportunities to militants and other squatters, who responded to the government's paralysis by rapidly expanding the number of occupied buildings.[159] The coincidence of three events greatly exaggerated the government crisis: the squatter movement, which had been growing gradually for almost two years; inept police actions, which provoked the December rioting by militant squatters; and the Garski affair, which began to blossom on the second day of rioting, when police raided the offices of Garski's firm.[160] Mayor Stobbe's leadership was extremely weak at this time, partly because of the internal conflict within the SPD that undermined his power during 1980. After Stobbe's departure, Vogel's government enacted only timid reforms, partly because it was weakened and its term of office drastically shortened by the campaign to force early elections. That campaign, in turn, was a highly contingent political event, since it briefly united two very odd political bedfellows, the AL and the CDU.

A brief look at two other cases also casts doubt on the idea that the structural influence of interest groups is decisive for explaining the differences between the Linden and Kreuzberg cases. In the Wedding borough of Berlin, institutional and social structural conditions were similar to those in Kreuzberg: large clear-cut renewal plans by the Construction Ministry, implementation by housing corporations, and a similar share of young people and university educated people at the outset of the conflict.[161] But when Young Socialists tried to organize tenants in Wedding beginning in 1969, they received very little support from residents or from the local Social Democrats.[162] Hence, disruptive and militant actions against clear-cut renewal policies remained limited in Wedding, and few squats occurred there in 1980–82, the period of the peak of the West Berlin squatter movement. Demolition and new construction were completed in the early 1980s, with no significant concessions to demands for neighborhood renewal.

The Nordstadt neighborhood of Hanover furnishes a different kind of counterexample. There, under the same citywide political institutions as in Linden, the local SPD organization did not support planning advisors to integrate local residents into the planning process when urban renewal began around 1986. Hence, with the support of conventional protesters, a disruptive and militant movement against urban renewal began to develop in 1987. The movement included long-term squats of seven buildings at a former chocolate factory, in which alternative and autonomist groups gained significant space for their projects.[163] As a result, disruptive and militant protests continued at high levels in Nordstadt in the 1990s, including the nationwide Chaos Days staged by autonomists there in the mid-1990s. Nordstadt, like Kreuzberg, became a nationally important center of autonomist activity, in a city without a powerful bloc of clear-cut renewal interests or special subsidies from Bonn.

In sum, political interactions were more important than structural conditions in producing strong militant movements. Despite similar structural conditions in Wedding and Kreuzberg, a strong militant movement developed only in Kreuzberg. And despite different structural conditions in Kreuzberg and Nordstadt, both neighborhoods experienced much militancy. The reason is that political interactions favorable to a militant movement developed in Kreuzberg and Nordstadt, but not in Wedding.

3 NUCLEAR ENERGY CONFLICTS AT WYHL AND BROKDORF

The national movement against nuclear energy in West Germany, which developed in the 1970s, was strongly rooted in regional protests against proposed nuclear facilities. The first two major conflicts were at Wyhl (Baden-Württemberg) and Brokdorf (Schleswig-Holstein). As in the urban renewal conflicts, Wyhl and Brokdorf exemplify large, sustained, influential protest movements with very different kinds of participation. But these conflicts were in rural areas, in *Länder* governed by Christian Democrats through the late 1980s. In both cases, utility companies, with the approval of *Land* officials, proposed nuclear plants in the early 1970s, and broad coalitions of protest groups from local villages and nearby cities mobilized in response. Protests became massive at Wyhl and Brokdorf and lasted about a decade in each case, pausing in the late 1970s and resurging in the early 1980s. In each case, protests grew because threatening state activities, alliances between protesters, bold tactics, elite support, and authorities' mistakes reinforced each other. Furthermore, both movements were influential, though in different ways. The second round of Wyhl protests, and the threat of escalating protests, led the *Land* government to abandon its proposed plant in 1984. Although the Brokdorf plant was built and put into operation in 1986, the long and intense Brokdorf protests contributed to a national stalemate on nuclear policy and the downsizing of the federal government's nuclear energy plans.

Yet the two conflicts also exemplify sharply contrasting experiences of the antinuclear movement. Wyhl is a case that combined highly disruptive, nonviolent protest with strong conventional actions, on the basis of strong cooperation among protest groups. The Wyhl protests centered on the illegal occupation of a nuclear construction site, leading to negotiations between *Land* officials and protesters, with very little militancy or violence. By contrast, at Brokdorf, authorities prevented any significant site occupation and protests took mainly conventional and militant forms. Mass demonstrations, involving large militant shows of force and small battles between militants and police, occurred repeatedly. The local citizen initiatives at Brokdorf largely demobilized, and although nonviolent protests continued, they became rather routine and lost their disruptive character. As in the urban renewal conflicts, the contrasting kinds of participation were due to differences in the timing of reforms, alliances among protest groups and elites, and the ways police responded to protests.

After describing the main events of the Wyhl and Brokdorf conflicts, I assess how well socioeconomic and institutional theories can explain them. Most of the chapter then provides an interactive political process explanation, which focuses first on the rising phase of protest. I simultaneously examine how large movements and opportunity expansion went hand in hand in both cases, and how political interactions led to divergent protest strategies in the two conflicts. Next, I explain why protests resurged in the early 1980s at Wyhl and Brokdorf, long after the initial peak in protest, and why they again took different forms. In the conclusion I compare and summarize the main dynamics of the two cases.

A Chronology of the Wyhl Conflict

In July 1973, the *Land* government of Baden-Württemberg and a *Land*-owned utility company, Southern Atomic Plant,[a] announced plans to build a nuclear electricity-generating plant in a wine-growing area near the small town of Wyhl. Opponents, including local farmers and students from the nearby university town of Freiburg, rapidly formed citizen initiatives, which united as the International Committee of Baden-Alsace Citizen Initiatives[b] in August 1974. They opposed the plant at first in conventional ways, by making formal objections, attending a public licensing hearing, and pursuing litigation in the administrative courts. In

---

a. Kernkraftwerk Süd was a wholly owned subsidiary of two electricity utilities.
b. Internationales Komitee der Badisch-Elsässischen Bürgerinitiativen.

February 1975, the groups illegally occupied the construction site, were evicted forcibly, and occupied the site again, this time for fourteen months.[1] The site occupations produced dramatic confrontations with police and generated much publicity for the emerging national antinuclear movement.

The occupations also led to major, but temporary reforms. The government halted construction within a few days, and a Freiburg administrative court blocked the plant's license in March 1975. In the wake of those concessions, the *Land* government and the Baden-Alsace Citizen Initiatives slowly negotiated an agreement, finalized in January 1976.[2] According to the Offenburg Agreement, the protest groups ended their site occupation in exchange for detailed studies of the effects the proposed plant would have on the climate and the environment and an amnesty for protesters.[3] In March 1977, the Freiburg court suspended the plant's building permit, halting construction for another five years.

However, when a higher-level court cleared the way for licensing to proceed, the Baden-Württemberg government announced plans to resume the project in 1982. In response, the Baden-Alsace Initiatives mobilized, once again in conventional and disruptive ways. They met with officials and held demonstrations, and effectively adapted the nonviolently disruptive approach they had used so successfully in the mid-1970s. Rather than propose another site occupation, the protest groups threatened a massive, multifaceted, decentralized campaign of nonviolent resistance. As in the earlier conflict, violence and other militant actions were rare and isolated. *Land* officials effectively abandoned plans for the Wyhl plant late in 1983, and, at the twentieth anniversary of the site occupation in 1995, the *Land* government (CDU-SPD) announced that the region would be declared a nature preserve.[4]

A Chronology of the Brokdorf Conflict

The Brokdorf conflict began at almost the same time and in very similar fashion. In November 1973, the *Land* government of Schleswig-Holstein and a utility company, Northwest German Power Plants,[c] announced plans to build a nuclear plant in an agricultural area (the Wilstermarsch) near the village of Brokdorf. Opponents formed the Lower Elbe Environ-

---

c. Nordwestdeutsche Kraftwerke.

mental Citizen Initiative,[d] which included local chapters from the marshes and western coast of the Elbe River and a large chapter in Hamburg. As at Wyhl, these protest groups initially used a mostly conventional approach, including speaking at public hearings and pursuing litigation in the administrative courts. But the *Land* government surprised opponents by secretly granting a construction permit and allowing construction to begin just after midnight on 26 October 1976. When protesters attempted to occupy the construction site four days later, they found that officials had fortified it in order to prevent a long-term occupation. Police violently evicted protesters and attacked nonviolent demonstrators with helicopters and tear gas at two demonstrations, at the end of October and in November 1976.

The police actions at the Brokdorf demonstrations triggered increased support for the antinuclear movement from some Social Democratic leaders, including federal cabinet members, and this led to major, though temporary reforms. In February 1977, a lower administrative court suspended the plant's license, which blocked construction. This partial success reinforced a split that was already developing in the antinuclear movement at Brokdorf. In late February 1977, thirty thousand protesters, including communists and undogmatic leftists armed with clubs and Molotov cocktails, demonstrated at the construction site, while between ten and thirty thousand people demonstrated nonviolently in Itzehoe, twenty kilometers distant.[5]

However, in 1981 an upper administrative court overturned the lower court's decision, and the Schleswig-Holstein government immediately resumed construction. The antinuclear movement responded with renewed protests, which again split between militant actions at the construction site and largely conventional ones elsewhere. In December 1980, about four hundred youths used fireworks, clubs, and one hundred Molotov cocktails against police at a demonstration involving between four and ten thousand people,[6] and between fifty and one hundred thousand people held an illegal demonstration near the plant site in February 1981, where militants battled with police at the end of the demonstration.[7] In these actions, hundreds or thousands of autonomists, undogmatic leftists, and members of communist groups participated along with much larger crowds of protesters who did not directly engage in violence. Similarly, forty thousand people demonstrated at the construc-

d. Bürgerinitiative Umweltschutz Unterelbe.

tion site in June 1986, with police and militants clashing at control points many kilometers from the site and at the site itself. There were also many other militant actions in the 1970s and 1980s, including violence at demonstrations in Kiel, Itzehoe, and Hamburg, and sabotage actions and firebomb attacks near the Brokdorf plant, which caused an estimated 10 million deutschmarks in damage.[e]

Most of the nonviolent wing of the Brokdorf antinuclear movement carried out conventional or mildly disruptive actions, including litigation and protest rallies led by the SPD in Schleswig-Holstein. By contrast, strongly disruptive protests at Brokdorf were unimportant. Although disruptive actions continued over a ten-year period after 1986, they were mainly symbolic and drew relatively small numbers of participants. Protesters who were connected with various church groups and nonviolent-action groups held symbolic blockades and vigils outside the nuclear plant's fence once a month for several years starting in June 1986.[8] In addition, blockade actions were held into the late 1990s, usually in connection with the transport of nuclear waste, leading to more than one hundred arrests over a period of years.[9]

Although the Brokdorf plant was completed and put into operation in 1986, the Brokdorf protests, along with those at Wyhl, contributed to major reforms in the national nuclear program. The anti-Brokdorf protests helped create a national stalemate on nuclear policy from 1977 to 1982 and a polarization on the issue within the party system, and thus contributed to a downscaling of the original nuclear program across West Germany. In 1985, the net generating capacity of West German nuclear plants was about 17,000 megawatts, far short of the 45,000 to 50,000 megawatts planned in 1974.[10]

The Limits of Socioeconomic and Institutional Explanations

SIMILAR SOCIOECONOMIC SETTINGS

As in the urban renewal conflicts, the different types of protest at Wyhl and Brokdorf cannot be explained by the socioeconomic settings, which

---

e. These included four firebomb attacks and eight attacks against power-line towers near Brokdorf in 1986 (Willems 1997, 326). Other militant actions included a one-hour battle between police and protesters led by a communist group in Itzehoe in October 1977, an attempt by several hundred leftists to storm the construction fence in Decem-

were very similar. Both nuclear plants were proposed in rural locations, with only villages and very small towns in the immediate vicinity. The town of Wyhl had 2,700 residents, and the town of Brokdorf about 1,000 in the 1970s. The local economies were strongly agricultural, with high shares of small producers in the population and little industrial development. Wyhl lies within the *Land* of Baden-Württemberg (population 10 million), in the southwest corner of Germany, bordering the Alsace region of France. The proposed plant site lay in rural Emmendingen County (population 130,000), within ten kilometers of several prosperous villages. Specialty farming such as tobacco, fruit, vegetables, and wine grapes, the latter in the renowned Kaiserstuhl area, provided good incomes to many residents.[11]

The site of the Brokdorf nuclear power plant is in Steinburg County (population 130,000) on the Elbe River in the largely rural *Land* of Schleswig-Holstein (population 2.6 million), in northern Germany. As at Wyhl, the region around Brokdorf was mostly agricultural, in this case producing dairy and beef products. Its marshlands and ponds also served as important breeding grounds for wildlife, and the area had been set aside as a tourist area in *Land* plans. Yet both sites were rather close to cities from which students and adult members of the educated middle classes could be drawn. Wyhl is about thirty kilometers from Freiburg, a city with 160,000 residents, while Brokdorf is about fifty kilometers from Hamburg, a city-state (*Land*) of 1.8 million. Freiburg and Hamburg each had major research universities with over ten thousand students in the 1970s.

Finally, although both regions had large, prosperous agrarian populations who were not accustomed to industrial development and were not in great need of new jobs, this social structural factor was not necessary for large antinuclear protests. Wackersdorf, where massive protests against a fuel-reprocessing plant occurred in the 1980s, lay in a rural area with declining steel and coal industries and an unemployment rate twice as high as the *Land* average.[12] Wackersdorf also shows that proximity to a city the size of Hamburg was not necessary for large militant actions. Although this conflict occurred in a rather remote rural location in Bavaria, it attracted large numbers of autonomists from West Berlin

---

ber 1979, violence by two hundred militants during a demonstration in Kiel in October 1986, and heavy riots in Hamburg in October 1986 (*KN*, 17 October 1977, 9 October 1986; ILSH 1979, 34–35; 1985–86, 65–66, 60–62).

and other distant cities.ᶠ The autonomists were able to sustain their mobilization at Wackersdorf because they had support from local protesters.[13]

SIMILAR POLITICAL INSTITUTIONS: FEDERAL AND *LAND*

The different protest strategies at Wyhl and Brokdorf cannot be explained by the conflicts' political institutional settings, which were also very similar. In the first place, the same public institutions and private bodies that governed federal nuclear energy policy also affected both conflicts. In the early 1970s, state regulation of nuclear generation in West Germany reflected a fusion between the interests and goals of administrative agencies and private actors. Nuclear energy in Germany was developed mainly by a few private firms, with coordination and subsidies from the federal government, and orders for plants coming from a small number of large, regional electricity-producing utilities. Similar overlaps in ownership or high-level personnel existed between the utilities and a pro-nuclear trade association on the one hand (the Atomforum), and the agencies responsible for safety evaluations (primarily the federal government's Reactor Safety Commission and the Technischer Überwachungsverein, a technical supervisory organization), on the other.[14] Moreover, the utilities were responsible for the energy forecasts on which the government's nuclear plans were based, which led in the 1970s to a bias in favor of overestimating demand and overbuilding generating capacity.

Responsibility in nuclear policy was divided between the federal and *Land* governments. The federal government had been involved since 1956, when it established the Ministry of Atomic Energy, and by the late 1960s, the Ministry for Research and Technology assumed responsibility for the nuclear program.[15] The *Länder* owned large shares of the electricity producers, and members of the *Land* government sat on the utilities' boards of directors. *Land* governments usually allowed electricity producers to select sites for plants, which were then approved post hoc by the *Länder*.[16] The state's dual roles as a promoter and a regulator of nuclear energy made it difficult for nuclear opponents to influence plans for nuclear expansion, especially since nuclear energy production requires long-term investments that make a shift in course very difficult to effect once a policy has been partially implemented.[17]

f. Hence, the Wackersdorf example undermines Koopmans's argument that the strength of leftist militants in Hamburg compared with Freiburg helps account for the differences between the Brokdorf and Wyhl cases (Koopmans 1995, 162).

However, the role of West German administrative courts, which oversaw nuclear plant licensing procedures, created the potential for nuclear opponents to delay plant construction in the 1970s. Although administrative courts normally are limited to enforcing rather than interpreting the law, a 1972 decision by the Federal Administrative Court[g] gave the lower administrative courts significant latitude in the nuclear policy area. The Court interpreted the federal Atomic Law to require that ensuring the safety of nuclear energy be given priority over promoting its use, and that plaintiffs be protected against the prejudicial effects of early construction.[18] Thereafter, administrative courts were to decide whether safety had been pursued adequately within the limits of available technology. The courts became open to considering the criticisms of nuclear experts, which grew beginning in the late 1960s.[19] Although there is no legal right to a clean environment or health, and associations or groups in class-action suits have no legal standing, individual freedom and property rights are protected under law. Moreover, many judges in the lower administrative courts sympathized with citizen initiatives. In the early 1970s, the federal government expanded the administrative court system as part of an expansion of government planning activities. The new generation of jurists was influenced by the student movement, and many of them sought to implement the participatory goals of the first Brandt government.[20]

Legal procedures also gave the lower courts important latitude. When a suit was brought against a plant construction permit, the permit was suspended automatically, but the *Land* government could reinstate it with an immediate effect order as long as the government provided an argument that an overriding public interest in construction existed. The plaintiffs could then ask the court for an injunction against the *Land* government's order, on the grounds that they were likely to win the main court case or that the government's reasoning about an overriding public interest was weak. Therefore, immediate effect orders became the main point of conflict between the *Land* governments and the administrative courts.[21] In addition, the Federal Interior Ministry oversaw the granting of permits and had some leverage over the *Land* governments, which became a factor when the antinuclear movement began to influence federal officials in the mid-1970s.[22]

The political settings at the *Land* level were also very similar for Wyhl

---

g. Bundesverwaltungsgericht.

and Brokdorf. In both *Länder,* the Christian Democrats led the governments through the late 1980s, with absolute parliamentary majorities. Baden-Württemberg has been governed since 1956 by the CDU, which had stable electoral results between 1972 and 1984 (52–57 percent of the vote) and ruled without a coalition partner from 1972 to 1992. Emmendingen County, site of the proposed Wyhl plant, gave the CDU an average share of the vote (54 percent) in the 1972 *Landtag*[h] elections. In Schleswig-Holstein, the Christian Democrats governed from 1950 to 1988. Between 1971 and 1987, their vote share was stable (48–52 percent), and their absolute majority of *Landtag* seats allowed them to govern alone.[23] In Steinburg County, the location of the Brokdorf plant, the CDU had slightly above-average strength, consistently gaining about two percentage points more than their *Land*-wide average. Thus, the CDU was locally popular in both places in the early 1970s, and yet local residents became strongly opposed to the CDU's nuclear policies and willing to protest against them.

The Rise of Major Protest Movements and the Divergence of Strategies

THE THREAT POSED BY THE NUCLEAR PROGRAM

As in urban renewal, large threats to residents were one cause of the massive protests at Wyhl and Brokdorf.[i] In September 1973, shortly before the price of oil rose worldwide, Brandt's SPD-Liberal federal government announced plans to expand the country's number of nuclear plants from eight to fifty, and the electricity supplied by them from 2,300 to about 50,000 megawatts, by 1985. These plants were projected to supply

---

h. The unicameral *Land* parliament.
i. However, threats were not sufficient to produce strong antinuclear protests in other cases. Eleven large commercial nuclear facilities were sited in West Germany between 1967 and the start of the Wyhl conflict, but local protest groups mounted substantial opposition in only two of them, and those were short-lived and unsuccessful protests (Kitschelt 1980, 199, 256). Kitschelt's explanation is that neither of these cases had large agricultural populations and prosperous agricultural economies that were threatened by nuclear energy. But the strong protests at Wackersdorf in the 1980s pose a counterexample to this social structural explanation. Rising opportunities seem to be a more important factor, because strong antinuclear protests did not develop until the Wyhl conflict, when protesters' actions were met with major support from political parties and major concessions by administrative court judges.

15 percent of the country's energy consumption and to greatly promote industrial development.[24] Government officials and leaders of utilities argued that the electricity was needed to meet future demand, which they predicted would rise at 8 percent per year, and hence to ensure continued economic growth and employment.[25]

Opponents argued that the West German nuclear energy program posed particular threats to residents in the localities where the new plants were to be sited. They argued that nuclear plants would expose residents to thermal and low-level radioactive pollution even under normal operation, and to the risk of major or even catastrophic accident (as later seen at Three Mile Island and Chernobyl). They also predicted that the further industrialization of regions around the plants would produce pollution over large areas, and that nuclear waste disposal would also involve pollution and other risks.[26]

In the areas around the proposed Wyhl and Brokdorf plants, a large majority of residents evidently felt threatened. According to a Federal Research Ministry study, 75 percent of the population in Emmendingen and Freiburg counties were opposed to the Wyhl plant.[27] In addition, in the 1976 *Landtag* elections, the pro-nuclear CDU suffered heavy losses in the Wyhl area, which was previously a stronghold for that party. A district near the plant elected a speaker of a citizen initiative from the Liberal Party to a *Landtag* seat, with some localities giving him 70 percent of the vote.[28] Similarly, in the Brokdorf area, a nonscientific survey in December 1973 found that 75 percent of residents were opposed to the plant.[29] As protests drew attention to nuclear energy, public opposition across West Germany increased dramatically, from 16 percent in 1975 to 43 percent in 1977, putting nearly half the population at odds with government plans.[30]

At Wyhl, threats to residents triggered protests in the early 1970s. In July 1973, Southern Atomic Plant proposed building a 1260 megawatt pressurized-water nuclear reactor at Wyhl, with a second reactor of the same type and size to be built later.[31] This proposal was part of much larger plans by several governments to industrialize the Upper Rhine in West Germany, France, and Switzerland. Officials intended to create "a second Ruhr Valley" in this region, with seventeen nuclear plants, sixteen conventionally fired power plants, oil refineries, chemical plants, and metalworking factories.[32]

The proposed Wyhl plant sparked the formation of a network of citizen initiatives from the rural areas of Baden Württemberg and neighboring France as well as in the city of Freiburg. Local residents, led by farmers and clergy, were concerned about effects on the local climate, safety, and the prospects of the further industrialization of their agricultural region. They had allies among leftist students and ecologists in Freiburg, who saw the Wyhl conflict as a chance to assert anticapitalist or environmentalist positions. The opposition of these groups led to the first significant conflict over a nuclear facility in West Germany, and it gave major impetus to a broader antinuclear movement there and in other countries, including the United States.[33]

The core of the antinuclear movement at Wyhl consisted of the region's citizen initiatives. These were composed of local residents from the traditional middle classes (well-off farmers and winegrowers, artisans, and tavern owners) and from the educated middle classes (pastors, teachers, physicians, and pharmacists), as well as leftist and environmentalist university students from Freiburg and the larger region.[34] Local notables, including Christian Democratic politicians, Protestant pastors, and the Social Democratic mayor of Weisweil, were prominent members, forming a conventional wing that was initially reluctant to use or endorse illegal methods.[35] Weisweil, a village four kilometers distant from the proposed plant, became a center of antinuclear protest, as did the village of Sasbach, the town of Emmendingen (population 20,000), and the city of Freiburg.[36]

In response to the plans of Southern Atomic Plant, members of twenty-one citizen initiatives formed an umbrella organization, the International Committee of Baden-Alsace Citizen Initiatives, in August 1974. This organization grew to include fifty-six groups by 1977, mostly from the West German side of the border, representing groups from Freiburg as well as the surrounding countryside.[37] About twenty-five to thirty leaders from the citizen initiatives met regularly. The initial goal of the Baden-Alsace Citizen Initiatives was to stop construction of the Wyhl plant, but they soon embraced the more radical goal of stopping all nuclear plant construction in West Germany. This shift reflected the arguments of scientific critics about the general safety and pollution problems of the technology. Hence, the citizen initiatives supplemented their initial slogan, "No nuclear plant in Wyhl," with "or anywhere else!"[38]

At Brokdorf, too, plans for a nuclear plant immediately led to the formation of protest groups. In November 1973, Northwest German Power Plants announced plans to build a 1300 megawatt pressurized-water reactor at Brokdorf, with a minority ownership by the Hamburg electricity utility. Nuclear opponents charged that the proposed plant was part of much larger plans by the *Land* government to promote industrialization in the Lower Elbe Valley, although the government gave assurances that the area immediately around Brokdorf could be developed for recreational rather than industrial uses.[39]

In response, in the winter of 1973–74, local farmers and other residents formed citizen initiatives, which were concerned about the plant's effects on thermal pollution in the river, its biological carrying capacity, fog, radiation, and the emergency cooling system.[40] These protest groups became part of the Lower Elbe Citizen Initiative, which was founded in November 1973. This organization had chapters in the rural areas near the proposed plant as well as in Hamburg, which made it politically very diverse and often obscured major strategic differences between its different chapters. In 1974, the board of the Lower Elbe Initiative was drawn from the villages around Brokdorf, though by 1976 most of its members were from Hamburg. Like the Baden-Alsace Initiatives at Wyhl, it drew on members of the traditional middle classes from the rural area around the plant (farmers and fishers) as well as members of the educated middle class (university students, lawyers, scientists, and white-collar workers) from the nearby cities.[41] In the first two years, the Lower Elbe Initiative focused on preventing the construction of the Brokdorf plant, but the experts and arguments it relied upon called into question nuclear energy technology in general.[42]

PARTICIPATORY RIGHTS COMBINED WITH POLICY INTRANSIGENCE

As in the urban renewal cases, protests were spurred by a combination of formal participation rights and intransigence by public officials in their pursuit of unpopular policies. The participation rights helped protesters to get organized and begin opposition activities, while the lack of major reforms led them to expand their protests. Moreover, the manipulation of official participation forums by *Land* officials helped win elite allies to the protesters' cause. This combination of responses by authorities also affected the types of protest. Procedural access led to conventional participation, but with poor and dwindling prospects of success in that arena, protest groups shifted toward disruptive or militant strategies.

Before utilities could be licensed to begin construction, the federal Atomic Law required that public notice be given and that the *Land* government carry out public licensing hearings. But these public participation rights did not give protesters any chance of influence over policy. There were strict limitations on the scope of participation and discussion at the hearings. Nuclear safety was included but environmental effects were not, and anyone who had not filed a written objection could not participate.[43] Moreover, authorities made clear that neither hearings nor court cases would alter their construction plans. However, individuals and local governments could appeal a *Land*'s licensing decisions to the administrative courts.

At Wyhl, the citizen initiatives used these participatory rights, along with other kinds of institutional access, to build public and elite support for their position. They attended the licensing hearing, lobbied the legislature, and campaigned on a local referendum measure. The Baden-Württemberg government's publicly stated intention of rapidly licensing the plant, regardless of public objections, made participation in the public licensing hearing seem pointless. Before the licensing process had begun, Economics Minister Rudolf Eberle published advertisements explaining "Why the Wyhl nuclear plant will be licensed" and *Land* Premier[j] Hans Filbinger (CDU) responded to demonstrations by insisting that "there can be no doubt that Wyhl will be constructed."[44] The impression of a foregone conclusion was reinforced by the *Land*'s large indirect ownership stake in the plant and the leading roles of Filbinger and Eberle on the board of one of the utilities that owned Southern Atomic Plant.[45]

The way that Eberle conducted the July 1974 public hearing also underscored the *Land* government's intransigence. Representatives of Southern Atomic Plant and others who had prepared favorable reports on the electricity producer's behalf held long speeches addressing each other. Although approximately ninety thousand people had signed a collective objection to the license and eight municipalities and fifty associations had also objected formally, only a few residents from the citizen initiatives were allowed to speak.[46] Their request for a continuation of the hearing was denied, and they walked out in protest.[47]

The citizen initiatives used the hearing as a springboard for further mobilization, while also beginning to shift toward a disruptive strategy. In August, they responded to Eberle's conduct of the hearing by holding a protest march of two thousand people to the construction site and founding the Baden-Alsace Initiatives. They issued a statement that listed a series of lessons learned from the public hearing, including govern-

j. Minister-Präsident.

ment officials' conflicts of interest and unwillingness to listen to critical scientific opinion. The groups concluded "that the government wants to implement its plans if necessary with violence and against the will of almost one hundred thousand petitioners; that we can represent our interests only ourselves, collectively and unified—because we will not tolerate this trampling on our rights."[48] In an important statement in late September 1974, Hans-Helmut Wüstenhagen, the speaker of a local environmental group, stated publicly that if the Wyhl plant were licensed, the citizen initiatives would occupy the site with up to two thousand people.[49]

The ineffectiveness of conventional efforts, exemplified by a frustrating lobbying expedition to the *Land* capital in December 1974, led the local citizen initiatives to publicly consider a nonviolent site occupation. When six hundred people from thirteen communities in the Kaiserstuhl area drove several hours to the *Land* capital in Stuttgart to meet with their elected representatives, their convoy of buses was met by police, led around the city for an hour, and prevented from parking near the *Landtag* building. Few deputies were willing to meet with them to hear their request that the parliament halt the permit process until all scientific issues were clarified. In response to this negative experience with police and *Land* politicians, the citizen groups' leaders announced that a site occupation would be possible as a last resort.[50] Yet the site occupation strategy remained a divisive issue within the Baden-Alsace Initiatives, since most local notables rejected illegal actions.

The ineffectiveness of conventional participation was also made clear in other ways. A Wyhl town referendum on the sale of land to the *Land* in January 1975 was manipulated and undermined when *Land* officials threatened to take the land by eminent domain; voters then narrowly approved the sale.[51] Perhaps most important was the *Land* government's apparent willingness to circumvent residents' court challenges, which represented their main chance to prevent construction. Ten days after the land-sale referendum, the Baden-Württemberg government moved quickly to grant Southern Atomic Plant an initial partial construction permit, on 22 January. After the lower administrative court in Freiburg advised the firm to delay construction pending a court decision, construction workers began clearing underbrush and erected a fence at the site in the early morning hours of 17 February 1975.[52] Protesters responded to this flouting of judicial authority by shifting to a disruptive strategy, as they tried to occupy the construction site twice within the next week.

At Brokdorf, protests initially unfolded in ways similar to those at Wyhl. Protesters had some institutional access, and this led them to mobilize initially in conventional ways. In 1974, groups in the Lower Elbe Initiative focused on winning support from local politicians and government officials, while in 1975–76 they put most of their energies into court challenges and into lobbying *Land* and federal politicians.[53] About twenty-one thousand formal objections to the plans were filed by October 1974, and 5,800 people filed objections in 1976 to a separate license concerning the plant's use of water from the Elbe River, an important water source for local agriculture.[54]

But the way that public officials conducted the hearings, in November 1974 and March 1976, made it clear that they would not budge on building the plant. Separate hearings were held for those living inside and outside a very small radius from the plant (four kilometers), thus separating the local citizen groups from their scientific experts and other outside supporters. Local residents were outnumbered inside the hall by officials, and outside the hall by hundreds of police, a display of force that further alienated the local opponents.[55] After a Liberal *Landtag* deputy supported the protesters' criticisms at the first Brokdorf hearing, authorities simply terminated it.[56]

In response, the antinuclear protesters in the area around Brokdorf added a nonviolent site occupation strategy to their conventional efforts. In the months before the March 1976 hearing, the Lower Elbe Initiative announced that it expected little to come from the public hearing and that it planned to occupy the construction site and nonviolently resist construction.[k] The citizen initiative feared that construction would begin before its court challenges would be heard, and concluded that a site occupation was needed to ensure that their court cases would be heard before the government created a fait accompli.[57]

MAKING ALLIANCES BETWEEN PROTEST GROUPS

At Wyhl and Brokdorf, cooperation between protest groups using complementary strategies was crucial in helping protesters to launch the kind of daring protests that could win elite allies, trigger mistakes in policing, and thus expand their opportunities. As in urban renewal, disruptive or

---

k. In its announcement, the Lower Elbe Initiative was joined by environmental groups from Hamburg and northern Germany (Radkau 1983, 449).

militant actions were more effective than conventional actions for gaining publicity, elite support, and concessions from authorities. For their part, groups using conventional methods lent a respectability to the antinuclear movement that made it easier for elites to endorse its actions, including the illegal site occupation attempts, and more difficult for authorities to repress such protests. In addition, the nature of the alliances that developed affected the types of protest in these two conflicts. At Wyhl, the alliance was between conventional and disruptive protesters, which promoted a nonviolent site occupation, while at Brokdorf, it quickly became one between disruptive and militant protesters, which promoted militant confrontations with police.

During 1975, the citizen initiatives at Wyhl nonviolently occupied the construction site twice, the second time for fourteen months. During the second occupation, the disruptive and conventional factions of the Baden-Alsace Initiatives formed and maintained a very effective alliance. These site occupations were the result of bold actions by some protesters from the citizen initiatives, who exercised nonviolent discipline. They gained rapid support from conventional protesters, even though local notables within the Baden-Alsace Initiatives initially opposed the actions.[l] Their nonviolently disruptive approach was inspired by the nonviolent activist Lanzo del Vasto and by two nonviolent conflicts in France in the early 1970s—a fast to protest the expansion of a military base at Larzac and the occupation of the planned site of a new lead works at Marckolsheim (Alsace). The Wyhl protests were influenced by activists who had taken part in those conflicts.[58]

During the second occupation, disruptive groups occupied the site while groups that preferred to use less risky methods provided political and material support. On 23 February, while a rally attended by between ten and twenty-eight thousand was concluding, a pastor suggested a nature walk around the site, and marshals suggested that everyone examine the fence closely. Protesters quickly used trees and ropes to pull down the fence in many places.[59] Although the citizen initiatives' leaders had been careful not to call for an occupation, three days after it occurred they decided to take responsibility for it publicly, and to help maintain it by organizing watches by residents of various villages on a fixed sched-

---

l. The notables feared being held legally accountable for damages, thought that illegal action might negatively influence the court case, and expected heavy police repression (Sternstein 1978b, 38).

ule.[60] Later, local residents collected money to build a Friendship House on the occupied site, and ran an on-site kitchen to cook meals for the occupiers.[61]

A high degree of unity among conventional and disruptive protesters at Wyhl continued for many months during the negotiation of the Offenburg Agreement, which helped make the site occupation long and effective. The *Land* government failed in its efforts to open a major split between the conventional and disruptive factions in the citizen initiatives.[62] A hard core of fifteen to twenty people lived at the site until November 1975, often joined by hundreds of people during the summer weekends. In addition, the impromptu Wyhl Forest Community College[m] held public educational events about nuclear energy and environmental protection in the Friendship House for seven months starting during the period of occupation, sometimes attracting hundreds of visitors.[63] After November 1975, several observers from the Baden-Alsace Initiatives maintained a presence at the site until April 1976, when the Offenburg Agreement went into effect.[64]

While conventional and disruptive protesters cooperated at Wyhl, they did not include militant groups in their alliance, even though students organized in communist groups and other left-wing militants from Freiburg repeatedly tried to mount collective actions in and around the site occupation. The leftists encouraged several dozen people from communist groups elsewhere in West Germany to travel to the site soon after the occupation.[65] But during the long months of the site occupation, when conflicts arose between tactical proposals by the communists and the nonviolently disruptive approach of the local citizen initiatives, the disputes were settled in favor of the latter.[66] Nonetheless, throughout the Wyhl conflict, minor violent incidents and threats occurred around the edges of the main events, such as protesters setting a construction vehicle on fire and throwing stones at police. These actions show that the conflict at Wyhl had the potential for more widespread militancy, yet they remained minor and isolated because they lacked support from other protesters and residents.[67]

Protests remained nonviolent at Wyhl partly because of efforts by protest leaders to maintain nonviolent discipline. When minor violent incidents between protesters and police occurred, Protestant pastors and members of a Freiburg nonviolence group, who were leaders in the citi-

m. Volkshochschule Wyhler Wald.

zen initiatives, stepped in to persuade demonstrators to stop throwing stones and to persuade police to retreat. The day that the second site occupation began, the citizen initiatives had two hundred marshals, who used megaphones to remind protesters and police that the demonstration was nonviolent. Although some protesters persistently sought violence, the main group responded directly with calls for nonviolence, and the militants remained isolated and ineffective.[68]

Alliances between protesters with complementary strategies were also important at Brokdorf. In the fall of 1976, disruptive and militant protest groups cooperated in repeated attempts to occupy the construction site, which led to mistakes in policing and increasing elite support for the antinuclear movement. The alliances between protesters at Brokdorf also promoted a shift toward militant actions at the construction-site fence, and away from nonviolently disruptive actions. A disruptive-militant alliance came to dominate the conflict because conventional participation seemed ineffective, authorities successfully blocked a nonviolent site occupation, and the rural citizen initiatives were organizationally weak in comparison to Wyhl.

Between October 1976 and February 1977, the antinuclear movement at Brokdorf split into two noncooperating factions, which carried out separate protests at the plant site and in the town of Itzehoe, on 19 February. One faction consisted of an alliance between disruptive and militant protesters, drawn mainly from Hamburg and other West German cities. They tried to protest near the construction site and to occupy it, or at least to threaten to do so. The most active part of this faction was the Hamburg chapter of the Lower Elbe Initiative, which was dominated by communist groups and other militant leftists.[n] One of these groups' leaflets called for occupying the Brokdorf plant site in order "to overthrow the capitalist state, to erect a dictatorship of the proletariat, and to develop the capacities necessary for these tasks."[69] The communist groups and the autonomous leftists argued that violence came from the state and needed to be resisted with violence.[70] The communists had been attracted to the conflict since the early months of 1976, and helped make the Hamburg section the largest part of the Lower Elbe Initiative

---

n. These included the Communist League, the Communist League of West Germany, the German Communist Party (DKP), the Communist Party of Germany (KPD), and the Communist Party of Germany/Marxist-Leninist (BUU 1977, 192–93; Willems 1997, 323; Trautmann 1978, 325; Joppke 1993, 103).

that year. In 1977, the Communist League° emerged as the driving force within the militant Hamburg faction, partly because its activists had recently been ejected from local trade unions and sought a new sphere of activity.[71]

This faction also included disruptive protesters who sought to occupy the site and did not openly endorse violence. Their actions began in the weeks after the surprise start of construction in October 1976, when tens of thousands of leftist protesters from Hamburg and elsewhere in West Germany came to two mass demonstrations, intending to occupy the construction site.[72] Many of these protesters wanted to avoid violence, especially against the police. But they entered a gray zone bordering on militancy when they attended demonstrations at the construction site, because major violence between the strongly organized militants and the police was expected there.

The other faction was made up of the local, rural citizen initiatives and nuclear opponents from outside the area who became disillusioned with the site occupation approach. These groups took part in the first two mass demonstrations, in October and November 1976. But within a few months, they retreated to conventional and mildly disruptive actions, such as rallies, while avoiding at all costs participating in further militant actions and police violence. By February 1977, the rural chapters of the Lower Elbe Initiative had separated from the Hamburg chapter, and other environmental organizations had distanced themselves from the communist groups.[73] As the rural citizen groups' capacity to mobilize declined rapidly, the SPD in Schleswig-Holstein came to lead this increasingly conventional wing of the Brokdorf antinuclear movement.[74] On 19 February 1977, this part of the movement demonstrated at a rally in Itzehoe, twenty kilometers from the construction site.[75] Itzehoe was chosen in order to maintain distance from the communist protesters and police, who were expected to battle at or near the construction-site fence.[76]

The split between the protest groups at Brokdorf, along with the repeated prevention of a site occupation, reduced the protesters' ability to pursue a nonviolently disruptive strategy. Soon after the November 1976 demonstration, the Wilster section of the Lower Elbe Initiative, consisting of the groups nearest to the plant, gave up on the site occupation strategy altogether, citing the risk to protesters' lives and health.[77] Fur-

o. Kommunistischer Bund.

thermore, locally based groups did not develop other methods of nonviolent resistance. They could have tried. After the violent November demonstration, some groups proposed nonviolent actions at sites away from the largest police deployments, such as road blockades or electricity consumption boycotts.[78] Threats to use this kind of decentralized approach were successful later, at Wyhl, in the early 1980s. But the Lower Elbe Initiative did not endorse a decentralized approach to nonviolent resistance, perhaps out of concern that violence would escalate between the police and militant protesters. Even large, fairly routinized protest demonstrations quickly faded, as many people feared to demonstrate in the polarized climate between militants and police, and the Federal Association of Environmental Citizen Initiatives[p] stopped endorsing mass demonstrations and site occupations.[79]

GAINING ELITE ALLIES

Early protests won elite allies for protesters in both cases, making large, sustained movements possible. Support from opposition parties, local government officials, interest group leaders, and church officials raised success chances and reduced the risks of repression, especially at Wyhl. Elite allies also affected the type of protest. At Wyhl, local elite allies aided the development of strong local protest organizations and hence made a nonviolent occupation possible. At Brokdorf, the protesters' inability to win many allies among local elites undermined that possibility, though protesters did gain important support from national elites, which allowed the Brokdorf opposition to grow.

At Wyhl, the protest groups' early, conventional actions gained them support from many local officials, politicians, churches, and interest groups. In turn, elite support gave the citizen initiatives credibility among local residents and helped open divisions among *Land*-level politicians, especially within the CDU. Elite divisions raised the chances of successful protests and thus encouraged further mobilization.

Local and *Land* organizations of all political parties, including the CDU, supported the citizen initiatives early in the conflict, despite the *Land* government's efforts to win the support of local politicians.[80] Local CDU organizations in Jechtingen and Sasbach informed the *Land* eco-

---

p. The Bundesverband Bürgerinitiativen Umweltschutz, a national umbrella organization for citizen initiatives active on environmental issues, became important in the national antinuclear movement during the mid-1970s.

nomics minister of their support for the citizen initiatives in November 1974. During the same month, the CDU's district organization in the village of Endingen sent an open letter to Filbinger requesting that the local population's wishes be respected.[81] Eight communities outside the town of Wyhl filed formal objections against the plant in the spring of 1974, and four villages filed appeals against the initial construction permit when it was granted in January 1975.[82]

Important support also came from the opposition parties in Baden-Württemberg and from the Protestant churches.[q] The SPD organization in Freiburg County announced opposition to the plant already in July 1973, and Social Democratic deputies made a motion in the *Landtag* in December to withhold approval for the site.[83] In November 1974, the Liberal Party gave the antinuclear protesters strong support by making an urgent motion in the *Landtag* to block the construction permit.[84] Furthermore, leaders in the Protestant churches provided crucial support for the Baden-Alsace Initiatives, and their support remained strong during the site occupation. The Protestant synod and bishops in Baden-Württemberg had opposed the plant as early as the summer of 1974, calling for further consideration of energy needs and the waste-disposal problem.[85] Protestant pastors also took major roles in the local citizen initiatives.[86]

By occupying the construction site in February 1975, the citizen initiatives gained additional elite support and hence expanded their political opportunities further. The local officials' opposition to the plant lent political legitimacy to the citizen initiatives, which initially helped prevent eviction by police and later helped the protesters gain negotiations with *Land* officials. Elite support made possible a site occupation that continued for over one year, an agreement with the government in January 1976 that delayed construction, and court decisions in 1975 and 1977 that blocked construction until 1982.

Local representatives of the Protestant Church provided important support to the site occupations. Pastors provided logistical aid for those occupying the site and helped keep actions nonviolent. The direct involvement of pastors inspired confidence in many residents that the cause was just, and this helped integrate the conservative, law-abiding parts of the Wyhl population into the antinuclear movement, while put-

---

q. The proposed site for the Wyhl plant lay in a largely Protestant area of Baden-Württemberg.

ting the moral weight of the Church behind the strategy of nonviolent resistance.

The site occupations also led to intensified support from the established political parties, especially at the local level, which probably helped reduce state repression. The eviction of the first site occupation outraged many local Christian Democrats, and they made their feelings known inside their party. When the site was successfully occupied three days later, the CDU's Emmendingen County organization continued to harshly criticize Filbinger.[87] The chair of a local CDU organization resigned his position after seeing the wife of a local politician hit by a water cannon. The local party organization in Bischoffingen dissolved itself, and many individual Christian Democrats tore up their party membership books in public.[88] The Emmendingen County organization of the CDU split between those who publicly resigned from the party, denouncing the "brutal police action," and the remainder, who wrote to Filbinger urging him to recognize that "the great majority of the population stands behind the protest action" and complaining about police provocations.[89]

The site occupations also gained the support of Social Democratic leaders at the *Land* level. After the first occupation was evicted, the chair of the Social Democratic parliamentary group in the Baden-Württemberg *Landtag*, who was a deputy from Freiburg, criticized the police actions. He said the police had used a disproportionate amount of force and the government should have waited for the administrative court decision.[90] Moreover, the chair of the SPD in Baden-Württemberg, Erhard Eppler, met with five hundred protesters at the construction site in June 1975, making a point of meeting them on the illegally occupied territory. This contrasted with a visit by Lothar Späth, the chair of the CDU group in the *Landtag*, who had come to the occupied site a few weeks earlier. Späth said that since Southern Atomic Plant would not give him permission to enter the site of the illegal occupation, he would meet with the nuclear opponents only at some location off-site. The three to four hundred people who had gathered at the construction site refused to meet him at a different location.[91]

At Brokdorf, the Lower Elbe Initiative also gained early support from elite allies, but in this case, the support came mainly from federal politicians and was initially due to the Wyhl site occupation, which continued from February 1975 to April 1976. The speaker of the citizen initiative, Rolf Hellerich, a farmer, met with the Christian Democratic and Social Democratic leaders of the Bundestag environmental committee in December 1975. He gained their agreement that no construction should start at Brokdorf before the main administrative court ruled on the plant's construction license. Politicians of all parties endorsed this position in the campaign for the Bundestag elections held on 3 October 1976, a position that Federal Interior Minister Werner Maihofer (Liberal Party) confirmed on television two weeks after the elections.[92] These statements by federal politicians gave a powerful boost to the Brokdorf protesters' chances of success and thus encouraged continued protests, which in turn triggered further expressions of support from politicians at the federal and *Land* levels. In addition, Protestant pastors from Hamburg and Bremen also gave much direct support to protesters at Brokdorf, by calling for demonstrations, leading church services at them, and trying to mediate between demonstrators and police. The February 1977 demonstration in Itzehoe was also endorsed by the *Land*-level SPD and Liberal Party organizations, the Federal Association of Environmental Citizen Initiatives, the German Communist Party, and the Young Socialists.

However, *Land* officials were able to prevent the Brokdorf citizen initiatives from gaining much support from local political elites. *Land* Premier Gerhard Stoltenberg (CDU) worked early and hard to win over local Christian Democratic politicians and interest groups. Stoltenberg and other *Land* officials met with local mayors in November 1973 and assured them the area around the plant would not be further industrialized.[93] By January 1974, the *Land* government had promised local governments substantial benefits in compensation for the disadvantages of proximity to a nuclear generating plant. The town of Brokdorf got a 2.5 million deutschmark swimming pool virtually for free, a new town hall, and annual tax revenue of 100,000 deutschmarks, rising to 2 million deutschmarks once the plant went into operation. These inducements helped convince local politicians to support the plant.[94] In addition, just before the surprise start of construction in October 1976, Stoltenberg personally met with five editors of local newspapers that favored the CDU and informed them of his plans, even though he kept the *Landtag* and the population in the dark.[95]

As a result, the level of local elite support for the Lower Elbe Initiative was lower than that enjoyed by the protesters at Wyhl. Other than one Liberal deputy in the *Landtag* and officials in eight village governments, local politicians from the established parties did not express strong opposition to the plant before the fall of 1976.[96] The Steinburg County government decided in February 1974 to approve the plant, on condition that facilities to promote tourism, such as roads, would be built simultaneously, and that recreational areas would be protected from traffic and construction.⁹⁷ The CDU organizations for Steinburg County and for the municipality of Wilstermarsch also came out in favor of the nuclear plant the next month.⁹⁸ Moreover, the *Land*'s farmer associations failed to come out against the Brokdorf plant, in contrast to the situation at Wyhl. Top officials from the *Land* Agriculture and Social Ministries met with the Schleswig-Holstein Farmer Association and apparently reassured many of its members.⁹⁹ This interest group became divided and opposed neither the plant nor the citizen initiatives.ʳ

The weak support from local politicians, local interest groups, and local notables made it difficult for the Lower Elbe Initiative to develop a strong organization in the areas around the plant. The citizen initiative had only 160 members as late as May 1975, and they collected only about one-third as many official objections to the plant's license as protesters had at Wyhl (27,000 versus 90,000). A nighttime demonstration and reconnaissance mission near the proposed plant site in March 1976 had a small turnout, disappointing its organizers.¹⁰⁰

The weakness of the local protest organizations had major effects on the types of participation that were likely to develop at Brokdorf. Organizational weakness in the rural areas limited the citizen initiatives' ability to imitate the disruptive strategy of the Wyhl groups, and it gave the leftist groups based in Hamburg more influence within the protest movement against the Brokdorf plant. Half of the members of a Lower Elbe Initiative committee that formed in October 1975 to plan the logistics of a site occupation were from groups that the *Land* authorities considered extremists.¹⁰¹ During 1976, the local chapters of the citizen initiative began to be overshadowed by Hamburg groups mainly interested in disruptive and militant protests. The Lower Elbe Initiative had difficulty with the organizational work for the two major demonstrations in 1976, and it had no marshals at the second of those protests, which helped make the demonstrations more chaotic and susceptible to manipulation by militants.¹⁰²

THE TIMING OF CONCESSIONS TO PROTESTS

Important concessions to protests occurred in both conflicts, but the timing of the concessions seemed to reward different kinds of protest strategies, and thus encouraged their later use by protesters.

r. However, other large associations from Hamburg, notably an association of fishers (14,000 members) and another of sailors (30,000 members), did oppose the plant by October 1974 (Trautmann 1978, 323).

At Wyhl, the second nonviolent site occupation led to rapid concessions by the *Land* government and the utility. A few days after the occupation began, Filbinger's cabinet, under pressure from local CDU organizations and *Landtag* deputies, announced that there would be no felling of trees, construction, or eviction of protesters until the administrative court ruled on whether the *Land* government's building permit was immediately effective.[103] Within a week, the Badenwerk utility removed its construction equipment.[104] Moreover, the following month, the Freiburg court blocked the plant's license. Since nonviolent disruption produced results, protesters were encouraged to maintain this strategy during the fourteen months of the site occupation, and to return to it in the early 1980s when the *Land* government renewed its threats to construct the plant.

By contrast, militant actions were the ones that seemed to produce results at Brokdorf, and this encouraged further militancy. The events at the October 1976 demonstration led Social Democratic leaders in the *Land* to move toward antinuclear positions. The Monday after the demonstration, the executive board of the Schleswig-Holstein SPD implicitly defended the protesters, since it criticized the *Land* government's methods and called for more citizen participation. The next day the party's board called for a halt to all nuclear plant construction, a surprising move that broke with the federal Social Democratic leadership.[105]

Similarly, immediately after the November 1976 demonstration, which included violence by protesters and police, leading *Land* and federal politicians publicly shifted to support the antinuclear groups.[106] While they were explicitly trying to win the support of the nonviolent opponents of nuclear energy, the timing of their statements seemed to reward the militant actions as much as the nonviolent actions at that demonstration. Leaders of the Schleswig-Holstein SPD accused the Christian Democratic *Land* government of using the police against nonviolent demonstrators in order to deter further protests. The Schleswig-Holstein Liberal Party responded to the police violence by calling for a stop to construction at Brokdorf.[107] Leading Social Democratic politicians both in and out of government, including Federal Research Minister Hans Matthöfer, Federal Justice Minister Hans-Jochen Vogel, Schleswig-Holstein party chair Günther Jansen, and North-Rhine-Westfalia's social minister Friedhelm Farthmann, called for more citizen participation. They criticized the police actions, called for more dialogue with the local population and citizen initiatives, and called for a popular referendum on nuclear energy.[108s] Jansen, who was present at the November demonstration, announced that he would ask the public prosecutor to bring charges against the responsible ministers, the police leaders, and one group of helicopter police for personal injury against demonstrators.[109]

Crucial concessions to militancy came from the Schleswig administrative court, which temporarily suspended construction in December 1976, soon after the violence at the November demonstration. The same court confirmed its decision by suspending the construction permit two months later, just ten days before a demonstration at the plant site at which great violence was expected.[110t] Politicians' expressions of support and the court decisions created the impression that threats and violence by demonstrators had prompted concessions where nonviolent actions had been ineffective. Hence, they probably reinforced the intentions of some protest groups to carry out militant actions, and the willingness of other groups to support such actions, at the mass demonstrations in 1977, 1981, and 1986.

PASSIVITY AND OVERREACTION BY POLICE AND OTHER PUBLIC OFFICIALS

In both conflicts, protesters' attempts to occupy construction sites triggered official responses that inadvertently aided the protest groups. Overzealous policing increased elite support for the antinuclear movement and increased solidarity among different protest groups, thus expanding opportunities and making large, sustained movements possible in both cases. Police actions also greatly affected the types of protest. Police passivity in crucial periods at Wyhl made a nonviolent site occupation possible there, while the continued use of massive, often undifferentiated repression at Brokdorf cemented a disruptive-militant alliance and led to repeated militant confrontations, while also preventing a nonviolent site occupation.

At Wyhl, the harsh responses of Baden-Württemberg authorities to the February 1975 site occupations strengthened the support that protesters received from their allies. The police delivered civil citations to those

---

s. Under pressure from the federal government, even Stoltenberg came to see the usefulness of distinguishing between the local farmers and urban militants. He held some discussions with the Lower Elbe Initiative in the winter of 1976–77 (Trautmann 1978, 329–30).

t. In October that year, the upper administrative court in Lüneburg upheld the Schleswig court's decision (*KN*, 18 October 1977).

occupying the site, at a hefty 200 deutschmarks per person, and warned protesters of criminal charges.[111] Filbinger declared that the protest was "steered by nationally organized extremists," and said that harsher police measures would be used if the present ones did not succeed. Seventeen Protestant pastors responded to Filbinger's perceived insult with a telegram informing him that the protesters were largely members of churches in the area. Additionally, the three pastors present at the first occupation attempt publicly endorsed the action in full.[112] Farmers and winegrowers also reacted strongly against what they saw as the *Land* government's attempts to defame them for opposing the nuclear plant.[113]

Police responses to the occupations also aided the protesters, because police vacillated between passivity and harsh actions. At 4:30 a.m. on 20 February, about six hundred riot police arrived at the occupied site, equipped with full riot gear, dogs, two water cannon, and a helicopter. After using barbed wire to separate 150 occupiers from their supporters, police tried to arrest only students and others who were not local residents, even though local protesters asked to be arrested too. Those arrested did not resist, and were dragged by their clothing and dropped in puddles of freezing water.[114]

The harsh police methods proved to be a mistake, as residents and outside observers saw these initial police actions as disproportionate and unfair. The eviction produced dramatic television footage favorable to the protesters, which a national television network broadcast one week later, without commentary and juxtaposed with long statements by nuclear opponents.[115] Rather than split the local protesters from the outsiders, the eviction and arrests helped unify the two forces, sparking increased protests in favor of the site occupation. The day after the eviction, five thousand people demonstrated near the site, and many of them had friendly conversations with police. Two days later, on Sunday, 23 February, between fifteen and twenty-eight thousand demonstrators arrived, including many from various parts of West Germany as well as France, Switzerland, and the Netherlands.[116]

At other times, police also aided the Wyhl site occupations by being hesitant and passive. The police who confronted protesters at the plant site during this period often sympathized with them and hence hesitated at crucial times. Partly this was due to mistakes by authorities concerning the deployment and training of the police officers. The riot police were mostly from the local area, and had been barracked for three weeks prior to the action. The training film shown them just before they left for Wyhl depicted students throwing stones at police in 1968. This film left the officers ill-prepared for the nonviolent and broad-based opposition that they met at Wyhl. In the first days after their arrival, they fraternized with local residents near the plant site. Police officers traded hot coffee for homemade soup and got into discussions about the environment.[117] Therefore, many police officers felt internally conflicted by their duties, and some went so far as to wear antinuclear stickers on their helmets or write critical letters to newspapers.[118] The chair of the police union later wrote to Filbinger that "the necessary feeling of legal and moral conviction was not fully present" and asked that the police not be expected "to carry on our backs politically and legally unclear situations."[119] Two companies of a hundred officers each never made it to the action. The men in one company had refused to go, while those in the other claimed to have gotten lost.[120]

A long-term site occupation without violent confrontations was possible largely because protest groups maintained nonviolent discipline and the police retreated rather than use a high degree of force against nonviolent demonstrators. At the second occupation, the police, who numbered only three hundred, initially retreated without using their water cannon.[121] Up to two thousand people then stayed on the site during the first night, erecting fifty tents and using felled trees to barricade all paths to it.[122] At 4 a.m. the next morning, eight hundred police returned with twelve water cannon and an abundance of tear gas, but did not try to retake the site, perhaps because their tear gas was useless in the thick fog and they had no gas masks themselves.[123] However, some sources said that secret negotiations between the citizen initiatives and key public officials led authorities to decide not to attack the site occupation.[124]

In the Brokdorf conflict, how the police and other authorities responded toward protesters also strongly shaped the types of participation. Authorities in Schleswig-Holstein acted aggressively to preempt and repress protests at Brokdorf, much more aggressively than Filbinger's government had done at Wyhl. From one point of view they were successful, since they prevented a site occupation and ultimately got the plant built. From another perspective, however, their strategy was mistaken, since it attracted many militants and led other protesters to support militant actions. Moreover, early mistakes in policing also greatly reinforced this tendency. The interactions surrounding the October and November 1976 demonstrations initiated a spiral of militant actions, undifferentiated police repression, the involvement of nonviolent protesters in militant actions, elites' apparent concessions to militancy, and apparently rising chances of success. The result was repeated confrontations between protesters and police forces over the next ten years, always involving militant threats and sometimes significant violence. Brokdorf became a focal point of a growing national antinuclear movement that helped undermine the national nuclear program.

At the same time, public officials in Schleswig-Holstein were very effective in preempting any kind of long-term site occupation, whether nonviolent or violent. The most important action by the authorities, on 26 October 1976, became known among opponents as the "Nacht und Nebel"[u] action. The *Land* government secretly granted a construction permit and allowed fortifications to be built at the proposed plant site, starting just after midnight, using two hundred construction vehicles guarded by a battalion of police. These measures contradicted the government's earlier promises that no construction would begin before the administrative courts had made a final decision. That night, the site was secured with a fence topped with coils of barbed wire, lookout posts, and dog patrols. Within two weeks, a concrete wall and a large, water-filled moat also protected the site.[125]

The Schleswig-Holstein government also mobilized more equipment and troops than their counterparts in Baden-Württemberg had. When about eight thousand people protested at the site on 30 October, they were met by 660 police who used horses, dogs, chemical mace, clubs, and water cannon. This force successfully drove off protesters who had temporarily occupied part of the site.[126] Twenty demonstrators were treated for eye injuries, and fifty-five were arrested. Two weeks later, on 13 November, 1400 police again acted very aggressively against crowds.[127] Police used sixteen water cannon, twelve dogs, and ten horses, and, in an extraordinary measure, federal border police with three helicopters were used directly against demonstrators. The injured included 79 police and up to five hundred demonstrators.[128] Unlike at Wyhl, most of the police deployed were from other *Länder*, which minimized the risk of fraternization.[129]

Police used aggressive and undifferentiated methods at the first two mass demonstrations. At the October demonstration, the communist ac-

---

u. Literally, "night and fog," though "cloak and dagger" might be a better translation. The German phrase carries undertones of Nazi repression, since it also refers to a 1941 decree by Hitler that resulted in the disappearance of many political opponents.

tivists initially were isolated in the crowd of eight thousand people, and their occasional slogans were whistled down or shouted down by the majority of the protesters. After the rally ended, members of several communist and undogmatic leftist groups broke through the construction fence in several places, and about two thousand nonviolent demonstrators followed them onto the site. A pastor from Bremen and citizen initiative leaders convinced the protesters to remain nonviolent, and pastors obtained an agreement from the police not to evict those occupying the site. Yet the police attacked them an hour later with water cannon, tear gas, clubs, horses, and chemical mace, aiming at nonviolent as well as violent protesters, and at local residents as well as outsiders.[130]

The police repression at the October demonstration led conventional and disruptive protesters to increase their support for the communist militants in the short term. Many members of the Lower Elbe Initiative, including Rolf Hellerich, the organization's speaker, were outraged at the harsh police measures at the October demonstration. They said that many protesters were treated for head wounds after being clubbed by police, and the next day between five hundred and four thousand people participated in a silent march at the construction site. The Lower Elbe Initiative announced its solidarity with the leftist protesters who had tried to occupy the site, and called for prison terms for leading public officials and some frontline police officers.[131]

Undifferentiated police repression at the November 1976 demonstration was, inadvertently, very effective in recruiting elite allies to the antinuclear movement. Police attacked nonviolent and local participants along with the urban militants, and prevented leaders of the Lower Elbe Initiative from reaching the site with loudspeaker cars, which reduced the influence of nonviolent protesters on the demonstration. Between twenty and forty-five thousand demonstrators forced their way through police lines to reach the construction site for a rally. Most protesters were peaceful and unprepared for any attacks by police, but the crowds included about three to four thousand communists and other urban leftists who came equipped with gas masks, helmets, and raincoats, for protection against police tear gas, clubs, and water cannon. About fifteen hundred members of communist groups broke through the fortifications at the site and fought a pitched battle with police. When demonstrators tried to pull down the fence, police fired tear gas canisters at them and into the crowd standing well behind them, including women and children. Then, when demonstrators tried to retreat from the site, police attacked them with clubs, tear gas, and helicopters.[132]

Many observers compared the unprecedented violence by both sides at this demonstration to a civil war. It triggered an immediate outpouring of support for the nonviolent elements of the antinuclear movement from leading Social Democratic and Liberal politicians at the federal level and in Schleswig-Holstein.

After the Peak of Protest

Even after the 1976–77 peak of protest, through the mid-1980s, protests remained strong at Wyhl and Brokdorf because both opportunities and threats increased. Protesters gained new elite allies as the Social Democrats debated nuclear energy and gradually shifted toward an antinuclear position, and the antinuclear Greens became established in many *Landtage*[v] and the Bundestag. After a hiatus, threats by officials increased once again when upper administrative courts lifted construction bans and the *Land* governments proceeded with their original nuclear plans in the early 1980s. In the Wyhl conflict, a decision of the upper administrative court in Mannheim on 30 March 1982 overturned the lower court's 1977 decision. The decision meant that construction of the Wyhl plant could proceed legally,[133] and it led to a second major wave of antinuclear protests in 1982–83. In the Brokdorf case, the lower administrative court in Schleswig reinstated the plant's construction permit in the summer of 1980, a decision confirmed by the upper court in Lüneburg in January 1981, and the *Land* government said it would resume construction. Protesters responded with intensified mobilization against the Brokdorf plant for the next five years. As in the rising phase of protest, the types of participation were affected by alliances between protest groups and support from elite allies. Those factors promoted conventional and disruptive participation at Wyhl, and mainly a combination of conventional and militant actions at Brokdorf.

CONVENTIONAL PARTICIPATION: INSTITUTIONAL ACCESS AND ELITE ALLIES

Conventional participation continued at high levels in both conflicts because nuclear opponents had institutional access and enjoyed much support from elite allies, who were comfortable with conventional actions.

---

v. Plural of *Landtag*.

Conventional protests remained important at Wyhl after 1982 also because the citizen initiatives there had gained informal procedural rights in the Offenburg Agreement. After the *Land* government renewed its nuclear plans in 1982, the Baden-Alsace Initiatives and other nuclear opponents asked for meetings with public officials, referring to the Offenburg Agreement's requirement that the parties to the conflict continue to hold discussions about controversial questions. Späth, who had become *Land* premier in 1978, promised to carry out discussions with farmers, professional and environmental associations, churches, and local government officials. During 1983, the Baden-Alsace Initiatives used conventional activities as a major part of their protests against the plant. Among other actions, there were two public assemblies opposing the plant, the first attended by six hundred people, and the second by three thousand, and the citizen initiatives collected 43,000 signatures on a petition against the plant.[134]

Conventional participation also continued at Brokdorf, as nuclear opponents pursued litigation in the administrative courts[w] and worked within various organs of the SPD at *Land* and federal levels.[135] After the 1977 protests, the *Land* SPD became a key elite ally of the Brokdorf nuclear opponents. Although the Greens did not enter the *Landtag* until 1996, the SPD became clearly antinuclear in Schleswig-Holstein in the late 1970s. Social Democrats campaigned in the 1979 and 1983 *Landtag* elections by promising to halt nuclear energy if they gained enough seats to replace the Christian Democrats in the *Land* government, which they failed to do until 1988.[136]

The Schleswig-Holstein Social Democrats and their chair, Günther Jansen, steered protesters toward rallies and assemblies, which were fairly predictable and conventional forms of protest. Soon before the February 1981 demonstration at the construction site, they held an assembly of three thousand people in a hall in Kiel, the *Land* capital, at which Jansen spoke against nuclear energy.[137] As in February 1977, this rally was explicitly designed to undercut support for the demonstration planned at the construction site, as well as to express opposition to nuclear energy.[138] Similarly, the *Land*-level SPD organized a demonstration

---

w. However, as part of its efforts to revive the nuclear program in 1982–85, the CDU-Liberal federal government under Chancellor Helmut Kohl (CDU) reduced and then eliminated the role of the lower administrative courts in decisions on large-scale technical projects such as nuclear facilities (Kretschmer 1988, 192–93; Nelkin and Pollak 1981, 166).

in Wilster, near the plant site, in June 1986, advertising it as a "family demonstration" to compete with a disruptive-militant demonstration planned at the plant site itself.[139]

DISRUPTION, MILITANCY, AND ALLIANCES BETWEEN PROTEST GROUPS

At Wyhl, preexisting alliances between protest groups made conventional and disruptive responses to the *Land* government's nuclear plans likely in the early 1980s.[x] A strong alliance already existed between groups that had used conventional and disruptive methods in the mid-1970s, including local groups and those from Freiburg. They responded to the 1982 Mannheim court decision by immediately carrying out a variety of conventional and disruptive actions. Within five days, farmers drove one hundred tractors in a spontaneous demonstration, and fifty citizen initiatives from the Baden and Alsace regions issued a declaration. Between four and ten thousand rallied in Freiburg, and between twenty and fifty thousand people demonstrated in the Wyhl forest.[140] Citizen initiatives held public discussions of the five-hundred-page court decision in every village in the area once the text was made available.[141]

The next year, this alliance of protest groups developed an innovative disruptive strategy. The Baden-Alsace Initiatives met with *Land* officials and threatened a large-scale campaign of nonviolent resistance. After a regional newspaper revealed the government's extensive policing plans in April 1983, the Baden-Alsace Initiatives and the Federal Association of Environmental Citizen Initiatives responded with a demonstration and detailed threats to carry out widespread civil disobedience if construction were to begin. In a major public statement, the citizen initiatives said that if necessary, they would consider the *Land* government's forces to be an occupying army. However, they would not become involved in any battles, but rather would use "all the means of nonviolent resistance" in order to "make South Baden ungovernable."[142] The scale of the confrontation was potentially massive, since *Land* officials said that they expected to use fifteen thousand police against a hundred and fifty thousand demonstrators.[143]

In meeting the threat of massive police mobilization, the citizen initiatives at Wyhl were creative in devising new disruptive tactics, rather than

---

x. Although militant groups were active in Freiburg, they remained marginal to the conflict and undertook few actions other than an attempt to bomb radiation measuring equipment near Wyhl (*International Herald Tribune*, 14 September 1983).

trying to simply replicate the 1975 site occupation. Like the government, they feared massive confrontations at the construction site that could be dominated by militants and police. By 1983, such confrontations had occurred repeatedly at widely publicized conflicts at Brokdorf and an airport expansion project near Frankfurt. The speaker for the Federal Association of Environmental Citizen Initiatives said that the protesters would try to occupy the site before a fence was built, but that the demonstrators would not "run against a barricaded construction site," as they had at Brokdorf.[144] An attempt to occupy the construction site was widely expected, as was the involvement of militants from across West Germany.

But rather than retreat from the disruptive strategy, as many antinuclear activists had done at Brokdorf, the Baden-Alsace Initiatives shifted to a decentralized approach to nonviolent disruption. At an April 1983 demonstration, their speaker threatened decentralized and multifaceted nonviolent resistance:

> No village needs to support and shelter the police troops. The region must become enemy territory for the police. Let's shut down public life in the cities and rural areas. Schoolteachers can refuse to teach. The pupils' organization has already announced a strike. We can shut down mass transit and the border crossings. We don't have to pay our electricity bills in full. Local government can use its self-administration rights and refuse to cooperate with the *Land* government. The men from Stuttgart can build their roads and pick up their taxes themselves.[145]

At Brokdorf, by contrast, alliances between protesters promoted militant rather than nonviolently disruptive actions after the 1976–77 peak of the conflict there. Not only were nonviolent protesters deterred by the threat of violence after November 1976, but they also found little support from rural residents. The rural citizen initiatives quickly decided to give up attempts to occupy the site and aligned themselves with the Social Democrats' largely conventional strategy. Residents of the area near the Brokdorf plant also withdrew their support from outside protesters, making a nonviolently disruptive approach more difficult. Many residents in the Wilstermarsch area were aghast at the equipment and hard tactics of both the leftists and the police. Militant violence was sometimes targeted at local interests, as when a small group threw Molotov cocktails into a building belonging to the Brokdorf village sewage plant, setting it on fire, during the February 1981 demonstration. Farmers became fearful of damage to their property, and they sometimes demonstrated against outside protesters or spread manure on their fields to try to deter them.[146] The lack of local support for nonviolent protests limited such actions to protests of very short duration, such as the symbolic blockades and vigils held regularly after 1986.

At the construction-site demonstrations, militants received important, though often merely tacit, support from disruptive protesters, who did not engage in violence themselves. As Rucht concluded, "The communist groups ... started violent conflicts while protected by the anonymity of large demonstrations."[147] Indeed, protest leaders deliberately blurred the distinction between nonviolent and violent actions. In their call to the 1981 demonstration, the organizers declared: "We don't want a confrontation with the state's apparatus, but we will defend ourselves against the violence that is practiced against us by means of the nuclear plant."[148] Similarly, the organizers of the June 1986 demonstration called ambiguously for "resistance" rather than "nonviolent resistance" and for "overcom[ing] our fear of confrontation with the state."[149]

SUPPORT FROM ELITE ALLIES

Another reason that the Wyhl protests in 1982–83 were nonviolently disruptive is that politicians and interest group leaders supported these kinds of actions, even more than they had in 1974–76. In the early 1980s, the vintners' and agricultural associations, five mayors, the Emmendingen County CDU organization, almost all local politicians, and the *Land*-level SPD, Liberal Party, and Greens all came out against the new plans to construct a nuclear plant.[150] Moreover, the Baden-Alsace Initiatives benefited from the rise of the Green Party, which entered the *Landtag* with 5.3 percent of the vote and nine seats in 1980, and from a gradual shift toward antinuclear positions within the SPD in the late 1970s. Immediately after the 1982 Mannheim court decision, the Greens' *Land*-level spokesperson announced that the party would make nuclear energy a major issue and would support the citizen initiatives in a campaign of nonviolent resistance.[151] The Social Democrats were slower to move, but in June 1983, the Social Democratic expert for internal security policy in Baden-Württemberg said his party would also call for nonviolent resistance.[152]

At Brokdorf in the 1980s, the types of protest were also affected by elite support. Militant actions got a boost because some elites gave more support to demonstrations at the construction site, which were widely expected to involve militants, than to purely nonviolent, disruptive methods. Although blockade actions, vigils, and other nonviolent protests took place frequently after 1986, they did not gain public support from the Social Democrats or Greens, which helps explain why public participation in them was limited, with none of those events attracting more than 150 people.

However, elite allies aided militant protests by sponsoring demonstrations at the construction site in 1981 and 1986, even though the leaders of these demonstrations deliberately conflated nonviolent and violent resistance. Several Green *Land*-level party organizations, some individual labor unions, and several environmental organizations supported the February 1981 demonstration.[153] These organizations had large followings, which along with the support of sixty citizen initiatives helped boost the turnout at the demonstration to about a hundred thousand, and thus facilitated militant actions. A large turnout was important for the militant strategy because it meant that non-militant protesters would be present in sufficient numbers to complicate the police's task of defending the site against militants without producing many injuries and much bad publicity. Similarly, the Greens helped organize a mass demonstration in June 1986, two months after the widely publicized, lethal nuclear accident at Chernobyl.[154] This demonstration drew between thirty and forty thousand people, including fifteen hundred autonomists who tried to reach the construction fence and clashed with police, resulting in over 180 injuries on both sides.[155]

Furthermore, as in 1976–77, politicians and officials appeared to make concessions to militant actions, and thus may have encouraged further militant activity. In February 1981, just after a violent anti-Brokdorf demonstration in Hamburg, the Hamburg SPD party conference voted narrowly (198 to 157) that the Hamburg electricity producer, which had a 30 percent share in the Brokdorf plant, should cease participation in the project. The next week, the SPD-Liberal government of Hamburg voted for a three-year delay in the plant's construction.[156]

Summary and Conclusions

MAKING OPPORTUNITIES

As in the urban renewal cases, large, long-lived protests developed in Wyhl and Brokdorf after unpopular policies prompted different kinds of protesters to join forces to mount risky actions (see Table 3 on page 222). Local, rural citizen initiatives, in alliance with young, urban protesters, attempted illegal site occupations, and they sometimes succeeded. Their attempts won publicity and support from political elites, especially in the SPD and Protestant churches, and led public officials to make mistakes in the use of police. Police overreacted in both cases, reinforcing solidarity among protesters and increasing the support of elite allies, which made effective repression more difficult. At Wyhl, police also became passive at crucial moments, which allowed a major illegal site occupation to continue for over a year. Moreover, in both cases, protests resurged in the early 1980s because of increased threats and opportunities. Courts reversed earlier decisions that had blocked plant construction, and elite allies from the SPD and Greens also gave strong support to antinuclear protesters.

POLITICAL INTERACTIONS AND TYPES OF PROTEST

Why did protesters at both Wyhl and Brokdorf shift from conventional to disruptive strategies? Why did the Wyhl conflict center on an almost entirely nonviolent site occupation, with only minimal property damage, while protests at Brokdorf shifted from nonviolent disruption to paramilitary confrontations and battles between protesters and police?

First, the types of participation at Wyhl and Brokdorf were strongly affected by the alliances that protest groups made, or failed to make, with each other (see Table 4 on pages 228–29). At Wyhl, a strong, durable alliance between conventional and disruptive protesters made a long, nonviolent site occupation possible. In the rising phase of the protest movement, the disruptive faction of the Baden-Alsace Initiatives, including many people from the Freiburg protest groups, led the way by initiating two site occupations. The conventional faction quickly provided political support and material assistance to the site occupiers, helping protect them from eviction by police by lending them the respectability of the local notables who led the rural citizen initiatives. In addition, nonviolent discipline by the protesters and persistent efforts to marginalize militant protesters also helped keep the Wyhl conflict peaceful.

In the Brokdorf case, the most important alliance was between militant and disruptive protesters, which allowed the militants to launch attacks against the construction site and engage police in bitter confrontations through 1986. Initially, in the October and November 1976 demonstrations, a broad alliance between local and urban groups, including conventional, disruptive, and militant protesters, developed under the pressure of undifferentiated police actions. However, this alliance was quickly transformed as state repression and militancy by communist groups increased. Conventional protesters turned away from future demonstrations at the plant site, where it was expected that large crowds would provide a favorable environment for militants to launch attacks on the construction site or police.

Yet militant and disruptive protesters continued to cooperate in attempts to occupy the construction site, leading to massive confrontations with police. Several thousand urban militants repeatedly tried to capture the construction site violently. Up to a hundred thousand disruptive protesters joined the militants at construction-site demonstrations, rather than innovating a decentralized approach to nonviolent protest. This larger mass of protesters sought a site occupation without violence against persons, and most of them did not actively engage in violence.

Nonetheless, they gave crucial assistance to the militants. In the first place, nonviolent protesters potentially would help the militants occupy the site if they managed to breach the fence. This had happened at the October 1976 demonstration, when militants confronted police and cut holes in the fence, and then nonviolent protesters streamed through the openings and established a brief, peaceful occupation. Furthermore, large numbers of protesters made it less likely that authorities would ban a demonstration or turn away all the protesters, and made it more difficult for police to search demonstrators for potential weapons[y] or prevent demonstrators from reaching the site.[157] In addition, militants could mix in with nonviolent protesters, making targeted repression more difficult, while undifferentiated repression might reinforce movement solidarity and trigger a political backlash, as it did after the November 1976 demonstration. Nonviolent protesters also gave the militants moral support, by giving them the sense that their cause was broadly supported, and lent them some legitimacy vis-à-vis the news media and public. Without a larger crowd of supporters, the negative publicity from purely militant demonstrations might have convinced the militants to give up after only a few months of activity, as occurred at a nuclear-energy conflict in Grohnde in 1977.[158]

Second, the amount and timing of support from elite allies also af-

---

y. These included offensive and defensive weapons, such as helmets, gas masks, raincoats, bolt cutters, wooden staves, and metal projectiles.

fected the kind of participation in these two conflicts. At Wyhl, early, strong support from local elites, even in the CDU, promoted a mix of conventional and disruptive strategies. Local elite support helped the rural citizen initiatives develop strong local organizations and helped protect the second site occupation from eviction. Local officials and party leaders lent respectability to the Baden-Alsace Initiatives, and this helped to limit police repression and make a strategy of nonviolent, illegal protest viable. Finally, in 1982–83, the citizen initiatives' elite allies announced their support for a campaign of widespread nonviolent resistance.

By contrast, at Brokdorf, the pattern of elite support promoted conventional and militant actions, but not nonviolent disruption. During the mid- and late 1970s, the scarcity of local elite allies undermined the nonviolently disruptive strategy. Although the local population was overwhelmingly opposed to the plant and some local governments joined the opposition, most local elites, including the county government and major rural interest groups, sided with the *Land* government or remained neutral. They did so partly because of Stoltenberg's lobbying and offering large material benefits to local governments in return for accepting the plant. The lack of local elite support made it difficult for the rural chapters of the Lower Elbe Initiative to become strong organizations capable of a nonviolent occupation, and made it easier for militants from Hamburg to dominate the conflict from November 1976 onward. Then, the *Land* SPD steered many protesters toward conventional actions beginning in the winter of 1976–77. Later, in the 1980s, leaders of the Greens and other elites gave important support to the militant strategy, by sponsoring demonstrations at the plant site, where it was expected that militants would attempt to storm the construction fence.

Third, the blockage of major reforms led protesters to shift away from a purely conventional strategy at Wyhl and Brokdorf, as it did in the urban renewal cases. At both nuclear sites, citizen initiatives used access to hearings, litigation in administrative courts, and other routine participation to oppose the proposed plants. But in the rising phase of the conflicts, public officials were plainly unwilling to give ground on their plans to build the plants, regardless of the scope or intensity of formal citizen participation, the arguments marshaled against the plants, or even the willingness of lower-level courts to delay construction. Therefore, the citizen groups in both cases shifted their strategies to include attempted nonviolent site occupations.

However, the timing of concessions to protests seemed to reward different strategies in the two cases, which is one reason why Wyhl remained nonviolent and Brokdorf did not. At Wyhl, the nonviolent site occupation triggered an immediate halt to construction, soon reinforced by a court order. Therefore, protesters remained focused on a strategy of nonviolent disruption and gave little support to those advocating a more militant approach.

By contrast, at Brokdorf, the *Land* government made no concessions to nonviolent attempts to occupy the site. But violence between demonstrators and police at the October and November 1976 demonstrations led federal government officials and *Land*-level Social Democratic politicians to shift toward antinuclear positions—apparently as a concession to the militant actions. Similarly, the Schleswig administrative court decisions in December 1976 and February 1977 were widely viewed as attempts to de-escalate the conflict and prevent further violence, but they also gave the impression that protests which threatened violence were effective at gaining concessions. This pattern of concessions encouraged militant protesters to attempt to violently occupy the site in 1977, 1981, and 1986. It also made it difficult for nonviolent protesters and their elite allies to resist the temptation to aid the militants by calling for large demonstrations at the construction site and rhetorically blurring the lines between violent and nonviolent resistance in the 1980s.

Finally, police actions contributed greatly to the nonviolence and disruptiveness of the Wyhl conflict and to the militant confrontations at Brokdorf. At Wyhl, the police initially overreacted and then underreacted, which greatly enhanced the chances for a nonviolent site occupation. Their first interventions were harsh and unpredictable, which increased the unity among local and outside protesters and their support from elite allies. But later, at crucial points in the site occupation, police hesitated, refused to obey orders, or retreated from actions, and they never tried to evict the second site occupation. The sympathy of some officers for the protesters, and strategic and tactical errors by the authorities who ordered the police actions, underlay the weakness of the police response. Elected officials may also have become less willing to use police aggressively as they became aware of the political costs.

Police practices at Brokdorf followed a different course altogether, one that erred on the side of overreaction. In the context of blocked reform and growing elite support for protest, this approach hindered a nonviolent site occupation but also promoted militant actions. The *Land* built strong fortifications, including moats and multiple barriers, before protesters could mobilize, making a site occupation much less likely.ᶻ Authorities also deployed police from outside the local area, who presumably were less likely to sympathize with the local population. Although demonstrators breached the construction-site fence at the October and November demonstrations, the police promptly drove them out each time.

At the same time, the harsh and undifferentiated repression at those two demonstrations increased the support of many nonviolent protesters for the militants. Hence, the policing strategy encouraged a series of large, confrontational demonstrations, at which protesters threatened violence against the construction-site fortifications and the police. This pattern of heavy state repression and solidarity between nonviolent and violent protesters continued until 1986, when the plant went into operation. However, authorities' innovation of new repressive tactics at Brokdorf in the 1980s—preventing protesters from reaching the site, searching and disarming demonstrators, and once even trapping eight hundred protesters for twelve hours—gave them an advantage that probably limited the militants' ability to carry out violence, especially after 1980.[159]

NATIONAL PROTEST CYCLES AND THE POLITICAL INTERACTIONS AT WYHL AND BROKDORF

Why did such different political interactions unfold at Wyhl and Brokdorf? A possible explanation is that the timing of these conflicts within the overall West German antinuclear movement made Brokdorf, the later conflict, more militant and violent. Thus, Koopmans argues that Wyhl's nonviolent site occupation exemplifies the early, creative phase of the antinuclear movement, while Brokdorf exemplifies the splitting of the movement into conventional and militant wings under the impact of reforms, repression, and the influx of militants seeking a popular cause.[160]

The cyclical theory can help explain the differences between the Wyhl and Brokdorf conflicts. Most of the actions and interactions I have analyzed were influenced by the position of these two conflicts in the national movement against nuclear energy. At Brokdorf, *Land*-level authorities responded to the Wyhl experience by surprising almost every-

---

z. By contrast, the security measures adopted by Badenwerk, the utility company at Wyhl, after the first, failed site occupation were limited to a single fence topped with barbed wire, which was rather easily breached or pulled down by protesters.

one with the start of construction, fortifying the site, and adopting more effective methods for deploying police than their counterparts in Baden-Württemberg had done. On the protesters' side, the national publicity given to the Wyhl conflict helped prepare disruptive and militant leftists to enter quickly into the Brokdorf conflict and to focus quickly on what became a quasi-military matter of trying to seize a site guarded by fortifications and a large police force.

However, its temporal position within the overall antinuclear movement did not determine the nature of either of these two conflicts. While the timing of each conflict's onset influenced the choices available to protesters, politicians, and authorities, the local processes of mobilization and alliance formation against nuclear energy operated in ways that were significantly autonomous from the national antinuclear movement. Indeed, an early position in the overall protest cycle did not guarantee that the Wyhl conflict would become a major example of nonviolent resistance. That conflict was open-ended, and its course depended on contingent interactions. Protests might have gone in a more militant direction if the *Land* authorities had tried to evict the second site occupation, if politicians had given less support to the nonviolent occupation, or if nonviolent discipline among the protesters had broken down. Nor was the Brokdorf conflict predestined to be dominated by intransigent authorities and militant protesters just because the conflict peaked in the fall of 1976, a year and a half after the Wyhl site occupation began. Protesters at Brokdorf might have innovated decentralized methods of nonviolent resistance, such as those successfully threatened at Wyhl.

Other possible paths for the Brokdorf conflict become clearer if we briefly examine the conflict over a nuclear fuel-reprocessing facility and waste disposal site at Gorleben (in Lower Saxony). Although the Gorleben conflict occurred later than both Wyhl and Brokdorf, the national context of the antinuclear movement did not force authorities to be intransigent and repressive or force protesters into supporting a militant strategy there. Rather, the Gorleben conflict, which began in 1977, was qualitatively intermediate between Wyhl and Brokdorf, and closer to the nonviolent course at Wyhl. At Gorleben, nonviolently disruptive protesters led by the Lüchow-Dannenberg Citizen Initiative carried out a great variety of strong, nonviolent protests from 1977 to 1985: demonstrations, site occupations, a two-month long antinuclear village, week-long marches to the *Land* capital, and blockades of streets. In the same period, communists, undogmatic leftists, and autonomists from cities in northern Germany also carried out sabotage actions and, for a few days in 1982, battled with police at Gorleben.[161]

The Gorleben conflict took a mainly nonviolent, disruptive course rather than a militant one largely because authorities made rapid concessions to nonviolent actions. A week-long march from the Gorleben area to the *Land* capital in Hanover attracted a hundred thousand people to a peaceful rally in March 1979, which occurred, coincidentally, just days after the widely publicized nuclear accident at Three Mile Island in Pennsylvania. The *Land* government in Lower Saxony, led by Ernst Albrecht (CDU), responded to this impressive action with a dramatic concession. The government postponed the construction of the reprocessing plant indefinitely, while continuing to pursue the construction of a long-term storage facility for spent nuclear fuel. The plant operator ultimately abandoned plans for a reprocessing plant in the Gorleben region in 1985. This shows that the hard line which Stoltenberg took in Schleswig-Holstein was not the only kind of response authorities could make, even in the intense phase of the antinuclear movement after 1976.

Nonviolently disruptive protesters also made different strategic choices at Gorleben than at Brokdorf. At Gorleben, they held to an explicitly nonviolent course from the start of the conflict, drawing on U.S. experience with affinity groups in nonviolent direct action. The Lüchow-Dannenberg Citizen Initiative managed to keep control of most protests, even after the forceful eviction of a month-long nonviolent site occupation in 1980 and later battles between militants and police in September 1982. In a crucial move, the local citizen initiatives at Gorleben responded to that violence by distancing themselves from the militants and simultaneously pursuing a series of nonviolent protests, using new tactics, in 1983–84. These included a long march to Hanover by 5,000 people, a symbolic human chain around the region by 15,000 people, and blockades and attempted blockades of streets leading to the short-term storage facility. Again, authorities responded to nonviolent protests with concessions, as the administrative court in Lüneburg blocked the operation of the short-term waste facility early in 1985.[162]

Hence, the split between nonviolent protesters and militants at Gorleben did not lead to demobilization of the disruptive forces as it had at Brokdorf. In short, given appropriate actions by authorities and disruptive protesters, a largely nonviolent protest movement was possible even in a case where protests began during the most confrontational phase of the West German antinuclear movement.

4 IMMIGRATION CONFLICTS IN MUNICH AND RENDSBURG COUNTY

In the period during and following German unification, immigration by asylum seekers, refugees, and ethnic German resettlers increased dramatically, and so did protests against foreigners. Most work on anti-immigration politics in this period has focused on waves of violence by right-wing skinheads and neo-Nazis against asylum seekers and other foreigners,[1] or on the activities of far-right parties.[2] But nonviolent protests by citizen initiatives opposed to immigration were also significant in the late 1980s and early 1990s, especially in the western *Länder*.[a] These groups formed an important part of a loose-knit anti-immigration movement in the early 1990s, which also included far-right parties, skinheads, and neo-Nazis. Although this movement's organizations were less stable and less well coordinated than the left-wing movements, the anti-immigration groups did have common goals, allies, and opponents, and they sustained a high level of mobilization from 1989 to 1993.[b] Together

---

a. On nonviolent protests by residents in West Berlin and the western German cities of Saarlouis and Hanover, see Dittberner 1986; Willems et al. 1993, 214–17; and Benzler 1997, 15. Nonviolent protests by resident groups were evidently more common in western than eastern *Länder*, though there is no systematic evidence on this point, since national newspaper studies pick up little of this kind of activity (Ruud Koopmans, communication to the author, 20 April 2005). Nonviolent protests did occur in eastern Germany. For example, in Oschatz (Saxony), 2,500 people demonstrated against plans to house 1,000 asylum seekers in that community (*Sächsische Zeitung*, Riesa ed. [*SZR*], 13 June 1992).

b. They shared the goal of opposing the arrival and presence of asylum seekers in Germany at the federal, *Land*, and local levels. Their common allies were those who called most strongly for restrictions on asylum rights, mostly Christian Democrats and

with violence by skinheads and neo-Nazis, and electoral successes by far-right parties, protests by citizen initiatives helped accelerate a national debate on asylum rights in 1991–93. Their mobilization led to a constitutional amendment, Article 16a of the Basic Law, that restricted asylum rights in May 1993.[c]

This chapter analyzes fifteen protest campaigns by citizen initiatives and more informal resident groups[d] in western Germany. The cases are drawn from a large, southern German city (Munich) and a mostly rural county in northern Germany (Rendsburg-Eckernförde County in Schleswig-Holstein) in 1989–93. The cases studied here exemplify nonviolent, largely conventional protests by groups opposed to the siting of shelters for asylum seekers in neighborhoods in western Germany. In all but one of the campaigns, citizen initiatives used petitions, meetings with public officials, or attendance at citizen assemblies and local council meetings, and ten of the fifteen cases involved no physical violence.

---

some Social Democrats, while their common opponents included much of the SPD, the Greens, and advocates for foreigners.

c. Article 16a blocks asylum seekers who arrive from a "persecution-free country" or via a "safe country," categories defined by the federal government to include all the countries bordering Germany and the countries from which most asylum seekers have originated.

Local citizen initiatives against asylum seekers influenced the debate on the amendment and its adoption in two ways. They helped convince urban leaders of the SPD, especially Oskar Lafontaine (premier of the Saar, a small urban *Land*) and big-city mayors such as Hamburg's Henning Voscherau, Munich's Georg Kronawitter, and Bremen's Klaus Wedemeier, that the anti-immigration cause was popular. Those officials were important in the SPD's shift toward a more restrictive position during the last months of 1992 (Braunthal 1994, 313–14; Lemke-Müller and Matthäi 1993, 575). Citizen initiatives also contributed greatly, though indirectly, to the increases in anti-foreigner violence, by triggering a major mistake by officials. By opposing the siting of asylum shelters in their neighborhoods, citizen initiatives in western Germany pressured local and *Land* officials to find other locations for these foreigners. This was one reason why a conference of *Land* officials decided that asylum seekers should be transferred from western to eastern Germany beginning in December 1990. For reasons discussed in Chapter 5, foreigners were especially vulnerable to attack in the eastern *Länder*. Therefore, this decision facilitated several massive waves of anti-foreigner violence, which began in eastern Germany in the spring of 1991 and continued through early 1993 (BV 1991, 75). The violence greatly accelerated the national debate on asylum rights and helped drive the Social Democrats toward accepting the restrictive constitutional amendment (Karapin 2003, 34–37; 1999; Koopmans 1996b).

d. For simplicity's sake, I will refer to them as citizen initiatives. They sometimes referred to themselves by other terms, such as "resident initiatives," and sometimes, as in the Kronshagen cases in this chapter, they consisted of ad hoc groups for which evidence of formal organization is lacking.

In this chapter, I explain why citizen initiatives protested against asylum seekers and why the Munich cases involved larger and more sustained protests than the Rendsburg County cases. I also explain why these neighborhood-level protest campaigns remained largely nonviolent, and why some cases involved a shift to disruptive or militant methods while others remained purely conventional. As in the urban renewal and antinuclear cases, the answers lie mainly in political interactions rather than socioeconomic factors. Protests grew because state actions threatened residents and protesters formed alliances with local elites. Protests remained mostly conventional because officials made substantial concessions in response to routine participation and elite allies did not support a shift toward disruptive or militant methods.

In the following sections, I discuss the basis for selecting these fifteen cases before examining how well socioeconomic and organizational theories can account for residents' protests against immigration in Munich and Rendsburg County. Then I describe how immigration around the time of unification led to cultural threats, rather than economic threats, to residents in many German localities. Next, I analyze one Munich case (Munich-Südpark) and one Rendsburg County case (Kronshagen) in their respective social and political contexts, focusing on how political interactions affected the rise of protest and the kinds of protest activities. I conclude by summarizing results from those two detailed cases and the fifteen cases in Munich and Rendsburg County.

Case Selection

In choosing local cases of protests by citizen initiatives, I looked for conflicts that varied widely in a large number of other ways, to see if common interactive processes were nonetheless at work in all or most of them.[e] The politics of asylum in this period were very complex, with conflicts at all levels of government and mobilization by anti-immigration and pro-foreigner groups, and sometimes by groups of foreigners. To make case selection manageable, I focused on protests by anti-immigration protest groups at the local level and defined cases in terms of conflicts over particular asylum shelters. Since nonviolent, anti-

---

[e]. This is a strategy of universalizing comparison (Tilly 1984a), using most-different systems (Przeworski and Teune 1970).

immigration citizen initiatives have been neglected in the literature, one of my aims was simply to show how common this kind of protest was in the early 1990s.

Hence, instead of looking for the largest conflicts in all of Germany, as I did when selecting urban renewal or nuclear energy cases, I started by choosing two quite different jurisdictions that represent much of the diversity of political and socioeconomic conditions found in western Germany.[f] One jurisdiction was the large city of Munich, in the southern *Land* of Bavaria. The other was the largely rural county of Rendsburg-Eckernförde in the mostly rural northern *Land* of Schleswig-Holstein. The two jurisdictions varied greatly on many dimensions in the early 1990s, including community size (large in Munich, small to medium in Rendsburg County);[g] population density (high in Munich, low in Rendsburg County);[h] unemployment rates (low in Munich, medium to high in Rendsburg County);[i] and foreigners as share of the population (high in Munich, low to medium in Rendsburg County).[j] They also varied in the partisan control of government[k] and the level of skinhead organization and militant attacks on asylum shelters (low in Munich, high in Rendsburg County).[l] Having so much diversity in these background variables

---

f. Eastern German cases of mobilization against immigration are treated in Chapter 5.

g. Munich had 1.3 million residents, with about 53,000 in each borough in 1992; Rendsburg County had 250,000 residents, with about 1,500 residents in the average town and 30,000 in the largest, the city of Rendsburg (SAM 1997; KRE 1995).

h. About 4,500 people per square kilometer in Munich and about 110 per square kilometer in Rendsburg County, compared with about 220 per square kilometer in Germany as a whole.

i. In 1992, these were 2.9 percent in Munich and 7.2 percent in Rendsburg County, versus 6.6 percent in western Germany (BFA 1993, 61, 65).

j. About 21 percent in Munich and 6.3 percent in Rendsburg County in 1991, versus 7.3 percent nationally (SAM 1997, 42; *Statistisches Monatsheft Schleswig-Holstein* 1992 [3], 54; data from Statistisches Bundesamt).

k. This was SPD-Green in Munich combined with control by the CSU in Bavaria. By contrast, the Rendsburg County parliament had a CDU-Liberal majority after 1990, while the Social Democratic controlled Schleswig-Holstein after 1988.

l. Bavarian authorities counted 240 right-wing skinheads in 1992 (BSI 1992, 46), while Schleswig-Holstein counted 220 (ILSH 1992a, 6), with a *Land* population only about one-fifth as large as Bavaria's. Skinhead organization in Munich was lower than average for Bavaria, while in Rendsburg County it was about average for Schleswig-Holstein (ILSH 1993a, 24). In terms of per capita right-wing arson attacks, Bavaria reported about 35 percent of the national average in 1992, while Schleswig-Holstein reported about 175 percent of the national average; these were the lowest and highest rates among the western *Länder* (PDS 1995, author's calculations).

meant they were unlikely to be causes of whatever common patterns I would find.

Within each of the two jurisdictions, I first identified ten localities with the largest conflicts concerning asylum shelters.[m] These were seven Munich boroughs (Moosach, Südpark, Hadern, Solln, Ramersdorf, Pasing, and Harlaching) and three small towns in Rendsburg County (Altenholz, Büdelsdorf, and Kronshagen). I summarize my findings concerning fifteen[n] conflicts in these ten localities in the conclusions to this chapter. For more in-depth study, I chose two local cases, Munich-Südpark (1992–95) and Kronshagen (1992–94).[o] The Südpark protests were larger, longer, and more diverse in methods than those in Kronshagen, which reflects general differences in the size and types of protests in Munich and Rendsburg County in 1989–93. The conclusions provide more information on the ways these two cases were typical of other protests in their respective jurisdictions.

The Limits of Socioeconomic and Organizational Explanations

According to ethnic competition theory, areas with higher unemployment, immigration, or proportions of working-class residents should have more protests against foreigners. However, in the fifteen cases in Munich and Rendsburg County, there is little evidence that these socioeconomic factors were related to the level or form of anti-immigration protests.

Protests by citizen initiatives did not depend on high unemployment or immigration rates. Munich had very low unemployment, at 2.9 percent in 1992, and Rendsburg County's rate was 7.2 percent, only slightly higher than the average for western Germany in 1992.[3] Nor were large

---

m. For each jurisdiction, I used two different local archives that contained clippings files (*Münchner Merkur*, Bayerischer Rundfunk, *Kieler Nachrichten*, Norddeutscher Rundfunk). I defined the largest conflicts as those for which the largest number of newspaper articles for the 1989–93 period were available.

n. The ten localities with the largest conflicts contained fifteen specific conflicts, because the very decentralized housing policies pursued in the three Rendsburg County towns produced multiple conflicts in each.

o. These time frames reflect the fact that protests in the local cases continued for some time after the national anti-immigration movement rapidly declined in 1993. Although protests in Kronshagen stretched over a two-year period, they consisted of a series of brief protests against different asylum shelters, most of them lasting only several months each, rather a sustained campaign against one shelter, as in Südpark.

concentrations of foreigners needed to provoke protests by citizen initiatives. Although foreigners made up about 21 percent of Munich's population in 1991, the foreign share was only 6.3 percent in Rendsburg County, slightly below the national average. Moreover, both locations had tiny populations of asylum seekers, who made up about 0.9 percent of the total population in Munich and about 0.8 percent in Rendsburg County in 1992.[4p] Concentrations of asylum seekers were not related to anti-immigration protests, either. In four of the five Munich boroughs that had the highest shares of asylum seekers,[q] there was no major opposition to asylum shelters.

Moreover, social structural differences within Munich, within Rendsburg County, and between the two places had little if any effect on the size or type of protest. The seven neighborhoods in Munich with the largest protests against asylum shelters included two comparatively working-class areas, three middle-class areas, and two relatively rich areas. Within Rendsburg County, the three towns with the largest conflicts also had quite different social compositions. Manual workers made up 34 percent of the population in Büdelsdorf, 20 percent in Altenholz, and only 15 percent in Kronshagen.[r]

Social structural differences also had little effect on the types of protest that anti-immigration groups used. Conventional methods predominated, occurring in fourteen out of fifteen conflicts (93 percent). At the same time, eight cases, slightly more than half the total, involved some unconventional protests. Anti-immigration groups used disruptive protests in four cases (all of them in Munich), used militant threats without violence in two cases, and physically attacked shelters in five cases.[s] Yet there was no relationship between the type of protest and the social composition of the local population in the fifteen conflicts. Protesters mounted conventional actions (such as meetings or petitions) in virtually all the cases, regardless of the neighborhood's social structure. Residents

---

p. In Südpark and Kronshagen, the shares were, at most, about 1.6 percent and 1 percent, respectively.

q. The boroughs of Neuhausen, Allach, Trudering, and Aubing.

r. The *Land* average was 30 percent; 1987 census data from Statistisches Amt Schleswig-Holstein, column 132.

s. Violent actions dominated only two of the conflicts (Altenholz-Klausdorferstrasse and Büdelsdorf-Birkenklause). Most militant actions were undertaken by skinheads, neo-Nazis, or unidentified groups. But in three Munich cases (Südpark, Hadern, and Harlaching), a group involved in nonviolent protests sometimes made militant threats, too.

were somewhat disruptive in a wide range of Munich neighborhoods: working-class Ramersdorf, middle-class Südpark and Hadern, and upper-middle-class Harlaching. Physical attacks on shelters also occurred in all kinds of neighborhoods, including one of four working-class areas (Büdelsdorf-Birkenklause), three of six middle-class areas (Munich-Hadern, Munich-Pasing, and Altenholz-Klausdorferstrasse), and one of five relatively rich areas (Munich-Harlaching).

Finally, while protests usually were sustained for several years in the Munich cases compared with only several months in Rendsburg County, it is difficult to explain this difference using the socioeconomic factors of ethnic competition theory. The only socioeconomic factor that correlates with this Munich-Rendsburg difference is the total foreign population share, which was three times as high in Munich as in Rendsburg County. However, the protests in these cases were directed against the relatively small groups of asylum seekers, not the much larger populations of guest workers. Asylum seekers were present in roughly similar proportions of the local population in Munich and Rendsburg County because of federal and *Land* policies for distributing asylum seekers. Moreover, unemployment is equally important in ethnic competition theory, and Munich had much lower unemployment than Rendsburg County.[t] Later in this chapter, I explain the difference in the longevity of protest across these two jurisdictions in terms of the support of elite allies for the protest groups.

Were these conflicts mostly nonviolent simply because militant groups were lacking in Munich and Rendsburg County? The available evidence suggests that skinhead and neo-Nazi groups were present in adequate numbers to make violent conflicts possible in both jurisdictions. Indeed, right-wing skinheads and anti-foreigner violence were very common in Rendsburg County. In 1992, police observed 220 skinheads in Schleswig-Holstein, and Rendsburg County was one of their centers of activity.[5] In Schleswig-Holstein, police recorded forty-seven right-wing arson attacks and sixty-five assaults in 1992–93.[6] Although Munich, and Bavaria as a whole, had less skinhead organization, skinhead activity, and anti-foreigner violence than the average for Germany in the early 1990s, the rates of activity were still significant.[7] Right-wing skinheads and neo-Nazis in Bavaria numbered 460 in 1992 and 520 in 1996, though authorities counted only about 20 right-wing skinheads in Munich in

---

t. The product of unemployment and immigration rates in the two jurisdictions was also not markedly different: 0.0061 in Munich and 0.0045 in Rendsburg County.

1991.[8] Yet in that city, newspapers reported at least nine demonstrations and other public actions by neo-Nazis, twenty-one assaults on foreigners, and ten attacks on foreigners' housing, mostly arson against asylum shelters, in 1989–93. Similarly, the seven conflicts over Munich asylum shelters analyzed in this chapter involved a significant amount of physical violence, including a total of four arson attacks against two of the shelters. Violence was clearly a possibility in Rendsburg County and Munich, yet most conflicts remained nonviolent.

Immigration, the Siting of Asylum Shelters, and Cultural Threats

Increased immigration was a major cause of protests by anti-immigration groups, but not for the reasons advanced by ethnic competition theory. Protests were triggered not by competition over jobs, housing, or other material goods, but by cultural threats that the newcomers posed to many Germans. Germans expected asylum seekers sent to their neighborhoods to be different from them in terms of propensity for cleanliness, noise level, sexual behavior, fighting, petty and serious crime, and other public behavior. Furthermore, the cultural threats posed by asylum seekers were not simply produced by their arrival and presence in Germany, but rather were strongly influenced by government decisions about where and how to house asylum seekers.

Immigration to Germany surged from 1988 to 1993. During those years, 1.4 million people from Eastern Europe, Asia, and Africa applied for political asylum in Germany, over one million ethnic German resettlers arrived, and so did at least 850,000 other refugees.[11] The surge in immigration was mainly due to the sudden freedom of movement for citizens of former communist countries, combined with civil conflict in parts of Eastern Europe. About half of all the people seeking asylum in Western Europe in this period applied for asylum in Germany, which was attractive because of its prosperity, comparatively generous asylum rights, geographic location on the eastern frontier of Western Europe, and large preexisting immigrant groups.[9] The asylum seekers' de facto ability to remain in Germany for long periods makes it appropriate to

---

11. Since many asylum seekers left the country again or gained a different legal status as de facto refugees, only about 550,000 asylum seekers were in Germany in 1993; data from Beauftragte für die Belange der Ausländer, "Daten und Fakten zur Ausländersituation," October 1994 press release, Table 12.

refer to conflicts about their arrival and presence as conflicts about immigration.ᵛ

The arrival of asylum seekers and other foreigners threatened many German residents. Their complaints included small matters that could be seen very differently by people from different cultures, such as how loudly people talk on the street, the noise level at parties, or whether to cook outdoors or indoors. While German residents' concerns about planned shelters included the potential for serious crime, most complaints about operating shelters concerned smaller issues. Germans complained about local environmental problems (such as noise and dirt), petty crime (shoplifting and trespassing), and violence among the shelter residents, which could be noisy or seem dangerous to neighbors.ʷ

A distaste for living near asylum seekers was very common across the German population. In a 1996 survey, a huge majority, 83 percent, agreed that there were "strong lifestyle differences" between Germans and asylum seekers, and 37 percent placed those differences at the extreme end of a seven-point scale (at "very strong"). Forty-seven percent said they would find "having an asylum seeker as a neighbor" to be "unpleasant," compared with only 15 percent who would find it "pleasant," thus making asylum seekers much less desirable as neighbors than Turks, ethnic German resettlers, Jews, or Italians.[10]

Government policies concerning employment and the distribution of asylum seekers greatly exacerbated the cultural threats that the newcomers posed to German residents. Beginning in 1980, asylum seekers were barred from employment for periods ranging from two to five years. After July 1991, they were allowed to work only if jobs were available that could not be filled by German or European Community citizens.[11] Limits on their employment made many asylum seekers dependent on social

---

v. In this period, over 90 percent of asylum applications were eventually rejected by German courts, which interpreted political persecution rather narrowly. However, the Basic Law (Articles 16 and 19) and judicial interpretations of it gave asylum seekers the right to full judicial review of their cases and allowed them to remain in Germany while their cases were decided. That took an average of six years. Furthermore, about 60 percent of those denied asylum remained in the country, often with toleration status (*Duldung*) from *Land* governments (Bade 1994, 110; Kanstroom 1993b, 190, 199; 1993a, 224–25).

Protests by resident groups were "anti-immigration," since they were usually directed against immigration, while I term violence against foreigners "anti-foreigner," since it was directed against foreigners as persons.

w. Unfortunately, the sources available to me did not report what the foreigners thought of the Germans' behavior.

assistance, which increased the resentment of many Germans, who viewed asylum seekers as abusing the system. It also forced the asylum seekers to be idle, which led to loitering, drunkenness, fighting, and petty crime by some of them.

In addition, a decentralized policy for distributing asylum seekers increased the chances of conflicts between them and German residents. Instead of allowing asylum seekers to concentrate in the larger cities, which already had higher proportions of foreigners (10 to 25 percent of the population in most major cities), government policy required them to live in many small towns and even villages where residents had little experience with foreigners. This problem was especially acute in the eastern *Länder* (see Chapter 5). It was exacerbated by inadequate funding for counselors, who worked in the shelters, supervised asylum seekers, and mediated between them and their German neighbors.[12]

The threats posed by asylum seekers were widely distributed across Germany because national policy decentralized the state's responsibility for the asylum seekers to a high degree. This policy created the potential for conflicts in probably more than a thousand different local jurisdictions, where asylum seekers remained under state authority while their applications were decided.[x] These conflicts concerned the entry of asylum seekers into German territory, into particular *Länder*, and into particular localities, and how and where they were to be housed.[y] Following a 1974 agreement among the *Land* governments, the Federal Office for the Recognition of Asylum Applicants distributed asylum seekers to the *Länder* in proportion to population. According to the Unification Treaty between West and East Germany, the new eastern *Länder* were added to this formula effective December 1990.[13] The *Länder*, in turn, distributed the asylum seekers to county and city governments, which distributed the newcomers to towns, villages, and neighborhoods within their borders. According to the Social Assistance Law, local governments were ultimately responsible for housing the asylum seekers and giving them social assistance payments. Although local governments generally had a claim for reimbursement from the *Länder*, this compensation was inadequate to cover their additional costs.[14]

x. *Land* governments required the vast majority of Germany's approximately 540 counties and 100 independent cities to house asylum seekers in the early 1990s, and a high proportion of local governments redistributed asylum seekers to multiple towns or neighborhoods within their borders.

y. Therefore, I consider them to be conflicts about immigration even though the borders in question were those of subnational entities rather than the national state.

The decentralized approach to housing created problems for local officials, which made it difficult for them to avoid making controversial decisions. Local governments had responsibility for housing asylum seekers and much discretion in doing so. Because renting or buying private housing was expensive in the early 1990s, officials usually decided to reuse old structures or build new ones in residential neighborhoods. But in those cases, land-use laws allowed neighbors to challenge the siting of such housing in court, based on specific preexisting planning documents[z] or arguments that the housing would present an "unacceptable burden" for neighbors.[15] Anti-immigration and pro-foreigner protesters complicated local officials' tasks further, by pressuring them to find housing that was comparatively safe from attacks by skinheads and neo-Nazis and that met minimum humanitarian standards.

Given all their constraints, public officials were likely to choose sites that many residents considered inappropriate, such as school or municipal gymnasiums, purely residential neighborhoods without commercial or public buildings, sites near schools or playgrounds, or open fields used for recreation. Furthermore, some politicians, including Munich's mayor,[aa] Georg Kronawitter (SPD), sometimes used highly visible sites in order to provoke local opposition.[16] They evidently did this in order to strengthen their arguments for restricting federal asylum rights or reducing the numbers sent to their jurisdictions. Officials also sometimes cut costs in ways that made conflicts among shelter residents and between them and neighborhood residents more likely, for example by housing asylum seekers in makeshift buildings or hiring inadequate staff to counsel and supervise them. Moreover, the administrative and political difficulties of finding a large number of suitable shelter sites often led officials to construct very large shelters with hundreds of residents, locate asylum shelters in sensitive areas, or overcrowd existing shelters. These practices exacerbated cultural conflicts by making the shelters much more visible and concentrating the potential problems associated with them.

Local Conflict Settings

MUNICH AND SÜDPARK

Munich is a large industrial and commercial city with 1.3 million residents. It is the capital of Bavaria, a *Land* with twelve million residents

---

z. *Bebauungspläne* and *Flächennutzungspläne*.
aa. *Oberbürgermeister*.

that has been governed by the CSU, which has had an absolute majority in the *Landtag,* since 1962. Despite its size, Munich's political institutions are relatively open to neighborhood-level protest groups. Borough-level political structures have existed since the 1950s, and in the late 1980s, Munich contained forty-one boroughs (reduced to twenty-five in 1992), each of which had a borough council. These councils met monthly, were usually open to public attendance, and usually allowed residents to speak, though they had no formal right to do so. In addition, the Bavarian *Land* constitution required citizen assemblies to be held at least once per year, called into session by the mayor with the agreement of the borough council. At assemblies, which were often well attended, all citizens could propose and vote on resolutions, though these had only an advisory character.[17] However, the borough councils were weak institutions with little power. Before 1996, the council was appointed by the borough-level political parties in accord with the city council election results in each borough. Before 2000, the boroughs controlled no separate budgets or administration, and they could pass only nonbinding recommendations to the city government.

The broad guidelines of Munich's asylum policy were made by the city's mayor, who was Kronawitter from 1984 to 1993, and the city council. The Social Democrats and Greens had a majority on the council from 1984 to 1996 and created a formal coalition from 1990 to 1996. In the early 1990s, the SPD-Green coalition preferred a more generous policy toward asylum seekers than did most Christian Democrats, while Kronawitter was prone to call publicly for restrictions on the entry of asylum seekers. But the most important decisions, including recommendations about where to site asylum shelters, were made by an ad hoc asylum commission.[bb] This commission consisted of top city officials, including the head of the Social Department (Hans Stützle, CSU). Borough councils normally had a chance to register their opinions on major decisions by the commission, which in turn required city council approval. The asylum commission also worked with the city's Social, Housing, and Construction departments,[cc] which sometimes became directly involved in siting conflicts. The commission officially tried to distribute the asylum seekers about equally across the boroughs and across more broadly defined areas of the city, a policy formalized in terms of a formula based

---

bb. The Staff for Extraordinary Events (Stab für aussergewöhnliche Ereignisse).
cc. The Sozialreferat, Wohnungsamt, and Baureferat.

90 percent on population and 10 percent on land area. However, the city administration often did not meet the goal of equitable distribution, since officials were limited by the availability of buildings and construction sites, and in some cases by political pressure.[18] The asylum commission made dozens of siting decisions in 1989–93, as the rate at which the *Land* of Bavaria sent asylum seekers to Munich rose sharply, to more than 150 per week during the first part of 1992.[19] In the early 1990s, about 12,000 asylum seekers lived in about ninety shelters in Munich.[dd]

The Südpark neighborhood is a mainly lower-middle-class area within a mostly middle-class residential section of Munich, just east of a large park in the southern part of the city. Originally part of the Waldfriedhofsviertel borough, the neighborhood became part of the Sendling-Westpark borough in 1992. Sendling-Westpark had about fifty thousand residents, with slightly lower shares of foreigners and manual workers than in the city, and comparatively few publicly subsidized apartments (18 percent of the housing units). The Südpark neighborhood itself has many small, owner-occupied, one- and two-family houses. It was classified as a purely residential area, though an industrial area dominated by Siemens lay just one kilometer to the southeast of the proposed shelter site, in a neighboring borough. In the 1990 city council elections, voters in Waldfriedhofsviertel gave 43 percent to the SPD, 30 percent to the CSU, 8 percent to the Greens, and 8 percent to the far-right Republikans party, almost identical with the citywide averages.[20] The borough council was led by Social Democrats in the early 1990s.

RENDSBURG COUNTY AND KRONSHAGEN

The conflict settings in Schleswig-Holstein contrasted sharply with those in Munich in institutional and social terms. Schleswig-Holstein is a mostly rural *Land* at the northern border of western Germany, with only 2.6 million residents and a much lower foreign population share (3.5 percent in 1992) than in Germany as a whole.[21] Governed by the Social Democrats alone between 1988 and 2000, the *Land* is divided into eleven counties, each with a county parliament,[ee] county administration, and ju-

---

dd. Only 30 percent of them were in shelters operated by the city. The remainder were in shelters run by the *Land*, which used Munich as the site for temporarily housing asylum seekers before they were distributed to other municipalities in Bavaria (*MM*, 22 December 1988; data from Flüchtlingsamt München).

ee. *Kreistag*.

risdiction over all the municipalities in its territory except the *Land*'s four largest cities. Rendsburg County, in the center of Schleswig-Holstein, contained about 160 municipalities with 250,000 residents in the early 1990s. It is mostly rural, with only about 30,000 residents in the largest municipality. The Christian Democrats and Liberals had a narrow majority in the county parliament in 1990–94. As the number of asylum seekers housed in Schleswig-Holstein rose from ten thousand at the end of 1990 to twenty-one thousand at the end of 1992,[22] Rendsburg County was responsible for receiving its share of the asylum seekers and apportioning them to its municipalities. In contrast to the Christian Democratic government in Bavaria, Schleswig-Holstein's SPD-led government pursued a policy of integrating asylum seekers into the local population, which included a highly decentralized housing policy.[23]

Political institutions in Kronshagen were fairly open to protesters, and yet, as in Munich, the degree of openness depended on how and when public officials chose to grant access to them. The municipalities in Rendsburg County were governed by councils, which elected the mayors until 1998. Councils and mayors together controlled the local governments' budgets, municipal property, and administrative staff. These officials decided where and how to house the asylum seekers sent by the county. If they chose, officials could make council meetings either open or closed to the public, and they could also hold citizen assemblies with an advisory character.

Kronshagen is a small, largely upper-middle-class town of 12,000 residents in Rendsburg County. It lies on the border to Kiel, a port city with 250,000 residents and the capital of Schleswig-Holstein. In the early 1990s, Kronshagen was home to many relatively high-income people who wanted to live in a small town and have short commutes to their jobs in Kiel. Hence, its shares of civil servants and white-collar employees (26 percent and 44 percent, respectively) were well above average when compared with Rendsburg County and the *Land*.[ff] In the 1990 town council elections, the CDU won twelve seats, the SPD ten, the Liberal Party one, and the Greens none. The Christian Democratic majority on the council chose Wolf-Dieter Wilhelms to be mayor beginning in October 1991. Under *Land* law, housing asylum seekers was a *Land* function

---

ff. The figures for the county were 14 percent and 35 percent and for the *Land* 12 percent and 38 percent, respectively (1987 census data provided by Statistisches Amt Schleswig-Holstein).

delegated to the municipalities, and hence fell within the mayor's authority as head of the municipality. In Kronshagen, the mayor had the power to choose sites, but the council retained the right to vote on expenditures for renting property or construction. Hence, the mayor was the leader in asylum policy, but he required council support.

Summary of the Protests in Südpark and Kronshagen

The residents of Südpark undertook a large amount of protest and used a broader range of tactics than most resident initiatives, while focusing on conventional and disruptive actions. The Südpark Citizen Initiative,[gg] which was formed in March 1992, began making challenges in the courts and attending borough council meetings the same month. It quickly came to focus on a dual strategy of increasing public support for its position while proceeding with litigation. The group's conventional actions included undertaking a series of court cases in 1992–94, attending borough assembly meetings, and participating in three well-attended citizen assemblies in April 1992, October 1992, and November 1994. The Südpark Initiative also issued press releases and wrote monthly reports on the activities at the asylum shelter, which they sent to the Protestant Church (which was the shelter's landlord), the political parties, and the city administration.[24]

In addition, the Südpark Initiative used mildly disruptive actions to try to mobilize residents, gain publicity, and motivate elite allies. Its members held a rally attended by five hundred people in late March 1992, shouted down some speakers at the April 1992 citizen assembly, and posed with signs during the filming of a news program that September. At the October 1992 citizen assembly, the Initiative's leader Heinz Schwindler demonstratively presented Kronawitter with a white umbrella, as symbolic protection from the criticism of the other Social Democratic leaders in Munich.

Beginning early in the conflict, the Südpark Initiative sometimes resorted to militant methods, which were mainly symbolic or verbal threats, though the group did not openly use or call for violence. On the stage at the March 1992 rally, the citizen initiative's speaker demonstratively broke a pro-foreigner banner that had been brought by a counter-

---

gg. Bürgerinitiative Slevogtstrasse/Südpark.

demonstrator.²⁵ This suggested a violent attitude toward local residents who might oppose the Südpark Initiative, and may have set the tone for later actions. Members of the group emphasized that they would fight the shelter "with all means," which some interpreted as a veiled threat to use or encourage violence. The citizen initiative also wrote an implicitly threatening letter to the city's Housing Department, which said that "the group might no longer be able to guarantee that one of the neighbors would not do something drastic."²⁶ Finally, the group's public statements may have encouraged someone to make an anonymous bomb threat to the asylum shelter in September 1992, a few days after the broadcast of a television program that dramatized problems at the shelter. The television program had stated, in a somewhat provocative way, that "under the surface there seems to be something simmering."²⁷ A pro-foreigner group in Südpark also reported receiving anonymous threats, including death threats, by telephone and mail.²⁸

In Kronshagen in 1992–94, four resident initiatives formed to oppose the siting of asylum shelters in the Kopperpahl, Eichhof, Wenden Strasse, and Drew Strasse neighborhoods. In most cases, the Kronshagen protesters opposed the construction of the asylum shelters, and they sometimes named alternative sites, even in the same neighborhood, or called on the town government to change a shelter's entrance from a residential street to another, busier street.²⁹ Compared with the Munich cases, the protests against asylum shelters in Kronshagen were very brief. Except for the Kopperpahl conflict, the newspaper record indicates that they all were resolved within a month or two.

In addition, unlike the protesters in Südpark, those in Kronshagen stuck to conventional methods. In the Kopperpahl neighborhood, residents used leaflets to publicize their cause and mobilize residents to attend a town council meeting; the hall could not contain the large turnout. The residents also brought a case to the Schleswig administrative court, which ruled against them before the start of construction.³⁰ In the Eichhof area, residents wrote an open letter to the mayor and the church that owned the property, eliciting public responses from both. The neighbors of the Wenden Strasse shelter simply met with the mayor to discuss ongoing problems and what could be done about them. Finally, in a conflict about a proposed shelter on Drew Strasse, residents overfilled the town hall to attend a council meeting, presented forty-nine signatures on a petition, and threatened litigation. The only departure from conventional methods came several years after these conflicts ended. In January 1996, a group of young men led by a neo-Nazi activist threatened and threw stones at the Eichhof shelter, in two incidents.[hh]

Authorities' Mistakes and Cultural Threats

Why were the protests in Südpark longer-lived and more unconventional than those in Kronshagen? Part of the answer is that in Südpark, provocative actions and other mistakes by government and church officials created a larger threat to local residents, and reforms were slower in coming. The city began building an asylum shelter on Slevogt Strasse in Südpark in March 1992. Although the shelter was very unpopular with residents, the city moved asylum seekers into the shelter in June and operated it for three years. The asylum seekers numbered about 300 people from many different countries including Romania, Russia, "Black African" countries, and Albania. City officials created a shelter that was larger than most city shelters,[ii] one designed to house 300 to 360 people in two-story buildings made of prefabricated containers. Moreover, the building site chosen was a green field, near a school and a nursery school, for which publicly subsidized housing or another nursery school had been considered. In addition, the city administration, led by the asylum commission, took several actions that seem unnecessarily provocative. City officials ignored advice to site the shelter at a nearby location that recently had held a temporary asylum shelter.[31] Officials also stated that they were not interested in citizen protests, and they tried to build and operate the Slevogt Strasse shelter without even issuing a building permit or concluding a lease with the property's owner.[32]

The behavior of the Protestant Church, which owned the land, also increased residents' mistrust. Although church officials tried to influence the size, duration, and staffing of the shelter, they did not publicly inform residents of their intentions. The Church demanded and received from

---

hh. The neo-Nazi activist had recently moved to Kronshagen from another *Land*, and according to a newspaper, the young men who joined him were probably mainly from Kiel. In the most severe of the attacks, they shouted slogans, marched to the shelter, demanded that the shelter's residents leave, threw stones, and finally tried to storm the building before police prevented them. The two African families in the shelter also threw stones. The families were briefly moved out of the shelter, but the neo-Nazis' victory was only temporary, as asylum seekers moved back in (*KN*, 27 January 1996).

ii. Only two shelters operated by the city of Munich in 1995 had space for more than two hundred people.

the city 100,000 deutschmarks per year in rent and promised to use the money for counseling the shelter residents. Counseling was considered important for reducing conflicts between shelter residents and other neighborhood residents, but no counseling was available for the first five months of the shelter's operation, and very little was provided during the next four months. Finally, in September 1992, it became known that the city planned to transfer the shelter to the *Land*, a move that probably would have led to a reduction in the around-the-clock security force and perhaps a reduction in the church-provided counseling.[33]

In response to these threats, neighborhood residents, including some who directly abutted the shelter site, formed the Südpark Citizen Initiative in March 1992. By November 1994, the group had about a hundred members, mostly middle-class people with modest incomes, about ten of whom were active. The citizen initiative raised 30,000 deutschmarks from its members for a series of court cases.[34] Although there was also opposition from a parents' council at the school and from other residents, the citizen initiative quickly became the dominant voice among those who opposed the shelter's construction and operation.[35]

Opponents felt politically marginalized as well as threatened by the prospect of authorities moving hundreds of new foreigners into their neighborhood. They argued that the procedure for siting it was too fast, discussion was inadequate, there was no building permit, and the city's asylum commission was acting arrogantly.[36] Signs at a rally in March 1992 asked: "Where are the rights of the citizens?" and "Deliberate provocation or political game?"[37] Opponents also claimed that the southern neighborhoods of Munich were being assigned more than their fair share of asylum seekers. This was accurate. If the Slevogt Strasse shelter had remained open in November 1995, Sendling-Westpark would have housed 785 asylum seekers, almost double the quota of 429 that was foreseen by the city's formula for distributing asylum seekers. This would have made Sendling-Westpark one of the five most "overburdened" boroughs in Munich.[38] Opponents also argued that the city had chosen a poor site, close to schools, which threatened the safety of their children. They argued that shelter residents, who would include many young men from different nationalities, would be sexually aggressive and get into loud fights, and that the shelter would create additional traffic and noise from police interventions, ambulances, and vehicles supplying the shelter.

Residents continued to feel threatened by the shelter after it went into operation, complaining mostly of noise, unsanitary conditions, and petty crime. Shelter residents fought among themselves, as first Africans and then Albanians tried to establish dominance.[39] Südpark Initiative members observed and documented the activities of shelter residents in painstaking detail, recording some serious problems, such as noisy fights, stabbings, thefts, and police interventions late at night. The group also documented many smaller matters, such as overflowing trash cans, odors coming from the site, Bangladeshi asylum seekers walking out to sell roses illegally, and bottles being dropped into public recycling containers after the permitted hour.[40]

The primary objective of the Südpark protesters was preventing the opening of the shelter, and, if that were unsuccessful, then getting it closed down. Other, more reformist demands included improving security nearby (through lighting and emergency telephones), building noise barriers between the shelter and its immediate neighbors, and maintaining the shelter's around-the-clock security force in the event it was transferred to the *Land*. A pro-foreigner group, Living Together in Südpark,[jj] also pressed the Church to provide around-the-clock counseling, and the Südpark Initiative joined in this demand four months later.[41]

Members of the Südpark Initiative also made radical demands, but built no bridges to neo-Nazis or skinheads. Their radical demands included dissolving the city's asylum commission, firing Hans-Peter Uhl (CSU), a top administration official[kk] on the asylum commission, and completely stopping the inflow of asylum seekers. Moreover, a general antipathy to foreigners lay just below the surface in many of the citizen initiative's actions, despite claims that the group was not xenophobic. For example, claims that Germans were disadvantaged relative to foreigners were evident at the group's March 1992 rally, where signs read, "Germans are *Asylanten*[ll] in their own country—economic *Asylanten* out!" and "Are we second-class citizens?"[42] The Südpark Initiative found itself somewhat on the defensive when the political climate in Germany shifted toward pro-foreigner and anti-Nazi sentiment after a deadly arson attack against Turkish residents in Mölln (Schleswig-Holstein) in November 1992. By April 1993, the citizen group's permanent sign read,

---

jj. Miteinander leben in Südpark.
kk. *Kreisverwaltungsreferent*.
ll. This was a slightly derogatory term for asylum seekers, used by the tabloid press and politicians who sought restrictive measures against them.

"We are against xenophobia, against violence, but also against the abuse of asylum."[43]

Compared with Südpark, the siting of asylum shelters in Kronshagen posed smaller threats to residents and hence triggered smaller, briefer protests. The town government's decentralized approach to housing asylum seekers spurred protests in four different neighborhoods, while also helping to limit the size of protests in each case. Between 1990 and 1994, about a hundred asylum seekers were distributed to Kronshagen, beginning with groups of Romanians. Conflicts over where to house the foreigners began in the summer of 1992.[44] The mayor and council agreed to house them in a highly decentralized way within the town, usually with no more than twenty to be housed in any one place, with no neighborhoods spared, and without focusing them in areas on the edge of town.[45] Officials were limited by a local shortage of housing and the failure of an army hospital in Kronshagen to make space available for asylum seekers.[46]

Local officials decided that the least unattractive option was to build small new shelters on previously unbuilt lots, at five different sites scattered around the town. When the first asylum seekers arrived, officials placed them in low-standard apartments on the western edge of the town in the Heischberg neighborhood. By June 1992, thirty-five were living there and another twenty-four in a former construction yard in the center of town on Wenden Strasse. As additional asylum seekers were assigned to Kronshagen, three new sites were proposed. First, in June 1992, the town government proposed container-style housing for ten to twenty people on a sports field in the northern Kopperpahl neighborhood, to be operated for five years.[47] Then, in October 1992, it proposed a small shelter in the backyard of a pastor's house that bordered the large Eichhof cemetery, to be operated for ten years.[48] Finally, in June 1994, the government announced plans for sixteen to twenty asylum seekers or ethnic German resettlers at a site just south of the town center, at the end of Drew Strasse.[49]

The proposed shelters threatened Kronshagen residents in a variety of ways and hence triggered protests. At the Kopperpahl site, members of a resident initiative thought that a shelter housing eighty to a hundred people would eventually be built, because the federal government had recently called for more large shelters. They also argued that the site was too valuable because it was the only green space in the area, used by children and old people, and that other areas of town had more green space.⁵⁰ In the Eichhof conflict, opponents complained about the proximity to a school and expressed concerns about increased noise, a general feeling of insecurity, and the endangerment of the old fruit trees and small animals that lived at the site.⁵¹ At the Drew Strasse site, neighbors said they were not opposed to foreigners or asylum shelters, but found this a bad site since it was located in a purely residential neighborhood, which had small summer houses in the back yards and an "idyllic" character. They expected a loss of security, orderliness, and cleanliness that would reduce the quality of life and property values.⁵² Finally, neighbors of the shelter operating on Wenden Strasse complained about problems with noise at night and people walking in and damaging their gardens. The problems, they said, were especially large in the summertime and were not caused by all the twenty-five asylum seekers living there, but only by several Gypsy families.⁵³

Gaining Elite Allies

Another reason that protests against asylum seekers were comparatively long and intense at Südpark is that the citizen initiative there gained much support from political elites. From the first months of the conflict, the Südpark Initiative was encouraged by a broad range of politicians, who represented the two major parties and the neighborhood, city, *Land*, and federal levels of government.

Leading Social Democratic politicians in southern Munich opposed the shelter as soon as the Südpark Initiative began to mobilize, as did the Sendling-Westpark borough council and several Christian Democratic leaders, one of whom spoke at the March 1992 rally. That month, Hans Bauer, the district chairperson for the SPD in southern Munich, argued that Slevogt Strasse was a bad site for the shelter. He said that the city administration was ignoring the borough council in this decision and encouraged residents to call the mayor or the responsible civil servants to register their opposition.⁵⁴ The March rally featured speeches by a *Landtag* deputy, Dorle Baumann (SPD), who expressed opposition to the site and to the city's secretive methods, and by the husband of a Christian Democratic councillor, who spoke on her behalf. Several weeks after that turbulent event, which was attended by five hundred people, Erich Riedl (CSU), a Bundestag deputy and Federal Economic Ministry official, provocatively declared that southern Munich should be free of asylum seekers.[55] Later, the chair of the new Sendling-Westpark borough council, Hans-Dieter Simeth, also opposed the shelter and pressed the Church to explain its plans.

Mayor Kronawitter also provided important support for the Südpark Initiative. He wrote to the group that its monthly reports on conditions at the shelter "took his breath away," and he stood on stage with the Initiative's leader Heinz Schwindler as they both expressed support for a constitutional amendment restricting asylum rights at the October 1992 citizen assembly.[56]

Elite allies also influenced the types of protest in Südpark, though in somewhat contradictory ways. Politicians' support for the Südpark Initiative encouraged it to continue its protests, which gave it the opportunity to experiment with disruptive and militant tactics. However, the citizen initiative's elite allies also expressed reservations that discouraged it from moving more strongly toward militant methods or radical positions. At times, Kronawitter tried to reassure the protest group that residents in other neighborhoods had found they could live near asylum seekers, and he contradicted their claims that no counseling was in place in 1993.[57] Similarly, Simeth, the borough council chair, warned against "emotionalization" by the Südpark Initiative, in a statement made soon after the bomb threat against the shelter.[58] Similarly, other residents in Südpark supported many of the citizen initiative's demands, but also with reservations that may have checked its tendency to endorse radical positions or use militant tactics. Majorities at three large citizen assemblies in 1992 and 1994 voted against most of the radical demands by the Südpark Initiative, such as dissolving the city's asylum commission, although they almost unanimously supported closing the shelter.[59]

By contrast, protesters in Kronshagen, who used purely conventional methods, failed to win elite allies, and this shortened their mobilization. Local political elites largely maintained a consensus on a decentralized approach to housing the asylum seekers and on the sites chosen by the mayor. When opponents mobilized, the mayor, town councillors, and church leaders, with one minor exception, gave them no public support, reiterated the need to house the asylum seekers somewhere, referred to the town government's policy of sparing no neighborhood, and sometimes accused opponents of xenophobia or a desire to shift problems onto their neighbors.

The importance of the missing elite allies can be seen in the one conflict that departed somewhat from the others in Kronshagen. In the Kopperpahl conflict, elites and higher-level officials gave some support to a citizen initiative, resulting in stronger protests than in the other three Kronshagen conflicts. After protests began, one Social Democratic town councillor announced that he now thought that a centralized approach to the housing issue would be better, since rising numbers of asylum seekers would make such a policy inevitable eventually.[60,mm]

After this minor episode of elite support, the Kopperpahl resident initiative gained further support from officials in the county and *Land* administrations. The conflict between those officials and the town government raised the chances of success for the resident initiative and thus spurred its protests. In July 1992, the Rendsburg County Construction Department refused to give the town permission to use the Kopperpahl site for housing, arguing that the emissions from a neighboring industrial area would be harmful to shelter residents.[61] After the town government threatened to bring an action in administrative court, county officials got advice from the *Land* Interior Ministry, which suggested allowing construction but limiting the shelter to families so as "to not injure the neighborly interests."[62] Thus, the Interior Ministry placed itself partly on the side of the Kopperpahl residents against the town government. The local opponents responded to this support from higher-level authorities by continuing to protest in a different, though still conventional way, by initiating litigation against the shelter in administrative court.

The Timing of Reforms

Why did the protesters at Südpark adopt a fairly broad repertoire of methods, while the Kronshagen groups limited themselves to conventional actions? Why was militant activity nonetheless limited to a marginal role in the Südpark conflict? The answers lie mainly in the timing of reforms, which also helps explain why the Südpark protests were longer than those in Kronshagen.

In Südpark, public officials and the property owner initially refused all reforms, but they adopted some changes within the first year of the conflict. Finally, continued pressure from residents led to the closing of the shelter. The timing of these reforms had somewhat contradictory

---

mm. His prediction proved wrong.

effects on the type of protest. Official intransigence early in the conflict led the Südpark Initiative to shift toward disruptive and militant tactics, while the later adoption of reforms limited the extent of that shift.

Protests had no influence on city officials, the property owner, or the courts for the first six months of the conflict, and major reform was delayed for over three years. City officials stated they were uninterested in citizen protests, and an administrative court ruled against the Südpark Initiative in March 1992, citing the emergency situation that the city government faced. In response, the citizen initiative shifted toward mild disruptiveness and implicit militancy in a rally held ten days later. Then, after the group lost the appeal of its administrative court case in June 1992, a bomb threat followed in September.

However, the Südpark Initiative's activities did trigger a series of small reforms about six months after the first protests, and the group ultimately won the closing of the shelter in 1995. The reforms helped prevent the citizen group from shifting toward a clearly militant strategy or escalating its disruptive actions. The city and Protestant Church made some important reforms beginning in September 1992, reducing the threat that the shelter posed to local residents. That month, the city began to provide an around-the-clock security force, and in October the city and Church agreed on a three-year lease, compared with the five years the city had originally sought. In November, the Church finally provided a social worker to counsel the asylum seekers, though only on a half-time basis.[63] Furthermore, in March 1993, the city's attempt to transfer the shelter to the *Land,* a move opposed by the Südpark Initiative, failed when *Land* officials said they were unwilling to take the shelter. The reason given was that the shelter's building permits were not in order, a reference to the litigation being pursued by the citizen initiative.[64]

Eventually, the Südpark Initiative gained major reforms through litigation and a 1995 decision by the Protestant Church. After a July 1994 court defeat, the citizen initiative won a partial victory when an administrative court ruled that the city had not provided enough staffing and that the shelter had too high an occupancy. Although the court refused to shut down the shelter, the Protestant Church then decided not to renew its lease with the city, which expired in 1995. Hence, the shelter was closed in October 1995, at a time when the overall numbers of asylum seekers and hence demand for shelters was lower than during the 1992–93 peak. Publicly, church officials said they had decided to build their own facilities on this lot, and eventually they did build a nursery school there.⁶⁵ Although it had taken over three years, the Südpark Initiative had won a major victory, which made further protests and tactical experimentation unnecessary.

By contrast, the mayor in Kronshagen made small reforms rapidly in response to protests in almost every case where groups mobilized.[nn] His responsiveness encouraged protesters in later conflicts in this town to use conventional methods, because they seemed to be somewhat effective. In addition, the reforms significantly reduced the threat to residents, making them less likely to support continued protests or a shift to riskier protest methods.

Although the reforms were small, the mayor made them very quickly compared with the drawn-out process in Südpark. At the Kopperpahl site, the mayor responded to protests by immediately agreeing to move the planned housing from the sports field to a site next to the field, and to change the type of construction from containers to inexpensive wooden houses. Opponents also won a change in the location of the Drew Strasse shelter and promises about counseling at Wenden Strasse.⁶⁶ These rapid reforms probably boosted the mayor's credibility on asylum policy and made it more difficult to mobilize opposition to his decisions about where to site the shelters.

Another reform that was made on a town-wide basis helped lessen conflicts between asylum seekers and long-time Kronshagen residents, and hence reduced a potential cause of longer protests. In response to resident concerns, town officials lobbied the district Employment Office for a counselor for asylum seekers. They obtained a part-time counselor in July 1992 and a full-time counselor in April 1993.⁶⁷ The latter arrived with extensive plans for building relations between asylum seekers and local residents. These included holding contact evenings for Kronshagen residents to meet the asylum seekers living in the Kopperpahl and Eichhof shelters, encouraging Kronshageners to sponsor specific asylum seekers through godparentships, and trying to integrate the asylum seekers into local associations and schools.⁶⁸ These efforts continued through the 1990s and ultimately led Kronshagen to win third prize in a Federal

---

nn. However, local anti-immigration groups had little effect on the locations of asylum shelters in Kronshagen, because the council usually strongly backed the mayor's decisions despite neighborhood opposition. The Kopperpahl and Eichhof sites were ready for asylum seekers by May 1993 (*KN*, 23 April 1993) and remained in operation through the late 1990s.

Interior Ministry competition for programs promoting the integration of foreigners.[69]

Summary and Conclusions

SÜDPARK AND KRONSHAGEN

In sum, protests in these two cases differed in size and duration because of differences in interactions between protesters, politicians, and authorities (see Table 3 on page 223). In both cases, threats of state action spurred protests. But in Südpark, protests were larger and longer-lived, because the threats were larger, elite support stronger, and the government much slower to make even minor reforms than in Kronshagen. However, large threats by themselves did not lead to large protests, since only one of the five Munich boroughs with the highest shares of asylum seekers had major protests against asylum shelters. Nonetheless, sufficiently large threats may have been necessary before processes of opportunity expansion could develop in Südpark. There, interactions unfolded that were qualitatively similar to the urban renewal and nuclear energy conflicts, though on a much smaller scale. The Südpark Initiative used some attention-getting tactics, it won significant support from politicians, and at first officials were largely intransigent and dismissive. This combination of factors helped the Südpark Initiative to mount relatively large protests and to sustain activity for three years, and it led them to shift, to some extent, toward disruptive and militant forms of protest. Therefore, this conflict was larger, longer, and more intense than most of the conflicts in Munich and Rendsburg County.

By contrast, in Kronshagen, protests against four shelters were brief, lasting only a few months in most cases. Protests occurred repeatedly because there was a repeated conjunction, in different neighborhoods, of threatening government plans and a high chance of success when it came to gaining modest reforms from the mayor. But opportunities never expanded much, and therefore the protests were short-lived, except at the Kopperpahl site. Protesters did not win elite allies, and hence opportunities for preventing or shutting down any of the four shelters sited in the early 1990s appeared to be minimal. This may have been due to the relatively small threats posed by the small asylum shelters and the inherent cohesiveness of local elites in a small town. Nonetheless, more politicians might have broken ranks if protesters had shifted away from purely conventional methods toward more attention-getting tactics. Protests remained small also because local officials adopted minor reforms rapidly, which significantly reduced the threats to residents posed by the asylum shelters.

The types of protest also differed across the two cases, with a conventional focus in both cases but also some disruptive and militant actions in Südpark. These differences were due to the timing of policy reforms and the role played by elite allies (see Table 4 on pages 228–29). In Südpark, public and church officials initially failed to make reforms, which encouraged a shift toward disruptive and militant tactics. But, beginning in September 1992, city and church officials also made a series of small concessions, and ultimately closed the shelter in 1995, which helped prevent a greater shift toward unconventional methods. In addition, elite allies supported the Südpark Initiative in its conventional and mildly disruptive tactics, while their public reservations discouraged the group from shifting toward a greater use of nonviolent disruption or militancy. By contrast, in Kronshagen, the conflicts remained purely conventional because local officials responded to conventional protests by rapidly adopting small reforms, thus encouraging similar protests at the next siting conflict. The reforms also eased local acceptance of the housing and thus undercut potential support for unconventional tactics. For their part, local elites in Kronshagen did not give support that would have encouraged long-lived protests, during which resident groups might have tried out disruptive or militant strategies.

MUNICH AND RENDSBURG COUNTY

The conclusions from these two cases are supported by examining the fifteen largest conflicts over asylum shelter siting in Munich and Rendsburg County from 1989 to 1993. Indeed, the types of protest in Südpark and Kronshagen were rather typical for their respective jurisdictions. In fourteen of the fifteen cases (93 percent), anti-immigration groups using conventional participation opposed shelter siting. Yet the disruptive and militant actions at Südpark were not exceptional. Some disruptive activity occurred in four of the fifteen cases (27 percent), and some militant activity occurred in seven cases (47 percent).

In all fifteen cases, the emergence of protests depended on threats produced by official decisions to house asylum seekers in particular locations. In every case, protests occurred immediately after residents learned about municipal plans to site a shelter. Residents responded to threats to public order and other matters of cultural friction between Germans and asylum seekers, rather than competition over jobs or housing.

Protests were sustained where citizen initiatives gained support from the leaders of local political parties and interest groups. Conflicts were sustained longer in Munich, where protests usually lasted for one or more years, than in most of the Rendsburg County cases, where they typically ceased after several months. The main reason for this difference was that elite allies supported protest groups much more often in Munich than in Rendsburg County.[oo] In all seven Munich cases, major-party politicians[pp] gave significant support to the opponents of asylum shelters, and in three of those cases, protests were sustained for several years after the peak of conflict.[qq] By contrast, only four of the eight Rendsburg County conflicts included elite support for the local opponents, as local elites often remained unified when making siting decisions and usually left negotiations and concessions to the town mayor.

Protest groups used broadly similar methods in Munich and Rendsburg County. Almost all used conventional methods, half of the cases used militant threats or violence, and about a third involved mostly minor, isolated physical attacks on shelters. The rates of conventional actions and militant violence were similar in both locations.[rr] However,

oo. The differences in elite behavior in Munich and Rendsburg County were partly due to political institutions and *Land*-level asylum politics. Political institutions were more complex in Munich, creating more partisan diversity among elites and officials, than in Rendsburg County. Furthermore, the CSU-led Bavarian government pursued a deterrence-based asylum policy, which increased conflicts between the *Land* government and the SPD-led Munich government. By contrast, the SPD-led government in Schleswig-Holstein pursued the integration of foreigners, which created fewer conflicts between the *Land* and municipalities than in Bavaria.

pp. At the borough level, there was a strong tendency for Christian Democratic politicians to support anti-immigration protest groups and for Social Democratic and Green politicians to support pro-foreigner groups. However, in two cases (Südpark and Ramersdorf), the borough-level Social Democrats provided early allies to the anti-immigration groups, and the city's Social Democratic mayor acted as an ally in two cases (Südpark and Hadern).

qq. Residents continued litigation and other routine participation for several years in Südpark and Solln, and small arson attacks on the shelter in Pasing were repeated during the peak of that conflict and afterwards. In eleven other cases, protests collapsed completely after officials put the shelter into operation in the neighborhood in question, or in one case, decided not to site it there.

rr. Two of seven cases in Munich and three of eight cases in Rendsburg County involved physical attacks on asylum shelters.

nonviolently disruptive protests occurred in four out of seven Munich cases and in no Rendsburg cases. This difference was partly due to the greater availability of elite allies in Munich, which allowed protests to continue for longer periods compared with Rendsburg County, thus providing more time for tactical experimentation. In addition, residents and politicians in major cities such as Munich might have been more willing to use or support disruptive protests than those in small towns like Kronshagen, since those in large cities may have been exposed to a more frequent use of disruptive tactics by urban, leftist protesters.

Nonetheless, the similarities in protest methods are more striking than the differences, especially when these cases are compared to those in the next chapter. Why were protests largely nonviolent, with a strong emphasis on conventional methods, in both Munich and Rendsburg County? One reason is that, in both places, residents quickly gained access to local officials, and this promoted conventional participation. Both formal institutions and customary interactions made it more likely that officials would grant access. In Munich, borough councils and citizen assemblies helped make officials accessible to protesters. In Rendsburg County, the small size of communities facilitated informal contacts between residents and officials, making it easy for protesters to approach officials and politicians by attending meetings, circulating petitions, and using other conventional methods. However, in both locations, officials had much discretion in deciding whether to hold open meetings, schedule citizen assemblies, or listen to protesters. They usually chose to give dissatisfied residents a chance to express their views conventionally.

In both Munich and Rendsburg County, too, local officials tended to adopt small reforms in response to nonviolent protests, which encouraged protesters to use similar methods in later conflicts. In seven of the ten cases for which enough information was available, officials adopted small reforms that were designed to placate protesters and reduce conflicts between asylum seekers and neighborhood residents. These reforms included reducing the size of shelters, increasing staffing, blocking or delaying transfer to the *Land* (in Munich), moving the site slightly in order to accommodate other uses (such as recreation), and building inexpensive wooden houses rather than using the more unsightly prefabricated containers. Furthermore, in Munich, opposition in Westkreuz, Moosach, and other neighborhoods led to the adoption of a citywide policy of providing a high level of counseling staff at shelters operated by the city.[70]

However, major reforms, such as closing or not building shelters, were seldom forthcoming.[ss] Why did anti-immigration protesters fail to shift toward a strong use of disruptive or militant methods, as occurred in the urban renewal and nuclear energy protests? One reason is that the small reforms reduced the cultural threats to most residents to manageable levels, and hence helped undercut the most intense opposition to the asylum shelters. Another is that alliances between resident groups and skinheads or neo-Nazis, which could have been a basis for disruptive or militant protests, did not emerge in Munich and Rendsburg County. In these ways, these conflicts were very different from those in Hoyerswerda and Rostock.

---

ss. In thirteen of fifteen cases (87 percent), local officials constructed shelters on the initially proposed sites. The resulting distribution of asylum seekers in Munich did not benefit richer or middle-class boroughs (data from Flüchtlingsamt München, author's calculations).

5 IMMIGRATION CONFLICTS IN HOYERSWERDA, ROSTOCK, AND RIESA

The anti-immigration movement of the 1990s involved an enormous amount of violence against asylum seekers and foreign contract workers.[a] The largest violent actions were the riots in the eastern German cities of Hoyerswerda and Rostock, which involved hundreds or thousands of adults openly supporting hundreds of skinhead youths and neo-Nazis, who besieged and attacked foreigners' housing for many days. The riots received nationwide news coverage and led authorities to remove hundreds of asylum seekers and other foreigners from these localities. The riots and the dramatic concessions to the rioters inspired right-wing youths and neo-Nazis to carry out hundreds of attacks on asylum shelters and other foreigner housing across recently unified Germany.[1] The anti-foreigner violence accelerated the national debate on restricting asylum rights,[2] as Christian Democratic leaders successfully pressured their Social Democratic counterparts to accept constitutional restrictions on asylum rights, in the form of an amendment to Article 16 of the Basic Law.[b] The political significance of the Hoyerswerda and Rostock riots

---

a. Across Germany, the main targets of attacks were asylum seekers, who were distributed to the eastern *Länder* beginning in December 1990. In eastern Germany, the victims of right-wing violence after unification also included foreign contract workers (*Vertragsarbeiter*) from Africa and Vietnam. They had been recruited by the East German state and worked under multiyear labor contracts, which expired as late as 1995. Although these workers were expected to leave the country after their contracts expired, after unification it was possible for them to remain in unified Germany by applying for asylum or living illegally.

b. Two days after the Rostock riots, Christian Democratic politicians told the Social Democrats to begin negotiations within ten days or face a vote on a constitutional amendment in the Bundestag. The head of the chancellor's office, Friedrich Bohl

reflected their duration, intensity, and number of participants, which made them the most serious attacks against members of ethnic minority groups in postwar Germany.^c

This chapter focuses on three conflicts in eastern Germany. The riots in Hoyerswerda (Saxony) and Rostock (Mecklenburg-West Pomerania) are examples of large, militant, violent protest campaigns against foreigners. Riesa is a contrasting case which exemplifies the low level of protest and the lack of strong militant actions that characterized immigration conflicts in many places in eastern Germany. I address two questions: Why did protests became so large in Hoyerswerda and Rostock, compared to Riesa? Why did the protests in Hoyerswerda and Rostock involve much more militancy and violence than conventional protests, while Riesa had a balance between a few, relatively minor militant actions and a small amount of conventional participation?

I contend that the size of protests and the incidence of militancy were not due to ethnic competition over material goods. Rather, protests became large and militant where ill-conceived government policies increased cultural threats, militant youths and adult residents formed alliances, access to officials and reforms was limited, and police were extremely passive. Where these factors were not present, as in Riesa, protests were small and militancy was minimized. Furthermore, when authorities made concessions to violence, in Hoyerswerda and Rostock, their actions encouraged further militant attacks on foreigners across newly unified Germany.

First, I describe the rationale for case selection and sketch the main events in the three cases. Then I examine the limits of socioeconomic and organizational explanations of anti-foreigner violence in these eastern German conflicts. The next section examines the political settings for

---

(CDU), said that political action must occur within weeks because, as a conservative newspaper paraphrased him, "asylum seekers were overtaxing the residents of villages and towns, the police, and the housing resources of Germany" (*FAZ*, 27 August 1992, 2). Bohl rejected the Social Democrats' demands for special police units to protect asylum seekers after the riots, on the grounds that it was pointless to "cure symptoms" when the real problem was the legal right to asylum. Social Democratic leaders called an emergency party meeting for mid-November 1992, which accepted the need to amend Article 16.

c. The only other attacks that came close were the September 1992 riots at Quedlinburg, in eastern Germany, where youths attacked an asylum shelter on four consecutive nights, with up to two or three hundred supporters watching (*taz*, 9, 11 September 1992).

immigration conflicts in Germany during the early 1990s. Policy legacies and rapid institutional change in the eastern *Länder* just after unification were important causes, but cannot fully explain the size and type of anti-immigration protests in these three cases. In the bulk of the chapter, I then analyze the three local cases, explaining the size and type of protests as the results of political interactions, and conclude with a comparative summary.

Case Selection

To examine the militant side of the anti-immigration movement, I initially sought locations with the largest violent protest campaigns. The main candidates were the six largest riots against foreigners, all of which took place in the eastern *Länder*. Of these cases, the Hoyerswerda and Rostock riots were the most intense and also had the largest effects on waves of shelter attacks and the national asylum debate.[3] In field work and in my analysis, I focused on Hoyerswerda because its riots occurred earlier than those in Rostock, and hence may have affected what happened there.[d] As a contrasting case for Hoyerswerda, I chose a case with comparatively little violence against foreigners. There were many such places in Saxony and the other eastern *Länder*. Although Saxony had the third-highest rate of anti-foreigner violence among the sixteen German *Länder* in 1991,[4] there was much variation in the nature of immigration conflicts within Saxony. In thirty of its fifty-four counties and independent[e] cities, more than half of the total, no major attacks against foreigners' dwellings were reported during the peak periods of violence.[f]

I chose Riesa County because it is in important ways typical of relatively low-violence localities in Saxony while it also resembles Hoyers-

---

d. However, the available evidence on Rostock suggests that political interactions similar to those in Hoyerswerda were the most important causes of the Rostock riots.

e. *kreisfreie*, i.e. free of county supervision.

f. These results are from my analysis of attacks reported in *die tageszeitung* and PDS 1993 from January to December 1991 and August to November 1992. I chose attacks on housing because they were the most intense form of xenophobic violence among the forms that occurred extensively, and hence were least susceptible to reporting biases. I defined major attacks as those involving either attempted arson, storming or besieging the building, injuries, or the flight or evacuation of the residents. Minor attacks typically involved the brief throwing of stones or the firing of a gun loaded with blank ammunition.

werda County on many dimensions. Compared with other localities in the *Land*, the counties of Hoyerswerda and Riesa each had a medium degree of urbanization, an average number of foreigners, a large group of asylum seekers, a large group of right-wing skinheads, similarly high levels of skinhead activity, and local governments effectively controlled by coalitions that included Christian Democrats and Social Democrats.[g] In combining low anti-foreigner violence with these structural features, Riesa is not an unusual case, but rather is representative of many other localities in eastern Germany.[5h] Because these two cases had similar contexts, the many socioeconomic and political institutional factors they shared are unlikely to be causes of the differences in their protests.

Summary of the Protests in the Three Localities

In Hoyerswerda and Rostock, protests were dominated by the militant actions of skinhead youths and their supporters. The peak of the Hoyerswerda conflict involved seven days of rioting that began on 17 September 1991. Attacks continued for four days against foreign contract workers' apartment buildings on Schweitzer Strasse and were followed by three days of crowds massing outside asylum seekers' housing on Müntzer Strasse, about three kilometers distant.[6] At the first location, the attackers used bottles, chains, clubs, baseball bats, and Molotov cocktails, threatened to burn down the building, and said they would continue their attacks until the foreigners had left. At the height of the rioting, fifty to one hundred youths attacked the foreign workers' housing while crowds of five hundred or more adults watched, shouted slogans, chanted, cheered, and hindered police. At this point, the attackers were joined by an additional hundred or more youths, many from the immediate

---

g. In 1992, the counties of Hoyerswerda and Riesa had populations of 101,000 and 89,000, and their largest municipalities had 62,000 and 44,000 residents, respectively. The foreign population in January 1992 was about 800 in Hoyerswerda County (0.8 percent) and 900 in Riesa County (1.0 percent) (data from BLR 1995; Statistisches Landesamt des Freistaates Sachsen; *Sächsische Zeitung*, Hoyerswerda ed. [*SZH*], 8 August 1991; and *SZR*, 31 March 1991).

h. Within Saxony, there was relatively low violence (i.e., no major attacks) against foreigners in 1991–92 in ten out of the nineteen localities (53 percent) that had large skinhead groups, in sixteen out of the twenty-nine localities (55 percent) that had stable or increasing shares of foreigners, and in thirteen out of the twenty-two localities (59 percent) that housed at least fifty asylum seekers by the end of 1993.

neighborhood, who took a supporting role, provoking the foreigners with words and gestures rather than physically attacking them. Throughout the riots, as well as in the weeks before, skinheads formed the driving force in harassing, provoking, and attacking foreigners, and other youths and adult neighbors took their cues from what the skinheads did. The attacks against the foreign workers continued until police massed outside their apartment buildings, at which point the attackers moved on to the asylum shelter at the opposite end of town.

The rioting at the second location, the Hoyerswerda asylum shelter, was less intense and included less active support from adult bystanders than the violence against the foreign workers. Although the crowds were large, ranging from about three hundred the first three nights to between six hundred and a thousand on the last day, those who gathered mainly watched as fifty or more youths attacked the shelter. The attacks against the asylum seekers continued until authorities removed the victims from Hoyerswerda County to undisclosed locations in Saxony.

The Rostock riots were even more severe. The attacks on a *Land*-run asylum shelter[i] in the Lichtenhagen neighborhood of Rostock continued over five nights in August 1992, with up to five hundred attackers led by skinheads and neo-Nazis, many of them from western Germany. Up to three thousand adults stood by, voiced support, and allowed attackers to disappear into their midst. On the third night, youths stormed the shelter and set it on fire, forcing more than one hundred foreign workers to flee.[7]

In these two conflicts, the violence greatly outweighed the small amount of conventional protest that occurred. In Hoyerswerda, nonviolent activity was limited to informal complaints by residents of the asylum shelter and their loud, angry attendance at a public meeting in August 1991.[8] In Rostock, residents merely had informal contacts with a city official.

By contrast, anti-immigration protests in Riesa were small in scale and involved a balance between conventional and militant actions. For most residents, the main form of participation in Riesa was attending a series of meetings with officials concerning the asylum shelter, where residents sometimes raised strong objections. Anti-foreigner militancy and violence were comparatively unimportant in Riesa. During the pe-

---

i. This was the central receiving station for asylum seekers for the *Land* of Mecklenburg-West Pomerania.

riod when such violence was peaking in eastern Germany, in 1991 and 1992, right-wing youths in Riesa County carried out only one very minor, hit-and-run attack against the local asylum shelter. In August 1991, people in a car and a number of motorcycles stopped on the road outside the shelter, and ten of them threw stones and bottles and yelled anti-foreigner slogans for five minutes. There was no property damage, and police were informed only late the next day.[9] Riesa's skinheads aborted a second attempted attack in September 1992, three weeks after the Rostock riots. After thirty to forty youths assembled outside the asylum shelter late one evening, they were met by a large number of police. Police and youths waited for two hours, and then the group of youths dissolved and most of them went home.[10] In both these skinhead actions against the asylum shelter, neighbors provided no public support.[j]

The Limits of Socioeconomic and Organizational Explanations

SOCIOECONOMIC FACTORS

Socioeconomic theories would explain the anti-foreigner violence in Hoyerswerda and Rostock as the result of increased competition for material goods between different ethnic groups. In Chapter 1, I showed that immigration, unemployment, and xenophobic attitudes have little relationship to the location and timing of anti-foreigner violence in Germany as a whole. Here I argue that ethnic competition cannot explain why the conflicts in Hoyerswerda and Rostock became violent and produced large riots, while the conflicts in Riesa and many other eastern German locations were small and largely nonviolent.

In the first place, the riots did not occur in the most economically distressed areas of eastern Germany. Hoyerswerda's unemployment rate was several percentage points below the average for Saxony, and youth unemployment was declining at the time of the riots there, dropping by a third from July through October 1991. Rostock's unemployment rate

---

j. The same was true during a third event, which took place two years after the peak of the anti-immigration movement. On the night of Hitler's birthday in April 1994, during a burst of neo-Nazi activities planned for that day, an unidentified youth threw a Molotov cocktail into the asylum shelter and fled in a car. Shelter residents put out the fire before it could cause much damage, and there were no injuries (*Sächsische Zeitung*, Dresden ed. [*SZD*]; *taz*, 22 April 1994).

was also below average.¹¹ Moreover, differences in economic distress cannot explain the differences between the Hoyerswerda and Riesa conflicts. In the early 1990s, Hoyerswerda and Riesa Counties both experienced a sudden loss of industrial jobs in their narrowly based economies (coal in Hoyerswerda, steel in Riesa). Economic insecurity was very high in both places. In 1991, 32 percent were officially unemployed or on short hours in Riesa, compared with about 22 percent in both categories in Hoyerswerda.¹² Although Riesa County had a higher unemployment rate than Hoyerswerda, this was counterbalanced by greater hopefulness about economic development, since new industrial jobs were planned and expected in Riesa County as early as April 1991.¹³

Furthermore, foreigners posed little competitive threat for jobs or housing in these cases. The foreign contract workers had the most dangerous or dirtiest jobs, which Germans normally were unwilling to take, such as jobs that involved working around phenol in the local coal-processing plant.¹⁴ Asylum seekers in Germany were completely banned from employment until July 1991, and after then they could receive work permits only if it could be shown that no European Community citizen could do the job. In Hoyerswerda, asylum seekers were not even required to do community work in exchange for social assistance, since local officials wanted to reserve these work opportunities for Germans.¹⁵ Thus, although unemployment was rising, there continued to be very little real job competition between the foreigners and the native population in Hoyerswerda. Nonetheless, "foreigners take our jobs away" was a frequent complaint of Hoyerswerda residents, which shows that subjective perceptions of ethnic competition can be produced in the absence of objective competition.

Nor were Hoyerswerda residents threatened by large or rising numbers of foreigners who would compete for housing. The foreign population of Hoyerswerda actually declined during the nine months before the riots, from 1,600 at the beginning of January to about 1,000 (1.7 percent of the city's population) at the beginning of September 1991.ᵏ Although 230 asylum seekers arrived in the spring of 1991, about 800 foreign workers left Hoyerswerda in the months before the riots. In any case, foreigners did not compete with Germans for apartments in Hoyerswerda, which had a housing surplus because of an overall decline in

---

k. The foreign share also declined in the county (data from Ordnungsamt der Stadt Hoyerswerda, July 1997, and author's calculations).

population.[l] Indeed, both the foreign workers and the asylum seekers in Hoyerswerda were living in buildings that had been occupied for years by foreign laborers, not by Germans. The potential for ethnic competition over housing was actually greater in Riesa, where the total number of foreigners was stable during 1991 and housing was scarce, with 3,500 households seeking apartments that year.[16]

SOCIAL MOVEMENT ORGANIZATIONS

Another possible explanation of anti-foreigner violence is that it depends on the organizational strength of right-wing skinhead groups. A loose network of skinhead groups became established in both East and West Germany during the late 1980s. By 1991, they had grown to include 6,500 members, the vast majority younger than twenty-five. The skinheads were especially concentrated in the eastern *Länder,* which had about 3,000 of them, almost half of unified Germany's total, though the East had only about 20 percent of the country's population.[17] The skinhead groups were loosely organized and consisted mainly of working-class teenage and young adult males. They emphasized group loyalty, hostility toward the mainstream adult society, and violence against relatively weak groups, especially foreigners, leftists, and homeless people, with an increasing focus on foreigners in the early 1990s.[18] Although many of them were initially apolitical and a few were leftist, most skinheads in both parts of Germany came under the ideological influence of neo-Nazis by the early 1990s. Aspects of neo-Nazi ideology appealed to the skinheads' distrust and hatred of foreigners and helped strengthen the skinheads' radical nationalism and xenophobia. Neo-Nazis failed to incorporate most skinheads into strongly organized neo-Nazi groups, and the skinheads' actions remained largely independent of neo-Nazi organizations. However, the two kinds of right-wing militants formed a loose alliance based on demands for "Foreigners out!"[19]

The growth of skinhead groups was necessary for violence on the scale experienced from 1991 to 1993, and can help explain the greater rate of violence in the East compared with the West. However, an examination of violence across the eastern *Land* of Saxony shows that the location of strong skinhead organizations was not the decisive factor explaining why some anti-immigration conflicts became violent and others did not. In

---

l. The city had lost 6,000 residents since its population peak of 71,000 in 1981.

Saxony, a large group of skinheads was available[m] in virtually every county and city, as was a significant group of foreigners,[n] yet major attacks such as throwing firebombs or storming foreigners' housing occurred in only about one-third of the localities.[o] In many counties, the largest anti-foreigner attacks were relatively minor actions, such as the firing of blanks at a workers' hostel from a passing car, throwing stones that broke several windows, or other small events not reported in the newspapers.

Of the fourteen localities in Saxony that had large skinhead groups, eight of them, about half the total, had significant violence against foreigners during the period studied. For example, although Hoyerswerda and Riesa both had large, active skinhead groups, only the former experienced significant militancy and violence against foreigners. Hoyerswerda's skinheads consisted of a hard core of about thirty youths who used neo-Nazi symbols and slogans and were prone to violence, and another twenty sympathizers who sometimes took part in actions.[20] In Riesa, there were twenty to thirty-five skinheads, who were about as active as those in Hoyerswerda.[p] Therefore, once conflicts over immigration began in Hoyerswerda and Riesa, large skinhead groups were available to try to make them violent. But in spite of a similar potential for violence, these two conflicts developed very differently.

There are several reasons why the presence of a local skinhead group did not translate directly into major attacks on local foreigners. As the contrast between Hoyerswerda and Riesa will show, some locations presented more favorable political contexts for skinhead violence than others. Moreover, even though skinheads in Saxony almost always attacked within twenty kilometers of where their group was based,[q] this gave them a number of targets to choose from. If the closest asylum shelter or for-

---

m. That is, a skinhead group with at least twenty members was either based in the locality or in an adjoining locality, and hence was within the range that many skinheads traveled in order to attack foreigners (Willems et al. 1993, 137; SIS 1993, 21; Wagner interview).

n. Of fifty-four localities, forty-nine had more than one hundred foreigners at the end of 1991, and forty had more than two hundred foreigners (data from the Zentrale Ausländerbehörde in Saxony and Statistisches Landesamt Sachsen).

o. Major attacks occurred in fifteen cases and were not reported in thirty cases, while nine cases could not be readily classified.

p. Local newspapers reported eleven crimes by skinheads in Riesa over a fifteen-month period in 1991 and 1992, compared with eight crimes in Hoyerswerda.

q. They did so 90 percent of the time (LKAS 1996, 40).

eign workers' housing did not present favorable conditions for an attack, right-wing youths could attack foreigners in a neighboring town or county where police were more passive or adult residents more supportive. Indeed, 30 percent of skinheads arrested in Saxony committed crimes in a locality neighboring the one in which they lived.[21] In addition, they could find other targets, such as homeless people or leftists, as they did in Riesa.

Policy Legacies and Political Institutional Change in the New Eastern *Länder*

Another explanation of the violence in eastern Germany concerns the legacy of communist policies and the rapid institutional changes involved in unification. The legacy of East German policies toward foreigners made protests by German residents against foreigners and immigration more likely in the eastern *Länder* than in western Germany. In the late 1980s and early 1990s only a tiny proportion of the population in the eastern *Länder*, about one percent, were foreigners, most of them laborers from Africa and Vietnam. East German policies actively discouraged and prevented social interaction between foreign contract workers and the German population.[22] Hence, Germans had little contact with foreigners and little experience with cultural differences, creating the potential for intense conflicts over cultural issues.

The lack of contacts between Germans and foreigners in residential areas in the 1980s made conflicts likely after eastern Germans suddenly gained western-style political freedom in 1989. After the hard-liner Erich Honecker resigned in October 1989 and the secret police[r] were dissolved in January 1990, East Germans began to enjoy freedom of expression, association, and assembly. Competitive national and local elections were held in March and May 1990, respectively. In addition, in a major mistake, federal authorities began to distribute 20 percent of new asylum applicants to the eastern *Länder* beginning in December 1990.[s] Twelve thousand asylum seekers arrived in Saxony in 1991,[23] setting the stage for conflicts between them and their German neighbors.

The collapse of communist political institutions and the subsequent

    r. In the Ministry for State Security, known as the Stasi.
    s. This decision was triggered in part by the resistance to asylum shelters mounted by citizen initiatives in western German localities since the late 1970s (see Chapter 4).

unification process also created an institutional vacuum in eastern Germany in the early 1990s. This made violence more likely and nonviolent protests less likely in the eastern *Länder* than in western Germany, without determining the nature of participation in the East. After the East German Communist Party and the secret police were swept away, they were not immediately replaced with institutions that could effectively maintain order and mediate between residents and the state, not even when East and West Germany were unified in October 1990.

With unification, eastern Germany suddenly received formal political institutions largely copied from West Germany, including elected *Land*, county, and town governments. However, state actors were unable to exercise much authority through these new institutions in 1990–91, since local public administration and police forces remained greatly inadequate during those years. Public administration was being reorganized and reduced in size, and local governments suddenly gained self-administration rights.[24] This made nonviolent conflict less likely, since routine access to local officials was often lacking and neither residents nor officials had much experience with democratic political processes.

In particular, the collapse of communism brought with it a temporary collapse in policing capacity. The secret police were dissolved at the start of 1990, and the regular police were demoralized and discredited. In 1990–91, the regular police in eastern Germany consisted of former East German "People's Police"[t] officers who wore their old uniforms. They were on probation until the end of 1991,[u] while they were being retrained and equipped to deal with crime in a society no longer controlled by the Communist Party and the secret police.[25] The police used vehicles and communications equipment that were less modern than some skinheads possessed, and they did not enjoy the confidence of the local population. In September 1991, before the Hoyerswerda riots, 81 percent of eastern Germans thought their police were incompetent.[26] On top of this, the reorganization of the complex police bureaucracy, which had three to four levels of command within Saxony, led to further uncertainty. Hence, policing became much less effective. For example, in Hoyerswerda County, the number of recorded crimes increased from 1,600 in 1989, to 3,800 in 1991, to over 10,000 in 1992, while the proportion of cases solved fell from 80 to 30 percent.[27]

---

t. Deutsche Volkspolizei.
u. In Hoyerswerda, they were on probation until October 1991.

Yet these political challenges cannot explain the differences between the Hoyerswerda and Riesa conflicts, or why riots occurred in only five locations in eastern Germany from 1990 to 1992.[v] In both Hoyerswerda and Riesa, officials faced the major tasks of rebuilding public administration and police forces, coping with rising crime, and responding to rapidly rising unemployment, as well as housing hundreds of asylum seekers who arrived in the spring of 1991. Facing the same tasks, they responded in different ways, which helps explain why these two conflicts took such different forms.

Finally, since the Hoyerswerda and Riesa cases occurred within the same *Land*-level opportunity structure, this cannot explain the differences between the two cases. Both localities lie in Saxony, an industrialized *Land* in the southeastern corner of Germany that borders Poland and the Czech Republic, with a population of 4.8 million in 1991. After the October 1990 *Landtag* elections, the government was controlled by the Christian Democrats, who won 54 percent of the vote and chose the western German politician Kurt Biedenkopf as premier. Besides Soviet military personnel, the *Land* had only 75,000 foreign residents in 1989, who made up 1.5 percent of the population; most of them were foreign laborers. During 1991 and 1992, federal officials distributed 23,000 asylum seekers to Saxony. Both the asylum seekers and the police were under the authority of the Saxony Interior Ministry, which was headed by Rudolf Krause (CDU), a nationalist right-wing politician who became an implicit ally of the militant anti-immigration groups. Krause left the CDU in May 1993 to join the Republicans, an anti-immigration party on the far right.[28] Right-wing militants were very strong in Saxony, where authorities counted six hundred right-wing skinheads and three hundred neo-Nazis in 1993, about double and triple the per capita averages for Germany, respectively.[29] In 1991–93 police in Saxony reported ninety-six arson attacks and assaults against foreigners, resulting in sixty-five injuries, which gave this *Land* one of the highest per-capita rates of right-wing violence in Germany.[30]

Authorities' Mistakes and Cultural Threats

Protests in Hoyerswerda and Rostock became very large partly because authorities made mistakes in how they housed foreigners, leading to

---

v. Nor can it explain why riots in four of those locations, including Rostock, did not occur until August and September 1992 (Karapin 2000, 321), well after the institutional vacuum was at its greatest.

major cultural conflicts between them and their German neighbors. Foreign contract workers, mostly men from Mozambique and Vietnam without families in Germany, had lived in Hoyerswerda County on three-year contracts since the early 1980s. They worked in a large plant producing coke and gas from brown coal, and in brown coal strip mines. Although their overall numbers had declined by almost half since the beginning of the year, about eight hundred contract workers were still in Hoyerswerda County in the summer of 1991.[31] About a hundred Mozambican and thirty Vietnamese workers were living in housing on Schweitzer Strasse at the time of the riots.[32] The decline in contract workers was partially offset by the arrival of 230 asylum seekers from over twenty nationalities, mainly from Romania, the former Yugoslavia, and Ghana. In the spring of 1991, county and city authorities decided to move the asylum seekers into a building on Müntzer Strasse in the city of Hoyerswerda.[33]

Local officials' policies toward the foreigners greatly aggravated the cultural conflicts between them and German residents. Both the foreign workers and the asylum seekers were housed in groups of over a hundred, which concentrated behaviors that many Germans found offensive or threatening. Moreover, officials housed both groups in the high-density Neustadt section, a maze of unadorned high-rises, which further intensified the problems between them and their neighbors. Some Germans lived in the same twelve-story apartment complex as the foreign workers, and many others lived in adjoining or nearby buildings.

The close proximity of Germans' and foreigners' housing helped create large cultural conflicts between these two groups.[w] In the early 1990s, the main complaints by Germans about foreign workers and asylum seekers in Hoyerswerda concerned loud late-night music, garbage, and reckless driving. Other complaints concerned sexual relations between foreign men and German girls or women.[34] Conflicts over noise were exacerbated by the fact that the Germans tended to work during the day, while many foreign laborers worked late shifts, and the asylum seekers had much time on their hands since they were not permitted to work at all. Small-scale conflicts between Germans and foreign workers had occurred since the 1980s, but open conflicts were largely suppressed until after the East German state collapsed and civil liberties were effectively introduced in 1989 and 1990.[35] Suddenly, the German residents of

w. Germans' resentment of foreigners in Hoyerswerda dated back to the 1970s and 1980s, when Hungarian, Polish, Algerian, Mozambican, and Vietnamese workers were housed there. Some East Europeans were paid in Western currency, a source of keen resentment, and some were said to be sexually involved with German women and girls.

Hoyerswerda could express their dissatisfaction with foreigners much more freely.

In 1991, these cultural clashes led directly to both nonviolent and violent protests against foreigners. Complaints by neighbors about the asylum shelter led to a public meeting in August 1991, at which the neighbors angrily described noise that began in the evening and went until 3:30 a.m., as well as nightly "car rallies" and other problems.[36] The riots against the foreign workers' housing began immediately after the foreigners, preparing to leave for their countries of origin, held a farewell party that bothered their German neighbors, who described the noise as especially loud. A few days later these neighbors formed the bulk of the crowds that participated in the first nights of rioting.

In a similar way, housing policy mistakes in Rostock led to intense cultural conflicts between several hundred asylum seekers, mainly Gypsies, and their German neighbors, and the conflicts fueled both nonviolent protests and riots. The Rostock-Lichtenhagen asylum shelter was badly overcrowded at times beginning in the summer of 1991. At one point, six hundred people were assigned to a building with three hundred beds, which forced up to two hundred Gypsies to live outdoors near the shelter.[37] In 1991 Rostock's mayor complained about the overcrowding to the *Land* Interior Ministry, which had jurisdiction over the asylum shelter, but the Ministry permitted overcrowding to continue. Beginning in May 1991, German residents complained about noise, begging, drinking, gambling on the street, and defecation on the lawns.[38] These concerns led neighbors to contact Rostock officials repeatedly, and later led between one and three thousand adult residents to participate in the August 1992 riots.

The influx of asylum seekers also posed cultural threats to Riesa residents. Two hundred sixty asylum seekers from at least twelve countries arrived in Riesa County in May 1991. In addition, Riesa had been home to foreign contract workers since the 1980s, when the East German state brought hundreds of workers to Riesa from Mozambique, Vietnam, and Angola. During 1991, the total foreign population of Riesa County rose slightly from 860 to 890, including the asylum seekers, making up about one percent of the population.[39] Conflicts between Germans and asylum seekers occurred over issues such as begging by Gypsy children in the streets, illegal trading by Vietnamese, and the theft of car radios, which were later found in the asylum shelter.[40]

Although reported in the local newspaper, these conflicts remained comparatively small and did not spur major protests against the asylum seekers. One reason is that authorities housed the new arrivals in ways that reduced the potential for friction. Riesa County officials housed the 260 asylum seekers, along with 200 ethnic German resettlers, in two buildings containing former workers' barracks on the edge of Zeithain, a town of 4,500 people about five kilometers from the city of Riesa.[41] The low density of this neighborhood may explain why there were no reports that neighbors complained of excessive noise from the asylum shelter.

Making Alliances Between Adult Residents and Militant Youths

As in the cases of leftist protest, alliances between different kinds of protesters were crucial for the development of large, unconventional protests in Hoyerswerda and Rostock. In Hoyerswerda, militant skinheads and adult German residents who lived near the foreign workers' housing formed an alliance based on the common goal of removing the foreigners. A frequent demand during the Hoyerswerda riots was "Foreigners out!" This demand was seen in graffiti and newspaper headlines. It was also heard in slogans propagated by skinheads and repeated by local residents in chants, spontaneous shouts, and interviews with reporters. The alliance between skinheads and adult Germans had begun well before the September 1991 riots. In May 1990, skinheads rioted against the foreign workers' housing, supported by up to fifteen hundred spectators.[42] Comments made by residents at the citizen forum in August 1991 show that adult residents approved of skinhead attacks on foreigners. In Riesa, there was no such alliance between young militants and adult residents, and that greatly undercut the chances for large militant protests.

The alliance between young militants and adults became very public on the first three nights of the Hoyerswerda riots, when hundreds of adult Germans actively encouraged attacks and passively interfered with the police trying to contain the situation. On the first night, while forty youths attacked the foreign laborers' housing on Schweitzer Strasse, many adult spectators gathered. In loud conversations, they insulted the police and demanded that they act against the Mozambicans inside the building.[43] On the third night, four to six hundred spectators, mostly neighbors of the foreigners, gathered, hindered the police, and called loudly for the German youths to burn down the building. Some spectators, led by skinheads, even fought against police.⁴⁴ Similarly, on the second night of rioting in Rostock, three thousand people watched, chanted anti-foreigner slogans, and applauded while five hundred youths attacked the asylum shelter with stones and Molotov cocktails.⁴⁵ In both cities, the adults' supportive actions greatly increased the intensity and duration of the violence. They also created a symbolically powerful backdrop for photographs and television reports of the rioting, which in turn greatly amplified the national effects of the violence.

This kind of open alliance between skinhead youths and adult residents was quite unusual. There was no such alliance in Riesa, where neighbors of the asylum shelter did not assemble at any of the skinhead actions against the shelter or otherwise provide public support for the "Foreigners out!" demand. Since they lacked public support for anti-foreigner violence, the skinheads did not attack foreigners in Riesa consistently or forcefully, and preferred instead to attack leftists or damage public property.ˣ Even at the Müntzer Strasse conflict in Hoyerswerda the alliance was much weaker than it was at the Schweitzer Strasse conflict, and this led to weaker attacks against the asylum seekers than against the foreign contract workers in that city.

Creating Access to Public Officials

The alliance patterns in Hoyerswerda and Riesa were different partly because of differences in the degree to which public officials set up procedures to routinely communicate with residents after conflicts began. Where residents gained easier access to officials, conventional participation was encouraged, official responsiveness was enhanced, and adult residents' support for militant actions was undercut. But in Hoyerswerda in 1991, resident participation mechanisms, such as public hearings, public dialogues between residents and officials, and well-publicized city

---

x. They were very active. In 1990–92, right-wing youths from Riesa injured five punk-rockers in a youth club, beat up a punk-rocker and injured many people in a bar, attacked a man from western Germany and a young couple, painted swastikas on buildings, shouted "Sieg Heil!" in discos, damaged train and bus stations, brawled in a disco and near soccer matches, desecrated a Soviet cemetery, sang a Nazi song and damaged a monument to the victims of Nazism, painted anti-foreigner graffiti, punched children at a soccer game, appeared on national television with Nazi symbols, and fought with leftists. In 1995, one of their leaders was stabbed to death in a fight with a seventeen-year-old leftist in a right-wing bar (*SZR*, various dates; *taz*, 9 January 1995).

or county council meetings, remained very limited. During all of 1991, there were no public meetings concerning the foreign workers' housing and only one concerning the asylum shelter, and that was not held until several months after the shelter opened.

By contrast, Riesa's officials made it easy for residents to participate in conventional ways.[y] Before the Zeithain asylum shelter was opened, officials initiated dialogues with residents in an effort to defuse opposition to the asylum seekers. They held at least four meetings with residents to discuss the issue and also discussed foreigners at a public county council meeting.[46][z] The first of these meetings was held in March 1991, two months before officials opened the asylum shelter. Residents sometimes expressed strong opposition at these meetings. Officials and two hundred soldiers engaged in a heated five-hour discussion about asylum seekers, crime, and border security in a meeting at the Zeithain army base. At a meeting held at the asylum shelter, a *Landtag* deputy called for "respectful coexistence," putting responsibility both on German residents to be more accepting of foreign mentalities and customs, and on foreigners to take account of the laws and customs of their host country.[47]

In Riesa, the public officials' approach to informing and meeting with residents made it likely that Germans who experienced cultural conflicts with the asylum seekers would have approached the county employees managing the shelter, the police, or the elected officials of Zeithain or Riesa County. Officials, in turn, probably would have found ways to reduce potential conflicts, just as they did by siting the shelter in a low-density area in the first place. Hence, the accessibility of local officials probably reduced the likelihood that adult residents would become dissatisfied enough to support militant actions.

Furthermore, many youths in Riesa were involved in local politics, which reduced their willingness to support the skinhead groups.[aa] For

---

y. In Riesa, it was normal for officials to hold hearings and discussions on a wide range of local public policy issues. In 1991 alone, the local press reported on seventeen public assemblies or open meetings between officials and citizens, five demonstrations, three petitions, and two founding meetings in Riesa (*SZR*, various dates in 1991). The contrast with Hoyerswerda was great. In the same period, Hoyerswerda's local newspapers reported only four assemblies, two demonstrations, and one petition.

z. Two of the meetings were led by Heiner Sandig (CDU), a *Landtag* deputy and its omsbudsperson for foreigner affairs, and another was held at the Zeithain shelter by a *Landtag* deputy from the Party of Democratic Socialism.

aa. In addition, municipal youth clubs maintained and extended their services in 1991, compared with the cuts and partial privatization they suffered in Hoyerswerda

example, in November 1991, youths carried out street protests and collected one thousand signatures on a petition for the retention of a youth radio station that the eastern *Länder* were considering shutting down. As part of this campaign, the Riesa youth clubs organized a music party attended by a city councillor and a representative of the city's Youth Department.[48bb] Routine political interactions between youths and the city government made many of Riesa's youths comfortable talking with local officials.[49] This did not prevent thirty youths from joining a violent local skinhead group, but it did hinder others from joining the skinhead actions, which never involved more than forty participants. By contrast, one or two hundred youths sometimes assembled to menace foreigners under the leadership of the Hoyerswerda skinheads.

A partial exception to the usual pattern in Hoyerswerda also shows the importance of residents gaining access to officials and winning concessions. At a late date, local officials gave some access to neighbors of the asylum shelter on Müntzer Strasse and began to adopt reforms. This began to steer the neighbors toward conventional protests and to produce policy reforms, which in turn prevented a strong conventional-militant alliance and reduced the intensity of militant actions in this Hoyerswerda neighborhood. In late August 1991, city councillors hastily organized a citizen forum to deal with conflicts surrounding the asylum shelter. This heated, two-hour meeting was attended by seventy people, who complained of late-night noise, reckless driving, children begging, and asylum seekers digging in the garbage. Officials emphasized that the shelter's neighbors would have to learn to live with the asylum seekers and accept the laws of unified Germany, but they also offered to try to reduce the problems for the neighbors. The mayor offered to see if additional police patrols were possible, and a county official suggested adding a second night-time counselor to the shelter and creating a committee of residents and asylum seekers. Officials also promised to meet again with residents a month later.[50]

At this citizen forum, local officials also improved the procedures for routine communication about problems between shelter residents and their neighbors. Officials told the shelter's neighbors how to get the authorities to deal with legal violations such as excessive noise. Before the

---

before the riots (*SZR*, 1 March, 17 December 1991, 23 November 1992; Specht 1992, 55).

bb. Jugendamt.

August meeting, most residents of Hoyerswerda did not understand where or how to make their complaints, nor why their complaints to the police led to no action.[51] In the East German system, such complaints went directly to the police, but after unification, legal violations needed to be reported first to the City Clerk's Office.[cc] Moreover, reports now needed to be directed against the residents of specific apartments rather than against a building as a whole. By contrast, there were no public meetings for the Germans who lived near the foreign workers on Schweitzer Strasse, even though officials knew that there were long-running conflicts between these groups. Hence, residents in that area did not learn how to make more effective complaints about their foreign neighbors, and they did not come to see nonviolent protest as a potentially effective form of participation.

This helps explain why adult neighbors gave much more support to the rioting outside the foreign workers' housing on Schweitzer Strasse than they did outside the asylum shelter on Müntzer Strasse. The crowd outside the Schweitzer Strasse apartments, consisting mainly of adult neighbors, chanted slogans such as "Foreigners out!" and "Burn the shack down!"[52] One night, four hundred German neighbors hindered police to the extent that the latter finally distributed fifteen hundred leaflets asking for the residents' cooperation.[53] By contrast, on Müntzer Strasse, neighbors of the asylum shelter gave much less support to the skinheads when they began to attack the shelter, and this helped limit the severity of skinhead violence at that location. The actions against the asylum seekers mainly took the form of a siege and threats rather than the kind of heavy, regular violence that skinheads had directed against the foreign workers on consecutive nights.[54] The spectators at the Müntzer Strasse attacks seldom applauded or cheered, and they did not chant, call for violence, or interfere with police. Indeed, the asylum shelter conflict might have remained largely nonviolent, if skinheads and crowds of supporting spectators had not first mobilized at the foreigners' housing and then moved to the asylum shelter.

Gaining Allies Among Public Officials

Another reason that the protests in Rostock and Hoyerswerda became so large is that initial protests led some public officials to express support

---

cc. Ordnungsamt.

for removing foreigners, which increased opponents' chances of success and encouraged them to mobilize further. In Rostock, neighbors who protested the shelter gained an overt ally in Peter Magdanz (SPD), the head of the city's Interior Department.*dd* Magdanz called publicly for the asylum shelter to be moved to another neighborhood, and raised hopes that this would happen by September 1992.[55] Yet the Rostock shelter, under the control of *Land* officials, remained open and overcrowded. A similar dynamic may have influenced the Hoyerswerda riots. At a citizen forum held in Hoyerswerda one month before the riots, acting mayor Klaus Naumann (SPD) told an angry crowd that he would talk with other officials about possibly moving the asylum seekers and would hold another meeting a month later, at the end of September 1991.[56] He thereby opened the possibility of getting the asylum seekers out of the neighborhood, inadvertently raising the opponents' perceived chances of success,*ee* which may have helped embolden the skinheads who started the Hoyerswerda riots. However, this does not explain why they attacked the foreign workers first, rather than the asylum seekers.

By contrast, public officials opened no opportunities for protesters in Riesa, which helped limit all kinds of anti-immigration protests there. Local officials in Riesa were unified behind a pro-foreigner position, and they gave no public support to opponents of the asylum shelter. Beginning in January 1991, county and city officials and *Landtag* deputies initiated an information campaign that was designed to reduce prejudices and gain the German residents' acceptance of asylum seekers and ethnic German resettlers in Riesa County. They caused several informative articles about asylum seekers to appear in the local newspaper in early 1991,[57] and held a series of public meetings. The proactive approach of local officials in Riesa, combined with vigorous policing, made it clear that the immigration issue was the authorities' domain and not the skinheads', and that there was no realistic chance of getting the asylum seekers removed from Riesa County.

Police Practices

Perhaps the most important difference between Hoyerswerda and Riesa was in police practices. Extreme police passivity made large riots possible

---

dd. Magdanz was the *Innensenator*.

ee. Ironically, Naumann clearly sympathized with the foreigners and was the only city official who tried to quell the mob during the riots.

in Hoyerswerda, as well as in Rostock, while the high level of carefully targeted police activity against skinheads in Riesa sharply limited antiforeigner violence there.

In Hoyerswerda, police did little in the face of rising skinhead activity for almost a year before the September 1991 riots. In the winter of 1990–91, skinheads gained visibility and public acceptance through vigilante activities that were tolerated by the police and welcomed by many Germans. While crime was rapidly rising, a thirty-year-old ex-convict formed a group of about ten skinheads called the New German Order,[ff] which was affiliated with the large neo-Nazi organization German Alternative.[gg] The New German Order patrolled Hoyerswerda streets, offered fearful women rides home late at night, took action against burglars and auto thieves, and sometimes handed them over to the police.[58]

Hoyerswerda police were also very passive when skinheads attacked foreigners. When thirty-five youths attacked a Mozambicans' dwelling on German Unity Day in October 1990, police did not intervene decisively for several hours. Nor did police respond when assaults on foreigners increased in the week before the September 1991 riots, when more than a dozen attacks were reported to them.[59] While skinheads were learning that they could attack foreigners with near impunity, many adult German residents came to see the skinheads' methods as the most effective ones for "doing something about the foreigners."[60] Some Hoyerswerda residents even came to see the skinheads as an alternative to the police. At the public meeting in August, local politicians felt compelled to publicly rule out relying on the skinheads as a possible solution to "the problem of the asylum seekers." Given the police passivity toward the skinheads, several highly publicized police actions in July 1991, against Vietnamese cigarette dealers and against Romanian men accused of raping a sixteen-year-old girl, conveyed the impression that the police were, if anything, on the side of the anti-immigration forces in Hoyerswerda.[61]

Finally, the intense rioting in Hoyerswerda and Rostock was possible because police and other authorities greatly facilitated violence with their extraordinary passivity. Hoyerswerda police did not seriously interfere with the assault against the foreign workers' housing on the first few nights of rioting in September, even though over forty skinheads were using Molotov cocktails and iron bars. A force level of one hundred police

ff. Neue Deutsche Ordnung.
gg. Deutsche Alternative.

officers was not reached until the third night of rioting, and the foreign workers' housing was not cordoned off until the fourth day. Eyewitnesses reported that "the police stand around, walk by, and do nothing" and that "the police seem scared."⁶² An early, decisive crackdown probably would have greatly reduced the scale of the rioting, since police were effective when they were deployed on the fifth and sixth days of rioting, and they had been effective during a one-day riot in May 1990.⁶³

This extreme failure of policing was due in part to general difficulties caused by the rapid collapse of the communist system. However, the failure of Hoyerswerda's police was also due to the lack of a will to intervene decisively in order to protect foreigners against skinheads who were supported by crowds of Germans. This lack of will was apparent in the local commanders, their superiors, and political authorities at *Land* and local levels. In particular, *Land* Interior Minister Rudolf Krause (CDU) often downplayed right-wing violence and was obviously uninterested in protecting foreigners.*ʰʰ* As crime rose during the summer of 1991 and police were criticized for colluding with neo-Nazi vigilantes in Dresden, the *Land* capital, Krause emphasized that Saxony should not become a police state.⁶⁴ In Hoyerswerda, he favored an evacuation of the foreigners rather than a crackdown on skinheads. Even on the fourth day of the riots, with the police still in a passive posture, Krause announced in Hoyerswerda that he wanted to avoid a large police action, and that asylum seekers should be fenced in or evacuated to an army building in a neighboring county.⁶⁵ After the riots, Krause was immediately replaced and the new interior minister began a crackdown on the far right.*ⁱⁱ* For their part, Hoyerswerda officials failed to respond to a police request for a ban on public assemblies, and the city's mayor, Armin Arendt (CDU), a recently elected western German, could not be found by police all week long.⁶⁶

Deliberate police passivity was, if this is possible, even more evident in the Rostock riots. Just before violence began there, senior police officials ignored specific warnings of an attack that had been made in anonymous phone calls and in two newspaper articles, and they drove to their homes

---

hh. The interior minister of Mecklenburg-West Pomerania, Lothar Kupfer (CDU), took similar positions during the Rostock riots (*taz*, 25 August 1992).

ii. Under the new minister, Heinz Eggert (CDU), the Special Commission for Right-Wing Extremism of the Saxony police (SOKO REX), which was created in July 1991, became very active. It carried out about six hundred searches, investigated about nine hundred suspects, and solved over 85 percent of its cases in its first eighteen months of work (*taz*, 2 October 1991; LKAS 1992a, 53).

in western Germany for the weekend instead. Hence, at first only thirty to fifty police officers were on hand, and they were overwhelmed by the 150 German youths who came to attack the shelter.[67] Police then permitted a siege of the asylum shelter, in which 230 people were housed, for three nights. The crucial interaction came on the third night, when police forces evacuated most but not all of the asylum seekers and then retreated. The police retreat allowed 70 youths to set fire to the nearly empty asylum shelter, along with adjacent apartments that housed over 100 Vietnamese workers.[68] The buildings burned for two hours before police finally cleared the way for firefighters, and the foreign workers were forced to flee over the rooftops.[69] A police commander on the scene later told an investigating panel that his superior had ordered him away, because "the police had an agreement with the rowdies and were supposed to keep their distance."[70]

Police practices could not have been more different in Riesa. Police there acted decisively against right-wing youths almost every time the latter threatened or engaged in large-scale violence. In 1991 alone, police in Riesa prevented rioting by large numbers of right-wing youths on seven occasions.[71] Police were quickly present on the scene, and sometimes had prepared in advance for their interventions. When the asylum shelter was approached by right-wing youths late in the evening in September 1992, the police were quickly present with a large force, which prevented any attempt at violence. The police did not allow Riesa's skinheads to undertake vigilantism or to dominate the streets during any period. Unable to act effectively against the asylum shelter, Riesa's skinheads sought victims in bars and discos, where the police were more reserved and the managers had limited ability to maintain order.[72]

The response of the Riesa police shows that an appropriate police strategy could overcome the institutional and social problems of policing in the eastern *Länder*. The Riesa police had all the difficulties typical of eastern German police forces. After unification, they confronted high and dramatically increasing general crime rates, which in 1992 reached the same level as in Hoyerswerda. The rate at which crimes were solved was similarly low in the two counties.[73] But the Riesa police were effective in the two priority areas in which they focused their resources: investigating murders and repressing crimes by right-wing youths.[74]

Because police leaders were interested in combating right-wing crime, the officers learned how to deal with it much earlier and more thoroughly than the police in Hoyerswerda. For example, in October 1990, Riesa police were hesitant to intervene in a youth club fight, fearing, they said, that they would lose their jobs if they made a mistake, since they were on probation until near the end of 1991. But after that club fight, even while they were still on probation, there were five more occasions when the police de-escalated fighting or prevented rioting by large numbers of youths in 1991. In addition, police leaders in Riesa were very open and communicative with the press and called on the public for cooperation.[jj]

The Timing of Concessions to Violence

Finally, the riots proved that violence was much more effective than nonviolent forms of participation. In Hoyerswerda, local and *Land* officials immediately gave in to the "Foreigners out!" demands.[kk] Authorities had the remaining foreign contract workers removed on the fifth day of the attacks and the remaining asylum seekers on the seventh day, while a thousand spectators applauded the departing buses.[75] No substantial numbers of asylum seekers were housed in Hoyerswerda during the rest of the 1990s, despite the *Land* government's stated policy of distributing asylum seekers across all localities. In addition, the Hoyerswerda riots and other anti-foreigner violence greatly reduced the number of asylum seekers in Saxony. An estimated six to ten thousand asylum seekers in Saxony had fled to western Germany by April 1992, and federal officials diverted some ten thousand asylum seekers intended for Saxony to other *Länder*. This reduced the numbers of asylum seekers in the *Land* to only about one-third of its quota.[76] Similarly, in the Lichtenhagen neighborhood of Rostock, about 230 residents of the asylum shelter were evacuated to shelters in other parts of the city on the third day of the attacks. The Lichtenhagen shelter was not reopened, and officials replaced it with a new asylum shelter in an army barracks in a distant Rostock neighborhood.[77]

Violence also increased the anti-immigration movement's chances of success in federal politics. Federal politicians responded to the riots by accelerating their debate on asylum rights.[78] Moreover, federal officials,

---

jj. For example, after one failed action in a bar, a police officer wrote a newspaper article in which he admitted that the police needed to reassess their approach (*SZR*, 13 March 1991).

kk. Nonetheless, several hundred foreigners continued to live in Hoyerswerda, though not in large, visible groups.

like many *Land* and local authorities, refused to crack down on right-wing militants. The federal prosecutor,[ll] Alexander von Stahl (Liberal Party), admitted the Hoyerswerda attacks had a "radical-right background," but he argued that such attacks were not organized by right-wing extremists and hence did not fall under his office's jurisdiction. Similarly, he emphasized nonpolitical motives for the Rostock attackers, such as frustration and rebellion against parents.[79]

This set of official responses—toleration of violence and concessions to it—encouraged attacks against foreigners immediately after the Hoyerswerda and Rostock riots in hundreds of locations in eastern and western Germany.[80] According to police data, right-wing attacks against persons, which had averaged about 50 per month during the three months before the Hoyerswerda riots, shot up to an average of about 145 per month for the next three months, including a total of 260 arson attacks against foreigners' housing. Similarly, right-wing attacks increased from an average of about 45 per month during the three months before the Rostock riots to an average of about 200 per month in the two months afterward, with arson attacks rising from 20 to 125 per month, mostly against asylum seekers.[81]

Concessions to earlier violence also underlay surges in violence beginning in November 1992 and May 1993, though the actors and dynamics were somewhat different than after the riots. In these two instances, federal politicians made what seemed to be major concessions to earlier waves of violence. Social Democratic leaders finally endorsed a constitutional restriction on asylum rights in mid-November 1992, in response to the months of violence that followed the Rostock riots. Later, as a delayed result of the shift in the SPD's position, the Bundestag and Bundesrat passed the constitutional amendment in May 1993. Each of these major concessions was followed by a dramatic, widely publicized arson attack by skinheads against Turkish guest workers, in Mölln (November 1992) and Solingen (May 1993), both in western Germany. Each of those attacks, in turn, triggered a wave of attacks by skinheads and neo-Nazis in many places in Germany.[82]

Violence escalated partly because the federal government, led by Chancellor Helmut Kohl (CDU), failed to crack down on anti-foreigner violence until after the arson murders of a Turkish guest worker family in Mölln in late November 1992. The Mölln murders led the govern-

ll. Generalbundesanwalt.

ments of Turkey, the United States, and Israel to strongly criticize the German government, and they also sparked massive demonstrations against right-wing violence throughout Germany, which mobilized about 2.9 million people in fifty-four demonstrations over three months.[83] In response, the federal government took some mainly symbolic but highly publicized measures, including federal prosecution of the Mölln arsonists, banning and raiding some neo-Nazi organizations, and Chancellor Kohl's attendance at a pro-foreigner demonstration. During this period, public opinion also began to turn away from support for right-wing extremism and violence. From October 1992 to January 1993, those sympathizing with forceful aggression against asylum seekers declined from 17 percent to 8 percent in the eastern *Länder*. National approval of the far-right Republicans also declined sharply, from about 8 percent to at most 4 percent during this period.[84] The federal actions and shift in public opinion made *Land* police and judges willing to act more vigorously against xenophobic violence. In 1993, police arrested a higher proportion of suspects than in 1992, and prosecutors and judges sought long sentences against perpetrators in high-profile cases such as Mölln.[85]

Summary and Conclusions

Why did large anti-immigration protests occur in Hoyerswerda and Rostock, but not in Riesa? Large protests were promoted in the two riot cases partly because authorities made mistakes in housing policy and hence greatly exacerbated cultural threats (see Table 3 on pages 222–23). Local officials in Hoyerswerda housed foreigners in dense urban areas, and *Land* officials repeatedly allowed overcrowding at the Rostock shelter, leading to severe conflicts between asylum seekers and German neighbors in both cases. In Riesa, officials avoided a major potential mistake when they sited the shelter in a low-density neighborhood, thus reducing potential cultural conflicts.

But at least as important were the daring actions by skinheads and the effective division of labor that they formed with crowds of adult residents in the riot cases. Another, relatively minor, factor consisted of elite allies for protesters in those cases. Once again, Riesa was the polar opposite. Adult residents gave no support to skinheads, elites gave no public support to residents opposed to the asylum shelter, and hence anti-immigration protests of all kinds were very limited there. In short, state-mediated cultural threats and opportunity-expansion processes, rather than ethnic competition over material goods, explain why protests were massive in Hoyerswerda and Rostock, while in Riesa only a handful of meetings and weak militant actions against the asylum seekers occurred.

Even though all three locations had foreigners, cultural conflicts between them and their German neighbors, and active skinhead groups, their anti-immigration protests took very different forms. Why did rioting predominate over conventional participation in Hoyerswerda and Rostock? Conventional protests were limited in the two riot cases because officials there either offered little routine access for protesters, as at Hoyerswerda-Schweitzer Strasse (see Table 4 on page 229), or granted only some last-minute access, as at Hoyerswerda-Müntzer Strasse.

Moreover, in the riot cases, the strong shift to militant actions was due to the blockage of reforms and the alliances that developed among different kinds of protest groups. As cultural threats continued, with either no reforms (Hoyerswerda-Schweitzer Strasse) or inadequate reforms (Rostock), adult residents in Hoyerswerda and Rostock shifted to a strategy of supporting militant actions. They became willing to support skinhead youths, and ultimately they assembled in massive, chanting, cheering crowds that encouraged the skinheads and discouraged and interfered with police interventions. Hoyerswerda-Müntzer Strasse is a partially contrasting case, with some important official concessions to the citizen forum in August 1991 and a reasonable expectation that more reforms might be forthcoming through conventional protests. Therefore, adult neighbors of that shelter gave less support to militant actions than occurred at Schweitzer Strasse and in Rostock. Riesa presents a complete contrast, since officials created smaller threats through the siting of the shelter and gave residents much routine access to discuss their concerns about the asylum shelter. Hence, adult neighbors gave no public support to the skinheads.

Another, crucial reason for the riots was the extremely passive response by police and local authorities when militants began to threaten and attack foreigners in Hoyerswerda and Rostock. Police had too few officers, did not act against the attackers, and indeed seemed to intentionally tolerate the attacks. This made it much easier for the skinheads to attack dramatically and repeatedly, and for adults to support them. In Riesa, by contrast, police acted decisively on many occasions to prevent skinhead violence, especially against foreigners.

Why did local political interactions favoring anti-foreigner riots develop in cities in eastern, and not western, Germany during the first two years after unification? Why were the waves of attacks on asylum shelters in 1991–92 especially strong in the East, despite its tiny foreign population share? The local processes that led to the riots in Hoyerswerda and Rostock were rooted in major problems created by national policy failures in East Germany and by the unification process.[86] The legacies of communist-era policies toward foreigners and the multiple problems involved in unification made it less likely that local and *Land* officials would respond to emerging problems. Hence, in the eastern *Länder*, intense cultural conflicts were more likely, local officials were less likely to grant routine access and adopt reforms, and police were less likely to act vigorously against anti-foreigner violence than in the western *Länder*.

And yet the violence in eastern Germany was also the result of frequent failures by local officials and politicians to cope with the problems they faced. The absence of major anti-foreigner violence in Riesa and in many other places in eastern Germany shows that the general conditions that characterized the eastern *Länder* in the early 1990s did not necessarily lead to violent conflicts. Indeed, local actors had much scope to reduce conflicts, steer them into nonviolent forms, and limit violence.

6 CONCLUSIONS

In the previous four chapters, I have analyzed nine case studies, which span three different policy areas, both left-wing and right-wing movements, and protests in the eastern and western *Länder*. I have looked for common elements that can explain why large, influential protests occurred in such varied social and institutional settings, and have tried to discover why very different kinds of protest developed in similar settings. This chapter begins with a comparative summary of the nine cases. To what extent did political interactions shape the protests in these cases, and were some interactions more important than others? In the next section, I turn to a comparison of leftist and rightist protests. Why did rightist protests involve very little nonviolent disruption and so much militancy, when compared with those on the left? The third section addresses a deeper question: Were these political interactions really driven by socioeconomic factors and political institutions, or were they substantially independent of them? Finally, how can protest groups, politicians, and public officials steer conflicts away from militancy and toward nonviolent forms?

Comparative Summary

EXPLAINING LARGE PROTESTS

The cases in this book varied greatly in the size and duration of protests, which permits assessing how well political interactions account for the differences. In Table 3, I have divided Kreuzberg into two cases (1969–76 and 1976–95), which produces a total of ten cases for the analysis here. These include six cases of large protests, of which four were long-lived movements (Hanover-Linden, Berlin-Kreuzberg in 1976–95, Wyhl, and Brokdorf) and two were large but brief campaigns (Hoyerswerda and Rostock). They also include two cases of small protests (Kronshagen and Riesa), and two intermediate cases (Kreuzberg in 1969–76 and Munich-Südpark).[a] The main conclusion from analyzing these ten cases is that large protests depended on mutually reinforcing actions by protesters, elites, and authorities. Large state threats, bold protest actions, alliances between protesters with complementary strategies, support from elites, policy intransigence, ill-timed procedural reforms, and mistakes in policing are close to being necessary conditions for large protests. Since most of these factors were present in the large protests and absent in the smaller ones, it is difficult to weigh the separate contribution of each factor.[b] These factors tend to occur together because they reinforce each other, in a variety of ways, some of which are suggested by the roughly chronological organization of the factors in the case chapters. Interactions between actors, more than intentional actions by particular actors, affected the course of protest.

Yet unpopular government policies always preceded mobilization by protesters and their allies. Could threats arising from state actions be the most important causes of large protests, driving the other variables? Indeed, such threats are closely related to both the size and the duration of protest. Kreuzberg, Wyhl, and Brokdorf had the largest and longest threats to residents, with policies directly affecting tens of thousands of people over more than a decade, and these cases also had the largest and longest protests.[c] By contrast, the asylum shelters in Kronshagen and Riesa were either small, modified to reduce conflicts with neighbors, or sited in low-density neighborhoods. In these relatively low-threat cases, protesters did not use daring tactics, alliances between protest groups did not develop, and elites did not support protesters. By contrast, all those

---

a. The intermediate cases involved protests that were larger and longer than Kronshagen and Riesa but smaller and shorter than the four long-lived movements and smaller than the anti-foreigner riots.

b. This is partly a product of the research design, which was geared more to explaining differences in the types of participation than in the size of protests.

c. In Linden, threats and protests over a twenty-year period were large, but, after 1973, they were smaller than those in Kreuzberg.

CONCLUSIONS 221

Table 3. Explaining the Size and Duration of Protests in Ten Cases*

Case	Bold protest actions	Protest group alliances	Elite support	Authorities' mistakes about policy reforms	Policing mistakes	Protest size and approximate duration
			Large protests			
Hanover-Linden	Squats	Conventional-disruptive	Major	Major but brief intransigence and procedural reforms	None	Large; 20 years
Berlin-Kreuzberg (1976–95)*	Squats	Conventional-disruptive-militant	Major	Long intransigence and procedural reforms	Passivity (squats) and overreaction (raids, arrests)	Very large; 20 years
Wyhl	Construction site occupation	Conventional-disruptive	Major	Long intransigence and procedural reforms	Overreaction (first occupation) and passivity (second occupation)	Very large; 9 years
Brokdorf	Attempts to occupy construction site	Disruptive-militant	Major (though not by local elites)	Long intransigence and procedural access	Overreaction to demonstrations	Very large; 12 years
Hoyerswerda	Vigilantism, riots	Conventional-militant	Minor	major but brief intransigence	Extreme passivity during riots	Very large; 2 years
Rostock	Riots, arson	Conventional-militant	Medium	Major but brief intransigence	Extreme passivity during riots	Very large; 2 years

Table 3. (Continued)

Case	Bold protest actions	Protest group alliances	Elite support	Authorities' mistakes about policy reforms	Policing mistakes	Protest size and approximate duration
Intermediate-sized protests						
Berlin-Kreuzberg (1969–76)*	Demonstrations, squat	No data	Very little	Major intransigence with procedural reforms	No data	Medium; 7 years
Munich-Südpark	Minor	None	Major	Medium intransigence and procedural access	None	Medium; 3 years
Small protests						
Kronshagen	None	None	None	Medium intransigence	None	Small; 2 years
Riesa	Medium (by skinheads)	None	None	Major intransigence	None	Small; 3 years

* I am treating Berlin-Kreuzberg (1969–76) and Berlin-Kreuzberg (1976–95) as two separate cases.

elements were present in the six high-threat cases in this book. Hence, a minimum threshold of threats to residents seems to be necessary before the processes of opportunity expansion can begin to produce large protests.

Threats are also closely related to the timing of protests. The formation of protest groups and initial public actions immediately followed the announcement of threatening policies. Furthermore, protests receded after officials adopted neighborhood renewal reforms in Linden and Kreuzberg and courts imposed construction delays in Wyhl and Brokdorf. Protests picked up again when officials threatened housing demolitions or nuclear plant construction years later. In Hoyerswerda and Rostock, the removal of large groups of foreigners greatly reduced the cultural threats that local residents perceived, and anti-foreigner protests immediately declined.

But threats arising from state actions did not determine the size of protests.[d] While large threats led to large protests in Kreuzberg in 1976–95 and at Wyhl and Brokdorf, similarly large threats triggered only small protests in the earlier phase of the Kreuzberg conflict, as well as in the Berlin-Wedding urban renewal area. Similarly, protests were much larger and longer-lived in Südpark than in Riesa and several other Munich neighborhoods, despite the similar level of cultural threats posed by shelters housing several hundred asylum seekers in residential neighborhoods in all those localities. Furthermore, protests against immigration collapsed not only when authorities removed threats (in Hoyerswerda, Rostock, and Südpark), but also when opportunities did not expand through alliances between protest groups, support from elites, and policing mistakes (the West German nuclear energy conflicts before Wyhl).

Large protests depended not only on threats by authorities, but also on daring actions and alliances between diverse protest groups, which triggered policing mistakes. Police sometimes became passive, allowing disruptive or violent activity to accelerate. West Berlin authorities did little to counter the first phases of the squatter movement, and police hesitated at the nonviolent occupation of the Wyhl nuclear construction site. Police commanders also allowed anti-foreigner riots to proceed unimpeded for days in Hoyerswerda and Rostock. Overreaction by police, in

---

d. Nor were threats determined by deeper political and economic structures, as seen in the significant range of threat levels provided by similarly situated officials in Chapters 2–5. This point is also discussed later in this chapter.

the context of strong public and elite support for protesters, was also a common feature in the large leftist protests. In the antinuclear movements at Wyhl and Brokdorf, and the urban renewal movement in West Berlin (through the late 1980s), police crackdowns increased both cooperation among protesters and elite support for the movements, and hence had the unintended effect of promoting further mobilization.

In addition, formal procedural access to decision makers, through committees, tenant advisors, hearings, or courts, seemed to be necessary for the long protest movements in urban renewal and nuclear energy. In the context of large threats to residents and blocked reform, authorities erred when they granted protesters greater institutional access through citizen participation measures. The urban renewal protesters at Linden and Kreuzberg benefited from procedural reforms, especially from the far-reaching measures promoted by the West Berlin construction minister, whose experiment in resident participation touched off a large squatter movement. Protesters also used citizen participation forums to help them build long-lived protests in the nuclear energy conflicts and in the Südpark immigration conflict. However, procedural access was not necessary for the large, short-lived protests in Hoyerswerda and Rostock, and by themselves, procedural reforms contributed only to small protests in the early phase of the Kreuzberg conflict.

In sum, many kinds of political interactions, which expanded opportunities in a spiraling way, were necessary for large protests to develop. Protesters could expand opportunities only where state actions were sufficiently threatening and elites were at least partially divided. Under those conditions, protesters could make their own opportunities by forming alliances with other kinds of protesters, mounting bold actions, and gaining open support from some political elites. This combination of factors often triggered mistakes by police, which inadvertently promoted larger and longer-lived protests.[e]

EXPLAINING LONG-TERM INCREASES IN PROTEST

In several ways, protest movements also helped increase opportunities for protesters in the long run in Germany.[1] Protests by left-wing groups led Social Democratic leaders to shift toward movement positions, and

---

e. However, relatively large, long protests could develop without policing mistakes, as they did in Linden, if many other conditions were favorable.

leftist movements helped the Greens become established in party systems at all levels of government, which gave leftist protesters long-term elite allies. In addition, former protesters rose into elite or government positions, especially through the Greens, and protests led municipal officials to continuously expand local citizen participation opportunities into the late 1990s.[f] As illustrated by the urban renewal and nuclear energy cases in this book, these changes promoted high levels of participation for many years after the peak of protest. Moreover, the left-wing movements were embedded in the politics of fairly stable government policies, such as energy, transportation, housing, and social services, which provided a long stream of new threats and opportunities. As the theory of new social movements emphasizes, extensive programs of state action were major underlying causes of the leftist movements.

For these reasons, the protests of the 1970s led to long-term increases in participation across Germany as a whole. Participation in citizen initiatives of all kinds rose in the 1970s and remained high during the 1980s and 1990s. The share of the population who said they had participated in citizen initiatives rose from 5 percent in 1980 to 12 percent in 1989 (West Germany) and 16 percent in 1992 (unified Germany).[2] Between 1984 and 1989, about 60 percent of West German respondents said they would "certainly" or "maybe" participate in a citizen initiative, making it the second most popular form of participation after voting. In 1992, the share rose to 75 percent (western Germany) and 83 percent (eastern Germany).[3]

The level of disruptive, nonviolent protests also increased. Some event data and survey sources show large fluctuations, while others show a rather continuous rise, but all show that nonviolent protests were more frequent in the 1970s than before 1968, and even more common in the 1980s and early 1990s than in the 1970s. Rucht's studies of protest event data, taken from national newspapers, show that the rate of rallies, demonstrations, blockades, and occupations doubled from the 1950–64 period to the 1965–79 period, and doubled again from the 1965–79 period to the 1980–94 period.[4,g] These results are supported by studies of partic-

f. Local officials continued to create new participatory institutions in environmental policy, under the rubric of sustainable development, in the late 1990s (ICLEI/DIFU 1999, 75; Rösler 2000, 21–22).

g. Presumably, these increases were caused mainly by left-wing protest movements other than the labor movement. The increase across the last two periods was not due mainly to an increase in strikes and other workers' actions, which were not a rising

ular left-wing movements, such as the women's, peace, environmental, squatter, antinuclear, and infrastructure-related movements.[5] Surveys also show an approximate doubling from 1974 to 1990 in the share of the population saying they had already participated in petitions, lawful demonstrations, and boycotts in the Federal Republic.[6] At the same time, violence by left-wing protest groups also increased sharply from the 1960s to the 1990s (see Chapter 1).

By contrast, the wave of anti-immigration protests in the 1990s did not lead to a long-term increase in protest participation on immigration policy. Right-wing violence, which was mainly against foreigners, fell dramatically after June 1993. From 1992–93 to 1995–97, right-wing arson attacks declined by 93 percent, attacks against persons by 45 percent, and total right-wing crimes by 63 percent. It is difficult to assess anti-foreigner violence from the 1980s to later periods because of reporting biases[h] and officials' failure to separately classify such violence before 1990. However, the available evidence suggests that levels of right-wing violence in the late 1990s and early 2000s may not have been significantly higher than in the 1980s. Right-wing arson and bomb attacks, which are reported more consistently than other categories, declined by 18 percent from 1985–88 to 2001–03, even though the data for the latter period include the eastern *Länder*.[7] In addition, right-wing violence in the late 1990s focused less on foreigners and more on other targets such as leftists than in the early 1990s.[8] Nonviolent anti-immigration protests also dropped dramatically after the early 1990s, though systematic data are not available. For example, Munich newspapers reported only four small protests against asylum shelters in 1997, compared with thirteen relatively large protest campaigns and many smaller ones in 1992.

Protest participation on the right did not increase much, if at all, in the long run largely because the anti-immigration movement did not expand opportunities in the ways that leftist movements did. Although anti-immigration protests led to a shift toward anti-asylum positions by

---

share of all actions over these periods, nor to anti-foreigner actions, which were only 28 percent of all actions related to foreigners (Neidhardt and Rucht 1999, 142, 148). Other investigators present data showing a long-term increase with large fluctuations (Koopmans 1992, 116; Dalton 1993, 191).

h. It is highly likely that media attention, especially after the Mölln murders, increased the willingness of residents to report crimes and of police to record and classify crimes as right-wing.

the major parties, the inter- and intraparty debate on asylum rights fell off precipitously in the wake of the 1993 constitutional reform.[9] Hence, protesters' chances to win further restrictions of immigration declined. Threats due to immigration also declined as asylum applications dropped, authorities implemented controls on ethnic German resettlers, and the German economy entered recession and higher unemployment, making Germany less attractive to immigrants. Right-wing protests were not very sustainable partly because right-wing protesters relied heavily on political opportunities provided by publicized immigration issues, which fluctuate dramatically along with immigration rates.

Yet anti-immigration protests might have remained at high levels after their 1992–93 peak if right-wing protesters had expanded their own opportunities in some of the ways that the leftist movements had. Unlike the Greens, far-right parties did not gain Bundestag representation and had only sporadic successes in local and *Land* elections. Moreover, they were usually fractious, ineffective, and marginalized by other parties in the *Landtage* or local parliaments where they won seats, and they gained virtually no government positions.[10] Nor did citizen initiatives opposed to immigration produce leaders who rose into government positions (such as Orlowsky and Momper did on the left), or win major procedural reforms like those in urban renewal. Finally, the violence against foreigners triggered a government-led crackdown after the Mölln arson murders in November 1992, which greatly reduced the facilitation of violence by police, prosecutors, and judges (see Chapter 5). Skinheads and other right-wing youths were especially vulnerable to a crackdown because their action repertoires and alliance patterns were narrow.[11]

EXPLAINING THE TYPES OF PROTEST

The conflicts analyzed in this book fall into three broad types (see Table 4). Some remained largely limited to conventional actions (Kronshagen), others included major disruptive, nonviolent protests as well as conventional participation (Wyhl), and in still others, militant actions became significant and overshadowed the other forms of participation (Brokdorf, Hoyerswerda, and Rostock). Two cases are intermediate: Kreuzberg lies between the disruptive and militant kinds of conflict, and Linden between the conventional and disruptive kinds. Two others are difficult to classify in these terms: Südpark was mainly conventional but included

Table 4. Explaining the Types of Participation in Nine Cases

Case	Alliances between protest groups; duration and strategies used[a]	Protest strategies supported by elite allies	Routine access created by officials[b]	Delays in major reforms[c]	Protest strategies that resulted in official policy concessions	Policing mistakes	Main types of participation
Kronshagen	None	None (few allies)	Medium; frequent informal contacts, council meetings	Long;[d] throughout conflict period	Conventional	None	Conventional
Hanover-Linden	Sporadic; conventional-disruptive	Conventional, some disruptive	Major; renewal commissions, planning advisors	Brief (one year)	Disruptive (squats)	None	Conventional & some disruptive
Wyhl	Long-lived; conventional-disruptive	Conventional, disruptive	Medium; manipulated hearings, Offenburg Agreement negotiations	Long (10 years)	Disruptive (site occupation)	Passivity, overreactions	Conventional & disruptive
Berlin-Kreuzberg	Long-lived; conventional-disruptive-militant	All strategies	Major; neighborhood committees, tenant advisors	Long (13 years)	Disruptive & militant (squats, riots)	Passivity, overreactions	Conventional & disruptive & militant

CONCLUSIONS 229

Table 4. (Continued)

Case	Alliances between protest groups; duration and strategies used[a]	Protest strategies supported by elite allies	Routine access created by officials[b]	Delays in major reforms[c]	Protest strategies that resulted in official policy concessions	Policing mistakes	Main types of participation
Brokdorf	Long-lived; disruptive-militant	Conventional, militant, mildly disruptive	Minor; only manipulated hearings	Long (over ten years)[e]	Disruptive & militant (demonstrations)	Overreactions	Conventional & militant
Hoyerswerda	Brief; conventional-militant (riots)	Conventional, militant	Minor; one assembly	Short; until riots	Militant (riots)	Passivity	Militant & some conventional
Rostock	Brief; conventional-militant (riots)	Conventional, militant	None; informal contacts only	Short; until riots	Militant (riots)	Passivity	Militant & some conventional
Munich-Südpark	None	Conventional, mildly disruptive	Medium; citizen assemblies	Medium (3 years)	Disruptive (demonstration), militant	None	Conventional, some disruptive, some militant
Riesa	None	None (no allies)	Medium; many informational meetings with discussions	Long; throughout conflict period	None	None	Some conventional & some militant

[a] Alliances among protest groups with complementary strategies promote a shift to riskier strategies.
[b] Promotes conventional strategies.
[c] A long period of official intransigence (failure to adopt major reforms) promotes a shift to riskier strategies.
[d] Officials made concessions within months, but the shelters were still built.
[e] Official intransigence continued after plant was finished.

some mild disruption and militant threats, while Riesa included minor conventional and minor militant actions.

How well do the interactive political processes proposed in Chapter 1 explain these differences between the cases? Alliances between protest groups, concessions by authorities, mistakes by police, and direct encouragement by elite allies emerge as the most important variables, although the creation of routine access and delays in major reforms also shaped the types of protest.

Without exception, the significant use of disruptive or militant methods depended on alliances between protest groups pursuing complementary strategies, just as proposed by the theory. The nonviolently disruptive cases, Wyhl and Linden, were marked by alliances between conventional and disruptive protesters, with the short-lived, sporadic squats in Linden reflecting the sporadic nature of the alliances among the protesters there. All four militant cases had fairly public alliances between militant groups and nonviolent protesters. The short-lived militant protests in Hoyerswerda and Rostock were based on short-lived alliances between militant youths and adult residents. By contrast, the one purely conventional case, Kronshagen, lacked such alliances, as did Südpark, which helps explain why the militant actions in that case remained minor.

Authorities' concessions to protests were also very important in promoting disruptive and militant actions. In Linden and at Wyhl, public officials made concessions to disruptive protests, and the same or different protesters tried to repeat those successes later. The same happened with militant protesters in Kreuzberg and at Brokdorf. Since authorities conceded little to nonviolent protests and then made major concessions to militant actions, protesters and their allies got the message that militancy was effective. Housing policy reforms immediately after the December 1980 riots in West Berlin, like the Social Democrats' shifts away from nuclear energy just after militant protests at Brokdorf, promoted militant protests in those cases in later months and years. This dynamic did not occur in Hoyerswerda and Rostock, simply because the removal of asylum seekers and foreign contract workers ended those conflicts. However, the highly visible concessions to violence in those cases triggered massive waves of anti-foreigner violence in many other locations across Germany.

The types of protest were also closely related to the nature of policing.

All the large-scale militant actions depended on major policing mistakes, ranging from passivity in Hoyerswerda and Rostock to overreaction at Brokdorf to a mix of both in Kreuzberg. The quality of policing was also important in the nonviolently disruptive cases. At Wyhl, police passivity made the site occupation possible, while in Linden, flexible police practices helped to limit disruptive actions and prevent militant ones. In Riesa, finally, police vigilance was a crucial factor in limiting militant actions against the asylum shelter.

Police mistakes, and their implications for later protests, were also affected by other political interactions. Police passivity in the anti-foreigner riots was partly due to the large crowds that supported the skinheads' actions. Police passivity in Kreuzberg was partly due to the blockage of housing reforms, and alliances between protest groups made it difficult for police in Kreuzberg, Wyhl, and Brokdorf to target disruptive or militant protesters with proportionate repression. Police overreactions would not have triggered large illegal protests in those cases if it had not been for alliances between protest groups, elite support for protesters, and the blockage of major reforms.

While elite allies consistently encouraged conventional participation, sometimes they also promoted disruptive and militant protests. Some politicians and other elites openly encouraged disruptive actions in Linden, Kreuzberg, and Wyhl and militant actions in Kreuzberg and Brokdorf. Their public statements helped shield risky protest actions from repression. Moreover, in Hoyerswerda and Rostock, militants benefited greatly from the implicit support of *Land* interior ministers from the right wing of the CDU, who helped produce police passivity and government concessions to militant violence.

By contrast, the effects of formal participation rights on the types of protest were rather limited. Although formal procedural access to decision makers clearly encouraged conventional participation, this factor cannot explain the kinds of participation that ultimately were most important. In five cases, protesters were offered or gained routine access, and they all had significant conventional activity (Kreuzberg, Linden, Wyhl, Brokdorf, and Südpark). However, even in the absence of formal institutions, protesters gained informal access to particular officials and participated conventionally in Kronshagen, Riesa, and Rostock. Furthermore, formal procedural access and major conventional participation did not prevent a shift to disruptive methods (in Linden and at Wyhl) or to militant methods (in Kreuzberg and at Brokdorf). Nor was routine access a necessary stepping-stone to unconventional forms of participation, which developed in Hoyerswerda and Rostock without formal participation procedures.

Finally, delays in major reforms were necessary though not sufficient for the development of unconventional protests. In Linden and at Wyhl, reforms were delayed until disruptive protests occurred, at which point major reforms helped pre-empt any shift to militant actions. In Kreuzberg and at Brokdorf, delayed reforms led to a shift toward disruptive actions and then, given continued delays, toward militancy. In Hoyerswerda and Rostock, the same process occurred, except the shift was directly from low levels of conventional participation to massive militant activity. Südpark also fits the general pattern, with authorities' intransigence leading to a minor use of disruptive and militant methods.

However, by itself, policy intransigence did not determine the type of protest, which also depended on many other political interactions. At both Wyhl and Brokdorf, authorities insisted on constructing nuclear plants despite strong opposition, and administrative courts suspended construction, but different kinds of protest developed in those two cases because of differences in alliances between protest groups, the concessions made to protests, and police practices. In addition, there was no shift in strategy toward disruptive methods in Kronshagen and Riesa, despite the blockage of major reforms. In those two cases, overall protests remained weak because officials reduced the threats that the asylum shelters posed, elite allies gave little support, and disruptive protest groups were unavailable to encourage citizen initiatives to try new tactics.

For each of the three different kinds of conflict—purely conventional, nonviolently disruptive, and heavily militant—a combination of factors, rather than a single one, produced the result. These political interactions tended to cluster together to produce either conventional, disruptive, or militant conflicts because the interactions that promote each type of conflict tend to reinforce each other.[j] Authorities' intransigence in the pursuit of unpopular policies can lead protesters to form alliances and shift

---

j. Another possibility arises from the research design, which involved the deliberate selection of unusually large and disruptive or militant conflicts in Chapters 2, 3, and 5. Since they were extraordinary conflicts, it is likely that they would result from the confluence of many factors. Another possibility, that one variable tended to drive all the others, is not supported by an examination of the cases from that point of view. The main candidate, threats arising from state actions, is discussed earlier in this chapter.

to riskier strategies, motivate some elites to support protests, and undermine the morale of police. Where intransigence proves counterproductive, it may force officials to eventually make concessions to disruptive or militant protests, thus encouraging unconventional protests later on. When protesters form alliances with each other and mount disruptive or militant protests, they may complicate the task of the police and gain attention that wins them elite allies, who provide some protection against state repression. Police mistakes may reinforce alliances between protesters as well as elite support for protest. Whether disruptive or militant protests predominate depends partly on accidents of timing—on what kind of protest tactics is being used when protesters succeed in expanding opportunities by winning increased support from elite allies, triggering a passive response from police, or gaining concessions from authorities.

However, a caveat about violence is needed. My theory is geared to explaining militant protest rather than violence as such. Militant protests often led to violence or included violence as the main tactic, but whether militant actions led to violence, and how large the violence became, depended on many situational factors. These included tactical decisions by police, protesters, and bystanders. At Brokdorf, the massive use of police seemed to be fairly effective at deterring major violence in 1977, 1981, and 1986, sometimes aided by the Communist League's tactical decision to refrain from violence and to prevent violence by other militants. In Kreuzberg, the shift to a de-escalation strategy by police triggered a shift in alliance patterns and led to reduced violence in the early 1990s, even though the autonomists continued to mount large, threatening demonstrations on each May Day. In Riesa, proactive policing prevented any major attacks on the asylum shelter and deflected skinheads to other targets, but if police had slipped up on just one night, skinheads could easily have carried out a major arson attack against the shelter. This suggests that relatively small amounts of violence, much smaller than the Hoyerswerda riots, could not be prevented by the same kinds of factors that prevented large militant protests, a point underscored by the small neo-Nazi attacks on the Eichhof shelter in Kronshagen in 1996. Another situational factor is the nature of the attempted violence. It is easier for police to defend a central, isolated target such as a rural construction site (Brokdorf) against violence than it is to defend many scattered targets such as decentralized asylum shelters (Kronshagen-Eichhof) or property in urban neighborhoods (Kreuzberg).

THE CYCLICAL THEORY AND ITS LIMITS

The interactive political process theory in this book is largely complementary with the theory of protest cycles or waves. Both theories focus on how interactions produce shifts in strategies among diverse, interrelated sets of protest groups and participants. However, the cyclical theory is designed to explain the development of a large set of interrelated movements at the national level, while the interactive theory aims to explain how protest develops in particular conflicts. The cyclical theory emphasizes the ways that national protest waves affect particular conflicts, while the interactive theory emphasizes the partial autonomy of subnational movements and campaigns, and the ways that particular conflicts may influence a national cycle. I argue that the position of a conflict in a national protest cycle is only one factor influencing the types of protest used in Germany, and that political interactions at the local or *Land* level are at least as important.

Tarrow, Koopmans, and others have argued that the early phase of a protest cycle is marked by innovative forms of disruption, that the peak involves a growth of mildly disruptive mass protests, and that after authorities respond decisively with reforms and repression, protest strategies become divided between institutional participation and militant violence.[12] Different authors offer somewhat different explanations for these shifts. These include the diffusion of new protest forms from "early risers" to other groups and learning by authorities, who initially overreact to protests with clumsy repression but gradually learn to make concessions to some protesters and to repress others with more effective methods.[13] A related argument is that, after the initial outbreak of disruptive protest, protesters and authorities increasingly adjust their actions to each other, which makes interactions more predictable, and hence initially disruptive actions such as demonstrations become fairly routine.[14]

The cyclical theory can help explain aspects of the interrelated left-wing movements in Germany, Italy, the Netherlands, and other countries. It helps explains why the proportion of nonviolently disruptive protests in Germany declined in the aggregate after the peak of mobilization and why militancy increased in the later phases. The inclusion of some protesters or constituents and the exclusion of others help explain Germany's mixture of long-term changes in participation on the left, including rises in conventional participation and militant violence. However, contrary to the cyclical theory, nonviolent disruption also rose in absolute terms, and it declined only slightly in relative terms.[15k]

Moreover, while the types of participation used in a protest movement or campaign change over time in some patterned ways, the cases in this book show that there are many patterns rather than one. Some conflicts in Germany shifted from conventional methods to include nonviolent disruption, some to include militancy and violence, and some toward a combination of disruption and militancy, while some remained almost completely conventional. Moreover, the evolution of protest types in many conflicts runs contrary to that predicted by the cyclical theory.

There are three reasons for this.[l] First, tactical innovation has not always followed a predictable course leading to greater control by authorities. Although there are tendencies for protesters to run out of surprising and effective ideas and for authorities to learn from their initial mistakes, the tendencies may operate too slowly or weakly to greatly affect a given conflict. In Kreuzberg, police failed to innovate for a decade, remaining by turns brutal and passive from 1980 until about 1990, when their shift to more consistent and targeted repression helped undercut local support for militancy. At Wyhl, both sides ramped up their strategies in the 1980s, but protesters kept the initiative by shifting from centralized nonviolent actions to threats of multifaceted, decentralized nonviolent resistance. At Brokdorf, authorities quickly learned how to prevent a site occupation, but not how to conduct meaningful citizen participation, which partly explains why that conflict became very militant.

Second, the actions of subnational authorities and elites have often run contrary to national trends in Germany. For example, the Schmidt governments (1974–82), faced with economic recession and an assassination campaign by the Red Army Faction, turned away from participatory reforms and toward the repression of protest in the mid- and late 1970s. But *Land* and local governments were often becoming more open to left-leaning movements in this period. Social Democratic governments

---

k. The cyclical theory can also help explain similar strategy shifts in individual national-level movements and even some subnational movements that involved much disruptive and militant action (Koopmans 1995, 136, 157–227; Tarrow 1989b, chaps. 7, 10–11).

l. The latter two of these are rooted in the decentralized nature of the German polity, which makes local and *Land* conflicts in many policy areas largely independent of each other, such as in urban renewal, transportation, nuclear energy, alternative and women's social services, and immigration. By contrast, the cyclical theory seems to assume highly interdependent conflicts.

were initiating or consolidating reforms in Hanover and West Berlin, and Christian Democratic premiers were reluctantly defusing nuclear energy conflicts in Baden-Württemberg and Lower Saxony. Even when developments among federal authorities and politicians affected protest movements, they did so in an uneven way mediated by local conditions. The Brandt government's democratizing reforms encouraged student activists to join with other residents in citizen initiatives, but these efforts grew into bigger protests in Linden than in Kreuzberg in the early 1970s. In the early 1990s, the Kohl government helped set the stage for a large and often violent anti-immigration movement, by promoting the rapid unification of East and West Germany and downplaying the problem of right-wing violence. But national politics did not determine the nature of local anti-immigration conflicts, as the diversity of nonviolent and violent protest campaigns in the western and eastern *Länder* shows.

Third, external movements have had only limited influence on local and *Land*-level conflicts.[m] At least in Germany, new strategies or tactics brought in from outside a particular conflict setting have flourished only if the protesters using them have found appropriate local opportunities. Although the alternative movement affected both Linden and Kreuzberg in the late 1970s, it had much less impact in Linden, where major policy reforms had been adopted and most protesters had been incorporated into neighborhood commissions five years earlier, than in Kreuzberg, where reforms were still blocked and hence threats and opportunities were growing when the alternative movement began to mobilize. Similarly, despite the presence of many neo-Nazis in Munich, they had little influence on the conflicts over asylum shelters there, because they did not form alliances with resident groups and elites did not encourage a shift toward militancy.

The importance of local or regional conditions in shaping the nature of participation is also shown by the willingness of committed activists on the left and right to travel some distance to participate in protests,

---

m. Although the case studies focus on certain geographical and policy areas, protest groups inspired by external movements or based in other localities also influenced these conflicts. Radical or antisystem students inspired by the student movement were active in all the left-leaning protests. The alternative, antinuclear, and autonomist movements influenced squatting in Linden and Kreuzberg. Communist groups and autonomists brought militancy to locally based protests at Brokdorf, as well as to Gorleben and Wackersdorf. On the right, neo-Nazi activists from western Germany helped turn skinheads into a clearly right-wing, anti-foreigner force in eastern Germany, and this helped make the Hoyerswerda and Rostock riots more militant and violent.

even when other conflicts or targets existed closer to home. Activists often chose locations where other protesters or elites seemed likely to support their preferred strategy. Indeed, the previous conflict history sometimes attracted activists to live in particular areas, thus reinforcing the effects of earlier protests on later participation. Disruptive and militant activists became concentrated in Kreuzberg, and disruptive protesters became concentrated in North Linden and Gorleben. Hanover-Nordstadt drew autonomists from other parts of Hanover and Lower Saxony, and after the unification of Berlin, many autonomists and people who sympathized with them shifted their squatting and rioting activity from Kreuzberg to East Berlin neighborhoods. About 30 to 40 percent of skinheads attacked targets in a locality other than the one in which they lived.[16]

Local conditions affected not only where disruptive or militant conflicts took place, but also the overall amount of such activity in Germany. Although activists were somewhat mobile, not all activists were able or willing to travel or move to conflict settings where their preferred strategies could flourish.[n] If significant amounts of disruptive or militant activity were to develop in a conflict setting, then an adequate combination of active protest groups (including respectable local residents and risk-taking youths), potentially supportive elites, and blundering authorities was needed. In Germany at least, there have been more risk-taking youths available than settings where disruptive or militant protests could take off. Therefore, those who helped create, or helped prevent the creation of, such settings influenced the total amount of disruptive or militant protest in Germany.

Finally, protesters in many of the conflicts analyzed in this book became models for groups elsewhere in Germany, and thus the local processes that promoted their protests influenced the national left- and right-wing protest cycles at least as much as the national cycles affected the local conflicts. The Baden-Alsace Initiatives' actions at Wyhl provided a model for nonviolent site occupations, and the West Berlin squatter movement inspired squatters in other cities. The campaigns by the Hamburg chapter of the Lower Elbe Initiative offered a model for militant actions at construction sites, and the Hoyerswerda and Rostock riots im-

---

n. The geographic limits on skinhead activities were stronger than those on communists or autonomists, reflecting differences in the activists' socioeconomic resources and degree of organization.

mediately inspired fire-bombings and other attacks on foreigners' housing throughout Germany. Without those particular local protests, and the local interactions that made them possible, the waves of leftist and rightist protest in Germany would have been less disruptive, less militant, and smaller.

Comparing Protests on the Left and Right

This study has emphasized some important similarities in left-wing and right-wing movements in Germany. The urban renewal, antinuclear-energy, and anti-immigration movements had many common elements: citizen initiatives formed by respectable, mainly middle-class residents; ideologically committed, highly organized activists from the fringes of the political system; and politicians from parliamentary parties who were inclined to support reformist demands and impede repression of the protesters. Both leftist and rightist movements grew by winning elite allies and triggering authorities' mistakes, used a wide range of participation forms, and where their protests were large and went beyond conventional methods, influenced significant policy reforms. High levels of militancy resulted on the left and the right from the same complex of causes, including delays in policy reforms, support for militants from other protest groups or elites, and policing mistakes.

However, there were also important differences between leftist and rightist protests. First, leftist protesters used nonviolently disruptive approaches much more than did the rightist groups, which were mostly limited to conventional and militant methods. The left-leaning citizen initiatives sometimes used disruptive methods, formed alliances with other nonviolently disruptive groups, and gave implicit support to communist and autonomist militants. By contrast, the citizen initiatives opposed to immigration mostly confined themselves to conventional means, even though knowledge of disruptive tactics was widely available in western Germany in the early 1990s, after two decades of leftist protests. The anti-immigration initiatives, which were led by adults, also remained isolated from neo-Nazi and skinhead groups. Although these diverse groups shared antipathy to foreigners, or at least to additional immigration, they seldom made contacts to each other, coordinated or joined in actions, or expressed public support for each other. Even in anti-foreigner riots, where adult residents supported militant protesters in broad daylight, they did so only briefly, only in five locations in eastern Germany, and only where police were extremely passive and officials were very unresponsive.º

A second major difference is that militancy was more important on the right than on the left. In studies based on national newspaper reports, the proportion of all protests that were violent was much higher for right-wing protests (about 67 to 77 percent of all protests) than for left-wing protests (about 19 percent).[17p] There were also important differences in the nature of militant actions. Leftist protesters mostly threatened and attacked property and police officers, the latter at violent demonstrations. By contrast, rightists focused on attacking relatively powerless people, especially foreigners, and sometimes police at riots or demonstrations. However, explaining why leftists and rightists engaged in such different kinds of militancy is beyond the bounds of this study.

In the following, I focus on the coarser-grained issue of the relative proportions of disruptive and militant actions. I explain why rightists used militancy more often, and nonviolent disruption less often, than leftists did. To a great extent, the answer lies in left-right differences in authorities' responses to violence, strategic innovation by committed activists, the activists' ideologically rooted attitudes toward democracy and the state, and mainstream party responses to the activists.ᑫ

o. Beyond six episodes of rioting against foreigners' housing in eastern Germany (Karapin 2000), evidence of adult residents directly and explicitly assisting skinheads in attacking foreigners is rare. An exceptional case occurred in the village of Dolgenbrodt in the eastern *Land* of Brandenburg, where it came to light that residents had collected money to pay attackers (*taz*, 24 August 1993, 1 February 1997).

p. While national newspapers are more likely to report violent protests than conventional actions, these biases are probably similar in coverage of the left and right.

q. One might argue that right-wing activists seldom used nonviolently disruptive methods because, unlike activists in leftist movements, they seldom came from middle-class backgrounds or had high levels of education. Of suspects in right-wing and anti-foreigner crimes, only about 5 to 10 percent had white-collar occupations, and only 2 percent had graduated from academic high schools or postsecondary institutions (BV 1993b, 94; Willems et al. 1993, 116, 122; author's calculations). By contrast, young, middle-class, highly educated people were strongly overrepresented in left-leaning citizen initiatives and in the environmental, peace, women's, and alternative movements (Brand, Büsser, and Rucht 1986, 102, 136, 179–80, 217; Koopmans 1992, 18).

However, social structure cannot explain why right-wing protests seldom involved nonviolently disruptive tactics. Working-class people in labor organizations often carry out nonviolently disruptive actions in Germany; indeed, these were very common during the 1990s (Rucht 2002, Tables 7.1–7.2). Moreover, a wide range of social groups were available in most conflict settings for the anti-immigration movement, and middle-

AUTHORITIES' RESPONSES TO VIOLENCE

One reason that militant actions and violence were comparatively strong on the right is that authorities and party politicians in Germany have had a greater tendency to condone militant actions by antisystem groups on the right than on the left, at least through 1992.[r] In Kriesi's terms, the prevailing strategy among German elites has been less repressive toward the right than toward the left.[18] According to national newspaper reports, police repressed only 25 percent of violent actions by right-wing protesters between 1991 and 1994, compared with 70 to 80 percent of violent protests by leftists between 1975 and 1989.[19] When skinheads and neo-Nazis acted violently against foreigners, many authorities did not take the political dimensions of their crimes seriously. Therefore, interior ministers and police were often reluctant to act against right-wing offenders, prosecutors often brought charges on lesser offenses, and judges imposed light or suspended sentences.[20] Official leniency toward rightists was most apparent before the Mölln arson attacks led to a shift in public sentiment and more aggressive efforts by many police, prosecutors, and judges.[21] By contrast, authorities usually acted promptly and often preventively against violence by communists and autonomists in urban renewal, nuclear energy, airport expansion, and other conflicts.[s] However, police passivity does not explain left-right differences in the use of nonviolently disruptive protests, since police repressed only 9 percent of such protests by rightists, compared with 20 to 50 percent of those by leftists.[22]

---

class adults without high levels of education were capable of using disruptive tactics, as they did in Südpark and Linden.

r. For example, leftists have been charged under antiterrorism laws (sections 129 and 129a of the criminal code, which includes "supporting a terrorist or criminal association") for offenses as minor as attending public meetings. But prosecutions of right-wing extremists under these legal provisions have been rare. For example, a federal appellate court in 1981 dismissed section 129a charges against the far-right paramilitary leader Karl-Heinz Hoffmann (Siegler 1993, 95–99; Schmidt 1993, 165ff.). See also Willems et al. 1993, Stöss 1991, and Funke 1993 concerning repression of right-wing protesters, and Brand 1988 and Komitee 1988 concerning repression of leftists.

s. Police repression of leftists sometimes took the form of overreactions that reinforced alliances between protesters and elites and hence spurred militant protests and often violence, e.g., in Kreuzberg and at Brokdorf. But on the whole, this effect seems to have been less important than the effects of police passivity toward right-wing protesters.

STRATEGIC INNOVATION BY COMMITTED ACTIVISTS

Committed activists—communists, Young Socialists, other leftist students, autonomists, neo-Nazis, right-wing skinheads—had crucial influence on the types of protest in left-wing and right-wing movements. Such activists often sought out local conflicts involving other residents, brought new tactics and organizing skills to those conflicts, and were willing to take risky actions. They were the early risers who adopted new methods and were imitated by others.[23] A crucial difference between the left and right lies in the degree of strategic innovation that occurred among committed leftists and rightists, especially when they became part of broader protest movements.

Although most leftist activists were initially suspicious of "bourgeois democracy," many of them gradually, though somewhat grudgingly, accepted parliamentary democracy and innovated nonviolently disruptive tactics. Inspired by the civil rights movement in the United States, West German student activists in the 1960s gained experience with protest methods, such as sit-ins, teach-ins, and happenings, that sought to avoid physical violence, attract attention, and make police seem ridiculous.[24] However, students also began to experiment with violent tactics such as arson and bombings in the late 1960s.[25] When leftist students joined or organized citizen initiatives in the early 1970s, nonviolently disruptive actions became part of those groups' repertoires. Leftist university students, organized in groups like the Young Socialists in Kreuzberg and Housing Emergency Action in Linden, developed a political strategy that combined the radical goal of a peaceful, democratic transition to socialism with nonviolently disruptive methods.

The nonviolently disruptive strategy had great potential for bringing together leftist activists and "ordinary citizens," usually middle-class adult residents who were inclined to conventional participation. Leftists and citizen initiatives found they could combine conventional and disruptive actions in ways that were, or became, acceptable to some politicians and authorities. For that reason, alliances between disruptive and conventional protesters also had the potential to open divisions among elites, ward off repression by state actors, and expand opportunities for further protests. Since nonviolent disruption was often effective where it was tried, other protest groups were encouraged to try this approach. The Wyhl occupation in 1975 was an important, nationally publicized example, but the repeated, successful use of disruptive methods in Linden two years earlier shows that protesters also learned from local examples. Moreover, allied conventional and disruptive protesters often gained elite support, as they did in Linden, Kreuzberg, and Wyhl, which further promoted the use of nonviolently disruptive methods.

By contrast, committed activists on the right have failed to innovate a nonviolently disruptive approach at any time in the postwar period, despite the opportunities presented by the broad-based protests against foreigners in the late 1980s and early 1990s. Committed right-wing activists remained focused on conventional and militant strategies. Conventional actions included the election campaigns of the far-right Republicans, German People's Union, and National Democratic Party.[t] By contrast, neo-Nazis seldom participated in electoral politics or other conventional activity, and their occasional protest marches were militant, ritualistic shows of force against police and leftist counterdemonstrators, rather than attempts to mobilize a broader public for nonviolently disruptive actions. Neo-Nazis' graffiti and other illegal publicity actions were nonviolent protests, but these actions usually conveyed militant threats, were seldom carried out openly, and were ill-suited to help the neo-Nazis win allies among relatively respectable residents or elites. Skinhead youths, who made up the bulk of the committed, dedicated, risk-taking activists on the right, showed little interest in a conventional or nonviolently disruptive strategy, in cooperating with middle-class citizen initiatives, or even in working with neo-Nazi groups.[26]

Lacking assistance or inspiration from nonviolently disruptive activists, citizen initiatives opposed to immigration pursued narrow local goals, relied mainly on conventional methods, and usually did not see a disruptive strategy as an alternative if conventional means failed. In these ways they were similar to citizen initiatives working on urban transportation or planning issues in the mid-1960s, before the student movement began to influence the tactics of those rather respectable protest groups.[27] The anti-immigration initiatives also remained locally isolated, without overt links to similar local groups or organizations capable of mobilizing people on a regional or national scale. There was no right-wing equivalent of the Federal Association of Environmental Citizen Initiatives, which was founded in 1972 with the encouragement of federal officials from the Liberal Party.[28] The lack of overarching organizations is one reason why the anti-immigration movement did not develop tactics (such

---

t. Nationaldemokratische Partei Deutschlands.

as demonstrations, occupations, blockades, or boycotts) where leading neo-Nazis or skinheads might have participated alongside nonviolent groups, gained policy influence, and come to see a nonviolently disruptive strategy as an effective means for advancing their vision of a foreigner-free Germany.

This failure to innovate nonviolently disruptive methods meant there was little middle ground on which right-wing activists, elites, and authorities could meet. Since committed right-wing activists remained limited to militant methods, politicians could not openly support them. Nor could elites try to de-escalate the national conflict over immigration by encouraging the anti-immigration movement to avoid militancy and instead use nonviolently disruptive protests, as they did at Wyhl and in North Linden.

Committed activists on the left and the right have also held very different attitudes toward democracy and the state.[29] The anti-authoritarianism of the student movement gave leftists an opportunity to embrace expanded democratic participation as an ideal, as seen later in the Greens' emphasis on grassroots democracy.[30][u] Left-wing activists came out of the student movement and the Extra-Parliamentary Opposition of the late 1960s, or were influenced by those movements and by leftist university politics in the 1970s. While socialist students in the 1960s opposed the Vietnam War, bitterly contested the adoption of a domestic Emergency Law, and advocated codetermination in the universities, they also developed a general, radical critique of all authority, both state and societal. Their anti-authoritarianism flourished when they sought to mobilize manual workers and socially marginalized groups.[31] Of course, opposition to authority did not necessarily translate into a commitment to deepening democracy or even an acceptance of the rules of representative democracy. Many activists in the student movement chose a path toward socialism or communism through political violence and proletarian dictatorship, joining terrorist groups like the Red Army Faction, various communist groups, or undogmatic left groups.[32] However, anti-authoritarianism led many leftists to advocate the nonviolent pursuit of socialism, from within democracy, and indeed through an expansion of democratic participation. Their strategic shift was both a cause and an effect of the new opportunities provided by the SPD and the Liberal Party from 1969 to 1972.

---

u. *Basisdemokratie.*

By contrast, during the 1980s and 1990s, neo-Nazis and right-wing skinheads remained committed to extremely authoritarian positions concerning the state, implying a return to a political system similar to the Third Reich.[33] Of course, this left them ill-prepared for democratic participation. Preferring strong state authority, but rejecting the authority of the democratic German state,[34] right-wing activists have seen a stark choice between working within the system's rules for conventional participation or violently opposing it.[v] Hence, they have been divided between electoral participation, in far-right parties which at least pay lip service to accepting the democratic system, and paramilitary training, threats, and violence by neo-Nazi and skinhead groups.[w]

RESPONSES OF THE MAINSTREAM PARTIES

The differences in strategic innovation on the left and right were also partly due to the ways the center-left and center-right parties responded to tactical experimentation by committed activists. On the left in the late 1960s, the reformist wings of the SPD and the Liberal Party formed an alliance with student activists who were willing to work within democratic institutions (see Chapter 1). A confluence of events made such an alliance more likely. The peak and dissolution of the student movement in 1968 and 1969 occurred just before the inauguration of the Brandt government in October 1969. The first Brandt government (1969–72) briefly created large opportunities for leftist activists in local political conflicts, by simultaneously expanding planning activities, institutionalizing citizen participation, opening the SPD to leftist activists, and calling on West Germans to "dare more democracy." In this period, "citizen initiatives" and "citizen participation" defined a meeting ground for many Social Democrats, Liberals, and leftist activists. These were elastic terms, which many understood to include leftist activists and disruptive, even illegal protest methods.

The Social Democratic reforms encouraged young people, especially

---

v. The glorification of violence in neo-Nazism may also predispose rightists to militant actions, yet communists and autonomists also have ideological affinity for violent opposition to the state, so this feature of far-right ideology cannot explain differences between leftist and rightist protest.

w. Since their approach mixed electoral and militant elements in the 1990s, it was broadly similar to Hitler's two-pronged strategy of parliamentary participation and threat of civil war in 1928–33. This suggests that ideological and strategic continuity from the interwar period to the present have gone hand in hand for far-right activists.

from the universities, to make the transition from left-wing student politics to citizen initiatives, where students and recent graduates worked with other residents on problems that had major local components.[35] Students who joined citizen initiatives or the Young Socialists had a chance to develop a kind of anti-authoritarianism that was, at least potentially, consistent with parliamentary democracy. Activists in the SPD's and the Liberal Party's local and youth organizations helped organize many citizen initiatives. Young Socialists influenced by the student movement saw this organizing work as part of a double strategy, which they endorsed at a 1971 conference. The double strategy combined a "long march through the institutions," including the SPD, with grassroots organizing.[36] Although the opportunities for the double strategy became sharply restricted at the federal level within a few years, as symbolized by the 1972 Radicals Decree, the effects of the double strategy reverberated in the environmental, urban, peace, and other leftist movements during the next twenty years. Those movements often used a general strategy of nonviolent disruption in pursuit of public debate and policy reforms, while they developed a range of specific tactics, including housing squats, boycotts, and blockades, throughout the 1970s and 1980s.[37]

By contrast, the Christian Democrats failed to systematically open their parties to radical nationalist activists, who joined far-right parties in the 1980s and 1990s. Some might argue that this was due to a general taboo among political elites against anything associated with the Third Reich.[38] Bans on Nazi symbols make much far-right propaganda illegal, and mainstream politicians who were willing to openly support citizen initiatives against immigration would not do the same for a group tinged with neo-Nazism. But there was also a strong taboo on associations with communism in West Germany in the 1960s and 1970s,[39] which was anchored in the Cold War division of Germany as well as anticommunist traditions in the major parties going back to the Weimar Republic. Yet protesters in the urban, environmental, and peace movements sometimes cooperated with communist activists, and later with autonomists, while still gaining important support from Social Democrats, Greens, and other elites. The protests at Brokdorf from 1976 to 1986 and in Kreuzberg during the 1980s are primary examples. Although communists and autonomists could be an embarrassment to the elite allies of left-leaning movements, elites and reformist protesters often succeeded in downplaying the roles of those antisystem activists and in focusing media attention on the activities and goals of more respectable groups. Therefore, although political-cultural taboos against communism and neo-Nazism have been important factors in protest politics, by themselves they do not explain the differences between the left and right.

Rather, what was different on the right was the failure of right-wing Christian Democratic politicians and right-wing activists to develop an alliance, which could have weakened the effects of the taboo the way a similar alliance did on the left. On the right in the 1990s, there were no developments similar to Brandt's "dare more democracy" slogan, the legal innovations in public participation, and the opening of the SPD and the Liberal Party to student activists from 1969–72.

The Christian Democrats' conception of representative democracy and the state hindered the formation of such an alliance. Christian Democrats retained a statist, election-centered view of democracy as they witnessed the student movement, the growth of left-wing movements in the 1970s and 1980s, and the rise of anti-immigration protest in the 1980s and 1990s. Their concept of democracy remained focused on local self-administration, parliamentary elections, and the parliamentary parties. The official Christian Democratic response to citizen initiatives, formulated in 1975, emphasized the integration of individual citizens through a citizen friendly administration, better provision of information, and routine participation in hearings, citizen assemblies, and advisory committees. Christian Democratic leaders argued that citizen initiatives represent only minorities, in contrast to the parliamentary majorities represented by governments, and they opposed the expansion of citizen participation rights in the late 1970s.[40]

Given their commitment to this conception of democratic authority, Christian Democrats have seldom accepted disruptive protests and have strongly criticized illegal protests. Even on the rare occasions when the party has helped organize protests, the activities have been quite conventional, such as the gathering of petition signatures against a major liberalization of the citizenship law in 1999.[41] Christian Democratic politicians never tried to integrate radical nationalists into a democratic kind of protest politics through a broader citizen initiative movement. This failure is striking since Christian Democratic leaders considered local politics important to their campaign for asylum restriction, and institutions for consulting residents on the location of foreigners, such as borough councils and citizen assemblies, were widely available in the 1980s and 1990s.

These differences in repertoires and alliance patterns help explain why right-wing protests of all kinds declined sharply after the peak of the immigration conflict in 1993, in contrast with the left-wing movements' continued high levels of protest. Differences in opportunity expansion and threats to residents, described above, were certainly important. But in addition, the right-wing protesters' heavy reliance on militant actions and the isolation of militants from nonviolent protesters also undercut the anti-immigration movement in the long term, by making the committed activists vulnerable to a crackdown. Because the Federal Republic has a largely centrist party system and fairly strong norms against political violence, authorities and politicians in Germany have found it easy to marginalize militants who lack allies among nonviolent protest groups, and to repress them. The crackdown after the Mölln murders was possible partly because skinheads had few overt supporters among elites or among respectable citizen initiatives who could appeal to elite support.

Structures or Interactions?

A primary claim of this book is that political interactions affect protests in ways that cannot be reduced to the operation of structural factors. Although the evidence here is from Germany, the claim has broad support from research on protest movements in other advanced industrial democracies. Protest grew with help from elite allies and authorities' mistakes in the U.S. civil rights movement,[42] leftist protest movements in Italy during the 1960s and 1970s,[43] the peace movements against Euromissiles in many West European countries,[44] anti-nuclear-energy movements in the United States and France,[45] and squatter movements in Britain, France, and the Netherlands.[46] There is also much evidence that interactive dynamics have influenced the types of protest in other Western countries, including the antinuclear movements in the United States and France,[47] militant protest in Italy and France,[48] and youth rioting in Britain, France, and Switzerland.[49]

THE PARTIAL AUTONOMY OF POLITICAL INTERACTIONS

The nine main case studies in this book provide much evidence that interactions among protest groups, politicians, and public officials affect protest. But are those interactions independent factors, or are they largely determined by political institutions and socioeconomic trends? In the first place, most structural explanations do poorly when applied to this set of cases. In particular, socioeconomic structures fail spectacularly as explanations: Kreuzberg and Linden had large protests without postindustrial social structures; riots in eastern Germany occurred where immigrant shares were small and declining and where economic distress was below average for that part of Germany; and pairs of cases in all three policy areas were marked by similar social structures yet very different types of protest. Political institutional theories perform somewhat better, but also have major failings. They cannot explain, for example, why there were very different protest types despite very similar political institutions in the nuclear energy and eastern immigration cases. By contrast, the political interaction theory is supported in almost every instance, and hence performs much better overall than the structural theories.

Nonetheless, for each of the policy areas and major cases examined in this book, it could be argued that particular structural factors—different ones for each policy area—drove the political interactions that are my focus and hence that those structural factors were really responsible for the size and type of protests. Indeed, these structures do influence protest dynamics. However, when the focus is broadened to include additional cases in the same policy area, the structural explanations appear inadequate. Though influenced by certain structural features, the political interactions were significantly independent of them.

In urban renewal, some have argued that because housing corporations had close connections to state actors in Kreuzberg, reforms were blocked, protests grew large and unruly, elites gave them support, and police became ineffective.[50] While this argument is plausible when comparing Kreuzberg with Linden, it breaks down when other cases are examined. Hanover-Nordstadt had institutions very similar to those in Linden, but when authorities blocked reforms and disruptive and militant protesters gained allies, an urban renewal conflict developed in Nordstadt that resembled Kreuzberg, with long, confrontational squats by autonomists. Conversely, Berlin-Wedding had institutions similar to those in Kreuzberg, but because urban renewal protesters there got little support from elites, they gained few concessions and their protests remained insignificant (see the conclusions to Chapter 2).

In nuclear energy, it has been argued that the Brokdorf conflict was much more militant than Wyhl because Brokdorf came later in the overall cycle of antinuclear protests in West Germany.[51] By the time major protests began at Brokdorf, in 1976, authorities had learned to effectively repress attempts at nonviolent site occupations, and militants had grown in numbers and in the degree of support they could expect from disruptive protesters. But if temporal position in the protest cycle determined the nature of antinuclear conflicts, then the Gorleben conflict (which began in 1977) and the second round of the Wyhl conflict (1982–83) would have been at least as militant as Brokdorf. Yet the Gorleben and later Wyhl conflicts were both dominated by nonviolently disruptive actions, because government officials made concessions to nonviolent protests and nonviolent groups did not ally with militants in those two conflicts. Instead, local protest groups devised disruptive strategies that did not rely on militants and did not give militants chances to take cover in crowds of nonviolent protesters (see the conclusions to Chapter 3).

In the immigration cases, it could be argued that the eastern conflicts were so violent because political institutions were underdeveloped and democratic experience lacking in the new eastern *Länder*, especially during the first years after unification. In this view, an underequipped, discredited police force could not hold back skinhead attacks on foreigners, while local officials could not provide adult residents with enough routine access to decision-making to prevent them from supporting rioters. Although the turmoil of unification made intense anti-foreigner violence possible in the East, the Riesa case belies a structural interpretation. In Riesa, with a public administration and police who shared the problems of their counterparts in Hoyerswerda, local officials opened access to residents who were concerned about the arrival of foreigners, while the police successfully made the prevention of anti-foreigner violence a high priority.

Another possible structural argument is that formally open political institutions were crucial for channeling anti-immigration protests in nonviolent directions. However, the three cases of nonviolent protests against immigration show that openness could be achieved in many different ways and did not depend on formal institutions. Access was provided through legally anchored borough councils and citizen assemblies in Munich, largely informal contacts between the mayor and residents in Kronshagen, and preemptive meetings initiated by local officials in Riesa. Furthermore, all these alternatives depended on officials deciding to grant access in response to individual complaints or collective protests, rather than merely on the prior existence of formal institutions.

STRUCTURES AS PERMISSIVE CONDITIONS FOR LARGE PROTESTS

Nonetheless, some structural conditions were important as permissive conditions that made large protests possible. In the first place, the availability of elite allies, a very important factor for the development of large protests, is affected by deeper socioeconomic structures and trends. Elites became more willing to oppose plans for clear-cut renewal and a large nuclear energy program when it became clear that the plans were based on unrealistic expectations about construction costs, income trends, and electricity demand, especially in light of the slowdown in economic growth after 1973. Before 1993, asylum rights in Germany were very generous compared to those in neighboring countries, and they clashed with the dominant ethnic-based discourse of citizenship in Germany.[52] The political problems posed by asylum seekers became much more apparent after 1989, with the collapse of communist regimes, the end of the Cold War, and the onset of large-scale immigration out of Eastern Europe, and hence elites became more willing to restrict asylum rights. However, these were permissive conditions, which merely made elite shifts and policy reform possible. They did not guarantee that elites would adopt reformist positions, that protesters would form alliances and launch bold actions, or that protests and elite support would influence and reinforce each other to produce rising opportunities and large protests. Furthermore, in most of this book's case chapters, similarly permissive socioeconomic conditions led to very different kinds of protest movements within the same policy area.

The Federal Republic's political institutions have presented additional permissive conditions, described in Chapter 1. Constitutionally provided civil liberties, backed by the courts, have protected the right to demonstrate and have limited state repression.[53] Other institutions made it likely that some potential elite allies would be available for protesters in many different policy areas, at all levels of government. Largely autonomous *Land* and local governments, the multiparty system undergirded by the proportional electoral system, factionalized political parties and related interest groups (especially churches), and independent courts result in a large number of elites and authorities. Given their large numbers, it is more likely that they will become divided, openly support protesters, or make mistakes that promote protests. In addition, federalism involves much policymaking and policy implementation by local and *Land* governments and administrative agencies, which are more accessible targets than the more distant federal government. The lower costs of taking action led protesters in Germany to focus most of their energies in subnational settings. Federalism and coalition government also make rapid reforms difficult in many cases, so that even if elite competition and opportunities for protest increase, threats due to state action may continue at high levels for a prolonged period. This creates ideal conditions for large protests. Specific requirements in federal law also created low-cost avenues for conventional protests. Provisions of the 1971 Urban Renewal Law required municipalities to consult with citizens, and the Atomic Law required the *Länder* to hold public hearings on facility siting.

At the same time, the low-mobilization cases (Kreuzberg in 1969–76, Kronshagen, and Riesa) show that open institutions are not sufficient to promote large protests. Large protests also require a minimum threshold of opportunities provided by elite divisions, as well as cooperation between protesters with a range of complementary strategies. Only when those conditions are present can protesters begin to win elite allies or force officials' mistakes. But adequate elite divisions are not always available, and cooperation among diverse protesters does not always develop. Indeed, the fact that seven of the book's nine main cases involved significant mutual reinforcement between protests and elite actions is a product of the research design, which focused on large protests. In Kronshagen and Riesa, cases chosen to represent the many minor immigration conflicts in Germany, protesters and potential protesters did not cooperate in the pursuit of diverse strategies, found little or no elite support, and had at most marginal effects on politics and policy.

THE ROLE AND LIMITS OF POLITICAL INSTITUTIONAL THEORIES

Political institutional theories make a number of predictions about protest in Germany, only some of which are borne out by the nine cases in this book. Institutional variations within Germany can help explain some differences among the cases. In line with the institutional theory, proactive policy reforms were found in some cases at the local level (neighborhood renewal reforms in Kreuzberg and Linden, counseling requirements in Munich), while only reactive, blocking reforms occurred in nuclear energy, a policy area shared by the *Land* and federal levels of government. Differences in interest group access to the state helped delay reforms in Kreuzberg longer than in Linden, although this was only one factor among others in explaining differences in the size and types of protest in those two cases.

But institutional variations cannot explain other major aspects of these cases. Policymaking structures are the most open and implementation structures weakest at the local level, and hence institutional theorists expect movements to be more conventional if the targets of protests are at the local rather than the *Land* or federal levels. But conflicts at the local level of government spanned a wide range, from largely conventional (Linden, Kronshagen, and Riesa) to disruptive (Kreuzberg and Linden) to militant (Kreuzberg, Hoyerswerda, and Rostock). Where the *Länder* rather than municipalities had jurisdiction, as at Wyhl and Brokdorf, the type of protest also varied. The independent courts, while markedly weakening the state's implementation capacities, did not produce mild-mannered, assimilative movements against nuclear energy, but rather encouraged disruptive or militant protests by making concessions to those kinds of protest.

Even the presence or absence of legally anchored public participation procedures was not the main determinant of the extent of conventional participation. What was crucial was whether authorities extended access, through expanded formal rights or other means, to groups that opposed policies. Legal participation rights were weak in most of the immigration conflicts, yet they all involved conventional protests because protesters demanded access and officials provided it, at least to some extent. Moreover, in the cases with formal participation rights, what those rights meant in practice varied greatly and depended on political interactions, because granting significant access was a process largely at the discretion of officials. Urban renewal protesters in West Berlin and Hanover were able to gain major expansions of participation rights, while antinuclear protesters at Wyhl gained only informal rights through the Offenburg Agreement, and protesters at Brokdorf gained little meaningful access to officials. In urban renewal, tenant advising and neighborhood commissions were crucial in shaping participation and implementing policy reforms, but these neighborhood-level institutions were the results of protests rather than part of the stable institutional framework in which the protests developed. Finally, as described above, formal participation rights by themselves do not explain much about the types of protests that developed. Whether protests remained conventional or became disruptive or militant depended on many other political interactions.

THE ROLES AND LIMITS OF POLITICAL ACTORS

Opportunity-expanding alliances between protesters and political elites were not simply created by the structural conditions in these cases. They required political actors on both sides to take appropriate, mutually reinforcing actions, and these were often not forthcoming. Opportunity-expanding alliances between protesters and elites did not develop in Kronshagen, Riesa, or in the first seven years of the Kreuzberg conflict. Moreover, in the high-mobilization cases on which this book focuses, such alliances helped create elite shifts and ultimately policy reforms that initially seemed highly unlikely (in Linden, Kreuzberg, and Wyhl). Squatting campaigns in Linden and Kreuzberg and nonviolent site occupations at Wyhl were exceptionally well-timed, carefully justified to bystander publics, and novel, suggesting that protesters in those cases had unusual political skill, luck, or both, and that their choices mattered. Similarly, disruptive protesters sometimes maintained nonviolent discipline and refused to support militant efforts (Wyhl and Gorleben) and sometimes chose to give militants much support (Kreuzberg and Brokdorf).

Similarly, many important actions by the protesters' opponents are difficult to derive from structural features, and the effects of these actions depended on accidents of timing. While small reforms or careful planning helped defuse conflicts over asylum shelters in Kronshagen and Riesa, there are enough examples of intransigent authorities in the other cases of this book to suggest that even reforms this small depended on political judgments and were not dictated by structural features. When protests started in urban renewal, officials could have ignored them, or changed their clear-cut plans, but instead they invited their opponents to participate in the planning process without changing their plans. Great inattentiveness or intransigence by elected officials and administrators in early phases of conflicts made hasty concessions appear necessary later, benefiting whichever protesters happened to be strongly mobilized at the time. Concessions benefited disruptive protesters in Linden and at Wyhl, militants in Hoyerswerda and Rostock, and all kinds of protesters in Kreuzberg. Police passivity could unexpectedly benefit disruptive protesters (Wyhl) or militant protesters (Kreuzberg, Hoyerswerda, and Rostock), while targeted and consistent policing, combined with a lack of elite allies for protesters, could make policy concessions unnecessary even in the face of strongly mobilized militants (Riesa).

Police practices, which depend heavily on situational factors, also had important effects on these protest movements. Allowing police to fraternize with protesters at Wyhl was a mistake that authorities could have avoided, as they did at Brokdorf. The undifferentiated use of police against militant and disruptive protesters, as in Kreuzberg in 1980–82 and 1987–89 and at Brokdorf in 1976, was another mistake that made those conflicts more militant. Authorities might have avoided this mistake by adopting early reforms and using police more selectively, as they did in Linden beginning in the early 1970s and in Kreuzberg, finally, in the 1990s. The amazing degree of police passivity in Hoyerswerda and Rostock was largely the result of attitudes and decisions by particular leaders, starting with the *Land* interior ministers in Saxony and Mecklenburg-West Pomerania, just as the extraordinary vigilance of the Riesa police was a result of the priorities and learning capacities of those who led the local police there.

At the same time, I am not arguing that protesters, elites, or officials could always, or even often, achieve what they set out to do. Even well-considered actions that were aimed at altering causal dynamics failed when they went contrary to other, powerful political interactions. For example, in Linden, leftist activists squatted buildings in the late 1970s and 1980s. They were newcomers to the neighborhood and did not gain support from local elites or from protest groups with ties to those elites. As a result, they won little for themselves or the neighborhood renewal agenda. In Kreuzberg, Construction Minister Klaus Franke tried but failed to undermine the neighborhood committees and tenant advising regulations after 1983. Those institutions, although only a few years old, were too strongly supported by a range of former protesters and local political elites. Both Orlowsky and the SPD-AL *Land* government tried to de-escalate the violent conflicts between autonomists and police on May Day in 1989, but they failed spectacularly, because police were passive and then overreacted during the riots, contrary to the government's stated policy.

In the nuclear energy and immigration conflicts, many plausible initiatives by authorities and opposition politicians also failed. Baden-Württemberg's premier, Lothar Späth, tried to use discussions to channel the second round of Wyhl protests into conventional forms in 1983, but he failed to prevent protesters from threatening a large campaign of nonviolent resistance. His efforts were overwhelmed by the strong alliance between conventional and disruptive groups, the sharp division among the parliamentary parties on nuclear energy, and the precedent set by the successful 1975 campaign at Wyhl. The Schleswig-Holstein Social Democrats tried to undermine support for the militants at Brokdorf by taking a clearly antinuclear position and avoiding demonstrations at the construction fence in the 1980s. But they faced a strong alliance between militant protesters, nonviolent demonstrators, and their elite allies, and hence failed to prevent large protests that included militancy and violence at the construction fence through 1986. The head of Rostock's Interior Department and the acting mayor of Hoyerswerda tried to mediate between German residents and asylum seekers, but they inadvertently contributed to rising expectations and militant protests. In sum, the efficacy of any action depended on how it fit, or failed to fit, into the web of interactions involving a large number of protest groups, political elites, and public officials.

Protest Movements and Democracy in Germany

AVOIDING MILITANT CONFLICTS

The path to reform in contemporary Germany sometimes has passed through militant threats or violence. But this is not inevitable. Militant conflicts can be avoided if protesters, authorities, and politicians respond appropriately to the opportunities and problems that arise in protest politics. Most protesters seek to increase participation, gain policy reforms, and avoid militancy and violence. But they face a core dilemma: how to avoid both too much conformity to existing political routines and too much disruption and confrontation. On the one hand, if moderate protesters eschew disruptive protest tactics, they may increase participation and gain some policy influence, but their effects will probably be limited because they lack the political resources to do well in conventional channels or to gain much elite support.[x]

On the other hand, if conventional protesters support disruptive actions, a shift toward militancy becomes possible, too. The conflict may become largely militant if protesters encounter conditions that are mostly outside their control: officials' failure to make policy reforms, a

---

x. This occurred in South Linden before the Kaplan Strasse squat and in Kronshagen.

strategic decision by militant groups to mobilize, police overreactions or passivity, and authorities' concessions to growing militant protests. In such cases, conventional and disruptive protesters are faced with a choice between supporting the militants, giving up disruptive actions in favor of conventional activity, or demobilizing altogether.[y]

But protest groups can try to steer between the horns of this dilemma by combining disruptive and conventional strategies and by trying to limit the scope of action for militants and repressive authorities alike. Innovating tactics and using decentralized methods is helpful. Taking this approach, protesters may be able to use disruption and radical demands to win allies, trigger official mistakes, expand opportunities for later participation, and win reforms. Although nonviolent protesters on the left and right in Germany have often chosen to support militants, they do not need to do so. The citizen initiatives at Wyhl and Gorleben chose disciplined nonviolent strategies that deliberately marginalized militants.

Yet avoiding the dilemma between too little disruption and too much opportunity for militants requires not only the right kinds of strategic decisions by protesters, but also the right kinds of responses by authorities. Public officials and political elites usually work to prevent the expansion of participation if it includes disruptive protests, since even reformists among them usually prefers only minor reforms and routine participation. But sometimes, as in Linden and at Wyhl, officials contributed to the development of nonviolent movements that expanded participation and resulted in major policy reforms—a kind of protest politics that deepens democracy. Officials aided its development by tolerating a degree of nonviolent disruption, making timely concessions to conventional and disruptive rather than to militant protests, and repressing militancy in decisive, proportionate, and well-targeted ways.

This combination of interactions occurred, mostly accidentally, at Wyhl. Yet what arises by accident can also be nudged into existence, if protesters, politicians, and officials find counterparts who would like to steer protest politics in a democratizing direction. The case of North Linden shows that nonviolent protest politics can be deliberately encouraged. There, reformist Social Democrats helped create protest groups

---

y. In West Berlin, Hoyerswerda, and Rostock, protesters largely supported the militants during crucial periods of protest, while at Brokdorf they split between these three responses.

and then helped sustain the groups by making concessions to their protest actions. This case also shows the limitations of elite-sponsored protest, since protest activities were subordinated to the Social Democrats' priorities. Hence, protest groups in that part of Linden did not undertake many disruptive actions, spark very widespread participation, or achieve much influence on policy after major neighborhood renewal reforms were adopted.

STABILITY AND CHANGE IN DEMOCRATIC POLITICS

Scholars have argued that Germany's main political institutions provide great stability to political contention and policymaking.[54] But, ironically, the features that often seem to give German politics great stability sometimes contribute to turbulent, unpredictable changes in politics and policies. When the system is running in normal mode, party and interest group leaders control debate and wrangle over incremental changes in policy. Citizens remain spectators except when they weigh in at staid intervals by participating in elections, which produce small changes in parliaments and occasionally influence changes in government composition. Citizen influence on policy is heavily buffered by the inertia of coalition governments, *Land*-federal relations, corporatist linkages, parapublic institutions, and judicial oversight, and by the grip of the parties on public discourse. Any change is very slow, and the system resembles smoothly running machinery that produces, with considerable expenditure of energy, a small and predictable product.

But sometimes the machinery runs haywire. When policymakers impose new threats, when protest groups form effective alliances and use innovative tactics, when they gain public support, and when some elites give support to protesters, then politics becomes contentious and unpredictable. At such times, protesters, politicians, and authorities take actions that reinforce each other, sometimes deliberately, but more often accidentally. As protests rise, the mechanisms of stability may become sources of change. *Land* and local governments, as well as lower-level courts, provide many points for access and potential paths for new demands to slowly, unevenly move upward in the system. Privileged interest groups, such as housing corporations or electricity utilities, may reveal themselves, to the public embarrassment of officials, to be democratically unaccountable organizations liable to provoke protests. The parties' domination of debate and government makes them visible targets for demands, while protesters use the parties' decentralized organizations and internal fractures as footholds. The smoothly operating machinery of German policymaking transforms into an awkward dance partner for protest groups.

The ultimate effects on policy and politics have always been buffered by the institutional machinery, but they also depend on how each partner chooses to deal with the other, and on when and where their dance steps happen to match up. Where their actions reinforce each other, different kinds of relationships can arise, marked either by mutually respectful, predictable deliberations, or by nonviolent, creative confrontations, or by violent threats, attacks, counterattacks, and exclusion. Officials, politicians, and protesters soon settle into more predictable relationships that are built up from this varied but finite repertoire. Through their relationships with politicians and officials, protest groups sometimes effect major changes in politics and policy. Together, they continually remake democracy in Germany.

NOTES

PREFACE AND ACKNOWLEDGMENTS

1. E.g., Tarrow 1989a and Koopmans 1993.
2. E.g., Rucht 1994, Koopmans 1995, and Kriesi et al. 1995.
3. Joppke 1990, 1993.
4. For a review of the structure-agent problem in recent social movement theory, see Lichbach 1998.
5. Karapin 2003 and 2002.

INTRODUCTION

1. Karapin 1993.
2. Neidhardt and Rucht 1999, 149–50; Koopmans 1995, 61.
3. See Adam 1998; Banaszak, Beckwith, and Rucht 2003; Björgo and Witte 1993b; Bodenschatz, Heise, and Korfmacher 1983; Brand 1985; Dalton and Kuechler 1990; della Porta 1995; della Porta and Reiter 1998b; Duyvendak 1995; Evans 1979; Ferree et al. 2002; Giugni, McAdam, and Tarrow 1999; Imig and Tarrow 2001; Jenkins and Klandermans 1995; Joppke 1993; Katsiaficas 1987; Katzenstein and Mueller 1987; Koopmans 1995; Koopmans and Statham 2000a; Kriesi 1993; Kriesi et al. 1995; Lipset and Altbach 1969; Meyer and Tarrow 1998b; Miller 1987; Nelkin and Pollak 1981; Rochon 1988; Rucht 1994; and Witte 1996.
4. Koopmans 1995, 1996; Kriesi et al. 1995.
5. Rucht 2003, 161.
6. On the role of mechanisms in theorizing, see Tilly 2001, 25, and McAdam, Tarrow, and Tilly 2001.
7. Bergmann 1994, 270; Koopmans and Olzak 2004, 217–18.
8. Exceptions include Kriesi 1995, Koopmans 1998, and Betz 1991 for left-right comparisons and Rucht, Blattert, and Rink 1997 for East-West comparisons.

CHAPTER 1

1. Koopmans 1992, 50, 53.
2. Ibid., 92–93; Markovits and Gorski 1993, 42–44.
3. Almond and Verba 1963, 428–29.

4. Ibid., 185; Dalton 1993, 182; Helm 1993, 13–14.
5. Rucht 2003, 159; 1998b, 38, 46–48.
6. Kirchheimer 1966.
7. Cooper 1996, 78–81.
8. Ibid., 73–74; Koopmans 1992, 93.
9. Murphy and Roth 1991.
10. The figures are for the 1990s (Conradt 1996, 270, 225, 265, 193), but the pattern was similar in the previous decades.
11. Koopmans 1992, 66.
12. Holtmann 1992; Katzenstein 1987, 54–57; Gerlach 1999, 163–64.
13. Gerlach 1999, 267–73; Gunlicks 1970.
14. Hübner and Rohlfs 1984, 404; Gerlach 1999, 276.
15. Braunthal 1994, 1996; Smith 1986; Merkl 1989, chaps. 13–14.
16. Cooper 1996, 54–60; Poguntke 1993, 148–51.
17. Nelkin and Pollak 1981, 165 and n. 31; Kitschelt 1979; Koopmans 1992, 98.
18. Neidhardt and Rucht 1999, 136; author's calculations; Rucht 2003, 159–60; Koopmans 1995, 107; Dalton 1993, 200 n. 16; Rink 2000, 97. Although Rucht's figures include anti-foreigner protests, these points still hold if one excludes such events, since only 7 percent of western German protests and only 0.2 percent of protest participants in his data were opposed to foreigners in the 1990s (Rucht 2003, 161).
19. Kriesi et al. 1992; della Porta and Rucht 1995.
20. Hofrichter and Schmitt 1991, 479, 481, 483; Pappi 1991, 463–64; Klingemann and Fuchs 1995, 253; Jennings et al. 1990, 60.
21. Conradt 1980; Helm 1993.
22. Conradt 1980, 256.
23. Inglehart 1977; Baker, Dalton, and Hildebrandt 1981.
24. Kitschelt 1989; Markovits and Gorski 1993, chaps. 6–7; Meng 1987.
25. E.g., Barnes et al. 1979; Inglehart 1977; Baker, Dalton, and Hildebrandt 1981; Dalton 1996; and Jennings et al. 1990. By contrast, work on these movements from political institutional and political process perspectives does examine violence on the left, and relates it to nonviolent protest (Joppke 1993; della Porta 1995; Koopmans 1995; Kriesi et al. 1995; Rucht 1999, 2002).
26. Habermas 1981; 1984, 392–93; Offe 1987, 73; Inglehart 1981, 884; Touraine 1981; Melucci 1980, 219–20; Cohen 1985, 666–69; Gorz 1982.
27. BV 1991, 19; 2003, 113.
28. Neidhardt and Rucht 1999, 151; Kriesi et al. 1995, 120; Rucht 2002; Tarrow 1989a.
29. BV 1991, 23, 33, 35; 1993b, 24, 34; 1998, 66; author's calculations.
30. Braunthal 1990b, 31–32; Brand 1988, 26–40.
31. Dennis 1993, 195, 197, 205–8, 211–15; Bleiker 1993, 14.
32. Gapper 2003.
33. Rucht 1996.
34. Münch 1993; Betz 1994, 61.
35. BV 1991, 76; 1993b, 79–80; author's calculations.
36. BV 1991, 76; 1992, 70; author's calculations.
37. E.g., Stöss 1991, Bergmann and Erb 1994a, Jaschke 1994, and Institut für Sozialforschung 1994. Popular accounts in this vein include Funke 1993, Siegler 1993, Schmidt 1993, and Lewis 1996.
38. E.g., Koopmans 1996b and 1996d.

39. An exception is Willems et al. 1993, 213–26; cf. also Benzler 1997 and Dittberner 1986.
40. Rucht 2003, 163.
41. Klandermans and Tarrow 1988; Kriesi 1995, 1993.
42. E.g., Inglehart 1977, 1990; Barnes et al. 1979; Kaase 1982; Dalton 1996; Baker, Dalton, and Hildebrandt 1981; Gabriel 1983, 78–84; and Habermas 1981 and 1984, 392–93; cf. also Meyer and Tarrow 1998a, 12–20, and Zald and McCarthy 1987.
43. Dalton 1996, 80; Kriesi 1995, 22.
44. Kitschelt 1989.
45. Kriesi 1995, 32; Dalton 1996, 76; Kriesi et al. 1995, 74.
46. Betz 1994; Kriesi 1995. For the theory of ethnic competition more generally, see Olzak 1992, 24–47, Olivier 1991, Blalock 1967, Barth 1969, and Bonacich 1972. These factors are also prominent in other socioeconomic explanations of racist violence, e.g., Lloyd 1993, 216–17, Lüdemann 1995, Heitmeyer 1993, 26, and Björgo and Witte 1993a, 7–9.
47. Data from the Statistisches Bundesamt, published in Beauftragte für die Belange der Ausländer, press release "Daten und Fakten zur Ausländersituation," October 1994, Table 1; Martin 1994, 216.
48. Krueger and Pischke 1997, 198–205. This analysis relied on newspaper reports of xenophobic violence and controlled for population density and many other variables.
49. Krueger and Pischke 1997, 201.
50. BV 1991, 76; 1993a, 59; 1993b, 79–80; author's calculations.
51. *Statistisches Jahrbuch deutscher Gemeinden* 1992, 492; *Statistisches Jahrbuch für die Bundesrepublik Deutschland* 1994, 72; author's calculations to produce an estimate excluding Berlin.
52. BV 1993b, 102; Krueger and Pischke 1997, 201.
53. Data from Bundesamt für die Anerkennung ausländischer Flüchtlinge.
54. Willems et al. 1993, 36, 40.
55. Husbands 1988, 706; 1989, 96; on cultural conflict in general, see Park 1950, 236–39.
56. E.g., Heitmeyer 1992 and 1993; Otto and Merten 1993, pts. 4–5; and Tuttle 1994.
57. E.g., Barnes et al. 1979.
58. BV 1993b, 94; Rucht 1980; Brand, Büsser, and Rucht 1986, 102–3; Willems et al. 1993; Rucht 1994, 174–76; Ellwein, Lippert, and Zoll 1975, 151.
59. Koopmans 1995, 210–15; Geronimo 1995; BV 1993b, 34; Rucht 2002; Willems 1997, 435–37.
60. Rucht 2002, Tables 7.1–7.2.
61. Rucht 1980, 1984.
62. BV 1993b, 94; Willems et al. 1993, 119–23.
63. Tarrow 1994, 115.
64. Kitschelt 1986, 63–64, 67–69; Koopmans 1992, 66–67, 70; Kriesi et al. 1995, 41–44, 213–15; Brand 1985, 323.
65. Kriesi et al. 1995, 34–35.
66. Kitschelt 1986; Kriesi et al. 1995; Koopmans 1995.
67. For similar developments in political opportunity theories, see Burstein 1991; Meyer and Imig 1993; Amenta, Curruthers, and Zylan 1992; and Wisler and Kriesi 1998.

68. E.g., Thelen and Steinmo 1992, 16; March and Olsen 1984; Hall and Taylor 1996; and Immergut 1998.
69. Della Porta and Reiter 1998a.
70. On the ways that political opportunity structures affect movements, see Tilly 1978 and 1995b; McAdam 1982; Tarrow 1989a and 1998; and McAdam, McCarthy, and Zald 1996a. These authors also argue that movements can affect their political environments (e.g., Tarrow 1994, esp. 96–97; McAdam, McCarthy, and Zald 1996b, 13, 26–28; McAdam 1996; and McAdam, Tarrow, and Tilly 2001, 243–44). For a critique, see Goodwin and Jasper 1999. For an explicitly interactive theory, see Joppke 1993, chap. 1, and for reviews of structure and agency issues within recent theories of protest, see Lichbach 1998 and Schock 2005.
71. McAdam 1996, 35–37; for similar points, see also Joppke 1993, Goodwin 2001, and Schock 2005.
72. For political opportunity work that emphasizes both institutions and processes, see Rucht 1994, chap. 10; McAdam 1996, 26–28; Gamson and Meyer 1996; and Koopmans 1995.
73. Gamson and Meyer 1996.
74. E.g., Tarrow 1989a, Koopmans 1993, McAdam 1983, and della Porta 1995.
75. E.g., McAdam, Tarrow, and Tilly 2001 and Tilly and Tarrow 2007.
76. McAdam, Tarrow, and Tilly 2001, 48–50, 243–44.
77. Tilly 1978, 52–56, 100.
78. Tarrow 1989b; McAdam 1996.
79. Tarrow 1994, 96–97; McAdam 1983; Joppke 1993, 200–201; 1992; Rucht 1994, 480–82; McAdam 1982, 146; della Porta and Reiter 1998b.
80. Gamson and Meyer 1996, 288.
81. McAdam 1983.
82. Gamson and Meyer 1996, 289; cf. Tilly 1999.
83. Tarrow 1994, 85–90; McAdam 1996, 27–28; Rucht 1998a, 113.
84. Grant and Wallace 1991, 1118–20.
85. Della Porta 1996.
86. Braunthal 1994, 123–25; Koopmans 1995, 93; della Porta and Rucht 1995, 249.
87. Markovits and Gorski 1993, 95.
88. Mez 1991, 384–85; Mewes 1998, 31–37; Markovits and Gorski 1993, 189–96; Kitschelt 1989. A right-wing element of the Greens lost intraparty conflicts in 1980 and formed a right-ecological party that gained negligible electoral support (Biehl and Staudenmeier 1995, chap. 2; Markovits and Gorski 1993, 193–96).
89. Die Grünen 1980; Frankland and Schoonmaker 1992, 126–45; Markovits and Gorski 1993, 152–85.
90. Papadakis 1989, 68–69.
91. Poguntke 1993, 175–78; Cooper 1996, 152–63; Kretschmer 1988, 186–87; Koopmans 1995, 145; Kriesi et al. 1995, 68; Kitschelt 1989, 241–42.
92. *Frankfurter Rundschau*, 31 October 1978; *Rheinischer Merkur*, 18 July 1980, 5; *Der Spiegel*, 16 June 1980, 34.
93. Münch 1993; Meier-Braun 1980; Perlmutter 1995.
94. Perlmutter 1995; Karapin 1999, 2000; Kuechler 1994.
95. Betz 1997.
96. On the promotion of violent protest, see Koopmans 1996b, 202–3.
97. Rucht 1990a; cf. also Willems 1997, 444–48.

98. Koopmans 1993, 641; Tarrow 1989a, 26–27, 310–19; 1989b, 55–56; Piven and Cloward 1979, 27–36; Tilly 1978, 52–59.
99. McAdam 1983.
100. Winter 1998, 70; cf. Gurr 1970, 255–59.
101. Rucht 1980, 1984; Kitschelt 1980; Bodenschatz, Heise, and Korfmacher 1987; Schnepf and Staubach 1988; Schneider-Wilkes 1995; Linse et al. 1988; Rucht 1998a, 121; Koopmans 1992, 125, 173, 180, 188; Gabriel 1983, 84–87.
102. Cooper 1996; Rucht 1998a, 121; Koopmans 1992, 200.
103. Roth 1980, 82; Rucht 1987.
104. Koopmans 1992, 98; Wollmann 1974; Nelkin and Pollak 1981, 32; Hager 1995, 68–70; 1993, 48 and n. 14; Rucht 1988a, 11.
105. Windhoff-Heritier and Gabriel 1983.
106. Willems 1996, 37; Willems et al. 1993.
107. For a list of 198 specific protest methods, see Sharp 1973, chaps. 3–8.
108. Bond 1994.
109. McAdam 1983; della Porta and Reiter 1998b; Meyer and Tarrow 1998b.
110. Schock 2005, 38–40; Sharp 1973, chaps. 3–8.
111. Rucht 1980; Kretschmer 1988, 84–85.
112. Rucht 1990b, 172; Joppke 1993, 53.
113. Tarrow 1989a, 311–17; Joppke 1993, 15–16, 53.
114. Tilly 1979, 1983, 1986; 1995b, 26–27; 1995a; Tarrow 1994, 1995, 1998; Traugott 1995a; Rucht 1990a.
115. This has been noted in the context of the diffusion of tactics from one movement to another (Rucht 1990a, 208; McAdam and Rucht 1993). Regarding concessions to violence, see Eckert and Willems 1986; Willems et al. 1993, 230–31; and Smelser 1962, 239–40.
116. Rucht 1990b, 173; Joppke 1993, 15, 17.
117. Traugott 1995b, 6; Smelser 1962, 231–36, 262; Keith 1993; Salert and Sprague 1980, 20–27.
118. Della Porta 1995, 78–80, 191; Rucht 1999, 372; Neidhardt 1992; Koopmans 1997, 153; Mason and Krane 1989; cf. Thompson 1971.
119. Winter 1998, 70; cf. Gurr 1970, 255–59.
120. Koopmans 1996d, 776; 1995, 260; author's calculations.
121. Minkenberg 1994, 180–83; Merkl 1993, 210–11; Maaz 1991; Tuttle 1994, 77; Krell, Niklas, and Ostermann 1996, 158–59; Heitmeyer 1993.
122. Minkenberg 1994, 180–83; Ireland 1997, 546–50.
123. Bergmann 1994, 267; Oesterreich 1993; Stöss 1993; Watts 1997, 149.
124. Bergmann 1994, 267 and n. 8.
125. Kuechler 1994; Willems et al. 1993, 40–41; Bergmann 1994, 266.
126. Rucht 2003, 163.
127. Erb 1993, 145–46.
128. Panayi 1994, 278; Merkl 1993, 213; Willems et al. 1993, 226–31; Wollmann 2002, 167, 171–72; Glaessner 2001, 18.
129. Bergmann and Erb 1994b, 83–85, 87; Wagner interview; Wagner 1995, 76 and n. 89.
130. Przeworski and Teune 1970; Tarrow 1999, viii.
131. Dion 1998; McAdam, Tarrow, and Tilly 2001, 80–84.
132. Bennett and George 1997.
133. Neidhardt and Rucht 1999, 149–50.

134. Brech and Greiff 1978; Schnepf and Staubach 1988; Brandes and Schön 1981; Hermann et al. 1987; Geronimo 1995.
135. Rucht 1980; Kitschelt 1980; Kretschmer 1988; Willems 1997.
136. Wagner 1995; Karapin 2002.

CHAPTER 2

1. Gerlach and Holland 1976, 266.
2. Buchholz 1973, 20; Gerlach and Holland 1976, 267 n. 11; Brech et al. 1977, 56.
3. Karapin 1993, 516, 520.
4. First Becker interview.
5. Hermann and Glöde 1985, 199; Katz and Mayer 1985, 33.
6. Koopmans 1992, 178, 180; Brandes and Schön 1981.
7. Hermann 1985, 116–37; author's calculations.
8. Geronimo 1995, 117; Hermann 1985, 122–23.
9. Orlowsky 1982, 5; first Eichstädt interview; Bodenschatz, Heise, and Korfmacher 1983, 109; Bodenschatz 1987, 207; Verein 1989b, 64.
10. Hermann and Glöde 1985, 99.
11. Karapin 1993, 505–7.
12. *Berliner Morgenpost (BM)*, 11 February 1988; *Die Wahrheit*, 28 April 1988; *taz*, 3 August 1988; author's observation of SO36 Neighborhood Committee meeting, 14 February 1989; Lautenschläger interviews.
13. Sauter and Anonymous interviews; *taz*, 3 May 1988; LVB 1992, 32.
14. *taz*, 4 May 1987, 5 May 1989; Verein 1989b, 79, 91.
15. Senator für Inneres 1982, 6–7; Willems 1997, 272; Geronimo 1995, 117; Hermann and Glöde 1985, 106.
16. Hellweg and Wend 1982, 44; Sauter, Anonymous, and second Eichstädt interviews.
17. Geronimo 1995, 117; Koopmans 1995, 211.
18. Wollmann 1974.
19. *Statistischer Vierteljahresbericht Hannover* 1976, IV, 81; for 1981 and 1986, data from Statistisches Amt Hannover.
20. FGW 1998, 111.
21. Sattler 1979, 258.
22. Kuhn and Krüger interviews; *HAZ*, 29 September 1981, 30 January 1986.
23. AGSTA 1979, 4–5, 13; Schnepf and Staubach 1988; Gerlach and Holland 1976, 265; Radek, Woite, and Wekel 1977, 29.
24. Habermann et al. 1977, 320.
25. Bennefeld et al. 1976, 12.
26. Senator für Bau 1964, 1–2; Bodenschatz 1987, 172–73; Knipp 1974, 23.
27. Pirker et al. 1975, 40.
28. Heise 1981, 81.
29. Bennefeld et al. 1976, 77.
30. Jung and Worbs 1976, 26.
31. Ibid., 26–27.
32. Habermann et al. 1977; Schnepf and Staubach 1988.
33. Pirker et al. 1975, 38–39, 55, 59–61, 65–66; Rädler and Wartenberg interviews; Büro für Stadtsanierung 1971; Egert et al. 1971.
34. Habermann et al. 1977; Schnepf and Staubach 1988, 99; Deiters interview;

HAZ, 9 June, 24 June, 7 July 1972; Brech and Greiff 1978, 173; Brech et al. 1977, 56; Buchholz, Reincke, and Wiecha 1973, 184.
35. Buchholz, Reincke, and Wiecha 1973, 195; Buchholz 1973, 14–15.
36. Brech and Greiff 1981, 822–23.
37. Habermann et al. 1977, 320.
38. Buchholz and Siemund interviews.
39. Buchholz 1973, 50–51.
40. Buchholz, Reincke, and Wiecha 1973, 190–91; Buchholz 1973, 13–14.
41. Buchholz 1973, 17, 19.
42. Autzen et al. 1984, 26–31; Becker 1981; Pirker et al. 1975.
43. Pirker et al. 1975, 57–58, 61; Heise 1981, 106–8, 117–19, 151–53 nn. 91, 103, 106.
44. Pirker et al. 1975, 62; Verein 1989b, 18.
45. Verein 1989b, 26, 34–35.
46. Dittrich and Habeny 1980, 9–11; Verein 1989b, 36–37.
47. Sonnewald and Raabe-Zimmermann 1983, 27–28.
48. Rädler interview; Verein 1989a, 55. Dargel (1982) provides a case study of real estate speculation, and Ulsen and Claassen (1982, esp. 38) an informative satire.
49. AL 1985, 129.
50. Verein 1989b, 43; Dieser and Kouvelis 1980.
51. Thörnig interview; Bürgerinitiative 1978.
52. Laurisch 1981; Bürgerinitiative SO36, "Bürger informieren zum Thema," press release, n.d. (approx. September 1984).
53. Buchholz, Reincke, and Wiecha 1973, 199, 205–6.
54. HAZ, 6 January 1973.
55. Spandauer Volksblatt (SV), 6–7 February 1979; Der Abend, 16 February 1979; Der Tagesspiegel (Tsp), 3 April 1979; Sonnewald and Raabe-Zimmermann 1983, 52.
56. Laurisch 1981, 62.
57. Brand, Büsser, and Rucht 1986, 174–78, 182–83; Roth 1985, 60–66; Kraushaar 1978.
58. Willems 1997, 270.
59. Langguth 1983, 33–35; Schaper 1984.
60. Laurisch 1981; Sonnewald and Raabe-Zimmermann 1983.
61. Geronimo 1995, 43–48.
62. Mulhak 1983, 225; Hermann and Glöde 1985, 107–11; Geronimo 1995, 118–20, 53–57, passim; Interim, 3 May 1989; cf. also the periodicals Provo and Radikal.
63. "TUWAT Spektakel in Bärlin ab 25.8.," 1981 leaflet; translation of this and other quotations in this book are by the author.
64. Leaflet quoted in Sonnewald and Raabe-Zimmermann 1983, 69.
65. Katz and Meyer 1985, 34.
66. Laurisch 1981, 199–202.
67. Thörnig interview; press release from Fuderholz and Reichardt, 17 December 1980; letter from Hans-Joachim Knipp, business manager, Urban Renewal Division, to Fuderholz and Reichardt, STERN archives, [December 1980].
68. Volksblatt Berlin, 28 April 1981; Senator für Inneres 1982, 16; Bodenschatz, Heise, and Korfmacher 1983, 324.
69. HAZ, 19 July 1972, cited in Buchholz, Reincke, and Wiecha 1973, 186.
70. Gerlach and Holland 1976; Holland interview.

71. Buchholz 1973, 17–19.
72. *HAZ*, 21 August 1973.
73. Buchholz 1973, 21, 23, 30, 34–35.
74. *HAZ*, 5 September 1973.
75. Buchholz 1973, 23.
76. Pirker et al. 1975, 64; Sonnewald and Raabe-Zimmermann 1983, 20; Wartenberg interview; Senator für Bau 1983, Appendix 44.
77. Hermann and Glöde 1985, 44; Bodenschatz 1987, 190; Sonnewald and Raabe-Zimmermann 1983, 26; Rädler interview.
78. Bodenschatz, Heise, and Korfmacher 1983, 105.
79. Eichstädt 1982; Orlowsky 1982.
80. First Eichstädt interview.
81. Bodenschatz, Heise, and Korfmacher 1983, 106–7; Eichstädt 1984, 42–45.
82. Thörnig interview; Verein 1989b, 49; Laurisch 1981, 100; *SV*, 30 November 1979; *Tsp*, 30 January 1980; KMI [1980].
83. Verein 1989b, 50; Laurisch 1981, 187.
84. *SV*, 22 June 1980; Laurisch 1981, 192, 198.
85. Open letter from Hardt-Waltherr Hämer to Dietrich Stobbe, 9 October 1980.
86. *taz*, 3, 17, 24 July, 11 November 1981; *Tsp*, 12 September 1981; open letter from the "Aktionskreis von Gewerkschaften in DGB 'für eine Wende in der Wohnungspolitik,'" to the DGB Berlin, 16 August 1981.
87. Fuderholz and Reichardt, International Building Exposition, press release, 17 December 1980; Laurisch 1981, 86–90; Bascon-Borgelt, Ganssauge, and Pallenberg 1984, 14.
88. E.g., Ingeborg Drewitz and Jürgen Müller-Schneck, "Morgen Leute, denkt nur nicht, wir räumen," *Die Zeit Magazin*, n.d., accessed in the collection of the Amerika-Gedenkbibliothek, West Berlin, in 1989.
89. Siemund interview.
90. *HAZ*, 14, 30 May 1973; Buchholz, Reincke, and Wiecha 1973, 199–200; Buchholz 1973, 16.
91. *HAZ*, 3 January 1973; Buchholz, Reincke, and Wiecha 1973, 199; Buchholz interviews.
92. Dittrich and Habeny 1980, 9–11; Verein 1989b, 36, 38.
93. Laurisch 1981, 34.
94. Verein 1989b, 53.
95. *Tsp*, 3 May 1980; Orlowsky 1982, 4; Sonnewald and Raabe-Zimmermann 1983, 55–56.
96. *Tsp*, 14 December 1980; *taz*, 15, 17 December 1980; *BM*, 17 December 1980; Schmolt 1984, 912; Laurisch 1981, 200; Mulhak 1983, 228.
97. *BILD*, *Tsp*, 17 December 1980.
98. Eckert and Willems 1986, 144; Hellweg and Wend 1982, 44; Mulhak 1983, 230; "Berliner Häuserkampf" 1987; Geronimo 1995, 116.
99. Aust and Rosenbladt 1981, 28.
100. *Tsp*, *Die Welt*, 28 November 1979; *Süddeutsche Zeitung (SüZ)*, 3 November 1980.
101. Hermann 1985, 117–29; Hermann and Glöde 1985, 150–52, 175.
102. Sonnewald and Raabe-Zimmermann 1983, 98–101, 120.
103. *taz*, 4 May 1981.
104. *Die Neue*, 13 December 1980; FGW 1981, 1; Hermann and Glöde 1985, 82.
105. Pursch 1981, 70; Hager 1995, 179.

106. Mulhak 1983, 226; Schmolt 1984, 912; Laurisch 1981, 202, 212.
107. Koopmans 1992, 184; Aust and Rosenbladt 1981, 22; Hellweg and Wend 1982, 44.
108. Mulhak 1983, 231.
109. Willems 1997, 276.
110. Bodenschatz, Heise, and Korfmacher 1983, 308; Senator für Inneres, Berlin (West), "Hausbesetzungen und Hausbesetzer in Berlin," 30 November 1982 press release, 6–7.
111. Laurisch 1981, 200.
112. International Building Exposition press release, 17 December 1980; Bürgerinitiative SO36 press release, 11 February 1981; Laurisch 1981, 199–202.
113. Gallus and Peter interviews; Gerlach and Holland 1976, 266–67, 271 and n. 16.
114. Henning and Burucker interviews.
115. *taz*, 24 May 1996.
116. Lautenschläger, Sütcü, Karaciyan, Thörnig, and first Eichstädt interviews.
117. Eichstädt 1982, 54–55 and n. 9.
118. Data are from the Urban Renewal Division and Verein SO36, and taken from Herberg-Reidenbach 1989, 23.
119. Grube, Burucker, Ützmann, and first Barkhoff interviews; *HAZ*, 2 February 1985.
120. Author's observation of SO36 Neighborhood Committee meetings, 14 February, 9 May 1989; Eichstädt 1982, 55; *taz*, 23 November 1988.
121. Göhler interview; *taz*, 3 April 1987, 13 July, 2 August, 2 September 1989; Kaczmarczyk 1982.
122. BAKU 1989; *HAZ*, 10 November 1985.
123. Schaper 1984.
124. Bodenschatz 1987, 205; Sattler 1979, 258; Sütcü interview.
125. Verein 1989b, 72.
126. Göhler and Sauter interviews; *taz*, 19 May 1989, 16 March 1990.
127. *taz*, 22 March 1989.
128. Sauter interview; *BM*, 23 January 1988; Verein 1989a; *taz*, 23 November 1988.
129. *BM*, 11 February 1988; *Die Wahrheit*, 28 April 1988; *taz*, 3 August 1988; author's observation of SO36 Neighborhood Committee meeting, 14 February 1989; Lautenschläger interviews.
130. *Berliner Zeitung*, 10, 22 August 1991; *BM*, 13 August 1991; *taz*, 29 January, 12 May, 6, 8, 15 July 1992, 4 May, 10 November 1994; *Tsp*, 27 August 1991, 10 June, 9 July 1992, 28 June 1994; Verein 1992.
131. *taz*, 4–5, 13 May 1987, 11 July, 22 October 1988; *Volksblatt*, *Tsp*, 13 June 1987; *Drucksache* (a local monthly periodical), 22 May 1987, 10–12; Verein 1988.
132. *taz*, 4 May 1987, 3 May 1988.
133. Verein 1989b, 73.
134. *Rotes Lindenblatt*, August 1981.
135. *BM*, 14, 19 April 1981; *Berliner Zeitung*, 7 May 1981; Infas 1981, 7; Willems 1997, 277; Sonnewald and Raabe-Zimmermann 1983, 128.
136. Hermann and Glöde 1985, 174; FGW 1981, 21.
137. FGW 1981, 21, 24–25; see also Infas 1981, 102.
138. *taz*, 24 May 1991, 9 May 1992.
139. *taz*, 11 June 1981; *HAZ*, 9 April 1981.

140. *Neue Press*, 15 April, 3 September 1981; *HAZ*, 2 April 1981; *taz*, 11 June 1981; Peter interview.
141. Verein 1989b, 79–80; *taz*, 4–5 May 1987.
142. *taz*, 19 May 1987, 5, 12 May 1989.
143. *taz*, 30 April 1988.
144. *taz*, 15, 18 June 1987; *Drucksache*, 3 July 1987; Gerhards and Rucht 1992, 560–61; Verein 1989b, 80.
145. *SO36: Der Verein informiert*, April 1989, 1–3.
146. *taz*, 22 March 1989.
147. *taz*, 5 April 1989, 30 April 1990.
148. *taz*, 30 April 1990.
149. *taz*, 3 May 1990, 4 May 1992.
150. *taz*, 30 April 1990.
151. *taz*, 3 May 1989.
152. *taz*, 3 May 1990, 3 May 1991, 2 May 1992, 3 May 1993, 3 May 1994, 3 May 1995, 2 May 1996, 3 May 1997.
153. Bodenschatz, Heise, and Korfmacher 1983, 396; Bodenschatz 1987, 190.
154. Kujath 1988, 134; Pelzinger and Riege 1981, 141–42.
155. Becker 1981; Selle 1986; Bodenschatz 1987, 176.
156. Köhnke and Landsfeld 1987; Heine and Kisker 1987, 10; Sonnewald and Raabe-Zimmermann 1983, 29.
157. Bodenschatz, Heise, and Korfmacher 1983, 396.
158. Sonnewald and Raabe-Zimmermann 1983, 57.
159. Rädler, Beran, and Meinhof interviews; Bodenschatz 1987, 201–2; Autzen et al. 1984, 30; BRBS 1988, 10.
160. Hermann and Glöde 1985, 82.
161. Karapin 1993, 506, 510.
162. Pirker et al. 1975; Rädler and Nowack interviews; Autzen et al. 1984, 18–25.
163. *taz*, 8 February, 19 April, 20 April 1988; *HAZ*, 3 November 1989; Grubert and Ronge interviews.

CHAPTER 3

1. Sternstein 1978a, 35ff.; Wüstenhagen 1975, 75–93; Rawlinson 1986, 37–41; Beer 1978a, 75–76; Rucht 1988b, 133–34.
2. *Frankfurter Allgemeine Zeitung (FAZ)*, *Neue Zürcher Zeitung (NZZ)*, 26 February 1975; *SüZ*, 27 February 1975; Rawlinson 1986, 40.
3. Beer 1978a, 79–80; Buchholtz 1978, 139.
4. *taz*, 17 February 1995.
5. *Die Welt*, *Kieler Nachrichten (KN)*, 21 February 1977; ILSH 1976, 43; Rucht 1980, 90; Nelkin and Pollak 1981, 67–68; Rucht 1980, 88–90; Trautmann 1978, 325–30.
6. Willems 1997, 319; *KN*, *Schleswig-Holsteinsche Landeszeitung (SHL)*, 22 December 1980; *Lübecker Nachrichten*, 23 December 1980; ILSH 1980, 35.
7. Willems 1997, 320.
8. *KN*, 6 June, 8 December 1986; 16 January, 7 September 1988, 22 May 1990.
9. *taz*, 23 November 1993, 26 April 1994, 21 March 1995, 27 August 1997.
10. Häusler 1988, 36; Kiersch and von Oppeln 1983, 125; Nelkin and Pollak 1981, 15–16.

11. Kitschelt 1980, 229; Beer 1978a, 72.
12. Kretschmer 1988, 173-74.
13. Ibid., 184-85.
14. Nelkin and Pollak 1981, 34.
15. Ibid., 15; Radkau 1983, 446.
16. Nelkin and Pollak 1981, 17; Kitschelt 1980, 165.
17. Nelkin and Pollak 1981, 14-18; Kitschelt 1980, 38-52; Radkau 1983, 19, chaps. II.4 and III.1.
18. Radkau 1983, 447-48 and n. 726.
19. Ibid., 446-50; Nelkin and Pollak 1981, 123-24; Kitschelt 1980, 199.
20. Nelkin and Pollak 1981, 165 and n. 31.
21. Ibid., 160-62; Kitschelt 1979, 14-15.
22. Kiersch and von Oppeln 1983, 26.
23. FGW 1998, 12, 14-15.
24. Nelkin and Pollak 1981, 15-16; Radkau 1983, 18-19.
25. Willems 1997, 321.
26. Joppke 1993, 27-30, 97-98; Rucht 1980, 74-78.
27. SüZ, 12 March 1975.
28. Buchholtz 1978, 128; Beer 1978a, 81.
29. *Norddeutscher Rundschau* (*NR*), 7, 22 February 1974; Nelkin and Pollak 1981, 64.
30. Joppke 1993, 117.
31. *Stuttgarter Zeitung* (*StZ*), 20 July 1973; Rucht 1988b, 141.
32. Rucht 1988b, 142.
33. Rucht 1980, 85-91; Joppke 1993, 101; Nelkin and Pollak 1981, 64 and n. 8.
34. Beer 1978a, 72, 74; Mossmann 1975, 140; Nössler and de Witt 1976, 232.
35. Sternstein 1978a; Nössler and de Witt 1976, 231.
36. Beer 1978a, 72.
37. Rucht 1988b, 145-46; Buchholtz 1978, 126; Sternstein 1978c, 52.
38. Rucht 1988b, 160; Beer 1978a, 87.
39. Kitschelt 1980, 228-29; Rucht 1980, 293; *KN*, 12 November 1973, 30 January, 13 November 1974.
40. *NR*, 24 December 1973; *KN*, 10 March 1976.
41. *NR*, *Wilstersche Zeitung*, 24 December 1973; Willems 1997, 323; Trautmann 1978, 322; BUU 1977, 192.
42. *NR*, 24 December 1973.
43. Thaysen 1980, 207; Nelkin and Pollak 1981, 32-34; Kiersch and von Oppeln 1983, 26.
44. Buchholtz 1978, 129; Wüstenhagen 1975, 61.
45. Rucht 1988b, 143 and nn. 30-32.
46. Beer 1978b, 107; *StZ*, 26 September 1974.
47. Rucht 1980, 83; Buchholtz 1978, 125; Nössler and de Witt 1976, 47.
48. Beer 1978b, 108.
49. *StZ*, 26 September 1974.
50. *StZ*, 18 December 1974; Wüstenhagen 1975, 61.
51. *StZ*, 10 January 1975; *SüZ*, 11 January 1975.
52. Sternstein 1978b, 38; Beer 1978b, 108; Buchholtz 1978, 132; *StZ*, 28 January, 19 February 1975.
53. Trautmann 1978, 321 and n. 53.
54. *KN*, 4 October 1974; Trautmann 1978, 324.

55. Willems 1997, 321.
56. Nelkin and Pollak 1981, 65; *Hamburger Abendblatt*, 16 November 1974.
57. BUU 1977, 58–60; Trautmann 1978, 321 and n. 54; *KN*, 4, 8 March 1976.
58. Rawlinson 1986, 12, 16–17, 33–34; Buchholtz 1978, 121–33; Rucht 1980, 83–84; McAdam and Rucht 1993, 57.
59. Rawlinson 1986, 39–40; Wüstenhagen 1975, 86; Rucht 1980, 85.
60. Sternstein 1978a, 38, 46.
61. Ibid., 47, 50.
62. *NZZ*, 21 October 1975; Sternstein 1978a, 45.
63. Beer 1978a, 95–126, esp. 110; Rucht 1988b, 137–39; *StZ*, 3 May 1980.
64. Sternstein 1978a, 41, 46, 48; Beer 1978a, 76, 79, 81; *StZ*, 8 November 1975; Rucht 1980, 87.
65. Sternstein 1978a, 44; *Die Welt*, 8 March 1976.
66. Mossmann 1975, 145–46; Sternstein 1978a, 43, 44, 45.
67. *StZ*, 29 August 1974, 7, 13 January, 22, 24–25 February 1975.
68. Rawlinson 1986, 37–39; Wüstenhagen 1975, 82–88; Rucht 1988b, 133; Sternstein 1978b, 46; *StZ*, 21, 24 February 1975.
69. Kommunistischer Bund Westdeutschland, "Deshalb haben wir beschlossen . . . ," leaflet, n.d., approx. September 1976.
70. Joppke 1993, 104.
71. Geronimo 1995, 105–6; Joppke 1993, 103–4.
72. Joppke 1993, 102; *SHL*, *KN*, 1 November 1976; *KN*, *Die Welt*, 15 November 1976.
73. *KN*, 9 December 1976, 7–8, 14 February 1977; Trautmann 1978, 330.
74. *Flensburger Tageblatt*, 3 November 1976; SPD Landesverband Schleswig-Holstein, "Weiterhin Baustop in Brokdorf," leaflet, n.d., approx. February 1977.
75. Willems 1997, 323.
76. Rucht 1980, 88–90; Nelkin and Pollak 1981, 68; Trautmann 1978, 325–30.
77. *Der Spiegel*, 22 November 1976, 82.
78. Kleinert 1981, 141–44.
79. Nelkin and Pollak 1981, 68.
80. Rucht 1980, 84.
81. Buchholtz 1978, 129–30; Rucht 1988b, 144; Nelkin and Pollak 1981, 62.
82. Rucht 1988b, 149; Buchholtz 1978, 132.
83. *StZ*, 28 July, 24 December 1973.
84. *StZ*, 9 November 1974.
85. *StZ*, 4 July 1974.
86. *StZ*, 7 March 1975; *SüZ*, 1 March 1976.
87. *StZ*, 24 February 1975.
88. *StZ*, 25 February 1975; *FAZ*, 26 February 1975.
89. *FAZ*, 25 February 1975; Wüstenhagen 1975, 79, 89.
90. *FAZ*, 22 February 1975.
91. *StZ*, 12, 18, 28 June 1975; Sternstein 1978a, 48–49.
92. Trautmann 1978, 325–26 and nn. 79–80; Rucht 1980, 89, 244 n. 48; Kretschmer 1988, 168–69 and nn. 13–15; Willems 1997, 322.
93. *KN*, 12 November 1973.
94. *KN*, 30 January 1974; Willems 1997, 321; Joppke 1993, 102.
95. Trautmann 1978, 327.
96. *Wilstersche Zeitung*, 21 December 1973; *KN*, 6 November 1974, 10 March 1976.
97. Trautmann 1978, 316; *KN*, 2 March 1974.

98. *KN*, 2 March 1974.
99. *KN*, 24, 26 July 1976.
100. Trautmann 1978, 323, 325–26.
101. ILSH 1976, 36.
102. *Der Spiegel*, 22 November 1976, 82.
103. *FAZ, NZZ*, 26 February 1975; *SüZ*, 27 February 1975; Rawlinson 1986, 40.
104. Wüstenhagen 1975, 90; Sternstein 1978a, 39.
105. *Flensburger Tageblatt*, 2–3 November 1976; *KN*, 3 November 1976.
106. Rucht 1980, 89.
107. *Hamburger Abendblatt*, 15 November 1976.
108. Rucht 1980, 89 and n. 48.
109. *KN*, 18 December 1976; Trautmann 1978, 328; Fach and Simonis 1987, 189–90.
110. *KN*, 15 November 1976.
111. *StZ*, 19 February 1975.
112. *StZ*, 19, 21 February 1975.
113. Buchholtz 1978, 132; Wüstenhagen 1975, 79.
114. Wüstenhagen 1975, 75–81; Rawlinson 1986, 37–39; Sternstein 1978b, 58; *StZ*, 21 February 1975; *päd-extra*, 15 March 1975.
115. Beer 1978a, 76.
116. *StZ*, 24–25 February 1975; Rawlinson 1986, 39; Wüstenhagen 1975, 82; Buchholtz 1978, 133; Sternstein 1978b, 65.
117. Rucht 1980, 241 n. 29; Sternstein 1978b, 47; *StZ*, 21, 24 February 1975.
118. Wüstenhagen 1975, 87–88.
119. *SüZ*, 12 March 1975.
120. Wüstenhagen 1975, 82.
121. *StZ*, 25 February 1975.
122. Wüstenhagen 1975, 86; *FAZ*, 26 February 1975.
123. Rawlinson 1986, 40.
124. Wüstenhagen 1975, 88.
125. *KN*, 27 October 1976; *Die Welt, Tsp*, 28 October 1976; *FAZ*, 1 November 1976; Brand 1988, 184; Nelkin and Pollak 1981, 65; Joppke 1993, 102.
126. *KN*, 2, 5 November 1976.
127. *KN*, 15–16 November 1976; *Die Zeit*, 10 December 1976.
128. Trautmann 1978, 327; Brand 1988, 184–85; Willems 1997, 322.
129. Rucht 1980, 241 and n. 29; *Die Welt, KN*, 15 November 1976.
130. *SHL*, 1 November 1976; *Frankfurter Rundschau (FR)*, 1 November 1976; *KN*, 1–2 November 1976; ILSH 1976, 21, 38; Trautmann 1978, 327 and n. 86; Rucht 1980, 89; Nelkin and Pollak 1981, 65–66.
131. *KN*, 1 November 1976; *Die Welt*, 2 November 1976.
132. *KN, Die Welt*, 15 November 1976; BUU 1977, 129–33; Trautmann 1978, 327; Rucht 1980, 243–44 and n. 47; Nelkin and Pollak 1981, 66; Kleinert 1981, 141.
133. *StZ*, 1 April 1982.
134. Rawlinson 1986, 50; *StZ*, 29 April 1982, 26 January, 19 March, 25 April, 30 June 1983.
135. *KN*, 18 October 1977, 2 October, 15 December 1979, 23 January, 31 July, 21, 25 August 1981.
136. *KN*, 15–16 November 1976; SPD Landesverband Schleswig-Holstein, "Weiterhin Baustop in Brokdorf," leaflet, n.d., approx. February 1977; *SüZ*, 29 January 1979.

137. *KN*, 20 February 1981.
138. *KN*, *Die Welt*, 6 February 1981.
139. *KN*, 27 May 1986.
140. *StZ*, 5 April 1982; *Unsere Zeit*, 6 April 1982; Rawlinson 1986, 48–49; Rucht 1988b, 157 and n. 94.
141. Rawlinson 1986, 49.
142. *Die Neue*, 15 April 1983.
143. *FAZ*, 21 April 1983.
144. *FAZ*, 21 April 1983; *Der Spiegel*, 2 May 1983.
145. *Die Neue*, 14 May 1983.
146. *KN*, 27 July, 6 August 1977, 25, 28 February 1981, 10 June 1986.
147. Rucht 1980, 91.
148. Willems 1997, 324–25.
149. Ibid., 325.
150. *FR*, 25 March 1982, 28 March 1983; *StZ*, 21 June 1983.
151. *StZ*, 3 April 1982.
152. *StZ*, 18 May 1982; *Der Spiegel*, 2 May 1983; *FR*, 23 June 1983.
153. Willems 1997, 323–24.
154. *KN*, 4 July 1986.
155. *KN*, 9 June 1986.
156. *KN*, 11 February 1981.
157. Geronimo 1995, 112–13.
158. Rucht 1980, 90.
159. *KN*, 23 February, 2–3 March 1981, 9 June, 4 July, 1, 4 October 1986; *Dittmarsche Landeszeitung*, 2 March 1981; ILSH 1981, 36; Kleinert 1981, 104–6; Geronimo 1995, 112–13, 163–65; Willems 1997, 319–20, 326–30; Associated Press, 9 June 1986; *taz*, 31 October 1986.
160. Koopmans 1995, 158–70.
161. Willems 1997, 334–48; Rucht 1980, 99–148; Joppke 1993, 109–16.
162. Willems 1997, 337.

CHAPTER 4

1. E.g., Björgo and Witte 1993b, Witte 1996, Koopmans 1996b, and Karapin 2002.
2. E.g., Betz 1994 and Schain, Zolberg, and Hossay 2002.
3. BFA 1993, 61, 65.
4. Data from Flüchtlingsamt München; SH Landtag 1991; 1994, 15; author's calculations.
5. ILSH 1992a, 6; 1993a, 21; 1993b, 18.
6. ILSH 1992b, 24.
7. BV 1991, 76.
8. BSI 1992, 46; 1996, 18; *Münchner Merkur* (MM), 9 October 1991.
9. Cornelius, Martin, and Hollifield 1994, 421; Martin 1994, 182.
10. ALLBUS 1996 survey, online codebook, accessed at www.social-science-gesis.de, Questions 37 (3), 38 (3); the latter data, from 1994, were provided by Institut für Demoskopie Allensbach.
11. Kanstroom 1993b, 197.
12. Linke and Ness 1992.

13. *taz*, 29 November 1990.
14. Thoma 1990, 143–44; Willems et al. 1993, 213–17.
15. Thoma 1990, 122–31.
16. *taz*, 14 February 1992.
17. Reissl interview.
18. Kurreck interview.
19. *taz*, 14 February 1992.
20. SAM 1997, 41–42; 1987, 179; *Münchner Statistik* 1990 (3), Table 4.
21. *Statistisches Jahrbuch deutscher Gemeinden* 1992, 482.
22. SH Landtag 1994, 15.
23. Data from Social Ministry, Schleswig-Holstein; SH Landtag 1994.
24. *SüZ*, 10, 13 March, 22 September 1992; *taz*, 12 November 1994; *Süddeutsche Zeitung-München Süd (SZMS)*, 16 April 1992; *MM*, 12 March, 22 October 1992.
25. *SüZ*, 23 March 1992.
26. *taz*, 12 November 1994.
27. *SüZ*, 22 September 1992.
28. *taz*, 12 November 1994.
29. *KN*, 18 June, 10 October 1992, 1 June, 16 October 1994.
30. *KN*, 18 June, 29 October 1992; Lubinski interview.
31. *SZMS*, 16 April 1992.
32. *MM*, 12 March 1992; *SüZ*, 15 October 1992.
33. *SüZ*, 22 September, 15 October 1992; *MM*, 22 October 1992.
34. *SüZ*, 23 March 1992; *taz*, 12 November 1994.
35. *SüZ*, 11 March 1992.
36. *SüZ*, 10–11 March; *MM*, 12 March 1992.
37. *SüZ*, 23 March 1992.
38. Data from Flüchtlingsamt München; author's calculations.
39. *SüZ*, 15 October 1992.
40. *MM*, 22 October 1992; *taz*, 12 November 1994.
41. *MM*, 22 October 1992; *SZMS*, *SüZ*, 16 April 1992; *SüZ*, 15 October, 23 December 1992, 15 April 1993.
42. *SüZ*, 23 March 1992.
43. *SüZ*, 15 April 1993.
44. *KN*, 22 September 1990, 12 June 1992.
45. Lubinski interview.
46. *KN*, 23 April 1993.
47. *KN*, 12 June, 29 October 1992.
48. *KN*, 10 October 1992.
49. *KN*, 1 June 1994.
50. *KN*, 12, 18 June 1992.
51. *KN*, 10 October 1992.
52. *KN*, 1 June 1994.
53. *KN*, 16 October 1992.
54. *SüZ*, 11 March; *MM*, 12 March 1992.
55. *FR*, 10 April 1992.
56. *SüZ*, 15 October 1992; *MM*, 22 October 1992.
57. *SüZ*, 11 March 1992, 15 April 1993.
58. *SüZ*, 22 September 1992.
59. *SZMS*, 16 April 1992.
60. *KN*, 18 June 1992.

61. *KN*, 21 July 1992.
62. *KN*, 29 October 1992.
63. *SüZ*, 15 October 1992; 15 April 1993.
64. *SüZ*, 22 September 1992, 15 April 1993; data from Flüchtlingsamt München.
65. *taz*, 12 November 1994; email communication from Michael Hoffmann, Sendling borough council, 29 April 2002.
66. *KN*, 18 June, 21 July, 16 October 1992.
67. *KN*, 12 June, 16 October 1992, 23 April 1993.
68. *KN*, 23 April 1993.
69. Lubinski interview.
70. Schneider and Reissl interviews.

CHAPTER 5

1. Lüdemann and Erzberger 1994; Esser and Brosius 1996; Willems 1997, 424–26.
2. Koopmans 1996a; Karapin 2000.
3. Karapin 2000, esp. 321.
4. BV 1991, 76.
5. Karapin 2002, 152.
6. All information about these riots is taken from *SZH, Lausitzer Rundschau*, Hoyerswerda edition (*LR*), *Hoyerwerdaer Wochenblatt* (*HW*), *Hoyerwerdaer Wochenspiegel, BILD* (Dresden edition), and *Dresdner Morgenpost* (*DM*), 19–27 September 1991.
7. *Ostsee Zeitung* (*OZ*), 24–25 August 1992; *taz*, 25 August 1992.
8. *SZH*, 29 August 1991.
9. *SZR*, 17 August 1991.
10. *SZR*, 14 September 1992.
11. *SZH*, 7–8 September 1991; *HW*, 16 August, 13 September, 11 October, 13 December 1991; BFA 1993, 263.
12. *SZH*, 8 August 1991; *SZR*, 31 March 1991; author's calculations.
13. *SZR*, 9 April, 1 August, 18 September 1991, 3 March 1992; Sandig interview.
14. Joedecke 1992, 77.
15. Kanstroom 1993b, 197 and n. 337; *HW*, 26 July 1991.
16. *SZR*, 10 April 1991.
17. BV 1991, 91.
18. Koopmans and Olzak 2004, 218.
19. Bergmann and Erb 1994b, 84–88; Farin and Seidel-Pielen 1993, chap. 4; Willems 1993; Wagner 1995.
20. Schmidt, Wagner, and Vogel interviews; see the riot sources cited in note 6.
21. LKAS 1996, 40.
22. Ireland 1997, 548–49; Minkenberg 1994, 183.
23. Data from Zentrale Ausländerbehörde, Saxony.
24. Merkl 1993, 213; Bergmann 1994, 270–71; Ireland 1997, 557; Thumfahrt 2002, 618–33; Wollmann 2002, 167, 171–72.
25. Willems 1993, 175.
26. *BILD* (Dresden edition), 9 September 1991.
27. *HW*, 7 December 1990; data from Polizeidirektion Bautzen.
28. *taz*, 3 February, 26 May 1993.

29. SIS 1993, 19; author's calculations.
30. LKAS 1992a, 7, 22; 1993, 6.
31. Data from Landratsamt Hoyerswerda.
32. *LR*, 26 September 1991.
33. Hockenos 1993, 24–25; *HW*, 22 February 1991, *SZH*, 4 April 1991.
34. *HW*, 26 July 1991; *SZH*, 19 July, 29 August 1991; *LR*, 29 August 1991.
35. Schmidt interviews; Joedecke 1992, 76–77; Hockenos 1993, 24.
36. *SZH, LR*, 29 August 1991.
37. *OZ*, 27 June 1991, 19 June 1992.
38. *OZ*, 18–19 June 1992; *Norddeutsche Neuste Nachrichten*, Rostock edition, 18 June, 14 July 1992; Funke 1993, 112.
39. *SZR*, 21 February, 7 March 1991; other data provided by Statistisches Landesamt Sachsen.
40. *SZR*, 26 July, 18 December 1991, 8 February 1992; *BILD*, 21 December 1992.
41. *SZR*, 7 March 1991; Sandig interview.
42. *taz*, 7 May 1990.
43. *LR*, 19 September 1991.
44. *taz, DM, SZH*, 21 September 1991.
45. *OZ*, 24–25 August 1992; *taz*, 25 August 1992.
46. *SZR*, 7 March, 2 December, 18 December 1991, 15 October 1992, 13 February 1993.
47. *SZR*, 2 December 1991.
48. *SZR*, 23, 26 November 1991.
49. Sandig interview.
50. *SZH*, 29 August 1991.
51. Schmidt interviews; *SZH*, 16, 29 August 1991; *LR*, 29 August 1991.
52. *HW, DM*, 20 September 1991.
53. *DM*, 20 September 1991; *SZH, taz*, 21 September 1991.
54. *SZH, Junge Welt*, 23 September 1991.
55. *OZ*, 25 June 1992.
56. *SZH*, 29 August 1991.
57. *SZR*, 23 January, 21 February, 7 March 1991.
58. Wagner 1994, 84–85; Wagner interview; *taz*, 23 September 1991; *SZH*, 19 July 1991.
59. *SZH*, 5 October 1990; *SZH, SZD*, 19 September 1991.
60. *SZH*, 5 October 1990.
61. *SZH*, 6, 19 July 1991.
62. Quoted in *Hoyerswerdaer Wochenblatt*, 20 September 1991; cf. also Willems et al. 1993, 227–28.
63. *taz*, 7 May 1990.
64. *SZH*, 8, 28 June 1991.
65. *SZH*, 21, 23 September 1991.
66. *SZD*, 21 September 1991; *taz*, 23 September 1991.
67. Willems 1997, 422.
68. Willems et al. 1993, 229–30; Siegler 1993, 64–66.
69. *taz*, 25–26 August 1992; Funke 1993, 128–45.
70. Schmidt 1993, 164–65; *taz*, 3, 6 February 1993.
71. *SZR*, 13, 18, 26 March, 13 April, 8 May, 17 August, 9 November 1991.
72. *SZR*, 13 April 1991, 29 August, 14 September 1992.

73. LKAS 1992b, 31; *SZR*, 28 January 1993; data provided by Polizeidirektion Bautzen.
74. *SZR*, 28 January 1993.
75. Willems et al. 1993, 228.
76. *DM*, 25 April 1992; *SZD*, 1 October 1992.
77. Ireland 1997, 557.
78. Karapin 1999, 436–37; 2000, 334, 336–37; Koopmans 1996a.
79. Siegler 1993, 79.
80. Willems et al. 1993, 226–31; Lüdemann and Erzberger 1994; PDS 1993.
81. Author's analysis of Federal Interior Ministry data.
82. Lüdemann and Erzberger 1994; Esser and Brosius 1996; Willems 1997, 424–26.
83. Data compiled by Günther Wehrmann, German Information Center, New York; cf. also Thränhardt 1995, 336; *taz*, 26 November 1992.
84. Thränhardt 1995, 336.
85. Karapin 1996.
86. Ireland 1997.

CHAPTER 6

1. For similar arguments about Germany and other industrialized democracies, see Koopmans 1993, 640–47; Koopmans 1996a; McAdam 1982, 146; Tarrow 1989b, 36, 51; 1989a, 21, 52–57, 338; McAdam, McCarthy, and Zald 1996b, 15; and della Porta and Reiter 1998b.
2. Dalton 1993, 200 n. 16; Rink 2000, 97.
3. Willems et al. 1993, 78.
4. Neidhardt and Rucht 1999, 152; author's calculations; Rucht 1998b, Table 1.
5. Koopmans 1992, 125, 180, 188, 200, 210; Neidhardt and Rucht 1999, 140.
6. Dalton 1996, 76.
7. Author's analysis of data from BV 1985-88 and 2001-03.
8. Koopmans and Olzak 2004, 219.
9. Koopmans and Rucht 1996, 282–84.
10. Butterwegge et al. 1997.
11. For an analysis similar in many ways, see Koopmans 1996c.
12. Tarrow 1989a; 1989b, 53–55, 79, 91–103; 1994, 153–69; Koopmans 1993; 1995, 137–39, 152, 155; Karstedt-Henke 1980; della Porta and Tarrow 1986, 611–13; della Porta 1995, 192.
13. McAdam 1983.
14. Della Porta and Reiter 1998a.
15. Koopmans 1993, 643; Rucht 2002, 37–41; 2003, 163.
16. LKAS 1996, 40; Willems et al. 1993, 137.
17. Koopmans 1995, 82; 1996d, 776; Koopmans and Rucht 1996, 275.
18. Kriesi et al. 1995, 33–37.
19. Koopmans 1997, 156; 1995, 138.
20. Willems 1993; Zimmermann 1994, 21; Saalfeld 1994, 16.
21. Koopmans 1997, 160.
22. Estimated from Koopmans 1997, 156; 1995, 138, 260.
23. Tarrow 1994, 155–56.

24. Brand, Büsser, and Rucht 1986, 65–66; Markovits and Gorski 1993, 65; Roth 1980, 79–80; Gilcher-Holtey 2001, 120–22.
25. Markovits and Gorski 1993, chap. 3.
26. Wagner 1995, 76.
27. Roth 1980, 78–79.
28. Koopmans 1992, 220–21.
29. For a study linking left-wing ideological goals with high levels of protest participation in the late 1980s in West Germany, see Opp et al. 1995.
30. See Markovits and Gorski 1993, 181–82.
31. Roth 1985, 35–36, 38; 1980, 80; Burns and van der Will 1988, 106–24.
32. Markovits and Gorski 1993, chap. 3.
33. Schwagerl 1993, 162–90.
34. Ibid., 23–37.
35. Burns and van der Will 1988, 164–204.
36. Markovits and Gorski 1993, 95; Rucht 1981, n. 22; Ellwein, Lippert, and Zoll 1975, 155; Roth 1980, 82; Braunthal 1994, 127; Koopmans 1995, 218.
37. Balistier 1996.
38. E.g., Betz 1997.
39. Koopmans 1992, 53.
40. Thaysen 1980, 200–201, 213.
41. Cooper 2002, 90, 94, 100.
42. McAdam 1982; 1983; Button 1989.
43. Tarrow 1989a; della Porta and Rucht 1995.
44. Rochon 1988.
45. Rucht 1990a; Joppke 1993.
46. Willems 1997; Bodenschatz, Heise, and Korfmacher 1983.
47. Rucht 1990a; Joppke 1993; Willems 1997.
48. Tarrow 1989a; della Porta 1995.
49. Willems 1997.
50. Bodenschatz, Heise, and Korfmacher 1983.
51. Koopmans 1995, 157–70.
52. Brubaker 1992; Koopmans and Statham 2000a, 2000b.
53. Braunthal 1990a.
54. E.g., Katzenstein 1987, 1989; Smith, Paterson, and Padgett 1996, 2–3; Edinger 1977; and Offe 1972.

REFERENCES

ABBREVIATIONS FOR NEWSPAPERS CITED

BM = *Berliner Morgenpost*
DM = *Dresdner Morgenpost*
FAZ = *Frankfurter Allgemeine Zeitung*
FR = *Frankfurter Rundschau*
HAZ = *Hannoversche Allgemeine Zeitung*
HW = *Hoyerswerdaer Wochenblatt*
KN = *Kieler Nachrichten*
LR = *Lausitzer Rundschau*, Hoyerswerda edition
MM = *Münchner Merkur*
NR = *Norddeutscher Rundschau*
NZZ = *Neue Zürcher Zeitung*
OZ = *Ostsee Zeitung*
SHL = *Schleswig-Holsteinische Landeszeitung*
StZ = *Stuttgarter Zeitung*
SüZ = *Süddeutsche Zeitung*
SV = *Spandauer Volksblatt*
SZD = *Sächsische Zeitung*, Dresden edition
SZH = *Sächsische Zeitung*, Hoyerswerda edition
SZMS = *Süddeutsche Zeitung-München Süd*
SZR = *Sächsische Zeitung*, Riesa edition
taz = *die tageszeitung*
Tsp = *Der Tagesspiegel*

INTERVIEWS CITED

In the following list, the interviewee's name is followed by the date of the interview, affiliation at time of interview, any relevant former affiliation, and place of the interview. All interviews were conducted by the author.

Anonymous autonomist. 22 April and 15 May 1989. West Berlin.
Barkhoff, Anna. 11 June 1990. Linden Self-Help Housing Cooperative (Wohnungsgenossenschaft Selbsthilfe Linden); formerly a community worker in South Linden. Hanover.

Barkhoff, Ernst. 3 June and 12 July 1990. Linden-Limmer SPD; formerly North Linden Tenant Group (Mietergruppe Linden-Nord). Hanover.
Becker, Wolfgang. 20 and 26 June 1990. Formerly Independent Citizen Initiative (Unabhängige Bürgerinitiative). Hanover.
Beran, Hans. 28 June 1990. Urban Renewal Division, City Planning Office, City of Hanover (Sanierungsabteilung, Stadtplanungsamt, Stadt Hannover). Hanover.
Buchholz, Götz. 6 March 1990 and 22 May 1990. Formerly Housing Emergency Action (Aktion Wohnungsnot) and Independent Citizen Initiative (Unabhängige Bürgerinitiative). Hanover.
Burucker, Dirk. 22 March 1990. Community worker, North Linden. Hanover.
Deiters, Georg. 23 June 1990. Independent Citizen Initiative (Unabhängige Bürgerinitiative). Hanover.
Eichstädt, Wulf. 7 April and 23 June 1989. STERN Society for Careful Urban Renewal (STERN Gesellschaft für behutsame Stadterneuerung); formerly Urban Renewal Division, International Building Exposition (Bereich Stadterneuerung, Internationale Bauaustellung). West Berlin.
Gallus, Helmut. 27 June 1990. Urban Renewal Division, City Planning Office, City of Hanover (Sanierungsabteilung, Stadtplanungsamt, Stadt Hannover). Hanover.
Göhler, Hans. 19 March 1989. Kottbusser Tor Neighborhood Committee (Erneuerungskommission Kottbusser Tor) and Kreuzberg Borough Construction Department (Kreuzberger Bau- und Stadtplanungsamt). West Berlin.
Grube, Rainer. 31 May 1990. Neighborhood Forum (Stadtteilforum) and North Linden Renewal Commission (Sanierungskommission Linden-Nord). Hanover.
Grubert, Christian. 16 July 1990. Former planning advisor in Hanover-Nordstadt. Hanover.
Henning, Bärbel. 18 June 1990. Formerly a community worker in South Linden. Hanover.
Holland, Klaus-Jürgen. 20 March 1990. Planning advisor in South and North Linden. Hanover.
Karaciyan, Mari. 9 May 1989. Working Group for Social Planning and Applied Urban Research (SPAS-Kreuzberg-Nord). West Berlin
Krüger, Detlef. 29 March 1990. Former housing policy speaker for the Hanover Green-Alternative Citizens List (Wohnungspolitischer Sprecher, Grün-Alternative Bürgerliste Hannover). Hanover.
Kuhn, Egon. 12 June 1990. Linden-Limmer SPD. Hanover.
Kurreck, Wolfgang. 29 April 1998. Director, Munich Refugee Office (Flüchtlingsamt München). Munich.
Lautenschläger, Ulli. 6 March and 29 June 1989. SO36 Association (Verein SO36). West Berlin.
Lubinski, Cord-Peter. 30 April 1992. SPD chair in the Kronshagen Town Council (Kronshagener Gemeindevertretung). By telephone from Kronshagen.
Meinhof, Gert. 7 June 1990. Working Group for Urban Rehabilitation and Renewal (Arbeitsgemeinschaft für Stadt- und Altbauerneuerung); formerly Independent Citizen Initiative (Unabhängige Bürgerinitiative). Hanover.

Nowack, Jürgen. 19 April 1989. Formerly Wedding Citizen Initiative (Bürgerinitiative Wedding). West Berlin.
Peter, Jonny. 1 June 1990. Society for the Promotion of Education, Work, and Culture (Gesellschaft zur Förderung von Bildung, Arbeit und Kultur). Hanover.
Rädler, Michael. 30 March 1989. SPD Kreuzberg. West Berlin.
Reissl, Alexander. 11 April 2002. Former SPD chair in the Munich-Moosach Borough Council (München-Moosach Bezirksausschuss). By telephone from Munich.
Ronge, Gerd. 14 June 1990. North Linden Tenant Group (Mietergruppe Linden-Nord). Hanover.
Sancho-Rico, Marliese. 22 June 1990. Formerly Independent Citizen Initiative (Unabhängige Bürgerinitiative). Hanover.
Sandig, Heiner. 27 August 1997. Saxony Landtag deputy (CDU). Dresden.
Sauter, Rainer. 13 February 1989. SO36 Association (Verein SO36). West Berlin.
Schmidt, Martin. 31 July and 1 August 1997. Former director of the Culture, Youth, and Sport Department (Dezernat für Kultur, Jugend und Sport), City of Hoyerswerda. Hoyerswerda.
Schneider, Christian. 29 April 1998. *Süddeutsche Zeitung* and Living Together at Westkreuz (Miteinander leben am Westkreuz). Munich.
Siemund, Christian. 11 July 1990. Formerly Housing Emergency Action (Aktion Wohnungsnot). Hanover.
Sütcü, Özalp. 11 April 1989. Dresdener Strasse Tenant Initiative (Mieterladen Dresdenerstrasse). West Berlin.
Thörnig, Raimund. 26 April 1989. Formerly SO36 Citizen Initiative (Bürgerinitiative SO36) and SO36 Association (Verein SO36). West Berlin.
Ützmann, Dieter. 16 March and 6 June 1990. North Linden Tenant Group (Mietergruppe Linden-Nord); formerly a planning advisor in Hanover-Nordstadt. Hanover.
Vogel, Friedhart. 29 July 1997. Superintendent, Protestant Church, Hoyerswerda. Hoyerswerda.
Wagner, Bernd. 14 August 1997. Former director, State Protection Division, Joint Criminal Office of the Eastern German *Länder* (Staatschutzabteilung, Gemeinsamen Landeskriminalamt). Berlin.
Warnken, Alke. 2 April 1990. Linden Construction Group (Lindener Baukontor); formerly a planning advisor in North Linden. Hanover.
Wartenberg, Gerd. 28 May 1989. Bundestag deputy (SPD); formerly SPD Kreuzberg. West Berlin.

BOOKS AND ARTICLES CITED

Adam, Barry. 1998. *Global Emergence of Gay and Lesbian Politics*. Philadelphia: Temple University Press.
    AGSTA [Arbeitsgemeinschaft für Stadt- und Altbauerneuerung]. 1979. "Fallstudie Sanierung Hannover-Linden Süd." Institut für Raumplanung, Universität Dortmund. July.

AL [Alternative Liste]. 1985. *Wahlprogramm der AL.* West Berlin: Alternative Liste.

Almond, Gabriel, and Sidney Verba. 1963. *The Civic Culture.* Princeton: Princeton University Press.

Amenta, Edwin, Bruce Carruthers, and Yvonne Zylan. 1992. "A Hero for the Aged?" *American Journal of Sociology* 92:308–39.

Assheuer, Thomas, and Hans Sarkowicz. 1992. *Rechtsradikale in Deutschland.* 2nd ed. Munich: C. H. Beck.

Aust, Stefan, and Sabine Rosenbladt. 1981. *Hausbesetzer: Wofür sie kämpfen, wie sie leben und wie sie leben wollen.* Hamburg: Hoffmann und Campe.

Autzen, Rainer, et al. 1984. *Stadterneuerung in Berlin.* West Berlin: Verlag Ästhethik und Kommunikation.

Backes, Uwe, and Eckhard Jesse. 1996. *Politischer Extremismus in der Bundesrepublik Deutschland.* 4th ed. Bonn: Bundeszentrale für politische Bildung.

Bade, Klaus. 1994. *Ausländer, Aussiedler, Asyl.* Munich: C. H. Beck.

Baker, Kendall, Russell Dalton, and Kai Hildebrandt. 1981. *Germany Transformed.* Cambridge: Harvard University Press.

BAKU [Gesellschaft zur Förderung von Bildung, Arbeit und Kultur]. 1989. *Viktoriastrasse: "Rettet die Viktoriastrasse."* Hanover: Gesellschaft zur Förderung von Bildung, Arbeit und Kultur.

Balistier, Thomas. 1996. *Strassenprotest.* Münster: Westfälisches Dampfboot.

Banaszak, Lee Ann, Karen Beckwith, and Dieter Rucht, eds. 2003. *Women's Movements Facing the Reconfigured State.* New York: Cambridge University Press.

Barnes, Samuel, et al. 1979. *Political Action.* Beverly Hills, Calif.: Sage Publications.

Barth, Fredrik, ed. 1969. *Ethnic Groups and Boundaries.* Boston: Little, Brown.

Bascon-Borgelt, Christiane, Karin Ganssauge, and Hans Pallenberg. 1984. *Auf guten Rat gebaut.* West Berlin: IBA.

Baylis, Thomas. 1993. "Transforming the East German Economy." In *From Bundesrepublik to Deutschland,* ed. Michael Huelshoff, Andrei Markovits, and Simon Reich, 77–92. Ann Arbor: University of Michigan Press.

Becker, Ruth. 1981. "Grundzüge der Wohnungspolitik in der BRD seit 1949." *Arch+*, no. 57/58 (July): 64–68.

Beer, Wolfgang. 1978a. *Lernen im Widerstand.* Hamburg: Verlag Association.

———. 1978b. "Die Motive des Widerstands gegen Atomkraftwerke und der Prozess der Mobilisierung breiter Bevölkerungsschichten." In *Widerstand gegen Atomkraftwerke,* ed. Hans-Christian Buchholtz, Lutz Mez, and Thomas von Zabern, 103–12. Wuppertal: Peter Hammer.

Bennefeld, Rolf, et al. 1976. *Untersuchungsbereich Linden-Nord Hannover: Sozialplanerische Erhebung.* Hanover: Landeshauptstadt Hannover, April.

Bennett, Andrew, and Alexander George. 1997. "Process Tracing in Case Study Research." Paper presented at the MacArthur Workshop, Harvard University, October.

Benzler, Susanne. 1997. "Migranten in Wartestellung." In *Fremde im Land,* ed. Klaus Bade, 213–48. Osnabrück: Universitätsverlag Rasch.

Bergmann, Werner. 1994. "Antisemitism and Xenophobia in the East German Länder." *German Politics* 3 (August): 265–76.

Bergmann, Werner, and Rainer Erb. 1994a. *Neonazismus und rechte Subkultur.* Berlin: Metropol.
———. 1994b. "Eine soziale Bewegung von rechts?" *Forschungsjournal neue soziale Bewegungen* 7 (February): 80–98.
"Berliner Häuserkampf aus Kreuzberger Sicht." [1987.] In *Spekulanten auf den Mond, damit sich Raumfahrt endlich lohnt.* West Berlin: n.p.
Betz, Hans-Georg. 1991. *Postmodern Politics in Germany.* New York: St. Martin's Press.
———. 1994. *Radical Right-Wing Populism in Western Europe.* New York: St. Martin's Press.
———. 1997. "Why Is There No Right in Germany?" Paper presented at the German Studies Association Annual Conference, Bethesda, Md., September.
Bezirksamt Kreuzberg von Berlin (Abteilung Jugendförderung). 1987. *". . . und die einen steh'n im Schatten."* Berlin: Bezirksamt Kreuzberg von Berlin.
BFA [Bundesanstalt für Arbeit], ed. 1993. *Arbeitsstatistik 1992.* Nürnberg: Bundesanstalt für Arbeit.
Biehl, Janet, and Peter Staudenmeier. 1995. *Ecofascism.* San Francisco: AK Press.
Björgo, Tore, and Rob Witte. 1993a. "Introduction." In *Racist Violence in Europe,* ed. Björgo and Witte, 1–16. New York: St. Martin's Press.
———, eds. 1993b. *Racist Violence in Europe.* New York: St. Martin's Press.
Blalock, Hubert. 1967. *Toward a Theory of Minority-Group Relations.* New York: John Wiley.
Bleiker, Roland. 1993. *Nonviolent Struggle and the Revolution in East Germany.* Cambridge, Mass.: Albert Einstein Institution, 1993.
BLR [Bundesforschungsanstalt für Landeskunde und Raumordnung], ed. 1995. *Laufende Raumbeobachtung: Aktuelle Daten zur Entwicklung der Städte, Kreise, und Gemeinden, 1992–93.* Bonn: Bundesforschungsanstalt für Landeskunde und Raumordnung.
Blumer, Herbert. 1978. "Social Unrest and Collective Protest." *Studies in Symbolic Interaction* 1:1–54.
Bobbio, Norberto. 1996. *Left and Right.* Chicago: University of Chicago Press.
Bodenschatz, Harald. 1987. *Platz frei für das neue Berlin.* West Berlin: Transit.
Bodenschatz, Harald, Volker Heise, and Jochen Korfmacher. 1983. *Schluss mit der Zerstörung?* Giessen: Anabas.
Bonacich, Edna. 1972. "A Theory of Ethnic Antagonism." *American Sociological Review* 37:547–59.
Bond, Doug. 1988. "Nonviolent Action and the Diffusion of Power." In *Justice Without Violence,* ed. Paul Wehr, Heidi Burgess, and Guy Burgess, 59–79. Boulder, Colo.: Lynne Rienner.
Brand, Enno. 1988. *Staats-gewalt.* Göttingen: Verlag die Werkstatt.
Brand, Karl-Werner. 1982. *Neue soziale Bewegungen.* Opladen: Westdeutscher Verlag.
———. 1985. "Vergleichendes Resümee." In *Neue soziale Bewegungen in Westeuropa und den USA,* ed. Brand, 306–34. New York: Campus.
Brand, Karl-Werner, Detlef Büsser, and Dieter Rucht. 1986. *Aufbruch in eine andere Gesellschaft.* 2nd ed. New York: Campus.

Brandes, Volkhard, and Bernhard Schön, eds. 1981. *Wer sind die Instandbesetzer?* Bensheim: Päd.-extra-Buchverlag.

Braunthal, Gerard. 1990a. "Political Demonstrations and Civil Liberties in Germany." *German Politics and Society* 19 (Spring): 41–54.

———. 1990b. *Political Loyalty and Public Service in West Germany.* Amherst: University of Massachusetts Press.

———. 1994. *The German Social Democrats Since 1969.* 2nd ed. Boulder, Colo.: Westview Press.

———. 1996. *Parties and Politics in Modern Germany.* Boulder, Colo.: Westview Press.

BRBS [Bundesminister für Raumordnung, Bauwesen und Städtebau]. 1988. *Städtebauförderung 1988–1990.* 2nd ed. Bonn: Bundesminister für Raumordnung, Bauwesen und Städtebau, June.

Brech, Joachim, et al. 1977. *Anwaltsplanung.* Bonn: Bundesminister für Raumordnung, Bauwesen, und Städtebau.

Brech, Joachim, and Rainer Greiff, eds. 1978. *Bürgerbeteiligung mit Experten.* Basel: Beltz.

———. 1981. *Anwaltsplanung in der kommunalen Planungspraxis.* 2 vols. Frankfurt: Haag und Herchen.

Brubaker, William Rogers. 1992. *Citizenship and Nationhood in France and Germany.* Cambridge: Harvard University Press.

BSI [Bayerisches Staatsministerium des Innern]. Various years. *Verfassungsschutzbericht.* Munich: Bayerisches Staatsministerium des Innern, published annually.

Buchholz, Götz. 1973. "Sanierung Linden-Süd (Teil 3)." Studienarbeit, Technische Universität Hannover.

Buchholz, Götz, Gerd Reincke, and Reinhard Wiecha. 1973. "Möglichkeiten der Beteiligung der Betroffenen an der Planung am Beispiel der Sanierung Linden-Süd (Teil 1)." Studienarbeit, Technische Universität Hannover.

Buchholtz, Hans-Christian. 1978. "Chronologie der Widerstandsbewegung gegen Atomkraftwerke am Oberrhein von 1971 bis 1977." In *Widerstand gegen Atomkraftwerke,* ed. Hans-Christian Buchholtz, Lutz Mez, and Thomas von Zabern, 121–40. Wuppertal: Peter Hammer.

Bühnemann, Michael, Michael Wendt, and Jürgen Wituschek, eds. 1984. *AL: Die Alternative Liste Berlin.* West Berlin: Litpol Verlag.

Bürgerinitiative [Bürgerinitiative SO36]. 1978. "Bürgerinitiative SO 36." *Stattbuch 1,* 882. West Berlin: Stattbuch Verlag.

Burns, Rob, and Wilfried van der Will. 1988. *Protest and Democracy in West Germany.* New York: St. Martin's Press.

Büro für Stadtsanierung und soziale Arbeit, ed. 1971. *Sanierung—für wen?* 2nd ed. West Berlin: Büro für Stadtsanierung und soziale Arbeit.

Burstein, Paul. 1991. "Policy Domains." *American Review of Sociology* 17:327–50.

Butterwegge, Christoph. 1996. *Rechtsextremismus, Rassismus und Gewalt.* Darmstadt: Primus.

———, et al. 1997. *Rechtsextremisten in Parlamenten.* Opladen: Leske und Budrich.

Button, James. 1989. *Blacks and Social Change.* Princeton: Princeton University Press.

BUU [Bürgerinitiative Umweltschutz Unterelbe]. 1977. *Brokdorf!* Hamburg: Verlag Association.

BV [Bundesamt für Verfassungsschutz]. 1993a. *Fragen und Antworten zum Rechtsextremismus in Deutschland.* N.p.: Bundesamt für Verfassungsschutz.

——. 1993b and other years. *Verfassungsschutzbericht.* Bonn: Bundesministerium des Innern, published annually.

Castles, Francis. 1978. *The Social Democratic Image of Society.* London: Routledge and Kegan Paul.

Cohen, Jean. 1985. "Strategy or Identity? New Theoretical Paradigms and Contemporary Social Movements." *Social Research* 52 (Winter): 663–716.

Collier, Irwin. 1993. "German Economic Integration." In *From Bundesrepublik to Deutschland,* ed. Michael Huelshoff, Andrei Markovits, and Simon Reich, 93–113. Ann Arbor: University of Michigan Press.

Conradt, David. 1980. "Changing German Political Culture." In *The Civic Culture Revisited,* ed. Gabriel Almond and Sidney Verba, 212–72. Boston: Little, Brown.

——. 1996. *The German Polity.* 6th ed. White Plains, N.Y.: Longman.

Cooper, Alice Holmes. 1996. *Paradoxes of Peace.* Ann Arbor: University of Michigan Press.

——. 2002. "Party-Sponsored Protest and the Movement Society." *German Politics* 11:88–104.

——. 2004. "Social Movements in the Federal Republic." In *Germany at Fifty-Five,* ed. James Sperling, 206–26. New York: Manchester University Press.

Cornelius, Wayne, Philip Martin, and James Hollifield, eds. 1994. *Controlling Immigration.* Stanford: Stanford University Press.

Crozier, Michel, Samuel Huntington, and Joji Watanuki. 1975. *The Crisis of Democracy.* New York: NYU Press.

D'Anieri, Paul, Claire Ernst, and Beth Kier. 1990. "New Social Movements in Historical Perspective." *Comparative Politics* 22:445–58.

Dalton, Russell. 1993. *Politics in Germany.* 2nd ed. New York: HarperCollins.

——. 1994. *The Green Rainbow: Environmental Groups in Western Europe.* New Haven: Yale University Press.

——. 1996. *Citizen Politics in Western Democracies.* 2nd ed. Chatham, N.J.: Chatham House.

Dalton, Russell, and Manfred Kuechler, eds. 1990. *Challenging the Political Order: New Social and Political Movements in Western Democracies.* Cambridge: Polity Press.

Dargel, Jörn. 1982. "z.B. die Wohnbau-Design." *Arch+*, no. 66 (December): 72–75.

della Porta, Donatella. 1995. *Social Movements, Political Violence, and the State.* New York: Cambridge University Press.

——. 1996. "Social Movements and the State." In *Comparative Perspectives on Social Movements,* ed. Doug McAdam, John D. McCarthy, and Mayer Zald, 62–92. New York: Cambridge University Press.

della Porta, Donatella, and Herbert Reiter. 1998a. "The Policing of Protest in Western Democracies." In *Policing Protest,* ed. della Porta and Reiter, 1–34. Minneapolis: University of Minnesota Press.

——, eds. 1998b. *Policing Protest.* Minneapolis: University of Minnesota Press.

della Porta, Donnatella, and Dieter Rucht. 1995. "Left-Libertarian Movements in Context." In *The Politics of Social Protest*, ed. J. Craig Jenkins and Bert Klandermans, 229–72. Minneapolis: University of Minnesota Press.

della Porta, Donnatella, and Sidney Tarrow. 1986. "Unwanted Children: Political Violence and the Cycle of Protest in Italy, 1966–1973." *European Journal of Political Research* 14:607–32.

Dennis, Mike. 1993. "The Vanishing Opposition." In *Parties and Party Systems in the New Germany*, ed. Stephen Padgett, 193–223. Brookfield, Vt.: Dartmouth.

Die Grünen. 1980. *Das Bundesprogramm*. Munich: Die Grünen.

Dieser, Hartwig, and Anastasie Kouvelis. 1980. "Die Betroffenheit der Mieter durch die ZIP-Modernisierung in Kreuzberg SO36." Zentralinstitut für sozialwissenschaftliche Forschung, Freie Universität Berlin. November.

Dion, Douglas. 1998. "Evidence and Inference in the Comparative Case Study." *Comparative Politics* 30 (January): 127–46.

Dittberner, Jürgen. 1986. "Asylpolitik und Parlament." *Zeitschrift für Parlamentsfragen* 17:167–80.

Dittrich, Christiane, and Achim Habeny. 1980. *"Strategien für Kreuzberg": Beschreiben eines Modells*. Dortmund: Institut für Raumplanung, Universität Dortmund.

Duntze, Klaus. 1972. *Der Geist, der Städte baut*. Stuttgart: Radius-Verlag.

Duyvendak, Jan. 1995. *The Power of Politics*. Boulder, Colo.: Westview Press.

Eckert, Roland, and Helmut Willems. 1986. "Youth Protest in Western Europe." *Research in Social Movements, Conflicts, and Change* 9:127–53.

Edinger, Lewis. 1977. *Politics in West Germany*. 2nd ed. Boston: Little, Brown.

Egert, Jürgen, Manfred Meisner, Walter Momper, and Gert Wartenberg. 1971. "Basisarbeit—Theorie und Praxis." In *Überwindet den Kapitalismus, oder Was wollen die Jungsozialisten*, ed. Norbert Gansel. Hamburg: Rohwohlt.

Eichstädt, Wulf. 1982. "Kreuzberger Stadtteilsyndikalismus." *Arch+*, no. 66 (December): 54–57.

———. 1984. "Die Grundsätze der behutsamen Stadterneuerung." *Baumeister* 81, no. 9:40–45.

Ellwein, Thomas, Ekkehard Lippert, and Ralf Zoll. 1975. *Politische Beteiligung in der Bundesrepublik Deutschland*. Göttingen: Otto Schwarz.

Erb, Rainer. 1993. "Gruppengewalt und Rechtextremismus in den neuen Bundesländern." In *Jahrbuch für Antisemitismusforschung*, ed. Wolfgang Benz, 140–64. New York: Campus.

Esping-Andersen, Gosta. 1985. *Politics Against Markets*. Princeton: Princeton University Press.

Esser, Frank, and Hans Brosius. 1996. "Television as Arsonist?" *European Journal of Communication* 11:235–60.

Evans, Sara. 1979. *Personal Politics: The Roots of Women's Liberation in the Civil Rights Movement and the New Left*. New York: Vintage Books.

Fach, Wolfgang, and Georg Simonis. 1987. *Die Stärke des Staates im Atomkonflikt*. New York: Campus.

Farin, Klaus, and Eberhard Seidel-Pielen. 1993. *Skinheads*. Munich: C. H. Beck.

Ferree, Myra Marx, et al. 2002. *Shaping Abortion Discourse*. New York: Cambridge University Press.

FGW [Forschungsgruppe Wahlen]. 1976. *Wahl in Baden-Württemberg.* Mannheim: FGW.
——. 1981. *Wahl in Berlin.* Mannheim: Forschungsgruppe Wahlen.
——. 1987. *Bundestagswahl 1987.* Mannheim: Forschungsgruppe Wahlen.
——. 1998. *Wahlergebnisse in Deutschland, 1946–1998.* Mannheim: Forschungsgruppe Wahlen.
Frankland, E. Gene, and Donald Schoonmaker. 1992. *Between Protest and Power: The Green Party in Germany.* Boulder, Colo.: Westview Press.
Funke, Hajo. 1993. *Brandstifter.* Göttingen: Lamuv.
Gabriel, Oskar. 1983. "Gesellschaftliche Modernisierung, politische Beteiligung, und kommunale Demokratie." In *Bürgerbeteiligung und kommunale Demokratie,* ed. Gabriel, 57–103. Munich: Minerva.
Gamson, William. 1990. *The Strategy of Social Protest.* 2nd ed. Homewood, Ill.: Dorsey Press.
Gamson, William, and David S. Meyer. 1996. "Framing Political Opportunity." In *Comparative Perspectives on Social Movements,* ed. Doug McAdam, John D. McCarthy, and Mayer Zald, 275–90. New York: Cambridge University Press.
Gapper, Stuart. 2003. "The Rise and Fall of Germany's Party of Democratic Socialism." *German Politics* 12 (August): 65–85.
Geiling, Heiko. 1996. *Das andere Hannover.* Hanover: Offizin Verlag.
Gerhards, Jürgen, and Dieter Rucht. 1992. "Mesomobilization: Organizing and Framing in Two Protest Campaigns in West Germany." *American Journal of Sociology* 98:555–96.
Gerlach, Irene. 1999. *Bundesrepublik Deutschland.* Opladen: Leske und Budrich.
Gerlach, Ulrich, and Klaus-Jürgen Holland. 1976. "Sanierung Hannover Linden-Süd." *Stadtbauwelt* 52:263–71.
Geronimo. 1995. *Feuer und Flamme.* Rev. ed. Berlin: Edition ID-Archiv.
Gilcher-Holtey, Ingrid. 2001. *Die 68er Bewegung.* Munich: C. H. Beck.
Giugni, Marco, Doug McAdam, and Charles Tilly, eds. 1999. *How Social Movements Matter.* Minneapolis: University of Minnesota Press.
Glaessner, Gert-Joachim. 2001. "Der neue Staatsinterventionismus." In *Umbruch in Ostdeutschland,* ed. Karin Bock and Werner Fiedler, 13–28. Opladen: Westdeutscher Verlag.
Goodwin, Jeff. 2001. *No Other Way Out: States and Revolutionary Movements, 1945–1991.* New York: Cambridge University Press.
Goodwin, Jeff, and James Jasper. 1999. "Caught in a Winding, Snarling Vine: The Structural Bias of Political Process Theory." *Sociological Forum* 14:27–54.
Gorz, Andre. 1982. *Farewell to the Working Class.* Boston: South End Press.
Grant, Donald, and Michael Wallace. 1991. "Why Do Strikes Turn Violent?" *American Journal of Sociology* 96:1117–50.
Gude, Sigmar. 1988. *Veränderung der Eigentümerstruktur in SO 36.* West Berlin: TOPOS.
Gunlicks, Arthur. 1970. "Intraparty Democracy in Western Germany." *Comparative Politics* 2 (January): 229–50.
——. 1986. *Local Government in the German Federal System.* Durham: Duke University Press.
Gurr, Ted R. 1970. *Why Men Rebel.* Princeton: Princeton University Press.

Habermann, Klaus, et al. 1977. "Hannover 1945–1975." Diplomarbeit, Lehrgebiet für Stadtbaugeschichte, Technische Universität Hannover.

Habermas, Jürgen. 1975. *Legitimation Crisis*. Boston: Beacon Press.

———. 1981. "New Social Movements." *Telos* 49:33–37.

———. 1984. *The Theory of Communicative Action*. Vol. 2. Boston: Beacon Press.

Hager, Carol. 1993. "Citizen Movements and Technological Policymaking in Germany." *Annals of the American Academy of Political and Social Science* 528:42–55.

———. 1995. *Technological Democracy*. Ann Arbor: University of Michigan Press.

Hall, Peter, and Rosemary Taylor. 1996. "Political Science and the Three New Institutionalisms." *Political Studies* 44:936–57.

Häusler, Jürgen. 1988. "Die (falschen) Väter des Erfolgs." *Forschungsjournal neue soziale Bewegungen* 1 (October-November): 36–42.

Heine, Michael, and Klaus Kisker. 1987. "Berlin im 'Aufschwung'!?" In *Wirtschaftswunder Berlin?* ed. Klaus Kisker and Michael Heine, 9–36. West Berlin: Edition Sigma.

Heise, Volker. 1981. "Bedingungen und Formen der Stadterneuerung in Berlin-West." In *Bedingungen und Formen der Stadterneuerung*, ed. Volker Heise and Jürgen Rosemann. Kassel: Gesamthochschul-Bibliothek.

Heitmeyer, Wilhelm. 1992. *Rechtsextremistische Orientierungen bei Jugendlichen*. 4th ed. Munich: Juventa.

———. 1993. "Hostility and Violence Toward Foreigners in Germany." In *Racist Violence in Europe*, ed. Tore Björgo and Rob Witte, 17–28. New York: St. Martin's Press.

Hellman, Kai-Uwe. 1996. "Rechtsextremismus als soziale Bewegung." *Berliner Debatte* 1:2–54.

Hellman, Kai-Uwe, and Ruud Koopmans, eds. 1998. *Paradigmen der Bewegungsforschung*. Opladen: Westdeutscher Verlag.

Hellweg, Uli, and Christian Wend. 1982. "Neue Träger." *Arch+*, no. 61 (February): 43–46.

Helm, Jutta. 1993. "The Study of Germany in Comparative Politics." In *From Bundesrepublik to Deutschland*, ed. Michael Huelshoff, Andrei Markovits, and Simon Reich, 11–29. Ann Arbor: University of Michigan Press.

Herberg-Reidenbach, Dorothea. 1989. *Sozialplan- und Mieterberatungsverfahren bei öffentlich geförderten Stadterneuerungsmassnahmen in Berlin (West)*. West Berlin: SPAS.

Hermann, Klaus. 1985. "Chronologie der Räumungen und Durchsuchungen sowie anderer wichtiger Ereignisse, die in Bezug zu den Instandbesetzungen standen, vom 10.10.1980 bis zum 27.9.1981." West Berlin.

Hermann, Klaus, and Harald Glöde. 1985. "Aufstieg und Niedergang der Hausbesetzerbewegung in Berlin." Diplomarbeit, Freie Universität Berlin.

Hermann, Michael, et al. 1987. *"Hafenstrasse."* Hamburg: Verlag am Galgenberg.

Hocke, Peter. 1999. "Determining the Selection Bias in Local and National Newspaper Reports on Protest Events." In *Acts of Dissent*, ed. Dieter Rucht, Ruud Koopmans, and Friedhelm Neidhardt, 131–63. New York: Rowman and Littlefield.

Hockenos, Paul. 1993. *Free to Hate*. New York: Routledge.
Hofrichter, Jürgen, and Michael Schmitt. 1991. "Eher mit- als gegeneinander." In *Neue soziale bewegungen in der Bundesrepublik Deutschland*, 2nd ed., ed. Roland Roth and Dieter Rucht, 469–88. Bonn: Bundeszentrale für politische Bildung.
Holtmann, Everhard. 1992. "Politisierung der Kommunalpolitik und Wandlungen im lokalen Parteiensystem." *Aus Parlament und Zeitgeschichte*, 22 May, 13–22.
Hübner, Emil, and Horst-Hennek Rohlfs, eds. 1984. *Jahrbuch der Bundesrepublik Deutschland*. Munich: Beck / Deutscher Taschenbuch Verlag.
Husbands, Christopher. 1988. "The Dynamics of Racial Exclusion and Expulsion." *European Journal of Political Research* 16:701–20.
———. 1989. "Racial Attacks." In *Traditions of Intolerance*, ed. Tony Kushner and Kenneth Lunn, 91–115. Manchester: Manchester University Press.
ICLEI/DIFU [International Council for Local Environmental Initiatives / Deutsches Institut für Urbanistik]. 1999. *Lokale Agenda 21 im europäischen Vergleich*. Bonn: Bundesministerium für Umwelt, Naturschutz und Reaktorsicherheit.
Ignazi, Piero. 2003. *Extreme Right Parties in Western Europe*. New York: Oxford University Press.
ILSH [Innenminister des Landes Schleswig-Holstein], ed. Various years. *Verfassungsschutz in Schleswig-Holstein*. Kiel: Landesregierung Schleswig-Holstein, published annually or biannually.
———, ed. 1992a. *Jahresbericht der Verfassungsschutzabteilung 1992*. Kiel: Innenminister des Landes Schleswig-Holstein.
———, ed. 1992b and 1993b. *Verfassungsschutzbericht*. Kiel: Innenminister des Landes Schleswig-Holstein, published annually.
———, ed. 1993a. *Skinheads in Schleswig-Holstein*. Kiel: Innenminister des Landes Schleswig-Holstein.
Imig, Doug, and Sidney Tarrow. 2001. *Contentious Europeans*. Lanham, Md.: Rowman and Littlefield.
Immergut, Ellen. 1998. "The Theoretical Core of the New Institutionalism." *Politics and Society* 26 (March): 5–34.
Infas [Institut für angewandte Sozialforschung]. 1981. *Berlin 1981*. Bonn: Institut für angewandte Sozialforschung.
Inglehart, Ronald. 1977. *The Silent Revolution*. Princeton: Princeton University Press.
———. 1981. "Post-Materialism in an Environment of Insecurity." *American Political Science Review* 75:880–900.
———. 1990. *Culture Shift*. Princeton: Princeton University Press.
Institut für Sozialforschung, ed. 1994. *Rechtsextremismus und Fremdenfeindlichkeit*. New York: Campus.
Ireland, Patrick. 1997. "Socialism, Unification Policy, and the Rise of Racism in Eastern Germany." *International Migration Review* 31:541–68.
Jaschke, Hans-Gerd. 1994. *Rechtsextremismus und Fremdenfeindlichkeit*. Opladen: Westdeutscher Verlag.
Jenkins, J. Craig, and Bert Klandermans, eds. 1995. *The Politics of Social Protest*. Minneapolis: University of Minnesota Press.
Jennings, M. Kent, et al. 1990. *Continuities in Political Action*. New York: Walter de Gruyter.

Jervis, Robert. 1997. *System Effects*. Princeton: Princeton University Press.

Joedecke, Rainer. 1992. "Willkommen in Hoyerswerda." *Kursbuch*, no. 107:69–108.

Joppke, Christian. 1990. "State and Movement in the West German Nuclear Energy Debate." Typescript. September.

———. 1992. "Explaining Cross-National Variation of Two Anti-Nuclear Movements." *Sociology* 26:311–31.

———. 1993. *Mobilizing Against Nuclear Energy*. Berkeley and Los Angeles: University of California Press.

Jung, Karin, and Dieter Worbs. 1976. "Was halten die Bürger von Sanierung und ihrer Beteiligung daran?" *Arch+*, no. 31 (September): 24–29.

Kaase, Max. 1982. "Partizipatorische Revolution." In *Bürger und Parteien*, ed. Joachim Raschke, 173–87. Bonn: Bundeszentrale für politische Bildung.

Kaczmarczyk, Armando. 1982. "'Erneuerungskommission Kottbusser Tor.'" *Arch+*, no. 66 (December): 51–53.

Kaltefleiter, Werner, and Robert Pfaltzgraff, eds. 1985. *The Peace Movements in Europe and the United States*. New York: St. Martin's Press.

Kanstroom, Daniel. 1993a. "The Shining City and the Fortress." *Boston College International and Comparative Law Review* 16:201–43.

———. 1993b. "*Wer sind wir wieder?*" *Yale Journal of International Law* 18 (Winter): 155–211.

Karapin, Roger. 1993. "New-Left Social Movements and Public Policy in West Germany, 1969–1989." Ph.D. diss., Department of Political Science, M.I.T.

———. 1996. "Explaining the Surge in Right-Wing Violence by German Youth." Paper presented at the conference "Cross-Cultural Perspectives on Youth, Radicalism, and Violence," University of Wisconsin at Milwaukee, August.

———. 1999. "The Politics of Immigration Control in Britain and Germany." *Comparative Politics* 31:423–44.

———. 2000. "Major Anti-Minority Riots and National Legislative Campaigns Against Immigrants in Britain and Germany." In *Challenging Immigration and Ethnic Relations Politics*, ed. Ruud Koopmans and Paul Statham, 312–47. New York: Oxford University Press.

———. 2002. "Anti-Minority Riots in Unified Germany." *Comparative Politics* 34:147–67.

———. 2003. "Protest and Reform in Asylum Policy." *German Politics and Society* 21 (Summer): 1–45.

Karstedt-Henke, Suzanne. 1980. "Theorien zur Erklärung terroristischer Bewegungen." In *Politik der inneren Sicherheit*, ed. Erhard Blankenberg, 198–234. Frankfurt: Suhrkamp.

Katsiaficas, George. 1987. *The Imagination of the New Left*. Boston: South End Press.

Katz, Steve, and Margit Mayer. 1985. "Gimme Shelter." *International Journal of Urban and Regional Research* 9 (March): 15–45.

Katzenstein, Mary, and Carol Mueller, eds. 1987. *The Women's Movements of the United States and Western Europe*. Philadelphia: Temple University Press.

Katzenstein, Peter. 1987. *Policy and Politics in West Germany*. Philadelphia: Temple University Press.

———, ed. 1989. *Industry and Politics in West Germany*. Ithaca: Cornell University Press.

Keith, Michael. 1993. *Race, Riots, and Policing*. London: UCL Press.

Kiersch, Gerhard, and Sabine von Oppeln. 1983. *Kernenergiekonflikt in Frankreich und Deutschland*. West Berlin: Wissenschaftlicher Autoren-Verlag.

Kirchheimer, Otto. 1966. "Germany: The Vanishing Opposition." In *Political Oppositions in Western Democracies*, ed. Robert Dahl, 237–59. New Haven: Yale University Press.

Kitschelt, Herbert. 1979. "Justizapparate als Konfliktlösungsinstanz?" *Demokratie und Recht* 7:3–22.

———. 1980. *Kernenergiepolitik*. New York: Campus.

———. 1986. "Political Opportunity Structures and Political Protest." *British Journal of Political Science* 16:57–85.

———. 1989. *The Logics of Party Formation*. Ithaca: Cornell University Press.

Klages, Helmut. 1981. *Überlasteter Staat, verdrossene Bürger*. New York: Campus.

Klandermans, Bert. 1990. "Linking the 'Old' and 'New.'" In *Challenging the Political Order*, ed. Russell Dalton and Manfred Kuechler, 122–36. Cambridge: Polity Press.

Klandermans, Bert, and Sidney Tarrow. 1988. "Mobilization into Social Movements." In *From Structure to Action*, ed. Bert Klandermans, Hanspeter Kriesi, and Sidney Tarrow, 1–38. Greenwich, Conn.: JAI Press.

Kleinert, Ulfrid. 1981. *Gewaltfrei Widerstehen*. Reinbek: Rowohlt.

Klingemann, Hans-Dieter, and Dieter Fuchs. 1995. *Citizens and the State*. New York: Oxford University Press.

KMI [Kreuzberger Mieterinitiativen]. [1980.] "Sind Polizeieinsätze die neue Form der Bürgerbeteiligung?" Approx. June.

Knipp, Hans-Joachim. 1974. "Kurskorrekturen bei den Berliner Stadterneuerungsprogramme?" *Bauhandbuch* 108:23–32.

Köhnke, Dietland, and Ralph Landsfeld. 1987. "Das Berlin-Förderungsgesetz." In *Wirtschaftswunder Berlin?* ed. Klaus Kisker and Michael Heine, 37ff. West Berlin: Edition Sigma.

Komitee [Komitee für Grundrechte und Demokratie], ed. 1988. *Jahrbuch 1987*. Sensbachtal: Komitee für Grundrechte und Demokratie.

Koopmans, Ruud. 1992. "Democracy from Below." Ph.D. diss., University of Amsterdam, October.

———. 1993. "The Dynamics of Protest Waves." *American Sociological Review* 58:637–58.

———. 1995. *Democracy from Below*. Boulder, Colo.: Westview Press.

———. 1996a. "Asyl." In *Kommunikation und Entscheidung*, ed. Wolfgang van den Daele and Friedhelm Neidhardt, 167–92. Berlin: Sigma.

———. 1996b. "Explaining the Rise of Racist and Extreme-Right Violence in Western Europe." *European Journal of Political Research* 30:185–216.

———. 1996c. "Noch einmal davongekommen." *Berliner Debatte* 1:51–54.

———. 1996d. "Soziale Bewegung von rechts?" In *Handbuch deutscher Rechtsextremismus*, ed. Jens Mecklenburg, 767–81. Berlin: Elefanten.

———. 1997. "Dynamics of Repression and Mobilization." *Mobilization* 2:149–64.

———. 1998. "Konkurriende Paradigmen oder friedlich ko-existierende Komplemente?" In *Paradigmen der Bewegungsforschung*, ed. Kai-Uwe Hellman and Ruud Koopmans, 215–31. Opladen: Westdeutscher Verlag.

Koopmans, Ruud, and Susan Olzak. 2004. "Discursive Opportunities and the Evolution of Right-Wing Violence in Germany." *American Journal of Sociology* 110 (July): 198–230.

Koopmans, Ruud, and Dieter Rucht. 1996. "Rechtsextremismus als soziale Bewegung?" In *Rechtsextremismus*, ed. Jürgen Falter, Hans-Gerd Jaschke, and Jürgen Winkler, 265–87. Opladen: Westdeutscher Verlag.

Koopmans, Ruud, and Paul Statham, eds. 2000a. *Challenging Immigration and Ethnic Relations Politics*. New York: Oxford University Press.

———. 2000b. "Political Claims-Making Against Racism and Discrimination in Britain and Germany." In *Comparative Perspectives on Racism*, ed. Jessika Ter Wal and Maykel Verkuyten, 139–70. Burlington, Vt.: Ashgate.

Kopke, Christoph, and Lars Rensmann. 2000. "Die Extremismus-Formel." *Blätter für deutsche und internationale Politik* 45:1451–62.

Kraushaar, Wolfgang, ed. 1978. *Autonomie oder Getto?* Frankfurt: Verlag neue Kritik.

KRE [Kreis Rendsburg-Eckernförde]. 1995. *25 Jahre Kreis Rendsburg-Eckernförde*. Rendsburg: Kreis Rendsburg-Eckernförde.

Krell, Gert, Hans Nicklas, and Anne Ostermann. 1996. "Immigration, Asylum, and Anti-Foreigner Violence in Germany." *Journal of Peace Research* 33:153–70.

Kretschmer, Winfried. 1988. "Wackersdorf." In *Von der Bittschrift zur Platzbesetzung*, ed. Ulrich Linse et al., 165–218. Bonn: J. W. Dietz.

Kriesi, Hanspeter. 1993. *Political Mobilization and Social Change*. Brookfield, Vt.: Avebury.

———. 1995. "Bewegungen auf der Linken, Bewegungen auf der Rechten." *Swiss Political Science Review* 1:9–52.

Kriesi, Hanspeter, et al. 1992. "New Social Movements and Political Opportunities in Western Europe." *European Journal of Political Research* 22:219–44.

Kriesi, Hanspeter, et al. 1995. *New Social Movements in Western Europe*. Minneapolis: University of Minnesota Press.

Krueger, Alan, and Jörn-Steffen Pischke. 1997. "A Statistical Analysis of Crime Against Foreigners in Unified Germany." *Journal of Human Resources* 32:182–209.

Kuechler, Manfred. 1994. "Germans and 'Others.'" *German Politics* 3:47–74.

Kujath, Hans. 1988. "Die Träger der sozialen Wohnungsversorgung." In *Sozialer Wohnungsbau im internationalen Vergleich*, ed. Walter Prigge and Wilfried Kaib, 123–41. Frankfurt: Vervuert Verlag.

Langguth, Gerd. 1983. *Protestbewegung*. Cologne: Bibliothek Wissenschaft und Politik.

Laurisch, Bernd. 1981. *Kein Abriss unter dieser Nummer*. Giessen: Anabas.

Lemke-Müller, Sabine, and Ingrid Matthäi. 1993. "Emanzipatorisches Modell oder strukturiertes Chaos?" *Zeitschrift für Parlamentsfragen* 24 (November): 566–87.

Lewis, Rand. 1996. *The Neo-Nazis and German Unification*. Westport, Conn.: Praeger.

Lichbach, Mark. 1998. "Contending Theories of Contentious Politics." *Annual Review of Political Science* 1:401–24.

Linke, Ursula, and Klaus Ness. 1992. "Von der GST zur ZAST." In *Fluchtpunkt Deutschland*, ed. Ralf Ludwig, Klaus Ness, and Muzaffer Perik, 124–36. Berlin: Schüren.

Linse, Ulrich, et al. 1988. *Von der Bittschrift zur Platzbesetzung*. Bonn: J. W. Dietz.

Lipset, Seymour Martin, and Philip Altbach. 1969. *Students in Revolt*. Boston: Beacon Press.

LKAS [Landeskriminalamt Sachsen]. 1992a and various years and n.d. *Dokumentation rechtsorientierte/fremdenfeindliche Straftaten im Freistaat Sachsen*. Dresden: Landeskriminalamt Sachsen.

———. [1992b.] *Polizeiliche Kriminalstatistik Freistaat Sachen 1992*. Dresden: Landeskriminalamt Sachsen.

Lloyd, Cathie. 1993. "Racist Violence and Anti-Racist Reactions." In *Racist Violence in Europe*, ed. Tore Björgo and Rob Witte, 207–20. New York: St. Martin's Press.

Lüdemann, Christian. 1995. "Fremdenfeindliche Gewalt und Lichterketten." In *Autoritarismus und Gesellschaft*, ed. Gerda Lederer and Peter Schmidt, 355–81. Opladen: Leske und Budrich.

Lüdemann, Christian, and Christian Erzberger. [1994.] "Fremdenfeindliche Gewalt in Deutschland: Zur zeitlichen Entwicklung und Erklärung von Eskalationsprozessen." Typescript.

LVB [Landesamt für Verfassungsschutz, Berlin]. 1992. *Verfassungsschutzbericht Berlin 1991*. Berlin: Landesamt für Verfassungsschutz, Berlin.

Maaz, Hans-Joachim. 1991. *Der Gefühlsstau*. Berlin: Argon.

March, James, and Johan Olsen. 1984. "The New Institutionalism." *American Political Science Review* 78:734–49.

Markovits, Andrei, and Philip Gorski. 1993. *The German Left*. New York: Oxford University Press.

Martin, Philip. 1994. "Germany." In *Controlling Immigration*, ed. Wayne Cornelius, Philip Martin, and James Hollfield, 189–225. Stanford: Stanford University Press.

Mason, T. David, and Dale Krane. 1989. "The Political Economy of Death Squads." *International Studies Quarterly* 33:175–98.

McAdam, Doug. 1982. *Political Process and the Development of Black Insurgency, 1930–1970*. Chicago: University of Chicago Press.

———. 1983. "Tactical Innovation and the Pace of Insurgency." *American Sociological Review* 48:735–54.

———. 1996. "Conceptual Origins, Current Problems, Future Directions." In *Comparative Perspectives on Social Movements*, ed. Doug McAdam, John D. McCarthy, and Mayer Zald, 23–40. New York: Cambridge University Press.

McAdam, Doug, John D. McCarthy, and Mayer Zald, eds. 1996a. *Comparative Perspectives on Social Movements*. New York: Cambridge University Press.

———. 1996b. "Introduction." In *Comparative Perspectives on Social Movements*, ed. McAdam, McCarthy, and Zald, 1–20. New York: Cambridge University Press.

McAdam, Doug, and Dieter Rucht. 1993. "The Cross-National Diffusion of Movement Ideas." *Annals of the American Academy of Political and Social Science* 528:56–74.

McAdam, Doug, Sidney Tarrow, and Charles Tilly. 2001. *Dynamics of Contention*. New York: Cambridge University Press.

Meier-Braun, Karl-Heinz. 1980. *Das Asylanten-Problem*. Frankfurt: Ullstein Verlag.

Melucci, Alberto. 1980. "The New Social Movements." *Social Science Information* 19:199–226.

Meng, Richard, ed. 1987. *Modell Rot-Grün?* Hamburg: VSA.

Merkl, Peter, ed. 1989. *The Federal Republic of Germany at Forty*. New York: NYU Press.

———. 1993. "Conclusion." In *Encounters with the Contemporary Radical Right*, ed. Peter Merkl and Leonard Weinberg, 204–27. Boulder, Colo.: Westview Press.

Mewes, Horst. 1998. "A Brief History of the German Green Party." In *The German Greens*, ed. Margit Mayer and John Ely, 29–48. Philadelphia: Temple University Press.

Meyer, David S. 1993. "Peace, Protest, and Policy." *Policy Studies Journal* 21:35–55.

Meyer, David S., and Douglas Imig. 1993. "Political Opportunity and the Rise and Decline of Interest Group Sectors." *Social Science Journal* 30:253–70.

Meyer, David S., and Sidney Tarrow. 1998a. "A Movement Society." In *The Social Movement Society*, ed. Meyer and Tarrow, 1–28. New York: Rowman and Littlefield.

———, eds. 1998b. *The Social Movement Society*. New York: Rowman and Littlefield.

Mez, Lutz. 1991. "Von den Bürgerinitiativen zu den Grünen." In *Neue soziale Bewegungen in der Bundesrepublik Deutschland*, ed. Roland Roth and Dieter Rucht, 379–91. Bonn: Bundeszentrale für politische Bildung.

Miller, James. 1987. *Democracy Is in the Streets*. New York: Simon and Schuster.

Minkenberg, Michael. 1994. "German Unification and the Continuity of Discontinuities: Cultural Change and the Far Right in East and West." *German Politics* 3 (August): 169–92.

Mossmann, Walter. 1975. "'Die Bevölkerung ist hellwach!'" *Kursbuch*, no. 39:129–53.

Mulhak, Renate. 1983. "Der Instandbesetzungskonflikt in Berlin." In *Großstadt und neue soziale Bewegungen*, ed. Peter Grottian and Wilfried Nelles, 205–52. Stuttgart: Birkhäuser.

Münch, Ursula. 1993. *Asylpolitik in der Bundesrepublik Deutschland*. 2nd ed. Opladen: Leske und Budrich.

Murphy, Detlef, and Roland Roth. 1991. "In (nicht mehr gar so) viele Richtungen zugleich." In *Neue soziale Bewegungen in der Bundesrepublik Deutschland*, 2nd ed., ed. Roland Roth and Dieter Rucht, 415–40. Bonn: Bundeszentrale für politische Bildung.

Neef, Rainer. 1981. "Wohnungsversorgung und 'neue Wohnungsnot.'" *Leviathan* 19:332–53.

Neidhardt, Friedhelm. 1992. "Gewalt und Gegengewalt." In *Jugend, Staat, Gewalt*, ed. Wilhelm Heitmeyer, Kurt Möller, and Heinz Sünker, 233–43. Munich: Juventa.

Neidhardt, Friedhelm, and Dieter Rucht. 1999. "Protestgeschichte der Bundesrepublik Deutschland." In *Eine lernende Demokratie, 1950–1994*, ed. Max Kaase and Gunther Schmid, 129–64. Berlin: Sigma.

Nelkin, Dorothy, and Michael Pollak. 1981. *The Atom Beseiged*. Cambridge: MIT Press.

Nössler, Bernd, and Margret de Witt, eds. 1976. *Wyhl: Kein Kernkraftwerk in Wyhl und sonst nirgends*. Freiburg: Inform Verlag.

Oesterreich, Detlef. 1993. *Autoritäre Persönlichkeit und Gesellschaftsordnung*. Weinheim: Juventa.

Offe, Claus. 1972. *Strukturprobleme des kapitalistischen Staates*. Frankfurt: Suhrkamp.

———. 1987. "Challenging the Boundaries of Institutional Politics." In *Changing Boundaries of the Political*, ed. Charles Maier, 63–106. New York: Cambridge University Press.

Olivier, Johan. 1991. "State Repression and Collective Action in South Africa." *South African Journal of Sociology* 22:109–17.

Olzak, Susan. 1992. *The Dynamics of Ethnic Competition and Conflict*. Stanford: Stanford University Press.

Opp, Karl-Dieter, et al. 1995. "Left-Right Ideology and Collective Political Action." In *The Politics of Social Protest*, ed. J. Craig Jenkins and Bert Klandermans, 63–95. Minneapolis: University of Minnesota Press.

Orlowsky, Werner. 1982. "Streiflichter Persönliches zur IBA." *Arch+*, no. 66 (December): 4–12.

Otto, Hans-Uwe, and Roland Merten. 1993. *Rechtsradikale Gewalt im vereinigten Deutschland*. Bonn: Bundeszentrale für politische Bildung.

Panayi, Panikos. 1994. "Racial Violence in the New Germany, 1990–93." *Contemporary European History* 3:265–87.

Papadakis, Elim. 1989. "Green Issues and Other Parties." In *The Greens in West Germany*, ed. Eva Kolinsky, 61–86. New York: Berg.

Pappi, Franz. 1991. "Die Anhänger der neuen sozialen Bewegungen im Parteiensystem der Bundesrepublik Deutschland." In *Neue soziale Bewegungen in der Bundesrepublik Deutschland*, 2nd ed., ed. Roland Roth and Dieter Rucht, 452–68. Bonn: Bundeszentrale für politische Bildung.

Park, Robert E. 1950. *Race and Culture*. Glencoe, Ill.: Free Press.

PDS [Partei des demokratischen Sozialismus], ed. 1993. *Über den schonenden Umgang der Bundesregierung mit dem Rechtsextremismus, Teil 4*. Bonn: Partei des demokratischen Sozialismus.

———, ed. 1995. "Neofaschistische Gewalt und Straftaten in der BRD (1985–1995)." PDS/Linke Liste im Bundestag, Bonn, July.

Pelzinger, Renate, and Marlo Riege. 1981. *Die neue Wohnungsnot*. Hamburg: VSA.

Perlmutter, Ted. 1995. "The Political Asylum Debates in Germany, 1978–92." Paper presented at the Annual Meeting of the American Political Science Association, Chicago, August–September.

Pfahl-Traughber, Armin. 1992. "Der Extremismusbegriff in der politikwissenschaftlichen Diskussion." *Jahrbuch Extremismus und Demokratie* 4:67–86.

Pierson, Paul. 1994. *Dismantling the Welfare State?* New York: Cambridge University Press.

Pirker, Theo, et al. 1975. *Stadtplanung, Sanierung und Bürgerbeteiligung am Beispiel Berlin-Kreuzberg.* West Berlin: Institut für Wohnungsbau und Stadtteilplanung, Technische Universität Berlin.

Piven, Frances Fox, and Richard Cloward. 1979. *Poor People's Movements.* New York: Vintage Books.

Poguntke, Thomas. 1993. *Alternative Politics.* Edinburgh: Edinburgh University Press.

Przeworski, Adam, and Henry Teune. 1970. *The Logic of Comparative Social Inquiry.* New York: John Wiley and Sons.

Pursch, Günther. 1981. *Die in Bonn.* Frankfurt: Ullstein.

Radek, Udo, Lothar Woite, and Julian Wekel. 1977. "Bürgerbeteiligung in Hannover-Linden—ein Modell?" *Arch +*, no. 35 (October): 29–39.

Radkau, Joachim. 1983. *Aufstieg und Krise der deutschen Atomwirtschaft, 1945–75.* Reinbek: Rowohlt.

Rawlinson, Roger. 1986. *Communities of Resistance.* London: Quaker Peace and Service.

Rink, Dieter. 2000. "Blockierte Entfaltung." *Berliner Debatte* 11:91–103.

Rochon, Thomas. 1988. *Mobilizing for Peace.* Princeton: Princeton University Press.

Rösler, Cornelia. 2000. "Lokale Agenda 21 in deutschen Städten." In *Lokale "Agenda 21" Prozesse,* ed. Hubert Heinelt and Eberhard Mühlich, 12–28. Opladen: Leske und Budrich.

Roth, Roland. 1980. "Notizen zur politischen Geschichte der Bürgerinitiativen in der Bundesrepublik." In *Parlamentarisches Ritual und politische Alternativen,* ed. Roth, 74–96. Frankfurt: Campus.

———. 1985. "Neue soziale Bewegungen in der politischen Kultur der Bundesrepublik Deutschland." In *Neue soziale Bewegungen in Westeuropa und den USA,* ed. Karl-Werner Brand, 20–82. Frankfurt: Campus.

Rothstein, Bo. 1990. "Marxism, Institutional Analysis, and Working-Class Power." *Politics and Society* 18:317–45.

Rucht, Dieter. 1980. *Von Wyhl nach Gorleben.* Munich: C. H. Beck.

———. 1981. "Die Bürgerinitiativbewegung als Teil einer intermediären politischen Kultur." *Journal für Sozialforschung* 21:389–406.

———, ed. 1984. *Flughafenprojekte als Politikum.* New York: Campus.

———. 1987. "Modernization and Protest Movements During the Social-Liberal Era in West Germany." Paper presented at the Annual Meeting of the American Political Science Association, Chicago, September.

———. 1988a. "Institutional Mediation Between Public Authorities and Their Challengers." Paper presented at the Annual Meeting of the American Political Science Association, Washington, D.C., September.

———. 1988b. "Wyhl." In *Von der Bittschrift zur Platzbesetzung,* ed. Ulrich Linse et al., 128–64. Bonn: J. W. Dietz.

———. 1990a. "Campaigns, Skirmishes, and Battles." *Industrial Crisis Quarterly* 4:193–222.

———. 1990b. "The Strategies and Action Repertoires of New Movements." In *Challenging the Political Order,* ed. Russell Dalton and Manfred Kuechler, 156–78. New York: Oxford University Press.

---. 1994. *Modernisierung und neue soziale Bewegungen*. New York: Campus Verlag.

---. 1996. "German Unification, Democratization, and the Role of Social Movements." *Mobilization* 1:35–62.

---. 1998a. "Komplexe Phänomene—komplexe Erklärungen." In *Paradigmen der Bewegungsforschung*, ed. Kai-Uwe Hellman and Ruud Koopmans, 109–27. Opladen: Westdeutscher Verlag.

---. 1998b. "The Structure and Culture of Collective Protest in Germany Since 1950." In *The Social Movement Society*, ed. David S. Meyer and Sidney Tarrow, 29–57. New York: Rowman and Littlefield.

---. 1999. "Konfrontation und Gewalt." In *Eigenwilligkeit und Rationalität sozialer Prozesse*, ed. Jürgen Gerhards and Ronald Hitzler, 352–78. Opladen: Westdeutscher Verlag.

---. 2002. "Gewalt und neue soziale Bewegungen." In *Handbook of Research on Violence*, ed. Wilhelm Heitmeyer and John Hagan, 461–78. Opladen: Westdeutscher Verlag.

---. 2003. "The Changing Role of Political Protest Movements." *West European Politics* 26 (October): 153–76.

Rucht, Dieter, Barbara Blattert, and Dieter Rink. 1997. *Soziale Bewegungen auf dem Weg zur Institutionalisierung*. New York: Campus.

Saalfeld, Thomas. 1994. "Xenophobic Political Movements in Germany, 1949–94." Paper prepared for presentation at the Annual Meeting of the American Sociological Association, Los Angeles, August.

Salert, Barbara, and John Sprague. 1980. *The Dynamics of Riots*. Ann Arbor, Mich.: Inter-University Consortium for Political and Social Research.

SAM [Statistisches Amt der Landeshauptstadt München], ed. 1987. *Statistisches Taschenbuch 1987*. Munich: Statistisches Amt der Landeshauptstadt München.

---, ed. 1997. *Statistisches Jahrbuch München 1997*. Munich: Statistisches Amt der Landeshauptstadt München.

Sattler, Martin. 1979. "Demokratie in Stadtteilen?" *Zeitschrift für Politik* 26:254–67.

Schain, Martin, Aristide Zolberg, and Patrick Hossay, eds. 2002. *Shadows over Europe: The Development and Impact of the Extreme Right in Western Europe*. New York: Palgrave.

Schaper, Burkhard. 1984. "Die Entstehungsgeschichte der AL." In *AL: Die Alternative Liste Berlin*, ed. Michael Bühnemann, Michael Wendt, and Jürgen Wituschek, 51–68. West Berlin: Litpol Verlag.

Schmidt, Michael. 1993. *The New Reich*. New York: Pantheon Books.

Schmitter, Phillippe. 1981. "Interest Intermediation and Regime Governability in Contemporary Western Europe and North America." In *Organizing Interests in Western Europe*, ed. Suzanne Berger, 285–327. New York: Cambridge University Press.

Schmolt, Martina. 1984. "Instandbesetzung." In *Stattbuch 3*, 910–17. West Berlin: Stattbuch Verlag.

Schneider-Wilkes, Rainer. 1995. "Erfolg und Mißerfolg bei Berliner Verkehrsbürgerinitiativen." Typescript. Freie Universität Berlin, May.

Schnepf, Marita, and Reiner Staubach. 1988. "Bewohnerorientierte Stadterneuerung (Langfassung)." Institut für Landes- und Stadtentwicklungsforschung, Dortmund.

Schock, Kurt. 2005. *Unarmed Insurrections: People Power Movements in Nondemocracies*. Minneapolis: University of Minnesota Press.

Schreiber, Helmut. 1982. *Wohnungsmodernisierung am falschen Ort?* West Berlin: ZI 6, Freie Universität Berlin.

Schwagerl, H. Joachim. 1993. *Rechtsextremes Denken*. Frankfurt: Fischer.

Selle, Klaus. 1986. *Bestandspolitik*. Darmstadt: Verlag für Wissenschaftliche Publikationen.

Senat von Berlin (West). 1983. "Über das Projekt 'Strategien für Kreuzberg.'" Abgeordnetenhaus von Berlin, *Drucksache* 9/1222 (4 July).

Senator für Bau- und Wohnungswesen, Berlin (West). 1964. "Stadterneuerung in Berlin: Erster Bericht an das Abgeordnetenhaus von Berlin." *Drucksache* IV/1556 (12 June).

———. 1983. "Stadterneuerung in Berlin: 15er Bericht an das Abgeordnetenhaus." *Drucksache* 9/1259 (2 September).

Senator für Inneres, Berlin (West). 1982. *Hausbesetzungen und Hausbesetzer in Berlin*. West Berlin: Senator für Inneres, November.

Sharp, Gene. 1973. *The Politics of Nonviolent Action*. Boston: Porter Sargent.

SH Landtag [Schleswig-Holsteinischer Landtag]. 1991. "Asylbewerber in Schleswig-Holstein." *Drucksache* 12/1298 (18 February).

———. 1994. "Zahlenmässige Entwicklung und Situation der Asylbewerberinnen und Asylbewerber in Schleswig-Holstein im Zeitraum 1990 bis 1993." *Drucksache* 13/2241 (20 October).

Siegler, Bernd. 1993. "Der Apparat und die Rechten." In *Der Pakt*, ed. Bernd Siegler, Oliver Tolmein, and Charlotte Wiedemann, 11–117. Göttingen: Verlag die Werkstatt.

SIS [Staatsministerium des Innern, Saxony]. 1993. *Verfassungsschutzbericht 1993*. Dresden: Staatsministerium des Innern, Saxony.

Skocpol, Theda. 1988. "Comparing National Systems of Social Provision." Paper presented at the International Political Science Association meetings, Washington, D.C.

Smelser, Neil. 1962. *The Theory of Collective Behavior*. New York: Free Press.

Smith, Gordon. 1986. *Democracy in Western Germany*. 3rd ed. New York: Holmes and Meier.

Smith, Gordon, William Paterson, and Stephen Padgett. 1996. "Introduction." In *Developments in German Politics 2*, ed. Smith, Paterson, and Padgett, 1–13. Durham: Duke University Press.

Smithey, Lee, and Lester Kurtz. 1999. "'We Have Bare Hands': Nonviolent Social Movements in the Soviet Bloc." In *Nonviolent Social Movements*, ed. Stephen Zunes, Lester Kurtz, and Sarah Asher, 96–124. Malden, Mass.: Blackwell.

Sonnewald, Bernd, and Jürgen Raabe-Zimmermann. 1983. *Die "Berliner Linie" und die Hausbesetzer-Szene*. West Berlin: Arno Spitz.

Specht, Walter, ed. 1992. *Sozialraum Hoyerswerda*. Stuttgart: Diakonisches Werk.

Statistisches Bundesamt. 1987. *Datenreport 1987*. Bonn: Bundeszentral für politische Bildung, Bonn.

Sternstein, Wolfgang. 1978a. "Der Alltag des Widerstands." In *Ökologiebewegung und ziviler Widerstand*, ed. Theodor Ebert, Wolfgang Sternstein, and Roland Vogt, 34–50. Stuttgart: Umweltwissenschaftliches Institut.

———. 1978b. *Überall ist Wyhl*. Frankfurt: Haag und Herchen.

———. 1978c. "Zur Organisationsstruktur der badisch-elsässischen Bürgerinitiativen." In *Ökologiebewegung und ziviler Widerstand*, ed. Theodor Ebert, Wolfgang Sternstein, and Roland Vogt, 51–56. Stuttgart: Umweltwissenschaftliches Institut.

Stöss, Richard. 1991. *Politics Against Democracy*. New York: Berg.

———. 1993. *Rechtsextremismus in Berlin 1990*. Berlin: Berliner Arbeitshefte und Berichte zur sozialwissenschaftlichen Forschung, Nr. 80.

Strom, Elizabeth. 2001. *Building the New Berlin*. Lanham, Md.: Lexington Books.

Tarrow, Sidney. 1989a. *Democracy and Disorder*. Oxford: Clarendon Press.

———. 1989b. *Struggle, Politics, and Reform*. Ithaca: Center for International Studies, Cornell University.

———. 1993. "Social Protest and Policy Reform." *Comparative Political Studies* 25:579–607.

———. 1994. *Power in Movement*. New York: Cambridge University Press.

———. 1995. "Cycles of Collective Action." In *Repertoires and Cycles of Collective Action*, ed. Mark Traugott, 89–116. Durham: Duke University Press.

———. 1998. *Power in Movement*. 2nd ed. New York: Cambridge University Press.

———. 1999. "Foreword." In *How Social Movements Matter*, ed. Marco Giugni, Doug McAdam, and Charles Tilly, vii–ix. Minneapolis: University of Minnesota Press.

Thaysen, Ulf. 1980. "Stellung der Parteien zu den Beteiligungsmöglichkeiten und Beteiligungsformen der Bürgerinitiativen." In *Bürgerinitiativen in der Gesellschaft*, ed. Volker Hauff, 187–232. Villingen: Neckar.

Thelen, Kathleen, and Sven Steinmo. 1992. "Historical Institutionalism in Comparative Politics." In *Structuring Politics*, ed. Sven Steinmo, Kathleen Thelen, and Frank Longstreth, 1–32. New York: Cambridge University Press.

Thoma, Achim. 1990. "Die Verteilung und Unterbringung von Asylbewerbern in der Bundesrepublik Deutschland unter besonderer Berücksichtigung der Lage der Kommunen." Doctoral dissertation, Universität Mainz.

Thompson, Edward P. 1971. "The Moral Economy of the English Crowd in the Eighteenth Century." *Past and Present* 50:76–136.

Thränhardt, Dietrich. 1995. "The Political Uses of Xenophobia in England, France, and Germany." *Party Politics* 1:323–45.

Thumfahrt, Alexander. 2002. *Die politische Integration Ostdeutschlands*. Frankfurt: Suhrkamp.

Tilly, Charles. 1978. *From Mobilization to Revolution*. New York: Random House.

———. 1979. "Repertoires of Contention in America and Britain, 1750–1830." In *The Dynamics of Social Movements*, ed. Mayer Zald and John D. McCarthy, 126–55. Cambridge, Mass.: Winthrop.

———. 1983. "Speaking Your Mind Without Elections, Surveys, or Social Movements." *Public Opinion Quarterly* 47:461–78.

———. 1984a. *Big Structures, Large Processes, Huge Comparisons.* New York: Russell Sage.

———. 1984b. "Social Movements and National Politics." In *Statemaking and Social Movements*, ed. Charles Bright and Susan Harding, 297–317. Ann Arbor: University of Michigan Press.

———. 1986. *The Contentious French.* Cambridge: Harvard University Press.

———. 1995a. "Contentious Repertoires in Great Britain, 1758–1834." In *Repertoires and Cycles of Collective Action*, ed. Mark Traugott, 15–42. Durham: Duke University Press.

———. 1995b. *Popular Contention in Great Britain, 1758–1834.* Cambridge: Harvard University Press.

———. 1999. "Conclusion." In *How Social Movements Matter*, ed. Marco Giugni, Doug McAdam, and Charles Tilly, 253–70. Minneapolis: University of Minnesota Press.

———. 2001. "Mechanisms in Political Processes." *Annual Review of Political Science* 4:21–41.

Tilly, Charles, and Sidney Tarrow. *Contentious Politics.* Boulder, Colo.: Paradigm Publishers, 2007.

Touraine, Alain. 1981. *The Voice and the Eye.* New York: Cambridge University Press.

Traugott, Mark. 1995a. "Recurrent Patterns of Collective Action." In *Repertoires and Cycles of Collective Action*, ed. Traugott, 1–14. Durham: Duke University Press.

———, ed. 1995b. *Repertoires and Cycles of Collective Action.* Durham: Duke University Press.

Trautmann, Günther. 1978. "Defizitärer Planungsstaat und politische Legitimität." In *Bürgerinitiativen und repräsentatives System*, ed. Bernd Guggenberger and Udo Kempf, 309–36. Opladen: Westdeutscher Verlag.

Tuttle, Dale. 1994. "The Assimilation of East Germany and the Rise of Identity-Based Violence Against Foreigners in the Unified German State." *German Politics and Society* 31 (Spring): 63–83.

Ulbrich, Rudi. 1988. "Entwicklung und Stand der Wohnungsversorgung." In *Sozialer Wohnungsbau im internationalen Vergleich*, ed. Walter Prigge and Wilfried Kaib, 80–93. Frankfurt: Vervuert Verlag.

Ulsen, Micha, and Susanne Claassen. 1982. *Das Abschreibungs-Dschungelbuch.* 2nd ed. West Berlin: Litpol.

Verein [Verein SO36]. 1988. *Rechenschaftsbericht 1987.* West Berlin: Verein SO36.

———, ed. 1989a. *... ausser man tut es! Kreuzberg—abgeschrieben, aufgestanden.* West Berlin: Verein SO36.

———. 1989b. *Sachbericht 1988.* West Berlin: Verein SO36.

———. 1992. *Rechenschaftsbericht 1991.* Berlin: Verein SO36.

Wagner, Bernd, ed. 1994. *Handbuch Rechtextremismus.* Reinbek: Rowohlt.

———. 1995. *Jugend-Gewalt-Szenen.* Berlin: DIP.

Walsh, Edward, and Rex Warland. 1983. "Social Movement Involvement in the Wake of a Nuclear Accident." *American Sociological Review* 48:764–80.

Watts, Meredith. 1997. *Xenophobia in United Germany.* New York: St. Martin's Press.

Willems, Helmut. 1993. "Gewalt gegen Fremde." In *Aggression und Gewalt*, ed. Baden-Württemberg Landeszentrale für politische Bildung, 161–79. Stuttgart: Kohlhammer.

———. 1996. "Mobilisierungseffekte und Eskalationsprozesse." *Berliner Debatte* 1:34–42.

———. 1997. *Jugendunruhen und Protestbewegungen*. Opladen: Leske und Budrich.

Willems, Helmut, et al. 1993. *Fremdenfeindliche Gewalt*. Opladen: Leske und Budrich.

Windhoff-Heritier, Adrienne, and Oskar Gabriel. 1983. "Politische Partizipation an der kommunalen Planung." In *Bürgerbeteiligung und kommunale Demokratie*, ed. Oskar Gabriel, 126–55. Munich: Minerva.

Winter, Martin. 1998. "Protest Policing und das Problem der Gewalt." *Forschungsjournal neue soziale Bewegungen* 11:68–81.

Wisler, Dominique, and Hanspeter Kriesi. 1998. "Public Order, Protest Cycles, and Political Process." In *Policing Protest*, ed. Donnatella della Porta and Herbert Reiter, 91–116. Minneapolis: University of Minnesota Press.

Witte, Rob. 1996. *Racist Violence and the State*. New York: Longman.

Wochenschau für politische Erziehung, Sozial- und Gemeinschaftskunde. 1991. *Deutschland von Rechts*, Nr. 6, Frankfurt am Main, November-December.

Wollmann, Helmut. 1974. "Das Städtebauförderungsgesetz als Instrument staatlicher Intervention." *Leviathan* 2:199–231.

———. 2002. "Local Government and Politics in East Germany." *German Politics* 11 (December): 153–78.

Wüstenhagen, Hans-Helmut. 1975. *Bürger gegen Kernkraftwerke*. Reinbek: Rowohlt.

Zald, Mayer, and Roberta Ash. 1966. "Social Movement Organizations: Growth, Decay, and Change." *Social Forces* 44 (March): 327–41.

Zald, Mayer, and John D. McCarthy, eds. 1987. *Social Movements in an Organizational Society*. New Brunswick, N.J.: Transaction Books.

Zimmermann, Ekkart. 1994. "Xenophobic Movements in Contemporary Germany." Paper presented to the conference "Challenges to Democracy." Tel Aviv University, May.

INDEX

Page numbers in *italics* refer to figures or tables.

access to officials, 7 n. n, 12, 14, 49, 192, 224, 228–29, 249. *See also* procedural reforms
   at Brokdorf, 128, 131, 148, 155, 231, 251
   in eastern Germany, 201, 218, 249
   in Hoyerswerda, 206–9, 217, 224, 232
   in Kreuzberg, 97–98, 111, 224, 231
   in Kronshagen, 174, 189, 231, 249
   lack of, 1, 3 n. f
   in Linden, 97, 111, 231
   at lower levels of government, 250, 257
   manipulated, 128, 130
   in Munich, 189, 231, 249
   in Riesa, 207–8, 231, 249
   in Rostock, 217, 224, 231, 232
   at Wyhl, 128–29, 148, 155, 231
administrative courts, 20, 224
   at Brokdorf, 120, 131, 139, 142, 145, 147–48, 156, 159
   Federal Administrative Court, 124
   in Kreuzberg, 93–94, 102
   in Kronshagen, 176, 183
   in nuclear energy policy, 124, 129, 148 n. w, 153, 155, 221, 232, 252
   in Südpark, 175, 184
   at Wyhl, 118–19, 130, 137–38, 141, 147, 149, 151, 156
advanced industrial democracies
   movements in, 6, 28, 33, 127, 234, 241, 247
   others compared with Germany, 18, 20
AL. *See* Alternative List
Albrecht, Ernst (CDU), 159
alliances between protesters and elites. *See* elite allies
alliances between protest groups
   at Brokdorf, 134–36, 142, 150–51, 154, 232, 240 n. s
   compared across cases, 220–21, 224, 230, 232, 251
   conventional-disruptive, 222, 256
   conventional-militant, 208, 222
   dilemmas of, 255–56
   disruptive-militant, 134, 142, 149, 222
   effects on size of protests, xi, 7–12, 37–38, 40, 43, 221
   effects on types of protest, 40, 48–49, 61, 228–29, 230, 255–56
   in Hoyerswerda, 205–6, 208
   in immigration conflicts, 247
   in Kreuzberg, 81–85, 102, 112, 231, 240 n. s
   in Kronshagen, 190, 220
   and large protests, 220–21, 222–23, 230, 253
   in Linden, 80–81
   in Munich, 190
   in nuclear energy conflicts, 117, 131–32, 147
   and policing, 51, 224, 231, 233, 240 n. s
   in Riesa, 206, 220
   in Rostock, 206
   in urban renewal conflicts, 80, 109
   at Wyhl, 118, 132–34, 149–50, 232
Alternative List (AL), 71, 94, 100–101, 103 & n. zzz, 107 n. bbbb, 115
   in Kreuzberg government, 100–101 & n. www, 107
   Kreuzberg section of, 89, 101–3, 107
   support for protests, 66, 96, 102–3 & n. zzz, 107, 111
alternative movement, 55 n. ll, 82–83 & n. aaa, 110, 239 n. q

alternative movement (*continued*)
  in Kreuzberg, 79, 83, 110, 236
  in Linden, 106, 110
  in Nordstadt, 116
  projects of, 83, 98, 116
  in West Berlin, 64, 66 n. q, 83, 84 n. bbb, 236
anti-foreigner violence, 13, 215. *See also* arson attacks; militant protests; riots
  East German policy legacies and, 200
  in eastern Germany, 26, 53–55, 162 n. c, 191 & n. a, 218, 239 & n. o
  effects of, 191, 214–15
  in Hoyerswerda, 50, 191, 193–95, 205–6, 209, 211
  increase in, 26, 29–30 & nn. s–t, 191–92, 215, 230
  in Kronshagen, 177, 233
  long-term changes in, 226
  in Munich, 164 & n. l, 166–68, 188 & n. rr
  organizational explanation of, 196–200
  political-process explanation of, 31, 45, 162 n. c
  prevention of, 14, 171, 213–14
  in Rendsburg County, 164 & n. l, 166–67, 188 & n. rr
  in Riesa, 55, 59, 195–96 & n. j, 206, 249
  in Rostock, 191, 193, 195, 206, 213
  in Saxony, 29 n. r, 193, 194 n. h, 199–200, 202, 214
  socioeconomic explanations of, 28–32, 192, 196–98
  unification and, 201, 249
  waves of, 162 n. c, 215, 218
  weak repression of, 214–16
anti-immigration movement, 3, 6–7, 15, 25–27, 161–62 & n. b, 236. *See also* anti-foreigner violence; immigration conflicts; neo-Nazis; skinheads
  citizen initiatives in, 15, 161, 227, 261 n. 39
  compared with others, 238–39
  defined, 7 n. m, 161
  elite allies for, 42–43
  explanations of, 26
  nonviolent protests in, 26–27, 161–62 & nn. a–d, 188–89
  opportunity expansion and, 42–43, 214–15, 226–27, 241–47
  tactics, 242–43, 247
  violence in, 54, 193, 214

antinuclear energy movement, national, 117, 119–20, 124, 127, 136 n. p, 145. *See also* Brokdorf; Gorleben; Wackersdorf; Wyhl
antisystem groups. *See* autonomists; communist groups; skinheads; terrorist groups
arson attacks. *See also* anti-foreigner violence; Mölln
  in Bavaria, 164
  at Brokdorf, 120–21, 150
  in eastern Germany, 26
  in Hoyerswerda, 194
  in Kreuzberg, 64
  leftist, 24, 241
  in Munich, 168, 188 n. qq
  in Riesa, 196 n. j
  rightist, national amount, 26, 215, 226
  in Rostock, 206, 213
  in Saxony, 193 n. f, 199, 202
  in Schleswig-Holstein, 167
asylum policy, 44
  constitutional amendment restricting (Article 16a), 26, 162 n. c, 182, 191, 215
  debate on, 42–43, 162, 191, 193, 214, 226–27
  in Kronshagen, 175
  in Munich, 172–73, 188 n. oo
  right to asylum, 168–69 & n. v, 250
  in Schleswig-Holstein, 174, 188 n. oo
asylum seekers, 30–31, 168–69
  ability to remain in Germany, 168, 169 n. v
  applications for asylum, 29–31, 168 & n. u
  ban on employment of, 30–31, 169–70, 197
  campaigns against, 4, 26–27, 37, 42, 161–62 & n. c
  counselling for, 184–85, 189
  crime by, 170, 179, 205
  distribution of, 44, 162 n. c, 167, 170–71, 172, 178
  evacuation from riot cities, 210, 212–14
  housing of, 31, 42, 44, 170–71, 174–75
  in Hoyerswerda, 194, 197–98, 203, 208, 214
  in Kronshagen, 177 n. hh, 180–83
  in Munich, 166, 173, 177–79, 184, 186
  in Rendsburg County, 166, 174
  in Riesa, 204–5, 207, 210

in Rostock, 204, 213
in Saxony, 194 n. h, 200, 202, 214
in Schleswig-Holstein, 174
social assistance for, 169–70, 197
violence against, 161 & n. a, 191 n. a, 209, 215. *See also* anti-foreigner violence; arson attacks; riots
authorities' mistakes. *See* concessions; mistakes; policing; policy reforms; procedural reforms; threats by officials
autonomist movement, 2, 82, 236 n. m
autonomists, 3 n. e, 21 n. d, 22, 24, 237 n. n, 241
at Brokdorf, 120, 152
in Kreuzberg, 2, 67, 82–84, 101–3, 106–9
in Linden, 64, 106
in Nordstadt, 64, 116, 237
social composition, 31–32, 69–70
violence by, 24, 58, 84, 101, 106–8, 244 n. v
at Wackersdorf, 122

Baden-Alsace Initiatives, 126–27
goals, 127
as model, 237
protests by, 118–19, 129, 132–33, 148–50, 153
social composition, 118
strategies, 130, 132
Baden-Württemberg (*Land*), 122. *See also* Wyhl
elections in, 125–26
government of, 125, 129, 236, 254
Landtag, 130, 137–38, 141, 151
Bavaria (*Land*), 164 nn. k–l, 167, 171–74, 188 n. oo
Berlin, unified (*Land*), 66 n. u, 70, 99 n. rrr, 102, 105, 237. *See also* West Berlin
Berlin-Kreuzberg. *See* Kreuzberg, borough of; Kreuzberg urban renewal conflict
Bodenschatz, Harald, 113–14
Bohl, Friedrich (CDU), 191–92 n. b
bold protests. *See also* innovation of tactics; disruptive protests; militant protests
compared across cases, 221, *222–23*
in immigration conflicts, 30, 216, 220
in the making of opportunities, 9, *37–38*, 40, 52, 131, 220–21
in nuclear-energy conflicts, 117, 131–32
in urban renewal conflicts, 83, 109

Brandt, Willy (SPD), 39
"dare more democracy" slogan, 44–45, 244, 246
federal government led by, 124–25, 236, 244
Brokdorf nuclear energy conflict
alliances among protest groups, 131–32, 134–36, 146, 150–51, 153–54
chronology of, 119–21, 147
compared with other nuclear conflicts, 58, 152–59
concessions to protests, 140–42, 152, 156
elite allies for protesters, 138–40, 141–42, 146–49, 151–52, 155
explanation of size of protests, 152–53
explanation of types of protest, 153–57
national protest cycles and, 157–59
Northwest German Power Plant, 119, 127
participatory rights, 128–29, 131
police overreactions, 142, 144–47, 156–57
political institutions, 123–25
reforms, blockage of, 131, 155, 158
rural citizen initiatives, 128, 135, 140, 150
selection of case, 59
site occupation, prevention of, 145–46, 157
site occupation strategy, 120, 131, 135–36, 140, 154
socioeconomic setting, 121–23
Steinburg County, 122, 125, 139–40
summarized, 117–18
threats posed by nuclear plant, 126, 127–28, 131, 147
Bundesrat, 19, 26, 215
Bundestag, 17, 138–39
asylum reform and, 26, 191 n. b, 215
minor parties in, 25, 147, 227

cases, choice of. *See* research design
chances of success, 9, 36, *38*, 39, 42, 49. *See also* interactive political process theory; making of opportunities
defined, 36
Christian Democratic Union (CDU). *See* Christian Democrats
Christian Democrats, 18 & n. b, 20. *See also* Christian Social Union; elite allies; *names of individual leaders*
as allies for anti-immigration protesters, 20, 26, 42, 161 n. b, 191 & n. b, 245
at Brokdorf, 125, 138, 139–40, 141, 148
conception of democracy, 246

Christian Democrats (*continued*)
   and far right, 215–16, 231, 245–46
   at Gorleben, 159, 236
   in government, 5, 8, 23
   in Hoyerswerda, 194
   in Kronshagen, 174
   in Linden, 71, 86
   and nuclear policy, 148 n. w
   in Rendsburg County, 164 n. k, 174
   in Riesa, 194, 207 n. z
   in Rostock, 212 & n. hh
   in Saxony, 202, 212 & n. ii
   support for disruptive protesters, lack of, 14, 53, 246
   in West Berlin and unified Berlin, 14, 65–67, 89, 96, 104, 114; and the Alternative List, 94, 115; and urban renewal policy, 91, 98, 104–5
   at Wyhl, 119, 125–27, 129, 136–38, 141, 151, 236
Christian Social Union (CSU), 18, 20. *See also* Christian Democrats
   in Bavaria, 5, 164 n. k, 172, 174, 188 n. oo
   in Munich, 172, 179, 188 n. pp, 191–92 n. b
   in Südpark, 173, 181
citizen initiatives. *See* Baden-Alsace Initiatives; Independent Citizen Initiative; Kronshagen; Lower Elbe Initiative; SO36 Citizen Initiative; Südpark Citizen Initiative
communist groups
   at Brokdorf, 120–21, 134–35, 145–46, 151, 233, 236 n. m
   at Gorleben, 158
   and Greens, 42
   in Kreuzberg, 83
   in leftist movements, 6, 13, 21–22, 24, 237–38, 240–41
   in Linden, 76
   social composition, 31
   and violence, 243–44
   at Wyhl, 133
comparison of cases
   in immigration, 186–90, 216–18
   in nuclear energy, 152–59
   size and duration of protests, 5, 219–24, 222–23
   types of protest, 5, 228–29
   in urban renewal, 109–16
concessions to protests, 12, 22, 43, 45, 50, 253
   to anti-foreigner violence, 214–16
   at Brokdorf, 141–42, 145, 152, 156
   compared across cases, 50, 52, 230–33, 249, 253
   to disruptive and militant protests, 256–57
   effects on types of protest, 41, 48, 50, 228–29, 230
   at Gorleben, 159
   in Hoyerswerda, 191–92, 208, 214–15, 217
   in Kreuzberg, 91–92, 103, 112
   in Kronshagen, 163, 188
   in Linden, 75, 90–91, 99, 112–13, 256–57
   in Munich, 163, 187
   in Rostock, 191–92, 214–15
   at Wyhl, 119, 125 n. i, 141, 156
contentious politics, theory of, 35–36
conventional protest groups. *See* alliances between protest groups; Baden-Alsace Initiatives; Independent Citizen Initiative; SO36 Association
conventional protests. *See also* types of protest
   actors preferring, 31–32, 241
   at Brokdorf, 118, 120–21, 134–45, 148–49, 155
   compared across cases, 5, 228–29
   conflicts dominated by, 4, 14–15, 227, 230, 235, 252
   defined, 2, 45–46
   explained, 11–13, 34, 40, 47–50, 52–53, 252
   in Hoyerswerda, 192, 195, 206–8, 217
   institutional explanation of, 32–33, 252
   in immigration conflicts, 26–27, 162–63, 166, 187–89
   in Kreuzberg, 66–67, 81–82, 96–99, 111
   in Kronshagen, 176, 182–83, 185, 187
   in Linden, 61–63, 75, 91, 96–97, 111
   as result of access to officials, 12, 96–100, 128, 231, 251–52
   in Riesa, 192, 195, 206–7
   in rightist protests, 238, 242, 244, 246
   in Rostock, 192, 195, 217
   socioeconomic explanations of, 27, 31–32
   in Südpark, 175, 187
   at Wyhl, 117–19, 130, 136, 147–49, 155, 254
conventional strategy, 46, 74
costs and risks of protests, 10, 12, 35–36, 38, 47–48, 50–51

alliances between protesters and, 38, 48
elite allies and, 39, 42
procedural reforms and, 45, 49, 78, 97, 251
courts, 20, 34, 55, 169, 171, 250. *See also* administrative courts
in Kreuzberg, 65, 95
cultural conflicts, 168–69, 221. *See also* asylum seekers
defined, 31, 168–69
in eastern Germany, 217–18
Germans' attitudes toward foreigners and, 54, 169
government policies and, 31, 44, 55, 169, 192
in Hoyerswerda, 203–4, 208, 221
in immigration conflicts, 168, 169–71
in Kronshagen, 181, 190
in Riesa, 204–5, 207, 216
in Rostock, 204, 221
siting of shelters and, 171, 202–5, 216
in Südpark, 177–79, 190
cycles, protest. *See* protest cycles

daring protests. *See* bold protests
del Vasto, Lanzo, 132
demonstrations. *See* disruptive protests; militant protests
Diepgen, Eberhard (CDU), 65, 106
differences between eastern and western protests, 53–55, 200–201, 218. *See also* anti-foreigner violence, in eastern Germany; eastern Germany; unification
differences between left and right. *See also* similarities
in alliances between protesters, 238–39
in attitudes toward democracy and the state, 241, 243–44
in attitudes toward violence, 244 n. v
in authorities' responses to violence, 240
explanation of, 14, 53, 239–46
in protests, 13, 21 n. e, 26
in mainstream party responses to them, 244–46
political-cultural taboos and, 43, 245–46
in reliance on militant threats and violence, 13, 53, 238
in social backgrounds, 238 n. q
in strategic innovation, 241–43
in types of violence, 13 n. r

in use of nonviolent disruption, 53, 238–39
disruptive protest groups. *See* Baden-Alsace Initiatives; Housing Emergency Action; Lower Elbe Initiative; SO36 Citizen Initiative; Südpark Initiative
disruptive protests. *See also* squats; types of protest
at Brokdorf, 120–21, 134–36, 152
cases involving, 5, 58–59, 227–28
compared across cases, 228–29
cyclical explanation of, 234–35, 248–49
defined, 2, 45–47
explained, 11–13, 40–41, 47–51, 221, 230–33, 255–56
at Gorleben, 158–59
in immigration conflicts, 26–27, 175, 187, 190
institutional explanation of, 33, 71, 252
in Kreuzberg, 64–67, 74 n. mm, 80, 91, 100–102
in Kronshagen, lack of, 187
lack of rightist, 238, 243–44, 246
in Linden, 63–64, 75–76, 86, 90–91, 100, 104
in Munich, 166–67, 189
national amount of leftist, 225, 238
socioeconomic explanation of, 31–32, 69–70, 113–16
in Südpark, 175, 184, 186–87
in urban renewal, explained, 110–13
at Wyhl, 119, 131–34, 149–50, 151, 153
disruptive strategy, 46–47, 50, 255–56, 241–43, 249
Dolgenbrodt attack on foreigners, 239 n. o

East Germany (German Democratic Republic). *See also* eastern Germany; unification
collapse of communism and democratization, 25, 29, 200–201, 203
Communist Party (SED), 25, 201
foreign contract workers in, 6 n. k, 191 n. a, 204
legacies of immigrant policies, 54, 200–201, 218
eastern Germany. *See also* East Germany; unification
administration and policing, 200–202, 213, 249
anti-foreigner violence, 26, 30, 53–55, 162 n. c, 191 & n. a, 218, 239 & n. o

eastern Germany (*continued*)
    asylum seekers, 162 n. c, 170, 200
    citizen initiatives, 225
    crime, 201, 213
    cultural conflicts, 217–18
    immigration, 8, 29–30
    immigration conflicts, 5, 59, 161 n. a, 192–94. *See also* Hoyerswerda; Riesa; Rostock
    leftist protests, 56 n. mm
    nonviolent protests, 53 n. ii, 161 n. a, 193
    political culture, 53–54, 200, 216
    skinheads, 55, 198, 236 n. m
    unemployment, 8, 25, 28–30, 196
Eggert, Heinz (CDU), 212 n. ii
elite allies for protesters. *See also* Alternative List; Christian Democrats; labor unions; Liberals; Protestant churches; Social Democrats
    at Brokdorf, 138–40, 141–42, 146–49, 151–52, 155
    effects on repression, 10, 12, 39–42, 48–49, 51, 231, 233, 238
    effects on chances of success, 10, 38–39, 38, 40, 42–43
    effects on types of protest, 12, 40, 48, 49, 228–29, 231
    in Hoyerswerda, 209–10
    in Kreuzberg, 76–77, 86–90, 96, 100–103, 107, 111
    in Kronshagen, 182–83
    in Linden, 85–86, 99–100, 111
    in Munich, 188–89
    in Riesa, lack of, 210
    in Rostock, 209–10
    in Südpark, 181–82
    as weak insiders, 39
    at Wyhl, 136–38, 151, 154–55
Eppler, Erhard (SPD), 138
ethnic competition. *See also* immigration; socioeconomic theories assessed
    and immigration conflicts, 8, 165–68, 192, 196–98, 216–17
    theory of, xii, 28–31, 36 n. x, 261 n. 46

facilitation of protests. *See also* policing; procedural reforms; repression
    as cause of protest, 10–11, 36, 44–45, 100 n. uuu
    defined, 36
Federal Association of Environmental Citizen Initiatives (BBU), 136, 139, 149–50, 242

Federal Constitutional Court, 18
Federal Interior Ministry, 124, 139, 185–86
Federal Office for the Recognition of Asylum Applicants, 170
Federal Republic of Germany; see Germany
Filbinger, Hans (CDU), 129, 137–38, 141, 143–44
foreign contract workers, 6 n. k. *See also* foreigners
    in eastern Germany, 191 n. a, 200
    in Hoyerswerda, 197, 203, 205–6, 211, 214, 230
    in Riesa, 204
    in Rostock, 213, 230
    as targets of violence, 161 n. a, 194
foreigners. *See also* asylum seekers; foreign contract workers
    as targets of violence, 13, 29–30, 55, 169 n. v, 198, 226
    attitudes toward, 31, 54, 179, 198
    defined, 6–7 n. k
    in East Germany, 200, 218
    in Hoyerswerda, 194, 197–98, 203, 214 n. kk
    integration of, 185–86, 188 n. oo
    in Kreuzberg, 72
    in Linden, 63
    locations of, 30, 44, 162 n. c, 170, 194 n. h, 199–20
    in Munich, 164, 166–67
    protection of, 45, 212, 249
    protest groups in favor of, 21, 162–63, 171, 175–76, 179, 216
    refugees, 29, 161, 168
    in Rendsburg County, 164, 166
    in Riesa, 194, 197–98, 207
    in Rostock, 221
    in Südpark, 173
Freiburg
    city of, 118, 122–23, 127, 133, 149, 153
    County, 126, 137

Gamson, Bill, xiii, 262 n. 72
German People's Union (DVU), 26, 242. *See also* political parties, far-right
Germany (Federal Republic of), xi n. a. *See also* East Germany; unification
    deficits in democratic institutions, 7, 17–18
    federalism, 19, 235 n. l
    amount of protest in, 5, 21, 24–26, 224–27

protest movements in, 5–7, 20–22
strengthening of democracy in, 22–23, 257–58
strengths in democratic institutions, 18–20, 250–51
Gorleben nuclear energy conflict, 158–59, 236 n. m, 237, 249, 253, 256
Green parties (Die Grünen, Bündnis 90/Die Grünen). *See also* Alternative List
  as allies for leftist protesters, 10, 22–23, 42, 97, 225, 243, 245
  at Brokdorf, 148, 152–53, 155
  in Berlin, 107
  in eastern Germany, 25
  in elections, 2, 19, 23, 42, 71, 147–48
  in Hanover, 2, 71, 97
  in Kronshagen, 174
  in Munich, 174, 172–73, 188
  in nuclear energy conflicts, 147, 151
  right wing of, 22 n. e
  at Wyhl, 151, 153
grievances, 28, 44 n. bb, 236 n. x. *See also* cultural conflicts; ethnic competition; threats by officials
Grohnde nuclear conflict, 58, 154
guest workers. *See* foreigners

Hamburg, 122
  government of, 152, 162
  as site of Brokdorf protests, 121, 122 n. e, 152
  as source of Brokdorf protesters, 120, 122–23, 128, 131 n. k, 134–35, 139–40
  utility company in, 127–28, 152
Hanover
  City Planning Office, 62, 70, 72, 75, 81, 85, 97
  Green-Alternative Citizen List, 71
  political institutions, 70–71
Hanover-Linden; see Linden
Hitler, Adolf, 145 n. u, 196 n. j, 244 n. w
Honecker, Erich, 25, 200
housing corporations, public. *See* West Berlin, housing corporations
Housing Emergency Action, 62. *See also* Linden
  alliance with Independent Citizen Initiative, 74 n. ll, 76, 80–81
  composition of, 75–76, 241
  elite support for, 111–13
  goals of, 76

protests by, 81, 86, 90–91
strategies, 80–81
Hoyerswerda immigration conflict
  access to officials, 206–7, 208–9
  alliances between protest groups, 205–6
  asylum seekers, 203–4, 208–12, 214
  citizen forum, 208–9, 217
  compared with other immigration conflicts, 216–18
  concessions to protests, 214
  cultural conflicts, 203–4
  elite allies, 209–10
  evacuation of asylum seekers, 214
  explanation of protests, 192, 216–18
  foreign contract workers, 203, 205, 211
  foreigners' housing, 194, 203, 205–6, 208–9, 217
  immigration, 197–98
  police actions against immigrants, 211
  police passivity, 210–12
  political institutions, 200–202
  selection of case, 193
  skinheads, 194–95, 199
  socioeconomic setting, 194 & n. g, 196–98
  spectators at riots, 195, 205, 209, 214
  summary of protests, 194–95, 209
  unemployment, 196–97
  vigilante activities, 211
  youth clubs, 207 n. aa

immigration, 28–30, 168–69, 227. *See also* asylum seekers; foreign contract workers; foreigners
immigration conflicts, eastern, 58, 216–18. *See also* Hoyerswerda; Riesa; Rostock; Saxony
immigration conflicts, western, 58, 186–90. *See also* Kronshagen; Munich; Rendsburg County; Südpark
Independent Citizen Initiative, 62–63, 97, 100. *See also* Linden
  alliance with Housing Emergency Action, 74 n. ll, 80–81, 86, 113
  alliance with Social Democrats, 109, 111
  composition, 73–74
  goals, 75
  protests by, 75–76, 85–86
  strategies, 74, 76, 91
innovation of tactics, 35–36, 38, 234, 256–57. *See also* bold protests
  by authorities, 157, 235, 246

innovation of tactics (*continued*)
  by leftist protesters, 109, 149, 154, 158, 235, 241–42
  by rightist protesters, 242–43
interactions between protesters, elites, and authorities, xii, 31, 40–41, 47, 48, 52, 219, 224, 252. *See also* interactive political process theory
  in advanced industrial democracies, 247
  partial autonomy from structural factors, 247–49
  role of actors in, 253–55
interactive political process theory, xi–xii, 7–8, 9–14, 35, 36 n. x, 37–52, 248
  summary of evidence for, 219–33
International Committee of Baden-Alsace Citizen Initiatives. *See* Baden-Alsace Initiatives

Jansen, Günther (SPD), 141–42, 148
Joppke, Christian, xii n. 3, 37 n. y, 262 n. 70

Kitschelt, Herbert, 32–33, 125 n. i
Kohl, Helmut (CDU), 148 n. w, 215–16, 236
Koopmans, Ruud, 35, 52 n. hh, 53, 123 n. f, 157, 234
Krause, Rudolf (CDU, Republicans), 202, 212
Kreuzberg, borough of, 68
  Construction Department, 71, 78, 91, 100–101, 103
  council, 78, 98
  government and administration, 66, 78–79, 90, 92, 102, 114–15
  police blockade of, 105, 106–7
  political institutions, 71
  SPD-AL coalition in, 66, 100–101
Kreuzberg urban renewal conflict. *See also* Berlin; SO36 Association; SO36 Citizen Initiative; West Berlin
  alliances among protest groups, 81–85, 110–11
  amnesty demand, 84, 96, 111
  Berlin Line, 93–94, 95, 104
  Careful Urban Renewal, 66, 88–89, 92, 99, 107
  chronology of, 64–67
  compared with other urban renewal cases, 109–16
  concessions to protests, 90–92, 112
  delays in reforms, 109, 111–13
  Dresdener Strasse Tenant Initiative, 82, 88, 98, 100

  early protests in (1969–76), 74 & n. mm
  elite allies, 76–77, 86–90, 96, 100–103, 107, 111
  explanation of types of protest, 3, 110–13
  explanation of size of protests, 3, 109–10
  Garski affair, 94, 115
  godparents, 89–90
  housing corporations, 113–14
  Kottbusser Tor area, 64, 68, 72, 77, 88
  May Day demonstrations and riots, 2, 67, 102–3, 106–9
  neighborhood committees, 98
  policing, 93–95, 106–8, 112–13
  political institutions, 70–71
  procedural reforms, 76–80, 96–99, 111
  real-estate speculation, 74 n. mm, 78–79, 82–84, 87, 93–94, 110
  rehab-squats, 82, 93, 104
  selection of case, 58
  shift to disruptive protests, 79–80
  SO 36 area, 64, 68, 72, 77–79, 83, 98, 106
  socioeconomic setting of, 66–70
  Squatter Council, 84, 96
  structural explanation of, assessed, 113–16
  summarized, 1–2, 61
  tenant advising, 97–98, 101–2
  threats of demolition and displacement, 72–74, 76–80, 87, 105
  threats of repression, 104
  types of protest, 61
Kronawitter, Georg (SPD), 162 n. c, 171–72, 175, 182
Kronshagen immigration conflict
  asylum shelters, 176–77, 180–81, 182–83, 185–86
  compared with other immigration conflicts, 186–89
  cultural threats, 180–81
  duration of protests, 165 n. o
  elite allies for protesters, lack of, 182–83
  explanation of protests, 186–87
  local conflict setting, 173–75
  political institutions, 174–75
  reforms, timing of, 185–86
  socioeconomic setting, 166, 174
  summary of protests, 176–77
Kupfer, Lothar (CDU), 212 n. hh

labor unions, 6, 17–18, 22
  in particular conflicts, 90, 109, 144, 152
  and Social Democrats, 20, 21

Lafontaine, Oskar (SPD), 162 n. c
leftist protests and movements, 20–22, 23.
    See also alternative movement; autonomist movement; autonomists; communist groups; differences between left and right; nuclear energy conflicts; similarities between leftist and rightist protests; squatter movement; student movement; urban renewal conflicts; women's movement; *names of particular conflicts*
    defined, 21–22 & nn. e–f
    explanations of, 27–28, 31–32
    amount of activity, nationwide, 21, 24, 224–26
    militancy in, 24 & n. k
    types of protest in, 53
Liberal Party (Free Democratic Party). See Liberals
Liberals. *See also* elite allies
    at Brokdorf, 131, 139, 141, 147, 152
    in Hanover, 71, 86, 97 n. 000
    nationally, 18, 20, 22–23, 25, 39, 148, 242–46
    response to Hoyerswerda, 215
    in West Berlin, 65 n. p, 67, 71, 87, 89–90, 94
Linden urban renewal conflict. *See also* Hanover; Independent Citizen Initiative
    alliances among protest groups, 80–81, 110
    chronology of, 62–64
    compared with other urban renewal cases, 109–16
    concessions to protests, 90–91
    disruptive protests in, 63 n. i, 104 n. aaaa
    elite allies for protesters, 85–86, 99–100, 111
    explanation of size of protests, 109–10
    explanation of types of protest, 110–13
    Kaplan Strasse squat, 62, 76, 81, 86, 91, 109
    North Linden, 63–64, 72–73, 93, 97, 99–100, 104–6
    North Linden Citizen Initiative, 63, 100
    North Linden Tenant Group, 63, 100
    planning advisors, 85–86, 97
    policing, 93, 105–6, 113
    political institutions, 70–71
    procedural reforms, 75–76, 96–97, 98–99, 111
    reforms, 112

    renewal commissions, 97
    selection of case, 58
    shift to disruptive protests, 75–76
    socioeconomic setting, 63, 67–68, 69
    South Linden, 72, 80, 97, 99, 110–11, 113
    summarized, 1–2, 61
    threats by officials, 72–76, 104, 111–12
    types of protest in, 61
Lower Elbe Initiative, 142 n. s, 146
    composition, 128, 134, 140
    divisions within, 135
    elite support for, 138–40, 155
    goals, 128
    strategies, 130–31, 134–36
Lower Saxony, 41 n. aa, 68, 71 n. gg, 158–59, 236–37

making of opportunities by protesters
    at Brokdorf, 131, 134–36, 138–40, 144–47, 152–53
    in Hoyerswerda, 205–6, 209–10, 214–15, 217
    in Kreuzberg, 76–80, 81–85, 86–90, 96–99, 100–103, 109–10
    on the left, 13, 39–42, 224–26
    in Linden, 75–76, 80–81, 85–86, 96–97, 99–100, 109–10
    in nuclear energy conflicts, 118, 131–32, 142
    on the right, 13, 42–43, 214–15, 226–27
    in Rostock, 206, 209–10, 214–15, 217
    in Südpark, 181–82, 186
    summary of evidence for theory, 219–27, 233, 241, 253
    theory of, 9–11, 36–45, 38, 40–41, 262 n. 70
    at Wyhl, 129–30, 131–34, 136–38, 142–44, 147–48, 152–53
marches, 64, 108, 129, 146, 158–59, 177, 242. *See also* disruptive protests; militant protests
McAdam, Doug, 34, 35–36, 37 n. y, 262 n. 70
media attention, 9, 37–38, 49, 226 n. h, 246
militant protest groups. *See* autonomists; communist groups; Lower Elbe Initiative; neo-Nazis; skinheads; squatter movement
militant protests. *See also* anti-foreigner violence; arson attacks; riots; types of protest; violence

militant protests (continued)
    at Brokdorf, 118, 120–21 & n. e, 141–42, 144–45, 149–52, 154
    compared across cases, 5, 228–29
    cyclical explanation of, 236–38
    defined, 2, 11 n. q, 47
    how actors can avoid, 255–57
    in Hoyerswerda, 192–93, 194–95, 205–6, 209, 211
    institutional explanation of, 33, 71, 248–49
    in Kreuzberg, 2, 65–67, 80–81, 83–85, 92, 102–3, 106–9
    in Kronshagen, 176–77
    by leftists, 24, 53, 239
    in Linden, 64, 105
    in Munich, 164, 187–88
    in Nordstadt, 64, 116
    political process explanation of, 11–14, 40–41, 47–53, 230–33, 240–44
    in Rendsburg County, 164, 166 & n. s, 187–88
    in Riesa, 192, 195–96
    by rightists, 53, 239
    in Rostock, 192–93, 195, 206, 213
    socioeconomic explanation of, 24, 69–70
    in Südpark, 175–76, 182, 184, 186–87
    at Wyhl, 119, 133
militant strategy, 47, 50, 152, 155, 184, 242
mistakes by officials, 9–11, 38, 43–45, 50–51, 222–23, 235, 253. See also concessions; policing; policy reforms; procedural reforms; threats by officials
    at Brokdorf, 134, 144
    defined, 10, 43
    facilitating, 44–45
    in Hoyerswerda, 202–4, 216
    in immigration conflicts, 162 n. c, 200, 202–5
    in Kreuzberg, 78, 80, 113
    in nuclear energy conflicts, 117, 131, 153
    in policing, 50–51, 220–24, 228–29, 231, 233, 254
    provocative, 43–44
    in Rostock, 204, 216
    in Südpark, 177–78
    in urban renewal conflicts, 61, 75, 109
    at Wyhl, 153, 254
Mölln arson attack, 179, 215–16, 226–27, 240, 247
Momper, Walter (SPD), 39 n. aa, 84, 101, 227
movement. See also leftist protests; rightist protests
    defined, 4 n. g
Munich. See also Südpark
    asylum commission, 172–73, 177–79
    asylum policy, 172–73
    asylum seekers in, 173
    elite allies in, 188–89
    immigration conflicts in, 165
    political institutions, 172
    explanation of protests, 187–90
    skinheads and neo-Nazis, 167–68
    social structure, 164
mutually reinforcing actions, xi, 8, 9–11, 36–37, 38, 232–33. See also interactions; making of opportunities
    in nuclear energy conflicts, 144–45

National Democratic Party (NPD), 25 n. m, 242. See also political parties, far-right
neighborhood renewal, 62–63
neo-Nazis, 25–26 n. m
    as activists in anti-immigration movement, 7, 13, 26, 55, 198, 236 n. m
    and authorities, 45, 216, 240 n. r
    goals and ideology, 26, 198, 244
    in Hoyerswerda, 211
    in Kronshagen, 177, 233
    in Munich, 168, 179, 190, 236
    in Rendsburg County, 166 n. s, 167, 190
    in Saxony, 202, 212
    and skinheads, 198
    strategies, 242–44
    symbols used by, 199
    taboo and 245–46
    violence by, 14, 26, 52, 161, 191, 196 n. j, 215
new politics theory, xii, 3, 8, 22–23, 27–28
new social movements theory, xii, 3, 21 n. d, 23–24, 27–28, 36 n. x, 225
nonviolently disruptive protests. See disruptive protests
Nordstadt (Hanover) urban renewal conflict, 58, 64, 106, 116, 237, 248
    Chaos Days, 64 & n. k, 116
nuclear accidents, 126, 152, 159
nuclear energy conflicts, 58, 125 n. i, 152–59. See also Brokdorf; Gorleben; Wackersdorf; Wyhl
nuclear energy policy, national, 56 n. nn, 121, 125–26
    debate on, 138–39, 141–42

INDEX   313

institutions making, 123–25
licensing procedures, 128–29

occupations of construction sites. *See* Brokdorf; Wyhl
occupations of housing. *See* squats
opportunities, expansion of. *See* making of opportunities
organizational explanations. *See also* skinheads
   in eastern Germany, 198–200
   in Munich and Rendsburg County, 167–68
Orlowsky, Werner, 100–103, 227, 254

participation, political. *See* conventional, disruptive, *and* militant protests
participation rights. *See* access; procedural reforms
participation, types of. *See* types of protest
Party of Democratic Socialism (PDS), 25, 207 n. 2
policing of protests. *See also* repression
   effects on size of protests, 222–23
   effects on types of protest, 12–13, 41, 48, 50–51, 228–29, 231
   on left and right compared, 240
   overreactions, 10–12, 231; at Brokdorf, 144–47, 156–57; in Kreuzberg, 94–96, 106–7, 108, 112–13; at Wyhl, 142–43, 156
   proportionate and differentiated, 12; in Kreuzberg, 108–9; in Linden, 93, 105–6, 113; in Riesa, 213–14, 217
   underreactions, 10, 12, 214–15, 231; in Hoyerswerda, 210–12, 217; in Kreuzberg, 93–94, 106, 108; in Rostock, 212–13, 217; at Wyhl, 143–44, 156
policy reforms, failure to adopt, 12. *See also* concessions; threats by officials
   at Brokdorf, 155
   effects on types of protest, 40, 48, 49–50, 228–29, 232
   in Hoyerswerda, 208–9
   in Kreuzberg, 66, 111–12
   in Kronshagen, 185–86
   in Linden, 112
   in Rostock, 210
   in Südpark, 183–85
   at Wyhl, 119, 155
political actors, xii, 23
   rationality of, 35
   scope for, 253–55

political elites, 7–12, 23, 35, 39–42, 224, 256. *See also* elite allies
   defined, 7 n. n
political environment, 33–34, 36–37, 61, 262 n. 70. *See also* interactions; political institutions
political institutions, creation of, 34, 96–99, 252
political institutional theory assessed, 8–9, 32–34, 240, 248–49, 249–52
   in eastern immigration conflicts, 200–202
   in nuclear energy conflicts, 123–25
   openness as permissive condition, 249–51
   in urban renewal conflicts, 70–71, 113–16
   in western immigration conflicts, 172, 174, 188 n. oo, 189
political interactions. *See* interactions; interactive political process theory
political opportunities. *See* making of opportunities; political institutions
political opportunity structures, xii, 9, 32–34, 262 nn. 70, 72
political parties, far-right, 25–26, 42, 161, 227, 242, 244–45. *See also* Republicans
political parties, left-ecological. *See* Alternative List; Green parties
political parties, mainstream, 19, 22–23, 55, 239, 245. *See also* Christian Democrats; Christian Social Union; Liberals; Social Democrats
political process theories, xii, 34, 36 & n. x, 261 n. 67. *See also* interactive political process theory
political processes. *See* alliances between protest groups; concessions; elite allies; policy reforms; policing; procedural reforms; threats by officials
procedural reforms, 40, 44–45, 48
   effects on duration of protest, 224
   effects on types of protest, 40, 49, 228–29, 231–32
   at Brokdorf, 128–29, 131
   in Hoyerswerda, 206–7, 208–9
   in Kreuzberg, 76–80, 96–99, 111
   in Linden, 75–76, 96–97, 98–99, 111
   in Munich, 172
   in Riesa, 207–8
   at Wyhl, 128–29, 147–48
protest cycles
   affected by local conflicts, 58–59, 237–38

protest cycles (*continued*)
   local settings and, 236–37
   and nuclear energy conflicts, 157–59, 248–49
   subnational actors and, 235–36
   and tactical innovation, 234–35
   and temporal position of conflicts, 56, 58, 234, 248–49
   theory of, xii, 35, 234
protest group. *See also* organizational explanations; *names of particular groups*
   defined, 3 n. f
Protestant churches and pastors
   as allies for leftist protesters, 6, 10, 22, 250
   at Brokdorf, 49, 121, 136, 139, 146, 153
   in East Germany, 25
   in Kreuzberg, 77, 88–90, 96, 102, 106, 109
   in Kronshagen, 176, 180
   in Südpark, 175, 177–79, 182, 184, 187
   at Wyhl, 127, 132–33, 136–38, 143, 148, 153
protests. *See* conventional, disruptive, leftist, militant, *and* rightist protests
provocation of protests. *See* policing, overreactions; policy reforms, failure to adopt; threats by officials
public opinion
   about anti-foreigner violence, 216
   about foreigners, 31, 54, 168–69
   about nuclear energy, 126
   and protests, 3 n. f, 38

Quedlinburg riots, 192 n. c

Reagan, Ronald, 105–7
reforms. *See* concessions; policy reforms; procedural reforms
Rendsburg County, 164, 174. *See also* Kronshagen
   CDU-Liberal majority, 174
   explanation of protests, 187–90
   immigration conflicts in, 165, 166 n. s
   political institutions, 174
   skinheads, 167
   social structure, 164
repression, 24–25, 38, 48, 234. *See also* policing
   alliances between protesters and, 10, 12, 48–49, 231, 241
   defined, 36
   elite allies and, 10, 12, 39–42, 48–49, 51, 231, 233, 238
   institutions and, 19, 250
   of leftists, 18, 24–25, 240
   of rightists, 214–16, 240
Republicans (Republikaner), 26, 173, 202, 216, 242. *See also* political parties, far-right
research design, 55–59, 220 n. b, 232 n. j
   choice of cases, 3–4, 5, 57–59, 163–65, 193–94
   comparative case study approach, 56
   research methods, 56–57
resettlers, ethnic German, 6 n. k, 29, 161, 168–69, 227
   in Kronshagen, 180
   in Riesa, 205, 210
Riesa immigration conflict
   access to officials, 207–8
   alliances between protest groups, lack of, 206
   asylum seekers, 204
   compared with other immigration conflicts, 216–18
   cultural conflicts, 204–5
   effective policing, 213–14
   elite allies, lack of, 210
   explanation of protests, 192, 216–18
   political institutions, 200–202
   selection of case, 193–94
   skinhead actions, 206 n. x
   skinhead group, 199
   socioeconomic setting, 194 & n. g, 196–98
   summary of protests, 195–96
   youth clubs, 206 n. x, 207 n. aa, 208, 214
   Zeithain asylum shelter, 205, 207 n. z
rightist protests and movements. *See also* anti-foreigner violence; anti-immigration movement; differences between left and right; neo-Nazis; similarities between leftist and rightist protests; skinheads
   defined, 26
   long-term trends, 226–27
   types of protest, 53, 241–47
   violence, 25–26 & n. m
riots. *See also* militant protests
   against foreigners in eastern Germany, 52, 55, 58, 192–93, 202
   at Brokdorf, 118, 120, 121 n. e, 146
   effects of anti-foreigner, 214–15

INDEX   315

explanation of anti-foreigner, 216–18
  at Gorleben, 159
  in Hamburg, 122
  in Hanover, 64 nn. j–k
  in Hoyerswerda, 59, 194–95, 204–5, 209–12
  in Kreuzberg, 2, 49, 61, 67, 101–8, 111–12
  in Riesa, 213–14
  in Rostock, 50, 195, 204, 206, 212–13
  in West Berlin, 50, 65, 84, 92, 94–95
risks of protests. See costs and risks
Ristock, Harry (SPD), 76–79, 87–88, 111
Rostock immigration conflict
  alliances between protest groups, 206
  arson attack, 195, 213
  concessions to protests, 213, 214
  cultural conflicts, 204
  elite allies, 209–10
  explanation of riots, 192, 216–18
  informal contacts with officials, 195, 204
  overcrowding of shelter, 204, 210, 216
  police passivity, 212–13
  spectators at riots, 195
  summary of protests, 195
Rucht, Dieter, xii n. 2, xiii, 151, 225, 262 n. 72

Sandig, Heiner (CDU), 207 n. z
Saxony (*Land*), 202
  anti-foreigner demonstration, 161 n. a
  anti-foreigner violence, 29, 193, 199
  asylum seekers, 195, 200, 202, 214
  interior ministers, 202, 212, 254
  low-violence localities, 193, 194 n. h
  police, 201, 212 n. ii
  skinhead groups, 198–200
Schleswig-Holstein (*Land*), 122, 173. See also Brokdorf; Kronshagen; Rendsburg County
  anti-foreigner violence, 164 n. l
  asylum policy, 188
  asylum seekers, 174
  CDU-led government of, 119–20, 125, 144–45
  Landtag elections, 125
  political institutions, 124–25, 173–74
  skinheads, 164 n. l, 167
  Social Democrats in, 121, 135, 141, 148, 255
  SPD-led government of, 173–74, 188
Schröder, Gerhard (SPD), 39 n. aa

Sharp, Gene, 37 n. y, 263 n. 107
shift to disruptive protests, 12, 40, 47, 49–50, 234–35, 243
  at Brokdorf, 155
  in Linden, 50, 75–76, 91, 112
  in Kreuzberg, 50, 75, 79, 93
  in Südpark, 50, 184–87, 232
  at Wyhl, 129–30, 155
shift to militant protests, 12, 40, 47, 49–50, 234–35, 255
  at Brokdorf, 134, 153–54
  in Kreuzberg, 80, 93
  in Hoyerswerda, 217, 232
  in Rostock, 50, 217, 232
  in Südpark, 50, 184–87, 232
similarities between leftist and rightist protests, 13–14, 26–27, 52–53 & n. ii, 238
  in their causes, 13–14 & n. r, 52–53, 55
size and duration of protests. See also making of opportunities
  compared across cases, 5, 219–24, 222–23
  explained, 36–45, 40–41
skinheads, right-wing
  alliance with neo-Nazis, 195, 198, 236 n. m
  alliances with adults, 205–6, 217, 231, 238, 239 n. o
  in anti-immigration movement, 7, 25–26, 161–62, 236 n. m
  attacks on foreigners, 26, 30, 55, 161, 171, 215–16
  and authorities, 45, 227, 240, 247. See also policing
  in Bavaria, 164 n. l, 167
  in eastern Germany, 55, 198, 236 n. m
  goals, 26, 55, 244
  in Hoyerswerda, 194–95, 199, 205, 209–12
  in Munich, 166 n. s, 167, 179, 190
  organizations, 164, 198–200
  in Riesa, 196, 199, 207–8, 211, 213, 216
  riots against foreigners, 14, 52
  in Rostock, 195, 217
  in Saxony, 198–200, 202
  in Schleswig-Holstein, 164 n. ll, 167
  social composition, 31
  strategies, 13, 241–44
SO36 Association, 65, 77, 81–82, 106. See also Kreuzberg urban renewal conflict
  alliance with SO36 Citizen Initiative, 81–82, 110
  and autonomists, 102, 107

SO36 Association (*continued*)
  composition, 98 n. qqq
  goals, 64, 91–92
  strategy, 81–82, 111
  tenant advising by, 98, 101–2
SO36 Citizen Initiative. *See also* Kreuzberg urban renewal conflict
  alliance with other protesters, 82, 84, 96, 110
  alliance with SO36 Association, 81–82, 110
  composition, 79–80
  goals, 64, 79–80
  squats by, 80, 82, 89, 91
  strategy, 111
Social Democratic Party (SPD). *See* Social Democrats; Young Socialists
Social Democrats. *See also* elite allies
  as allies for anti-immigration protesters, 26, 42, 161 nn. b–c
  as allies for leftist movements, 3, 6, 10, 17–18, 22–23, 39–42, 224, 243–46
  and asylum rights, 162 n. c, 191 & n. b, 215
  at Brokdorf, 49, 120–21, 135, 138–39, 141, 147–48, 155–56
  concessions to leftists, 230, 235–36
  democratic reforms by, 39, 42, 44–45, 244
  factions in, 20, 87
  in government, 5, 56 n. nn
  in Hanover, 2, 63, 71, 85–86
  in Hoyerswerda, 194, 210
  in Kreuzberg, 66, 76, 91–92, 100–104, 107–9, 114–15
  in Kronshagen, 174, 183
  in Linden, 73–74, 85–86, 90–91, 97, 100, 104–5, 111, 256–57
  in Munich, 164 n. k, 171–72, 175, 188 nn. oo–pp
  in party system, 18, 21, 23
  in Riesa, 194
  in Rostock, 210
  in Schleswig-Holstein, 164 n. k, 173–74
  in Südpark, 173, 181
  support for disruptive protests, 14, 53
  in urban renewal conflicts, 115–16
  in West Berlin, 2, 65, 71, 77, 87, 89, 93–94, 100–101, 113–15
  at Wyhl, 127, 137–38, 151
socioeconomic theories
  of leftist protests, 8, 27–28, 31–32
  of rightist protests, 8, 28–32, 165–68

socioeconomic theories assessed, 8–9, 22–24, 27–32, 125 n. i, 239 n. q, 248
  at Brokdorf and Wyhl, 121–23
  in Hoyerswerda and Riesa, 194 & n. g, 196–98
  in Kreuzberg and Linden, 63, 66, 67–70
  in Munich and Rendsburg County, 164, 166–67
Solingen arson attack, 215
Späth, Lothar (CDU), 138, 148, 254
squats, housing
  in Kreuzberg, 80, 82, 89, 91, 93, 104, 107
  in Linden, 62, 76, 81, 86, 91, 109
squatter movement in West Berlin, 65–66, 82–85
Stobbe, Dietrich (SPD), 65, 89, 94, 115
Stoltenberg, Gerhard (CDU), 139, 142, 155, 159
strategic interaction, 14, 45, 52, 56. *See also* interactions
strategies. *See* conventional, disruptive, *and* militant protests *and* strategies
structural theories of protest, xii. *See also* political institutional theory; socioeconomic theories
  assessed, 8–9, 213–16, 247–55
  structures as permissive conditions, 18–20, 250–51
structure-agent problem, xii, 34, 250–55, 262 n. 70
student movement, 20, 39, 42, 44, 82 n. aaa, 124, 236 n. m, 242–46
  influence in Kreuzberg, 74, 88
students, university
  at Brokdorf, 122, 128
  in citizen initiatives, 20, 245
  in Kreuzberg, 1, 64, 69–70, 74 & n. mm, 79
  in Linden, 62, 74 n. ll, 76
  strategies of, 32, 84, 241, 243, 245
  at Wyhl, 118, 122, 127, 133, 143–44
success chances. *See* chances of success
Südpark Citizen Initiative, 186
  composition, 178
  goals, 178–80, 184
  strategies, 175–76, 182, 184–85, 187
Südpark immigration conflict. *See also* Munich
  asylum shelter, 177, 184
  compared with other immigration conflicts, 186–89

cultural conflicts, 178–79
duration of protests, 165 n. o
elite allies for protesters, 181–82
explanation of protests, 186–87
Living Together in Südpark, 179
local conflict setting, 171–73
militant threats, 175–76
organizational explanations and, 167–68
Protestant Church, 174, 177–78, 179, 182, 184, 187
Protestant Church, 177–78
reforms, 183–85, 186, 232
summary of protests, 175–76

tactics, protest. *See* innovation of tactics; conventional, disruptive, *and* militant protests
Tarrow, Sidney, xii n. 1, xiii, 35–36, 37 n. y, 234, 262 n. 70
tenant advising, 97–98, 101–2
terrorist groups
  leftist, 24–25, 82, 95, 243
  rightist, 240 n. r
Third Reich, 43, 54, 244–45
threats by officials. *See also* cultural conflicts; policy reforms
  at Brokdorf, 126–28, 131, 147, 158
  defined, 36 & n. x
  effects on size of protests, 10–11, 38, 40, 43–44, 220–23, 222–23, 232–33
  effects on types of protest, 40, 49–50, 228–29
  in Hoyerswerda, 203–4
  in Kreuzberg, 72–74, 76–80, 87, 104–5, 109, 113
  in Kronshagen, 180–81
  in Linden, 72–76, 104, 111–12
  in Riesa, 204–5
  in Rostock, 204
  in Südpark, 178–79, 184, 186, 232
  at Wyhl, 125–26, 128–30
Tilly, Charles, xiii, 35–36, 37 n. y, 259 n. 6, 262 n. 70
timing of reforms. *See* concessions; policy reforms
types of protest. *See also* conventional, disruptive, *and* militant protests
  defined, 45–47
  compared across cases, 5, 228–29
  dilemmas in choosing, 255–56
  explanation of, 38, 45–51, 40–41, 61, 227–38, 230–32, 255–56

in leftist and rightist movements, 53, 238–39

unconventional protests, 18, 21, 27–28, 45–46. *See also* disruptive *and* militant protests
unemployment. *See* ethnic competition; socioeconomic theories assessed
unification of Germany. *See also* East Germany; eastern Germany
  and administrative problems, 55, 201–2
  and anti-immigration movement, 6, 25, 191 n. a, 218, 236
  leftist protests after, 21, 56 n. mm, 99 n. rrr, 102, 105, 237
  and policing problems, 54–55, 201, 209, 213
  and political institutions, 19, 25, 200–201, 249
Treaty regulating, 170
urban renewal conflicts, 58, 109–16. *See also* Kreuzberg urban renewal conflict; Linden; Nordstadt; Wedding
Urban Renewal Division, International Building Exposition, 66, 88–89, 98–99
  support for protests, 81, 84, 89, 96, 109, 111
Urban Renewal Law, 70, 98 n. ppp, 251
urban renewal policy. *See also* Kreuzberg urban renewal conflict; Linden; Nordstadt; threats by officials; Wedding
  federal subsidies, 70, 72, 78, 88, 114
  in Kreuzberg, 72–74, 76–80, 88
  in Linden, 72–76
  neighborhood renewal, 62–63
  in Wedding, 115

violence. *See also* anti-foreigner violence; militant protests; riots
  at Brokdorf, 120–21, 134–36, 141–42, 145, 147, 151–52
  in eastern Germany. *See* anti-foreigner violence, in eastern Germany; *names of particular conflicts*
  explanations of, 8–9, 28–32
  in Hoyerswerda, 191, 194–95, 209–12
  in Kreuzberg, 2–3, 65–66, 84, 92, 95, 103 & n. zzz, 107–8
  by leftists, 13–14, 21, 23–24, 53, 260 n. 21
  in Munich, 168, 188
  by police, 80, 106, 120, 130, 134–35, 141,

318 INDEX

violence (*continued*)
146–47. *See also* policing, overreactions
and protest strategies, 46–47
in Rendsburg County, 166 n. s, 167, 188
in Riesa, 15, 193–94, 196, 213–14
by rightists, 13–14, 53. *See also* anti-foreigner violence
in Rostock, 191, 195, 212–13
situational causes of, 11, 47, 233
at Wyhl, 118–19, 133–34
Vogel, Hans-Jochen (SPD), 65, 93–94, 115, 141
Voscherau, Henning (SPD), 162 n. c

Wackersdorf nuclear energy conflict, 58, 122–23, 125 n. i, 236 n. m
Wedding (Berlin) urban renewal conflict, 74, 115–16, 221, 248
Wedemeier, Klaus (SPD), 162 n. c
Weizsäcker, Richard von (CDU), 65, 95, 104
West Berlin (*Land*)
construction ministers, 64, 66 n. q, 98, 105, 114–15, 224, 254
Construction Ministry, 71, 78–79, 87–88, 92–93, 98–99, 101, 114–15
federal subsidies to, 68, 73, 78, 88, 113–14, 116
governments, 65, 94, 101
housing corporations, 113–14
interior ministers, 66 n. q, 95 n. nnn, 105, 107–8
parliamentary elections, 67, 71, 87, 91, 93–94, 100, 115
political institutions, 70–71
political prosecutor, 89, 94–95, 111–12
unification with East Berlin, 66 n. u, 99 n. rrr, 102, 105
West Germany. *See* Germany
western Germany
anti-foreigner violence in, 29–30, 53, 164, 215, 218
cases in, 5, 32, 56
political culture, 31, 54
nonviolent anti-immigration protests in, 26–27, 55, 58, 161–62, 164–65
protests in, 13–14, 52, 225, 238
skinheads and neo-Nazis, 55, 195, 236
Willems, Helmut, 37 n. y, 161, 261 n. 39
women
and foreigners, 203, 211
issues concerning, 20, 100, 235
as protesters, 146
women's movement, 6, 21–22, 28, 42, 55 n. ll, 226, 239
Wyhl nuclear energy conflict
alliances among protest groups, 131–34, 149–50, 153
Alsace (France), 122, 132, 149
chronology of, 118–19, 147
compared with other nuclear conflicts, 152–59
concessions to protests, 140–41, 156
decentralized disruptive strategy, 149–50
elite allies for protesters, 136–38, 151, 154–55
Emmendingen County, 122, 125–26, 138, 151
explanation of size of protests, 152–53
explanation of types of protest, 153–56
fraternization of police and protesters, 144, 254
Kaiserstuhl region, 122, 130
nonviolent discipline, 133–34, 144
nuclear plant, 126
Offenburg Agreement, 119, 133, 148, 252
participatory rights, 128–29, 147–48
pastors, 127, 132–33, 137, 143
policing, 142–44, 156
policy reforms, blockage of, 155
political institutions, 123–25
rural citizen initiatives, 126–27
selection of case, 59
site occupations, 132–33
socioeconomic setting, 121–23
Southern Atomic Plant, 118, 126–27, 129–30, 138
summarized, 117–18
threats posed by nuclear plant, 125–30

Young Socialists
at Brokdorf, 139
double strategy of, 39, 241, 245
in West Berlin, 74, 115, 241